TRADE UNIONS IN BRITAIN

Errata

P.viii, Chapter Six *delete* p.155 *insert* p.157.

P.319 *delete* diagram and *substitute*:

Size of union

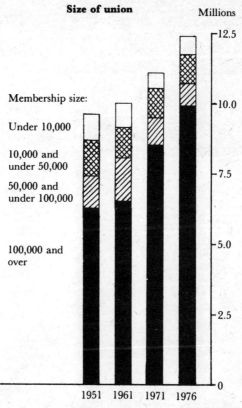

Millions

Membership size:

Under 10,000

10,000 and
under 50,000

50,000 and
under 100,000

100,000 and
over

1951 1961 1971 1976

Source: Department of Employment.

TRADE UNIONS
IN BRITAIN

Ken Coates and Tony Topham

SPOKESMAN

First published in 1980 by:
Spokesman
Bertrand Russell House
Gamble Street
Nottingham

Photoset and Printed in Great Britain by
Bristol Typesetting Co. Ltd.
Barton Manor
Bristol

Cloth ISBN 0 85124 293 6
Paper ISBN 0 85124 294 4

This book is gratefully dedicated to

Bill Jones

on the occasion of his eightieth birthday

Contents

Chapter One
Trade Unions and their Setting   1
  (a) Some Definitions
  (b) The Components of Trade Unionism
  (c) The Conditioning Social Context
  (d) Concentration of Capital and Power
  (e) Division of Labour and Alienation
  (f) Trade Union Objects
  (g) Postwar Growth: A Resumption of a Longer Trend

Chapter Two
Trade Union Structure   25
  (a) Types of Unions
  (b) 'Vertical' and 'Horizontal' Structures
  (c) 'Open' and 'Closed' Structures
  (d) Demarcation and Disputes Between Unions
  (e) Organisational Success
  (f) Structural Reform
  (g) Change and Democracy
  Appendix: Mergers

Chapter Three
Trade Union Government   61
  (a) Problems of Trade Union Democracy
  (b) Basic Units of Organisation
  (c) Relations Between Members and Organisers
  (d) Elections
  (e) Separation of Powers
  (f) Leadership Succession
  (g) Opposition
  (h) Lay Government versus Professionalism
  (i) Communications
  Appendix: Questionnaire on Democracy

Chapter Four
  The TUC   94
      (a) The Origins and Development of the TUC
      (b) 'Tripartism'
      (c) The TUC and Legislative Onslaughts
      (d) The 'Social Contract'
      (e) The Growth of Quangos
      (f) The Functioning of Congress
      Appendix: General Council involvement in public bodies

Chapter Five
  Shop Stewards and Workplace Trade Unionism   134
      (a) The Development of Workplace Representation
      (b) The Functions of Shop Stewards
      (c) Joint Consultation
      (d) Steward Organisation in the Plant
      (e) Relations with the Unions
      (f) Combine Organisation

Chapter Six
  Collective Bargaining   155
      (a) The Range of Trade Union Methods
      (b) Collective Bargaining Institutions
      (c) Local and Plant Bargaining
      (d) The Subjects of Bargaining
      (e) The Results of Collective Agreements
      (f) Procedures
      (g) Arbitration and Conciliation
      (h) Incomes Policy
      (i) The Experience of State Intervention
      Appendix: A Procedural Agreement

Chapter Seven
  Strikes   196
      (a) The Occurrence of Strikes
      (b) Measuring Strikes
      (c) Historical Patterns
      (d) International Comparisons
      (e) General Explanations of Strikes
      (f) Causes of Unrest in Britain
      (g) Unofficial Stoppages
      (h) Recognition Strikes
      (i) Financing Strikes

Chapter Eight
Industrial Democracy   232
    (a) Three Periods of Concern: A Historical Background
    (b) The Limitations of Joint Consultation
    (c) The Content of the Modern Movement
    (d) Encroachment of Powers
    (e) Planning Agreements
    (f) Alternative Corporate Plans
    (g) Worker Directors and the Bullock Report
    (h) The New Worker Co-operatives
    (i) Problems of Technological Innovation

Chapter Nine
Trade Unions and the Law   264
    (a) Judges and the Law
    (b) The Outlook of Trade Unionists
    (c) The Development of Labour Law
    (d) From Donovan to the Industrial Relations Act
    (e) The 1974 Legislation and After
    Appendix: TUC Response to Governmental Proposals for
    Law Reform: 1979

Chapter Ten
Trade Unions and the Labour Party   302
    (a) The Scope of Political Action
    (b) Labour Representatives in Parliament
    (c) Affiliations to the Labour Party
    (d) TU Participation in Labour Party Management
    (e) The Problem of the Block Vote
    (f) Determining Conference Arrangements
    (g) Conclusion

Chapter Eleven
International Affiliations   329
    (a) TUC International Links
    (b) The International Organisations
    (c) The Growth of Regionalism
    (d) Some Criteria for International Organisation
    Appendix: The Commonwealth Trade Union Council

Conclusion   357

Acknowledgements   359

Glossary of General Acronyms   360

Indices   363
    (a) Index of Trade Unions and their Acronyms
    (b) Index of Works Consulted and Bibliography
    (c) General Index

List of Tables

I:1 Percentage of Trade Unionists in Total Labour Force 7
I:2 UK Enterprises with over 200 Employees in the UK 13
I:3 Union Membership and Density 14
I:4 Unionisation in Larger Manufacturing Establishments 16

II:1 Comparison of Industrial Structures, TGWU and GMWU 31
II:2 Distribution of TU Members by Industrial Group 38
II:3 Unions with over 250,000 members, 1962 and 1977/79 43
II:4 Number of Unions Analysed by Size of Unions 44
II:5 Membership of Unions Analysed by Size of Unions 45
II:6 Mergers Between Unions 50

III:1 The Organisation of USDAW 63
III:2 Number of Members per Full-Time Officer in Certain Unions 70
III:3 Full-Time Local Officers: Shop Steward Responsibilities and Contacts 71
III:4 Ratio of Members to Full-Time Officers, TGWU 72
III:5 Union Journals, Costs and Advertising Revenue 87
III:6 Union Journals, Circulation and Distribution 88

IV:1 TUC Growth 111
IV:2 Elections to the General Council 114
IV:3 Public Appointments 125
IV:4 Quango Costs 125
IV:5 TUC General Council Participation in Public Bodies 128

VI:1 Bargaining Structure in 1973 165
VI:2 Payment by Results 169
VI:3 Gross Earnings and Agreements 173
VI:4 Conciliation Cases by Cause of Disputes 179
VI:5 Income Shares as % GNP 186
VI:6 Gross Weekly Earnings: Differentials 188

VII:1   Number of Strikes, Workers Involved, Striker-days   202
VII:2   British Strikes, 1939–45   205
VII:3   International Comparisons of Strikes in Certain Industries   210
VII:4   Striker-days per 1,000 workers, Internationally   211
VII:5   Disputes in the OECD Nations   212
VII:6   UK Strikes by Cause 1938–66   219
VII:7   UK Strikes by Cause 1977–78   220
VII:8   Striker-days, by Cause   221
VII:9   The Percentage of Strikes, and Striker-days, Accounted for by Official Strikes 1961–77   225

X:1   Union Sponsored MPs   304
X:2   Individual Union Sponsorships   306
X:3   Labour Party: Affiliated Unions, 1977   308
X:4   Labour Party: Largest Affiliations, 1970–77   312
X:5   League Table of % TUC Members Affiliated to Labour Party, 1977   313
X:6   % Contributions to Political Funds   314
X:7   Labour Party and TUC Membership   317
X:8   TU Representation on NEC of Labour Party   318
X:9   Labour Vote and % Electorate, 1951–79   325

XI:1   Estimated TUC International Expenditure, 1977   329
XI:2   International Expenditure as % Total Revenue   331
XI:3   TUC Expenditure on International Works as % of Total Expenditure, 1923–5   332
XI:4   Breakdown of Headings of TUC International Expenditure   333
XI:5   ICFTU Membership Trends   341
XI:6   ICFTU Membership by Regions   341
XI:7   Companies Financing AFL-CIOs Overseas Work   344
XI:8   Membership of the ETUC   346

Introductory Note

Any book on industrial relations is bound to be stiff with initials. Not only do the Trade Unions themselves delight in acronyms which make a complicated puzzle, but they also multiply joint bodies, confederations and alliances, each of which is normally known by some abbreviation or other.

A list of all the Unions which are named in this book will be found in the index of Trade Unions on page 363. Each acronym commonly used by such unions is de-coded in that index, which is cross-referenced.

A variety of other industrial relations bodies are also normally referred to by their initials. A list of these bodies will be found in the glossary on page 360.

Chapter One

Trade Unions and their Setting

Some Definitions

'A trade union, as we understand the term, is a continuous association of wage-earners for the purpose of maintaining or improving the conditions of their employment.' It was in this way, back in 1894, that Sidney and Beatrice Webb opened their classic work on the *History of Trade Unionism*.[1]

In commonsense terms, there is still merit in this definition. But in 1920, when they re-edited the work for students of the Workers' Educational Association, the Webbs deleted the word 'employment', and added the wider term 'working lives'. They made this change, they insisted, because they had been accused of assuming that unions had 'always contemplated a perpetual continuance of the capitalist or wage-system'. 'No such implication', they sternly added, 'was intended'.

More recently, critics have objected to even the modified formula, on the grounds that it places too much emphasis on the continuity of association.[2] In truth, many working-class initiatives are spontaneous, and only take on 'continuity' by accident. The TUC itself began as an ad hoc conference on threatened legal changes, and could easily have finished its career as a one-off event, if not quite a one-night stand.[3] Many trade unions may trace their original formation to a particular dispute, or trauma, out of which developed a permanent organisation. Such development does look a bit haphazard to any outside observer. What is it that turns one indignant demonstration, or strike, into the root of a new organisation, while a seemingly identical event next day, or in the next town, provokes no such continuity? These questions recur in every generation. During the extraordinary upsurge of factory occupations in 1971 and the following years, there were more than two hundred 'work-ins' or 'sit-ins'.[4] Of these, perhaps half a dozen evolved into permanent workers' producer co-operatives, of which a few survived.[5] Is the history of 'continuous associations' of self-management organisations to be written about the survivors only? But some of the failures are as interesting as the successes. Is our concern to be restricted, in this case, to people who sought 'continuity' for their initiative? But the handful of co-ops were part of a wider movement in which co-operative objectives played a relatively minor role. Whatever we think about these questions, it is difficult to understand trade unionism as a living movement in terms of its continuity alone. This was, mercifully, adequately recognised in the law governing trade unions from 1871 onwards. Consolidating various laws of 1871, 1876 and 1913, we arrived at a legal definition of a trade union which said it was:

> 'any combination, whether temporary or permanent, the principal objects of which are under its constitution statutory objects, namely the regulation of the relations between workmen and masters or between workmen and workmen, or between masters and masters, or the imposing of restrictive conditions on the conduct of any trade or business, and also the provision of benefits to members, whether such combination would or would not, if the Trade Union Act, 1871, had not been passed, have been deemed to be an unlawful combination by reason of some one or more of its purposes being in restraint of trade.'[6]

Although the recognition that temporary associations could be regarded as trade unions was vital for the protection of strikes, and much to be preferred as a legal provision to any attempt to limit legal protection to permanent bodies, this definition was generally felt to have been outdated, long before it was at last revised.

The official Donovan Report which was published in 1968[7] suggested that it was also too wide, since it dealt with employers' organisations under the same framework as unions themselves, which does not accord with any commonsense view. The Royal Commission also disliked the imprecision of the term 'workmen'. They wished to have it replaced by the word 'employee', and they suggested revisions of the provisions concerning 'restrictive conditions'. After a long debate and after the volcanic upheaval of the Industrial Relations Act of 1971, trade union law was finally resolved in the Trade Union and Labour Relations Act of 1974, which offers the following definition of a trade union:

> 28.—(1) In this Act, except so far as the context otherwise requires, 'trade union' means an organisation (whether permanent or temporary) which either—
> (a) consists wholly or mainly of workers of one or more descriptions and is an organisation whose principal purposes include the regulation of relations between workers of that description or those descriptions and employers or employers' associations: or

(b) consists wholly or mainly of—

    (i) constituent or affiliated organisations which fulfil the conditions specified in paragraph (a) above (or themselves consist wholly or mainly of constituent or affiliated organisations which fulfil those conditions), or

    (ii) representatives of such constituent or affiliated organisations:

and in either case is an organisation whose principal purposes include the regulation of relations between workers and employers or between workers and employers' associations, or include the regulation of relations between its constituent or affiliated organisations.

As we have just said, employers' organisations had been defined (somewhat paradoxically) as trade unions in the earlier legislation, but from 1974 onwards their role has been treated separately, no doubt in part because of the Royal Commission's recommendation. We pass over this complex issue since it is outside the area of our concern in this book. Returning to the unions, we should note that the current legal meaning of the words 'trade union' still preserves any element of protection which spontaneous organisations (however ephemeral these might have been) have traditionally been able to derive from the archaic wording of the Act of 1871 and its successors. Otherwise, it is considerably closer to normal usage. Nonetheless, it remains a legal formula, rather than a sociological description. If we are to approach closer to an appreciation of what unions are about, we must look elsewhere.

Refreshingly direct, and free from the common jargon of bureaucracy, is the long statement put in by the TUC itself to Lord Donovan's Commission: this sets out some of the basic reasons why it is right for a democratic state to safeguard the rights of independent trade unions.

'The status of the employed person in an industrial economy is one of dependence on earnings with little or no individual power of direct decision. The individual contract between an employee and an employer does not reflect a position of equal strength on the two sides. Equality before the law is only relevant to the observance of the contract and not to its terms or to the procedure by which it is made. In these circumstances the economic freedom of the individual employee is very small. This must be the starting point of any objective examination of the rights and needs of employed persons. These fundamental rights and needs deriving from the nature of the employment relationship are in essence permanent and enduring, though they lead to changes in substantive terms, for example in the level of wages, as the years go by.

It would be generally recognised that employed persons can justly claim the right to have their interests taken into account . . .

Trade unions are the unique means whereby men and women in employment can themselves decide how their interests can best be furthered. Workpeople have the right to combine to form their own organisations and through this means to advance and protect their interests.

Thus the essential characteristic of free trade unions is that they are responsible to the workpeople themselves who comprise their membership and cannot be directed by any outside agency . . .

Recognition of the fact that the interests and preferences of individuals and groups are different, according to the perspective of each of them, is embodied in the structure of individual trade unions and in the trade union movement as a whole. Recognition of the legitimacy of distinct and often diverging interests is also the basis of bargaining between trade unions and employers. Bargaining depends on each side recognising the legitimacy and representative capacity of the other. A bargain is a method of reconciling differences in the interests of both sides. Just as trade unions, whilst being responsible to their membership, recognise that other people have their own interests, they expect that their interests, too, should be recognised and respected by other people.

These rights which employed people claim cannot be recognised and conceded on a theoretical or abstract plane and then not be recognised and not be conceded when they are translated into trade union function and trade union practice. That they are recognised in this country is not due to the intellectual or moral force of the arguments advanced above but to the efforts of working people in asserting them and exercising them.'[8]

The TUC was compelled to pay special attention to the problems which are involved in the very idea of an 'employee'. Not so long ago, British laws referred to all employees as 'servants'. This reflects a distasteful relationship because it implies that employers are 'masters', as the 1871 legislation still specified. We should remember that this fundamental attitude dates from a time when 'democracy' itself was a most controversial concept, linked in the minds of the Establishment with anarchy and mob-rule.

Indeed, it is remarkable how modern sound some of the very earliest writings of political economy when they consider this question. Adam Smith, for instance, writing in *The Wealth of Nations*, which founded modern economics in 1776, says 'we rarely hear . . . of the combinations of masters, though frequently of those of workmen. But whoever imagines, upon this account, that masters rarely combine, is as ignorant of the world as of the subject. Masters are always and everywhere in a sort of tacit, but constant and uniform combination, not to raise the wages of labour above their actual rate . . . Masters, too, sometimes enter into particular combinations to sink the wages of labour even below this rate. These are always conducted with the utmost silence and secrecy, till the moment of execution . . .' On the other hand, even two hundred years ago, when labourers combined 'whether their combinations be offensive or defensive, they are always abundantly heard of.'[9]

Recognising this fact, which is still very much a part of contemporary life, the Trade Union Congress added to its Royal Commission statement these cautiously defensive remarks:

'Arising out of their status as employed persons, dependent on earnings, dependent on securing and retaining employment, workpeople know that to exercise their rights they must find a means to redress the balance of unequal strength vis-a-vis their employers. Whilst the position of the individual employee, both in law and in practice, is one of subordination, individual employees together recognise that it is through combination that they can develop a means, the essential means which they possess, to harness their own potential strength. It is in the nature of the employment situation that working people readily identify themselves with their fellows in groups. This feeling of collective identity enhances the economic freedom of the individual, a freedom which rests on the knowledge that unity is strength.

Just as the bargaining strength of the individual is enhanced when he combines with his fellow workers in a group at a place of employment, so on a wider plane trade unions grow in size and extent to become whatever may be the most effective combination of workpeople to advance and protect those interests, arising from their employment, which they have in common.'[10]

The Components of Trade Unionism

Sociologists, who do not always write as clearly as the TUC, have offered a variety of divergent efforts to bend the efforts of science in order to determine what constitutes a trade union. R. M. Blackburn, for instance, employs the concept of 'unionateness', which braids seven distinct strands:

'1. It regards collective bargaining and the protection of the

interests of members, as employees, as its main function, rather than, say, professional activities or welfare schemes.
2. It is independent of employers for purposes of negotiation.
3. It is prepared to be militant, using all forms of industrial action which may be effective.
4. It declares itself to be a trade union.
5. It is registered as a trade union.
6. It is affiliated to the Trades Union Congress.
7. It is affiliated to the Labour Party.'[11]

As Blackburn points out, these seven strands are not equally internally consistent. The first few can be a matter of degree, while the last four are clear characteristics which an organisation 'either has or does not have'. Within such a view, different unions may be more, or less, 'unionate' when contrasted at the same time; while the same union may become increasingly 'unionate' as it develops. NALGO, the Local Government Officers' Association, and the NUT (Teachers' Union) both resisted affiliation to the TUC over a long period of time, and even, at one moment, struggled to set up an alternative national centre for Professional Workers. When they finally took the plunge, their identification with traditional unionism was obviously the more complete for so doing. If they were tomorrow to follow the Colliery Officials into the Labour Party, their 'unionateness' would be even firmer in its consistency. (Blackburn was aware of the grey areas on the margins of his subject, because he was involved in a study of the Bank Employees, who subsequently so far forgot their unionate manners as to allow themselves to be suspended from membership of the TUC, after they had refused to implement its policies on the 1971 Industrial Relations Act.) Unions which would never have contemplated the thought, a few years ago, have recently been greatly more prone to link up with the TUC: which now includes not only the two mass professional associations just named, but also the Association of University Teachers, the British Association of Colliery Managers, the Institute of Professional Civil Servants, and a number of other representatives of the higher salariat. 'Unionateness', here, must still, surely, be rather evidently in the balance. At the same time, the growth of organisations which have always been quite unambiguously 'unionate' has, in some cases, become quite spectacular. The result is a dramatic increase in the proportion of the workforce which belongs to unions.

Today more than half the workforce in Britain is organised, and in 1978 112 unions, with 11,865,390 members, were affiliated to the TUC. Well over 300 unions, mostly small in membership, did not

Table I:1
Percentage of trade unionists in total labour force

	(a) Labour Force 000s	(b) Trade Union Members, 000s	% (b) of (a)
1969	23,603	10,472	44.4
1970	23,446	11,179,	47.7
1971	23,231	11,127	47.9
1972	23,303	11,349	49.4
1973	23,592	11,444	49.2
1974	23,689	11,755	50.4
1975	23,553	12,017	51.0
1976	23,713	12,376	52.2

belong to the TUC. On the lists of the Certification Officer, the official responsible for maintaining lists of trade unions, there were, in all, at the beginning of 1978, 485 unions. There is a time lag in officially reporting the precise membership of these unions, so the most recent available figure from this source is for 1976: it then ran at 12,133,000. The discrepancy between this and the figure cited above reflects changes in the basis of calculation used by the Department of Employment, but on any account, either assessment represents an extraordinary vote of confidence in trade unions. This is the more remarkable because their membership has been sharply increasing at a time of rising unemployment, during which the official tally of workless has drifted up to 1,400,000, while reasonable estimates of the real weight of the problem (which is understated in the official statistics) fix it at something nearer to two million.[12] Simultaneously, traditionally well-organised industries have continued to decline, and lay off workpeople. At the same time there has also been a considerable shift of labour into hitherto far less well-organised service industries. Whilst manual workers have consolidated very strong levels of unionisation, there has recently been significant growth among white-collar workers and women. We shall return to these questions: here it is enough to note that the late 'seventies saw British Trade Unions stronger in number than they had ever been, directly representing a majority (albeit a small one) of the employed population, and, apparently, still growing. The garden in which their organisations were rooted, however, was changing rapidly.

When the Royal Commission on Trade Unions sat, under Lord Donovan's chairmanship, during the mid-'sixties, it circulated unions with a booklet which spelt out the areas upon which it was seeking information. This included a suggested classification of types of organisation: and it provoked an interesting reply from the Transport and General Workers' Union, which was entered into the evidence it offered the Commission.

> 'It is our view that the classification of types of trade union quoted in the Commission's booklet, i.e., "craft", "general", "industrial" and "white-collar" is not really appropriate to the present pattern of industry.
>
> With one or two exceptions, it is impossible to isolate a "craft" today. New skills are constantly developing and entry to them is by a variety of methods, sometimes in maturity. Apprenticeship itself—the traditional way into the "craft"—is steadily becoming more liberal in the education and training it offers, and may equip a youngster with more than one skill.
>
> The attempt to define an industry is even more frustrating. What is the Engineering Industry? Or the Chemical Industry? Or plastics? Or food?
>
> We consider it wrong, socially and industrially, to separate "white-collar" employees from others, since their problems are identical in essence, and increasingly so in detail.
>
> It seems to us, therefore, that the modern union is bound to become a "general" one, and that these things are necessary to enable unions to do their work well:—
>
> (1) They must be large enough to bargain effectively for their members over the *whole* area in which they are employed, and they must be able to give the kind of service—including specialised technical, legal, research and educational provision—that is necessary if members' interests are to be promoted effectively.
>
> (2) They must have effective provision in their constitutions to ensure that their members' "trade" or industrial interests are studied and controlled by members of the trade, and that full-time officers of appropriate experience are available.
>
> (3) They must have plenty of well informed and adequately trained shop stewards, who are recognised by members and employers as responsible officers of their union.
>
> (4) They must have constant contact with other unions whose members are or may be employed in the same industries or undertakings. This contact should be at all levels (including that of shop stewards) and it should be concerned with common problems of wages and working conditions, as well as questions of membership.'[13]

We shall consider these traditional typologies ('craft', 'industrial', 'general' and so on) in detail in our next chapter: but it is appropriate to note this response as one very successful answer to the shifting stresses of the changing labour market. Here we find an explicit recognition of these pressures, and a deliberate strategy for dealing with them. Sometimes, it is true, less foresight is shown by unions: but once one organisation adapts to meet new challenges, others will not only follow very quickly, but also profit from any previous example by avoiding its mistakes. If unions develop at an uneven rate, and are 'unionate' to different degrees, they also tend to learn from each other. This sometimes enables them to *combine* features of development which were previously evolved separately, leapfrogging whole stages of transition which were necessary to the first innovators. New initiatives may sometimes be diffused at the speed of television transmission, speedily and cleanly.

Social historians have often noted the contextual limits of union organisation: how, in many countries, unions have grown through similar successive phases. First, spontaneous uprisings, outbreaks of rioting or machine breaking; then, local associations of craftsmen; later, national organisations, industrial movements involving semi-skilled along with the skilled. Stages like these are not neatly sealed off from each other like geological sediments, though: if a metaphor from the earth sciences applies to unions, we are bound to see that such deposits are jumbled by successive earth-movements which bend and shear the strata, and yet allow all kinds of otherwise anachronistic bodies to live on, apparently unharmed, in little time-capsules of their own. In Britain, these processes have left us with an exceptionally complicated trade union legacy.

The Conditioning Social Context

What is quite plain is that the unions never develop in a vacuum, and that the social and economic environment in which they grow exercises a continuously changing influence upon that growth. In the year of Robert Owen's Grand National Consolidated Trade Union (1834) there were 298 miles of railways. By 1848, the year of Chartism's last great upheaval, about 5,000 miles existed. In 1868, there were, by the time of the birth of the TUC, 12,319 miles.[14] Legislation bringing limited liability companies into being was approved in 1855, partly because of the pressures of scale involved in these developing railway networks: no traditional commercial partnership accepting full, conventional responsibility for its deeds could possibly extend its operations over a national modern railway system. (Neither could the vast capital commitments of the necessary related steel industry be undertaken by old-style entrepreneurs.) We shall return to the question of the effects of successive developments of new forms of company structure: it is enough here to note that in this complex skein, the type of trade union which had been just imaginable in 1834 had become perfectly physically possible by 1868.

The closer linkages of modern communications (newspapers, as well as transportation systems) not merely brought hitherto separate areas and trades within reach of one another, but at the same time integrated their economic experience, and intensified the need for their co-operation. Karl Marx pithily summarised the growth processes of modern capitalism:

> 'The battle of competition is fought by cheapening commodities. The cheapness of commodities depends, *ceteris paribus*, on the productivity of labour, and this again on the scale of production. Therefore, the larger capitals beat the smaller . . . The credit system becomes a new and formidable weapon in the competitive struggle, and finally it transforms itself into an immense social mechanism for the concentration of capitals . . . Centralisation completes the work of accumulation by enabling the industrial capitalists to expand the scale of their operations.'[15]

National trade unions grow up as an answering response at a certain point in this evolution, and national centres like the TUC emerge at another. Yet, if these are experiences which are in some degree common to a variety of national movements, it should be re-emphasised that such movements may, each, learn from all the others, thus foreshortening the perspective of development as one lesson follows another. Because unions develop consciously, they need not passively reflect what happens to them, but may, in some circumstances, initiate actions which can control, or even determine, to a greater or lesser extent, the environment in which they have to operate. For all that, it seems clear that, over the century, trade union history does undoubtedly involve a great deal of purely defensive response.

Concentration of Capital and Power

Nowhere is this clearer than in the most recent phase of capital concentration, the great postwar economic explosion which has meant that a relatively small number of transnational companies have come to dominate the major markets of the world. The vast scale of much modern production, the prodigious research costs involved in high technology, the close protective association of big industry with Governments, the nervous alignments which partition access to raw materials as well as capital: none of these is entirely a new phenomenon. What has been new has been the rapid growth of explicitly multinational operations, institutionalising all these processes into a tiny handful of nuclei, each operating on a truly universal scale. Since the mid-'sixties at least half the American companies with annual sales of a billion dollars or more have either owned a quarter or more of their assets abroad, or secured a quarter or more of their sales abroad, or both. In Britain, in 1970 'the top hundred manufacturing firms in Britain had controlled some half of manufacturing output. In 1950 they had controlled only a fifth, and in 1910 only 15 per cent. On any reasonable projections, the top hundred are likely to proceed from strength to superstrength, and control two thirds of manufacturing around 1980. Newbould and Jackson have made even more dramatic speculation that in the foreseeable future, unless countervailing action is taken, *three quarters* of the non-nationalised sector of British industry could be controlled by as few as *twenty-one* private companies.'[16] As Stuart Holland explains, this has serious implications for conventional economic theory: 'Such companies span the previous gap between micro- and macro-economic theory. The competitive firm of microeconomical theory was too small to influence macro-economic aggregates such as national investment, trade and employment. Even in collusion, it was generally held, they could not seriously influence the price level set by sovereign consumers. Such theory still has relevance to the thousands of small companies which the giants are squeezing into the bottom half of industry. But *in between* these micro-economic firms and the macro-economic level of government policy, the new giants have introduced an intermediate or *meso*-economic sector. Put more simply, these are the big league firms which now command the heights of British industry and dominate the thousands of small league firms.'[17]

Throughout the '50s and '60s the fastest growth tended to occur in the overseas subsidiaries of such companies. Banks have joined and stimulated these processes. A key constituent in them has been the growth of military-based orders and research, which have both stimulated, in particular, aircraft, motors and electronics industries. As the benefits of governmental finance of research and development are converted to profitable private investment, so growth has simultaneously facilitated the evasion of obligations to governments: taxes in particular. The device of transfer pricing, in which a company's subsidiaries exchange products at purely fictional prices in order to rearrange surpluses in the most beneficial areas from a taxation point of view, has become both widespread and sophisticated. Dr Penrose cites one multi-national company which, 'to her knowledge, prepares "three sets of accounts, one for internal accounting purposes, using costs prices, one for the internal revenue authorities, and one for shareholders" ".[18]

Michael Barratt Brown cites, from *Fortune* magazine, a classic case of the manipulation of cross-frontier cash payments:

> ' "One of our Danish subsidiaries," it said, "had excess cash which it lent to another Danish subsidiary that was receiving goods from the Swedish subsidiary. The Danish company prepaid its account with the Swedish subsidiary, and this money financed the movement of Swedish products into the Finnish subsidiary. What did the manoeuvre accomplish? If Finland had been required to pay for the goods, it would have had to borrow at 15 per cent, the going Finnish rate. If the Swedish subsidiary had financed the sale, it would have had to borrow at about 9 per cent. But cash in Denmark was worth only 5 per cent to 6 per cent. Moreover, Danish currency was weak in relation to the Swedish: by speeding up payments to Sweden we not only obtained cheaper credit, we hedged our position in Danish kroner as well." '[19]

Such movements of capital not only threaten the national management of economic affairs, a question which has been elaborately treated elsewhere, they also are a major weapon against effective trade union bargaining, as Stuart Holland has cogently insisted:

> 'Such transfer pricing in multinational trade weakens union wage bargaining power by understating real profits made in the UK'.[20]

All this argues the necessity of a new style of international trade union organisation, and of a system of combine union committees, to which we will return in later sections of this book. Here it is sufficient to note the extent of the challenge, and to note the shape of the terrain it occupies. This was carefully documented in the report of the Bullock Committee which enquired into the question of industrial democracy, and produced the following analysis of the structure of British industry.[21]

In table I:2, the figures given in brackets report the numbers of subsidiaries of overseas-based transnational companies. We see that some 2,100 companies employed 200 or more people in the UK at the time of the enquiry: of these, a third (738 enterprises) employ 2,000-plus people. 100 of these firms are foreign-based transnationals. Another table from the same source reveals an even greater degree of concentration: 155 enterprises employ 10,000 or more UK employees apiece. Thus, more than ¼ of the British workforce, or more than 7 million people, are employed in large firms in the private sector, many

Table I:2

United Kingdom enterprises with over 200 employees in the United Kingdom

ANALYSIS BY INDUSTRY AND NUMBER OF EMPLOYEES

Standard Industrial Classification order	Sector	No. of UK employees							
		201–500	501–1,000	1,001–2,000	2,001–5,000	5,001–10,000	Over 10,000	Total over 2,000	TOTAL
		Number of enterprises (of which controlled from overseas)							
I–III	Food, drink and tobacco	21 (3)	30 (7)	28 (4)	20 (4)	9 (3)	22 (f)	51 (8)	130 (22)
IV–V	Petroleum products etc. and chemicals etc.	34 (18)	31 (19)	24 (11)	21 (9)	8 (3)	7 (1)	36 (13)	125 (61)
VI–XII	Metal manufacturing, engineering, shipbuilding, vehicles	55 (17)	140 (30)	138 (31)	125 (34)	45 (9)	48 (10)	218 (53)	551 (131)
XIII–XV	Textiles and clothing	11 (1)	44 (4)	44 (2)	37 (3)	8 (—)	10 (—)	55 (3)	154 (10)
XVI–XIX	Other manufacturing	32 (5)	78 (5)	62 (8)	57 (7)	35 (1)	17 (3)	109 (11)	281 (29)
XX and XXII	Construction, transport and communications	32 (2)	44 (3)	55 (2)	40 (1)	16 (—)	11 (—)	67 (1)	198 (8)
XXIII	Wholesale and retail distribution	43 (10)	65 (4)	55 (7)	59 (5)	17 (1)	22 (3)	98 (9)	261 (30)
XXIV	Insurance, banking, finance and business services	124 (19)	73 (6)	37 (1)	32 (1)	18 (—)	11 (—)	61 (1)	295 (27)
XXVI	Miscellaneous services	17 (6)	21 (6)	18 (4)	22 (1)	12 (—)	9 (—)	43 (1)	99 (17)
	Total	369 (81)	526 (84)	461 (70)	413 (65)	168 (17)	157 (18)	738 (100)	2,094 (335)

Source: Department of Industry

Table I:3
*Union membership and density by industry in the United Kingdom,
1948 and 1974*

Industry*	1948			1974		
	Labour force (000s)	Union member-ship (000s)	Density (%)	Labour force (000s)	Union member-ship (000s)	Density (%)
Agriculture and Forestry	785.9	215.7	27.4	415.5	92.3	22.2
Fishing	37.7	14.9	39.6	12.2	7.4	60.5
Coal mining	802.7	675.3	84.1	314.0	302.1	96.2
Other mining	81.4	37.0	45.5	50.6	26.2	51.8
Food and drink	597.4	227.4	38.1⎫	783.9	401.1	51.2
Tobacco	49.1	26.1	53.1⎭			
Chemicals	426.8	127.3	29.8	483.6	247.4	51.2
Metals and engineering	3,676.1	1,837.5	50.0	4,118.0	2,862.7	69.4
Cotton and man-made fibres	395.2	276.6	70.0⎫	596.7	243.8	40.9
Other textiles	533.3	180.4	33.8⎭			
Leather	79.0	24.7	31.2	44.0	20.5	46.6
Clothing	429.1	145.5	33.9	345.8	207.7	60.0
Footwear	139.5	92.8	66.6	87.1	68.8	79.0
Bricks and building materials	172.2	70.1	40.8	171.9	69.4	40.4
Pottery	75.3	31.3	41.5	60.5	56.8	93.8
Glass	68.1	28.2	41.3	74.5	58.5	78.5
Wood and furniture	279.8	122.0	43.6	289.6	102.0	35.2
Paper, printing and publishing	455.5	264.1	58.0	596.1	426.6	71.6
Rubber	97.9	48.5	49.6	127.2	71.1	55.9
Construction	1,353.7	613.2	45.3	1,428.8	388.1	27.2
Gas, electricity and water	322.9	218.3	67.6	352.3	324.0	92.0
Railways	694.9	612.1	88.1	224.0	217.0	96.9
Road transport	490.6	295.0†	60.1†	468.3	445.4†	95.1†
Sea Transport	120.8	108.0	89.3	90.6	90.3	99.6
Port and inland water transport	155.7	123.2	79.1	81.5	77.2	94.7
Air transport	32.1	13.0	40.5	79.8	74.7	93.6

Table I:3 (cont.)

Industry*	1948			1974		
	Labour force	Union member-ship	Density	Labour force	Union member-ship	Density
	(000s)	(000s)	(%)	(000s)	(000s)	(%)
Post Office and telecom-munications	353.2	283.4	80.2	509.7	448.1	87.9
Distribution	2,167.9	325.3	15.0	2,810.1	321.8	11.4
Insurance, banking and finance	425.9	137.1	32.2	680.5	305.1	44.8
Entertainment and media services	238.4	95.7	40.1	189.6	123.0	64.9
Health	525.9	204.6	38.9	1,175.2	715.8	60.9
Hotels and catering	708.1	n.a.	—	824.2	42.5	5.2
Other professional services	276.8	n.a.	—	470.2	17.6	3.7
Education and Local Govern-ment	1,280.5	792.2	61.9	2,752.4	2,356.0	85.6
National Govern-ment	724.1	480.6	66.4	623.7	564.5	90.5

Notes:

*The following industries are not included in this table: miscellaneous transport services, other manufacturing (less rubber), business services (property owning, advertising and market research, other business services, central offices not allocable elsewhere), other miscellaneous services (betting and gambling, hairdressing and manicure, laundries, dry-cleaning, motor repairers, distributors, garages and filling stations, repair of boots and shoes, and other services). Union density in this heterogeneous group of industries was less than 3 per cent in 1974; total employment was 2.4 million.

†These figures are substantially overstated since it has not been possible to disaggregate the membership of the Commercial Trade Group of the Transport and General Workers' Union into those employed by haulage firms and those employed by manufacturing concerns. Union membership among the latter group should be classified to the relevant manufacturing industry.

Source: R. Price and G. S. Bain: *Union Growth Revisited.* B.J.I.R. xiv, 3.

Table I:4

Unionisation in larger manufacturing establishments in the United Kingdom, 1948 and 1974

	1948		1974	
	Labour force (000s)	Density (%)	Labour force (000s)	Density (%)
All manufacturing	6,709.3	52.2	7,778.9	62.2
Excluding employment in establishments with less than 100 workers	5,193.9	67.4	6,292.4	76.9
Excluding employment in establishments with less than 200 workers	4,268.4	82.1	5,422.5	89.2

Source: Price and Bain, op. cit.

of which are multinational. An equivalent number of people work in the combined public sector, including nationalised industries and national and local government and welfare services.

Trade union membership is heavily concentrated in these sectors, and so are some kinds of trade union problems. As Lord Bullock reported, unionisation is stronger in the larger enterprises: table I:4 reveals the degree of this concentration, and shows how far it has been increasing. In table I:3, we can follow the actual state of organisation, as it has been declining (in agriculture, wood and furniture, construction, or distribution) or increasing (everywhere else). These tables present us with a 'bird's eye view' of British trade unionism today, and provide a useful starting-point for the detailed studies which follow in the remaining chapters. They show clearly the density of organisation achieved by trade unions in Britain after almost 200 years of continuous history. Table I:3 shows that over the post-war period, only seven industry groups out of 33 experienced a decline in trade union density; some of the gains in the other sectors were of huge dimensions. Table I:4 indicates the overwhelmingly representative nature of trade unionism in the larger manufacturing sector of the economy, and the gains made there since 1948.

Although all this is useful and revealing information, it cannot easily be boiled down to tell us anything direct about any particular union or group of unions, because their structure is so complex that almost no industry is without its confusion of overlapping and even contending organisations. This is the central problem to be considered in our next chapter.

Division of Labour and Alienation

Concentration is one side of the process of development to which trade unions must react. The other side of it is the evolution of an ever more minute division of labour, involving those whom it entraps in paying more and more restrictive attention to smaller and smaller details. Once again we may find this problem clearly stated at the beginning of the industrial revolution by Adam Smith. He saw this principle as the first maxim of the new science of political economy, so much so that he began *The Wealth of Nations* with a description of a visit to a pin factory, where because of their obsessive specialisation on particular tasks, ten men could 'make upwards of forty-eight thousand pins in a day', whilst, had each worked separately, 'they certainly could not each of them have made twenty, perhaps not one pin in a day'.[22] The kind of centralisation which has grown up in the intervening two hundred years has not only concentrated power far beyond the dreams of eighteenth century manufacturers, it has also sharpened down the division of labour to a point where the founder of cybernetics has complained that in modern industry, people are only used to a millionth of their capacities.[23]

The two-way effect of capitalist industrialism, therefore, is to secrete vast agglomerations of unaccountable power at the top, while at the ground-level it affords individual people less and less opportunity to explore and develop their all-round abilities in the course of their work. This restriction of personal growth has profound implications for democracy, as was pointed up as long ago as 1835 by the distinguished philosopher of liberalism, Alexis de Tocqueville:

'When a workman is unceasingly and exclusively engaged in the fabrication of one thing, he ultimately does his work with singular dexterity; but at the same time he loses the general faculty of applying his mind to the direction of the work. He every day becomes more adroit and less industrious; so that it may be said of him that in proportion as the workman improves the man is degraded. What can be expected of a man who has spent twenty years of his life in making heads for pins? and to what can that mighty human intelligence, which has so often stirred the world, be applied in him, except it be to investigate the best method of making pins' heads? When a workman has spent a considerable portion of his existence in this manner, his thoughts are for ever set upon the object of his daily toil; his body has contracted certain fixed habits, which it can never shake off: in a word, he no longer belongs to himself, but to the calling which he has chosen. It is in vain that laws and manners have been at the pains to level all barriers around such

a man, and to open to him on every side a thousand different paths
to fortune; a theory of manufactures more powerful than manners
and laws binds him to a craft, and frequently to a spot, which he
cannot leave: it assigns to him a certain place in society beyond
which he cannot go: in the midst of universal movement it has
rendered him stationary.

In proportion as the principle of the division of labour is more
extensively applied, the workman becomes more weak, more
narrowminded, and more dependent. The art advances, the artisan
recedes. On the other hand, in proportion as it becomes more
manifest that the productions of manufactures are by so much the
cheaper and better as the manufacture is larger and the amount of
capital employed more considerable, wealthy and educated men
come forward to embark in manufactures which were heretofore
abandoned to poor or ignorant handicraftsmen. The magnitude of
the efforts required, and the importance of the results to be
obtained, attract them. Thus at the very time at which the science of
manufactures lowers the class of workmen, it raises the class of
masters.

Whereas the workman concentrates his faculties more and more
upon the study of a single detail, the master surveys a more
extensive whole, and the mind of the latter is enlarged in proportion
as that of the former is narrowed. In a short time the one will require
nothing but physical strength without intelligence; the other stands
in need of science, and almost of genius, to insure success. This man
resembles more and more the administrator of a vast empire—that
man, a brute. The master and the workman have then here no
similarity, and their differences increase every day.'[24]

H. G. Wells took this prediction literally when he wrote his novel
The Time Machine,[25] in which time-travellers voyage out into a future
in which 'masters' and 'workmen' have become two completely
different species. Of course, de Tocqueville's account of what might
happen to industrial civilisation is a gross over-simplification, precisely
inasmuch as it leaves out of account the inevitable responses of trade
unions, by far the most powerful countervailing tendency. To confront
the 'master', his 'brutes' must organise themselves: and in arguing with
him they are liable to refine their alternative picture of what the
working collective might be doing, and how it might be organised.

Yet there are constant difficulties in this process. First, in modern
industrial societies, the vital information upon which decisions are
taken is increasingly concentrated at the top, and selectively manipul-
ated to facilitate obedience below. Second, workpeople always *begin*

from 'the certain place in society beyond which they cannot go', which is a space in the pre-established division of labour. If they organise themselves as pin-makers, this is a major achievement: but they will soon then need links with wire-drawers, and then with iron and steel workers, and at the same time with the garment workers who employ their products. Here in a sentence we have compressed the whole of that century of historical struggles which we were just discussing, from the spontaneous growth of local trade associations up to the formation of a Congress of all the Trades, the TUC. But even once this is accomplished, and a vast democratic achievement it is, the work is only beginning. As we have already seen, the division of labour in modern industry is not something fixed and unvarying. It shifts and starts like the fragments in a kaleidoscope. New inventions, and indeed, whole new technologies, constantly recast the whole social industrial organisation. Yesterday's pin maker is today's chemical worker, or maybe tomorrow's computer operator. Not only do individuals shift their places: more urgently, from our point of view, whole types of skill are displaced, requiring convulsive re-organisations in work processes. And all these changes imperatively require similar vast adaptations in trade union organisation.

Trade Union Objects

This said, it is important to stress that trade union adaptation is not simply a matter of defensive administration. It is also, and in some ways crucially, a question of what the trade union itself is in business to do. Is it primarily concerned to help workpeople adjust to what the late C. A. R. Crosland called 'the technological imperatives', or is it an instrument for changing the status of labour, and ultimately abolishing the condition of 'employee'?

Richard Hyman has summarised the implications of the not uncommon view that modern unions are mainly, if not entirely, about fixing wages and conditions through the machinery of collective bargaining, in a telling paragraph:

'If unions have to accept the capitalist arrangements of industry—the structure of ownership, of economic priorities and of managerial authority—then they can be expected to provide no more than a limited range of improvements in the worker's situation. The reasonable member, in turn, will view his union as no more than a fairly narrow service agency; so long as it delivers the goods he has no cause to worry about its internal government. It would be as pointless to tell his full-time official how he should go about his job as it would be to tell his greengrocer.'[26]

He cites an eminent labour lawyer who lays down precisely such a restrictive dictum:

'Management can legitimately expect that labour will be available at a price which permits a reasonable margin for investment, and labour can equally legitimately expect that the level of real wages will not only be maintained but steadily increased. Management can claim a legitimate interest in obtaining for each job the most qualified worker available; labour can claim a legitimate interest in obtaining a job for each worker who is unemployed. Management can and must always expect that the arrangements of society (through law or otherwise) ensure that labour is as mobile as possible in the geographical as well as in the occupational sense; labour must always insist that workers enjoy a reasonable measure of job security so as to be able to plan their own and their families' lives. Management expects to plan the production and distribution of goods or supply of services on a basis of calculated costs and calculated risks, and requires society to guarantee the feasibility of such planning by protecting it against interruption of these processes; labour well realises that without the power to stop work collectively it is impotent, and expects to be able to interrupt the economic process if this is necessary in order to exercise the necessary pressure. Management's interest in planning production and in being protected against its interruption is the exact equivalent to the worker's interest in planning his and his family's life and in being protected against an interruption in his mode of existence, either through a fall of his real income or through a loss of his job. All this is palpably obvious, except for a person blinded by class hatred either way.'[27]

It is, of course, obvious that this view of 'legitimacy' would exclude any activity concerned with reversing the overall social position in which capital employs labour. Yet in fact, very few even of the most conforming trade unions are able to set their present-day assumptions within such a blinkered framework. One does not have to accept any dire perspective of social revolution to reject such arbitrary boundaries: collective wage bargaining is repeatedly constrained or even totally abrogated by governmental action in these times, and this recurrently makes even the most elementary questions of wages and working hours into key political issues. In some degree, the *more* a modern trade unionist places his faith in reforming devices, whether they be pay policies or 'social contracts', the *less* can he afford to treat his representatives as autonomous specialists, let alone to relate to them as he might to his greengrocer. To the extent that collective bargaining itself is extending its influence: spilling over from areas of wage-determination into questions of industrial policy, investment decisions and product-mixes, this narrow view becomes even less tenable. Hyman quite rightly insists that trade union purposes

'must be defined in terms of the members' own aspirations'.[28]

But these have always been changeable, and seldom more so than now.

Naturally, workpeople's aspirations change with changes in the overall political and economic climate. Just as people alter their immediate monetary demands, as they feel their needs altering, so too can they modify their picture of what kind of society they would most desire to live in, and what sorts of reform they see as most urgently necessary. Union rule books sometimes freeze these objectives for posterity: until 1977, for instance, the TUC rules still included machinery for initiating industrial action against future wars, while, in contrast, a number of affiliated bodies maintain rules committing them to support reforms which have long since been achieved. Nonetheless, there are certain broad objectives which recur from one rule book to the next, and from one generation to the next.[29] These concern the issues of power, control, and social accountability. Thus, the TGWU rules include as a main membership commitment the need

'to endeavour by all means in their power to control the industries in which their members are engaged,'

whilst the first aim of the AUEW is

'the control of industry in the interests of the community'.

The Foundryworkers' constitution speaks of

'developing and extending the co-operative system until a co-operative commonwealth is established which shall labour and produce for the good of all'.

The NUR sees these perspectives more doctrinally as requiring

'the supercession of the capitalist system by a socialist order of society'.

All these organisations, and many others, are affiliated to the Labour Party, which is pledged by rule to aim to secure 'the best obtainable system of popular control of each industry in service', in an often-forgotten section of its celebrated clause IV, the rule governing its commitment to social ownership.

We have argued elsewhere[30] that although the chosen means by which workers have pursued these goals have varied widely over the two centuries since the beginnings of the industrial revolution, it is easy to discern a strong thread of continuity, in which workpeople repeatedly reject the status of subordination and the deeply-felt lack of responsible citizenship which have uninterruptedly been imposed upon them, as a basic assumption of entrepreneurial thought and managerial practice, ever since the days of Richard Arkwright and his pioneering mills. The democracy of trade unions is strongly influenced by such objectives: many activists are motivated to voluntary service by the commitment to social change which they hold out; while they are still commonly felt to imply an alternative model of what is considered desirable conduct, which is seen as very distinct from the ethics of the rat-race in which so many of today's workpeople feel themselves to be entrapped.[31] Above all, such aims put a firm question-mark over the alleged immutability of the given, inherited division of labour, and in particular over the separation of mental from manual labour, within which modern workers are caught no less remorselessly than were their grandparents before them.

Postwar Growth: a Resumption of a Longer Trend

This alienation has in no way diminished with the rapid postwar concentration of industrial power, both in nationalised and in private multinational monopolies. As such companies have become stronger, so technologies have changed more fleetingly, and so the process of workers' organisation becomes more fluid and difficult. Whilst material living standards have been greatly improved, and expectations have developed accordingly, the individual worker in 1980 is commonly employed by a more arbitrary and unaccountable power than would have been imaginable in 1945. Even Governments have been known to quail at the hint of the displeasure of this power.

The more remarkable perhaps, at a time of such convulsions, is the continued, indeed continual, expansion in union strength, in the years since 1945.

This post-war growth of trade unionism is often contrasted with the period from 1926 to 1940 when trade union membership was in decline, and the inference is drawn that unionism undergoes periods of secular rise and fall. In fact, a much stronger case can be made for the belief that trade unionism (in Britain at least, where the continuity of the movement has been unbroken by war-time disruption or revolution), has exhibited a long-term historical tendency to grow, quantitatively, and to become more 'unionate' qualitatively, at least since the 1850s. A detailed historical analysis is not possible within the scope of this book, but it is argued here that the period of decline and quiescence, between 1926 and 1940, is best seen as an interruption to the historical trend. This is an important consideration at a time when nostalgic anti-trade union feelings are being successfully generated by the mass media and by some right-wing politicians, and an impression is being fostered that trade unionism can somehow be put in its (subordinate) place again—as it was between the wars. It should be evident that nothing short of a gigantic social and political upheaval could produce such an undesirable result.

NOTES

1. London, 1894: new edition, WEA, 1920. Translated into Russian by no less a person than Lenin, this book has repeatedly been quarried and requarried by authors and journalists of almost every imaginable persuasion, and criticised and recriticised by generations of sociologists of industrial relations. Nonetheless, it retains considerable value for the modern student.
2. Cf. V. L. Allen: *The Sociology of Industrial Relations*, Longman, 1971, Chapter 3.
3. The record of the founding Congress confirms this. It was republished in 1969, to commemorate the TUC centenary.
4. Cf. Ken Coates: *Work-ins, Sit-ins and Industrial Democracy*, Spokesman, 1980.
5. Cf. Ken Coates (ed.): *The New Worker Co-operatives*, Spokesman for IWC, 1976.
6. N. A. Citrine: *Trade Union Law* Stevens, 1950, p. 296 and following for a comprehensive discussion.
7. HMSO: Cmnd 3623, p. 205 et seq.
8. TUC: *Trade Unionism–Evidence to the Royal Commission*, 1966, pp. 29-31.
9. *The Wealth of Nations*, Everyman's Library edition, p. 59 et seq.
10. TUC: *Trade Unionism*: cited in footnote 8 above.
11. R. M. Blackburn: *Union Character and Social Class*, Batsford, 1967, p. 18.
12. *Full Employment*: Spokesman, 1978, Ch. 5.
13. TGWU: *Minutes of Evidence to Donovan Commission*, 15.3.1966 (30) p. 1181.
14. V. L. Allen, Ibid. pp. 125 et seq.
15. *Capital*, Volume 1, Chapter XXV 2.
16. Stuart Holland: *Strategy for Socialism*, Spokesman, 1975, p. 17.
17. Ibid.
18. Cited in Michael Barratt Brown: *From Labourism to Socialism*, Spokesman, 1972, p. 55.
19. M. Barratt Brown, op. cit., p. 56.
20. Stuart Holland, op. cit., p. 29.

21. HMSO Cmnd 6706, p. 9. See also pp. 8–19.
22. Book 1, Chapter 1. Everyman edition, pp. 4–11. Since 1776 informed commentators have nearly all reinforced Adam Smith's assumptions, until Stephen Marglin published his important essay: *What do bosses do?* See Andre Gorz: *The Division of Labour*, Harvester Press, 1976.
23. Norbert Weiner, *The Human Use of Human Beings*, Boston 1950.
24. Alexis de Tocqueville, *Democracy in America*, OUP, World's Classics, p. 427.
    Not that de Tocqueville took his own argument to the consistent conclusion drawn by Wells. On the contrary, as is clear from his notebook, published in English as *Journeys to England and Ireland* (edited by J. P. Mayer) Faber, 1958, De Tocqueville clearly thought that 'the gradual development of democratic principles must follow the irresistible march of events'.
25. H. G. Wells *The Time Machine*.
26. Richard Hyman, *Industrial Relations—A Marxist Introduction*, Macmillan, 1975, p. 85.
27. Otto Kahn-Freund, *Labour and the Law*, Stevens, 1972, pp. 52–3.
28. Ibid, p. 84. Hyman cites J. Child, M. Loveridge and M. Warner: 'Towards an Organizational Study of Trade Unions', *Sociology* 7, 1. They develop the distinction between 'administrative rationality' and 'representative rationality', or more baldly, between implementation on the one hand and determination of policy on the other. Too many commentators, says Hyman, quite rightly, blur this distinction, to the disadvantage of democracy.
29. For an account of union objectives in an earlier period, cf. W. Milne-Bailey: *Trade Union Documents*, Bell, 1929, Part I.
30. *Industrial Democracy in Great Britain*, Vols. 1–4, Spokesman, 1975–?
31. Some powerful accounts of this feeling are to be found in the two volumes of Ronald Fraser: *Work*, Penguin Books, 1968.

Chapter Two

Trade Union Structure

Types of Unions.
As may be seen in the tables presented in the last chapter, trade unions are considerably more successful in some industries than in others. In some sectors they are better organised and more rationally put together than in others, and in some areas they are more representative than elsewhere. How do unions recruit, and how do they organise their members? Obviously, there is no simple answer to these questions: unions come in a wide variety of sizes, shapes, and 'types': their classification is no longer the simple matter it used to seem.

The traditional discussion of trade unions divides them into three types: craft, industrial and general unions. Nowadays, the categories of 'occupational' and 'white-collar' unions are often added to this list. It is necessary first to explain this classification, which arose out of a process of evolution, although we shall see that it is now anything but adequate to explain present-day trade union structure.

Craft unionism customarily based itself on the principle of recruiting membership from some distinct skilled trade or occupation, normally entered through apprenticeship. The object was to ensure that all workers who went through such an apprenticeship, and qualified as tradesmen of a particular craft, became members of a trade union catering exclusively for it. A union which organised on this principle would enrol possessors of the skill, regardless of which industry or service might employ them; so that carpenters would belong to an exclusive carpenters' union whether they worked in the shipbuilding or in the house-building industries, for example.

The advantages of this form of organisation to its members were clear. By controlling the numbers of appentices admitted into the trade, and by regulating the length and nature of apprenticeship, the union could control the supply of its type of labour to the employers and it thus placed itself in a strong position to name the price for that labour. Craft unionism sought also, by virtue of the same control, to ensure greater security of employment for its members. Other favourable characteristics of this model of organisation included the fact that it generated fraternity amongst the members, based on their sense of a shared skill and relative equality of earnings. Because their aim was to restrict the supply of their skill, craft unions were not primarily concerned with maximum size; hence the internal problems of democratic administration and communication amongst the membership were less acute than in large organisations. Possession of a valuable skill which is widely in demand ensures a high degree of labour mobility amongst craftsmen, today, no less than in the past. But the value of particular skills varies and because this is so, craft unions have commonly been undermined.

In a dynamic economy, with constantly developing technology, the strongpoint of the craft is liable to be by-passed by technical change. The pace of this change has increased since the hey-day of craft organisation in the 19th century and in one industry after another the terrain has been completely altered. Many examples spring to mind, from the shipwrights, (craftsmen originally specialising in the skills of wooden shipbuilding) who were overtaken by prefabricated shipbuilding, to the vehicle builders (who carried on the hand-skills of the era of coach building for the horse-drawn road vehicle, and the rolling stock of the railway age) who were by-passed by the semi-skilled processes of assembly-line technology in the mass production of motor cars. Today, printing, the bastion of special skills, is being reduced to a new set of processes by the technology of offset lithography, which challenges not only the old-established trades, but also the traditional male monopoly of them.

A craft union caught in such circumstances has two options; to seek to preserve its pure form and witness a relentless decline in its numbers and bargaining strength, (to the point at which it may cease to be a viable organisation and be taken over by a larger union): or to alter its rules in order to admit other categories of membership; other crafts, or semi-skilled workers. In either case the structural consequence is the downfall of pure, single-craft unionism. This process, which is a continuing one, accounts in considerable degree for the prevalence of hybrid union forms in British trade union structure. A further disadvantage of the craft union is that its relatively small membership gives it little political influence: its vote at TUC and Labour Party Conferences will usually be negligible. Furthermore, its financial base will usually be insufficient to provide many of those services—research, education, legal advice—which members of a modern trade union find increasingly necessary. Moreover, whilst the fraternity of its membership may be strong within its ranks, craft unionism may foster a sectional outlook which militates against the growth of any wider sense of identification with the working class as a whole.

Craft unionism then, is important not for it present position since it has been in decline for many years, but for its residual influence on trade union structures, and the contribution it has made to the inheritance of sectionalism. Of course, all trade unions have some kind of sectional base, and even within the most 'General' of organisations, there exist groupings of particular occupations having strong sectional loyalties. Trade unions could hardly ever 'take off' as permanent bodies without this immediate sense of group identity; but it is one of the virtues of trade unionism that it has shown a persistent tendency to evolve ever wider forms of association, from such sectional origins.

We may at first sight readily identify an 'industrial union' as an organisation which seeks to recruit all the workers within a given industry, regardless of their occupations. On this principle, all employees of the railways, whatever their actual jobs, should belong to a single inclusive union for railway workers. The advantages claimed for this type of organisation are numerous. It will be larger than a cluster of purely occupational unions, and will represent the united strength of all the industry's workers, thus overcoming some of the sectionalism of craft or occupational groupings. It eliminates the problem of multi-unionism at all those levels in the industry where collective bargaining takes place, and this greatly simplifies the processes involved: a factor which in recent years has recommended this form of organisation to many employers. It brings any possible demarcation disputes within the confines of a single union, and makes it possible to resolve them through the normal processes of union decision-making. To an earlier generation of syndicalist militants, industrial unionism was the means through which class struggle could be waged until the moment of revolution, and thereafter it was the institution for the democratic administration of socialised industry. Rather oddly, perhaps, industrial unionism has also been a deliberate theory of trade union organisation for those whose aim is to re-order industrial relations on more rational lines, in order the better to administer the *present* state of things.

Industrial unionism in Britain, despite the advocacy of such incompatible schools of theorists, has not been a very successful means of organisation, for a number of reasons. In the first place, craft, sectional, and occupational unionism during the nineteenth century often established themselves *across* industrial boundaries, or as tightly-organised segments *within* an industry, before industrial union organisation was advanced. This has often meant that industrial unions have been frustrated in their ambitions to become the sole force within their chosen field.

On the railways, for instance, clerical workers have preferred to maintain their own white-collar union of railway clerks (later to embrace all salaried staff) and train drivers have evolved a form of craft unionism to organise foot-plate workers. The National Union of Railwaymen was thus faced with two stubborn forms of sectional unionism which refused to merge into an industrial organisation. Complicating matters still further, the skilled men in the railway workshops have preserved their membership of appropriate craft unions, which themselves maintain membership in dozens of other industries.

The National Union of Mineworkers represents the nearest approach in modern Britain to a fully inclusive industrial union in a major industry, though even here supervisory grades have a separate union (the National Association of Colliery Overmen, Deputies and Shotfirers), as do colliery managers, in the British Association of Colliery Managers. The National Union of Public Employees has often claimed to be an industrial union, but its membership is mainly divided between what may be considered to be two distinct industries, local government and the health service, and while in both cases it co-exists with others organising similar grades of workers, it is weak among skilled workers, technicians, and white-collar staff. The most common union structures nowadays found within particular industries are the 'multi-craft' form (found in shipbuilding, and printing) or the combination of craft and general unionism, sometimes (as in steel) with an industrial union representing the most characteristic specific skills and processes in the industry. Thus the possibility of pure industrial unionism has usually been pre-empted by the existence of prior organisation along craft or general union lines.

But there are other objections to industrial unionism, quite apart from these purely practical considerations.

In fact, the drawing of boundary lines to demarcate one industry from another is often a difficult or arbitrary process. When coal was the only source of fuel and power, the coal-mining industry defined itself fairly readily as self-sufficient for purposes of trade union organisation. But in an era when gas, oil, electricity and atomic energy, to say nothing of potential future alternative sources of power, offer themselves as alternatives, it is highly questionable whether a union confined to one section of the *fuel and power industry* constitutes an adequate long-term form of defensive organisation. Shifts in the balance between alternative power sources imply serious permanent effects upon employment patterns, and a trade union which aims to exercise influence and control over the planning of an industry's future, must be flexible enough to follow, indeed, to anticipate such changes, in the interests of its members' job security. Unions which have defined their area of recruitment in terms of particular industries at a certain stage of economic history find themselves vulnerable to large-scale shifts of resources caused by structural economic change. Thus, as coal has declined, so has the membership of the NUM, from 613,000 in 1952, to 256,000 in 1979. Similarly, the decline of the railway industry in the face of competition from road transport has reduced the membership of the National Union of Railwaymen from 396,000 in 1952, to 180,000 in 1979. The railwaymen's difficulty is indeed very similar to that of the miners: only by embracing the whole transport industry, rather than the dwindling railway section alone, could a union develop a relevant industrial strategy.

Change is the rule, wherever trade unions operate, and even if we could draw boundaries which were appropriate for today's industrial structure, they would need to be re-drawn for every new generation. It is not simply that technology changes the division of labour within industries: the organisation of large conglomerate companies increasingly disregards the industrial boundaries of the past. Nowadays the giant companies hedge their bets. Trade unions in ICI, for example, confront a common employer which spreads its manufacturing activities across a whole complex of 'industries': textiles, agricultural fertilisers, plastics, heavy industrial chemicals: whatever, indeed, the company decides to do next.

The third 'traditional' category, that of general unions, appears to suffer none of the disadvantages of craft and industrial unionism. By definition, general unions recruit across both occupational and industrial boundaries, and in theory they recognise no restrictions on their potential membership. In practice, of course, because of their historical origins in particular sectors of the economy, their membership is 'weighted' around cores in specific industries and occupations. Yet they have shown themselves flexible enough to take in new occupations, skills, and industries as these have arisen in the course of technical and economic change. Both the two largest general unions began life in the late 1880s, organising particular groups of unskilled workers. The main parent of the Transport & General Workers' Union was the Dock, Wharf, Riverside and General Labourers' Union, and the chief forerunner of the General and Municipal Workers' Union was the National Union of Gasworkers and General Labourers of Great Britain and Ireland. We should note the significance of the phrase 'and general labourers' in the titles of both these pioneering organisations. It tells us that, *from the outset*, these unions deliberately intended that their recruitment should not be restricted to specific industries or occupations. The reason for this is not hard to find; unlike the craftsmen, dockers and gasworkers were in no position to construct a tightly exclusive barrier around their occupations. Because their jobs were casual and relatively unskilled, all 'general labourers' were potential blacklegs threatening effective trade unionism anywhere unless all could be enrolled in the union. Thus the general unions felt it necessary to construct organisations having all the flexibility which other forms of union denied to themselves. It is small wonder that they have flourished and grown to their present dominant size (although the difference in relative success between the TGWU and the GMWU is worthy of serious attention, as we show below.)

With skill levels diversifying, and a growing level of universal literacy, the most obvious advantage of the general union is no longer confined to its appeal to the unskilled. Nowadays, the ability to adapt organisation and recruitment to the shifting patterns of occupations and industries gives general unions a strong capacity to survive and to grow.

By virtue of their size, such unions can afford to provide far more extensive services for their members than can smaller organisations. Such services may well include the development of specialist groupings of members and officers catering for particular occupations and industries. Indeed, a union's willingness to do this has a strong influence on its potential for retaining its existing membership. It acts as an insurance against any tendency for minority groups to develop sectional attitudes which might lead to breakaway unionism; and it provides an incentive, attracting new groups and smaller unions to merge their forces into the larger collective.

The key example of the flexibility of general unionism is provided by the shifting patterns of membership in the TGWU, which organises its members into broad industrial groupings. As its original base in the port transport industry has declined between 1950 and 1977 from 86,000 to 56,000 with the mechanisation of cargo handling, its membership in the road commercial industry has grown from 162,000 to 214,000; and that in engineering, from 197,000 to 269,000.

At the beginning of 1977, the TGWU membership was organised into major sections as Table II:1 shows.

These are tabulated, for convenience, alongside the industrial sectors of the GMWU. This table not only underlines the point that organisation into industrial subsections can be both fluid and stable, according to need: it also shows that where two or more general organisations co-exist in the same sectors, liaison can become complex, where subsections are defined according to different principles. All the same arguments which tell so strongly in favour of a general union, weigh rather powerfully against there being more than one such union in the same time and place!

Table II:1
Comparison of industrial sectors, TGWU and GMWU

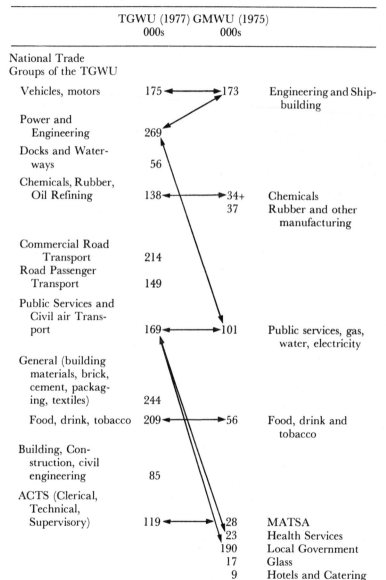

	TGWU (1977) 000s	GMWU (1975) 000s	
National Trade Groups of the TGWU			
Vehicles, motors	175	173	Engineering and Ship-building
Power and Engineering	269		
Docks and Water-ways	56		
Chemicals, Rubber, Oil Refining	138	34+ 37	Chemicals Rubber and other manufacturing
Commercial Road Transport	214		
Road Passenger Transport	149		
Public Services and Civil air Trans-port	169	101	Public services, gas, water, electricity
General (building materials, brick, cement, packag-ing, textiles)	244		
Food, drink, tobacco	209	56	Food, drink and tobacco
Building, Con-struction, civil engineering	85		
ACTS (Clerical, Technical, Supervisory)	119	28 23 190 17 9	MATSA Health Services Local Government Glass Hotels and Catering

The last and most obvious great advantage of general unions, is that their numbers enable them to play a major role in the decision-making machinery of the Labour movement as a whole; their block vote and influence at Labour and TUC Conferences is consistent and large.

Yet there are also disadvantages attached to great size. Most obviously there is a danger that bureaucratic and remote methods of policy-making may undermine internal democracy. Furthermore, in purely industrial terms, a large general union very rarely punches it full weight; within its ranks may be large groups of low paid workers for whom only a major industrial action by the whole union would suffice to raise them from their poverty. Yet unions will rarely contemplate such a deployment of their potential strength, partly because of the political implications, and partly through fear that its members in the better-paid sectors might not respond to a call for action on behalf of poorly paid members in a Wages Council industry.

In sum: the traditional classification of unions into craft, industrial, and general unions applies, in pure form, to the merest minority of unions.

Since most existing unions do not fall neatly into any of the time-honoured categories, scholars have offered alternative and supplementary terms, such as 'occupational union', and 'white-collar' or 'non-manual' union. 'Occupational' unions are those which organise workers in a particular occupation or related groups of occupations which are more loosely homogeneous than the apprentice-based craftsmen. Some of these occupational unions, such as the Association of Professional, Executive, Clerical and Computer Staffs, range over many industries rather like a craft society, whilst others, for example, the Fire Brigades Union, confine their recruitment to one occupation within a wider industry. 'White-collar' or 'non-manual' unionism clearly describes a sector of the movement which is readily identifiable and of growing significance. But apart from unions which concentrate exclusively on non-manual occupations, the large general and semi-industrial unions usually include white-collar sections of their own. Moreover, technical change in industry, bringing the growth of new occupations like computer staffs and technicians, increasingly tends to blur the once clear distinction between non-manual and manual occupations. A worker in a computerised office may become increasingly difficult to distinguish from a worker in a computerised factory.

'Vertical' and 'Horizontal' Structures

All this has led to the formulation of other attemps to explain trade union structure. It is sometimes said that unions are organised along either 'vertical' or 'horizontal' principles. A horizontal union recruits from a grade or grades of workers spread across industrial boundaries —all clerks in the clerks' union, all supervisors in the supervisors' union, and so on. This principle corresponds closely to, and therefore includes, the craft organisations—all fitters in the fitters' union, all plumbers in the plumbers' union, and so on. The vertical union on the other hand, aims to recruit all workers, whatever their grade or occupation, with a common industrial background, and thus corresponds to the industrial classification. These categories are useful, in that they draw attention to recognisable tendencies in union organisation and recruitment strategies. They further indicate the astonishing degree of complexity of structure which emerges from the simultaneous and historical pursuit of both (opposing) principles by different trade unions in Britain.

If we represent just a very small selection from the total pattern of industrial and occupational employment, and examine the fortunes of different trade union types within it, we can establish the picture of complexity and competing forms of organisation. We take a selection of industries, and a few broad categories of occupation, and picture them on a chequer board of vertical and horizontal columns.

	Steel	Railways	Civil Service	Local Government	Chemicals	Engineering
Supervisors	1	2	3	4	5	6
Clerks	7	8	9	10	11	12
Engineering Crafts	13	14	15	16	17	18
General and semi-skilled	19	20	21	22	23	24

It would require a major essay on its own to describe in full detail the trade union pattern which occupies all 24 of the segments in our diagram. A general summary must suffice. Supervisory workers are one of the major recruitment areas for the Association of Scientific,

Technical, and Managerial Staffs, and they are very successfully pursued therefore on horizontal lines. (471,000 people were enrolled in ASTMS in 1979). Nonetheless, in square 1, ASTMS immediately confronts the Iron and Steel Trades Confederation, a vertical or industrial union, as well as an internal management association, in British Steel. On the railways (square 2) supervisors are organised by either the vertically orientated National Union of Railwaymen, or the sectional Transport Salaried Staffs Association. In the Civil Service (square 3) there are purely sectional unions like the Inland Revenue Staff Federation, or the more widely based Civil and Public Service Association, catering for some supervisory grades. In Local Government, NALGO (National and Local Government Officers Association), square 4, occupies almost the whole territory. In chemicals, ASTMS has a clearer field (square 5), but the two major general unions also recruit here, for each of their white-collar sections. Supervisors in engineering (square 6) are one of the founding bases of the ASTMS, but even here competition is encountered from the Technical, Administrative and Supervisory Section of the Engineering Union. Clearly there is no possibility of ASTMS becoming an all-inclusive horizontal union for supervisors across all industrial boundaries. (Of course, a different selection of industries, taken to include insurance, finance, or higher education, would have revealed far more hopeful fields for ASTMS recruitment).

The Association of Professional, Executive, Clerical and Computer Staff is a horizontal union with its base in the clerical occupations, yet in squares 7, 8, 9 (steel, railways and the civil service), and 10 (local government) it encounters the same obstacles to recruitment as the ASTMS. Similarly in square 11 (chemicals), whilst doing rather better, it also encounters competition from the white collar sections of the TGWU and the GMWU. It has better fortune in square 12, (engineering). The engineering craft occupations, organised into the Amalgamated Union of Engineering Workers, have through prior craft organisation successfully pursued horizontal unionism for these grades of its membership right across the industrial field, so that squares 13 to 18 are largely the preserve of the AUEW. This effectively frustrates any hope of all-inclusive *vertical* unionism in almost any industry, as well as inhibiting it in those we have selected. The general unions, the TGWU and GMWU, have a mixed experience of the fortunes of horizontal unionism in our selected industries. In steel (square 19) the vertical union of steel process workers, the ISTC, recruits the more skilled grades, but has left room for both general unions amongst the less skilled manual workers. In the railways (square 20), the vertical NUR effectively bars the way to any recruitment by horizontal general unions. In the civil service (square 21), there is scope for the two giants, although a sectional union for manual workers within the Civil Service, (the Civil Service Union) enrols 47,000 members. Local Government (square 22), provides ample scope for the GMWU and the TGWU, but strong and successful competition is provided by the National Union of Public Employees. In chemicals, (square 23), the two general unions have major representation of process manual grades, although they are joined here by a third general union, USDAW. In engineering (square 24), the two general unions have large membership, but compete for them with the AUEW which has *vertical* union ambitions in that industry.

If we cast our eyes down the vertical columns, we find that vertical unionism is most strongly represented in our selection by the NUR on the railways, though as we have seen it is incomplete even there. In steel and engineering, there are species of partially successful vertical unionism (ISTC and AUEW respectively) whilst in the civil service, chemicals, and local government, vertical unionism as such hardly exists as a distinct form.

Any exercise of this kind, then, examining trade union coverage across, or up-and-down, the industrial boundaries, merely reveals the extraordinary complexity of organisation. Vertical and horizontal types exist as tendencies, rarely all-embracing, whilst some organisations combine both horizontal and vertical features. Others again, purely sectional-occupational unions, confine their recruitment to a single square on the board, pursuing neither horizontal nor vertical ambitions.

'Open' and 'Closed' Structures

We turn now to a more recent, and in many ways the most fruitful, method of examining structure. This, originated by Professor Turner,[1] identifies types of trade union by their different recruitment strategies, and distinguishes two basic methods, 'open' and 'closed'. A union is open when it is actively recruiting, or seeking mergers with other unions, in new occupational or industrial areas, and is closed when it concentrates on its existing territory, aiming to make that a strong-point of organisation and bargaining strength. A union, in the course of its history, may be closed at one time, open at another. Moreover it may at the same time be closed in some directions (e.g. vertically) whilst being open in others (e.g. horizontally). The extremes of the two strategies are represented by a completely closed single-craft or occupational union, and by a completely general, open union. In the course of time, a once-closed union may consider that this strategy has been undermined by changes in employment demand in its territory, and revise its rules to admit new occupations. This is the process by which the once pure craft unionism of the old Amalgamated Society of Engineers has been transformed into the near general unionism of the Amalgamated Union of Engineering Workers, with its engineering, foundry, construction and technical sections. Within a broadly open union, there may develop strong points of organisation around particular occupations, which the members and union then aim to close against indiscriminate new recruitment, by control of entry into the occupation. This is what has happened in the docks section of the TGWU, where the statutory dock labour scheme of employment gives the dockers a right of veto over any decision by employers to recruit new workers. In this case, the dockers' former dependence on the open strategy of general unionism gave way, after the second world war, to a sense of self-sufficiency which led to a serious breakaway union movement in the ports. This has only been contained and reversed because the union leadership's response to the challenge was to make the docks section more democratic and responsive to members' wishes.[2]

There is no doubt that the most recent trends in organisation point to the attraction for many unions of a more open strategy than has been traditional. One after another, unions in the 'sixties and 'seventies have changed their titles to indicate their entry into new fields of enrolment. Thus the Clerical and Administrative Workers' Union became the Association of Professional, Executive, Clerical and Computer Staffs, and the Civil Service Clerical Association became the Civil and Public Services Association. Sometimes the words 'and allied workers' or 'and allied craftsmen' are added to a title, as in the case of the agricultural workers and the patternmakers, with the same intent. Every possible variant on the open/closed theme is present in British trade union structure, so much so that some writers have now abandoned the old classifications and created a new terminology. Thus John Hughes speaks of 'sectoral-general' unions, to describe those like USDAW, NUPE and the AUEW; of 'occupational (non-manual) sectoral' to describe NALGO, and of 'occupational-industrial' to describe the former Gas Staffs Association.[3]

In reality, the structure is so complex as almost to defy classification: unions are undergoing an evolutionary and continuing process which invites comparison with the Darwinian process of natural selection, or, closer to industrial experience, with the growth of conglomerate and hybrid forms of company organisation.

Demarcation and Disputes between Unions
    In one important respect however, the trade union movement acts

to prevent the full impact of the law of the survival of the fittest. Through the operation of the famous 'Bridlington Rules' (adopted at the TUC Congress in Bridlington in 1939)[4] the TUC ensures that competition between unions for members is regulated. According to these rules, unions must not recruit members from another union whilst that union is engaged in a trade dispute, or whilst the members are in dispute with that union, or in arrears with their contributions. Unions may not commence recruitment in an area where another has enrolled a majority of the workers. The TUC, which operates a disputes procedure to enforce these rules, and can make them effective where it chooses by the threat or the execution of a decision to expel the offending union, at one time interpreted them in such a way as to simply preserve the vested interests of existing trade unions, even where their 'majority' of members was a thing of the past.[5] There have frequently been complaints by smaller unions that these rules were 'bent' to accommodate the interests of the larger affiliates of the TUC. Sometimes, certainly, the rules operated to prevent a dynamic and expanding union from moving into a territory occupied by a complacent and ineffective union, and this has led in some cases to the virtual protection of *non*-unionism.

In more recent years, however, the TUC disputes committee has adopted a more rational and intelligent interpretation of the rules, to prevent a union from claiming sole rights within an area whilst any large numbers of workers remain unorganised. Some critics have suggested that the rules should be re-written to allow the TUC (in cases which reach its Disputes Committee) to operate a positive policy which deliberately favours a rationalisation of union structure, aimed at reducing or eliminating multi-unionism within any given area of recruitment.

Organisational Success

One way of testing the relative effectiveness of different forms of trade union structure is to examine the degree of organisation reached (trade union membership as a proportion of employees) in different sectors of the economy, and to ask what kind of unionism prevails in each sector. When Professor Clegg did this, using data from 1964, he found that:

'The highest degree of organisation is found in an industrial union, the Mineworkers, but another industrial union, the Tailors and Garment Workers, comes near the bottom. The second industrial group in terms of organisation, national government service, is covered by a bewildering variety of separate unions, whereas the distributive trades, near the bottom of the list, have only one union, the Shop, Distributive and Allied Workers. One industrial group in which craft unions figure strongly, paper and printing, comes fairly near the top of the list, whereas another, construction, comes surprisingly near the bottom. The two general unions are the most important unions in the fourth and fifth groups on the list—gas, electricity and water, and transport and communications (excluding railways)—but they are equally important in the food, drink, and tobacco group near the bottom of the table.'[6]

Here are his figures, together with a second column giving broadly comparable information for 1974 with the rank order for the latter year entered for comparison. Although there have been remarkable gains in many sectors, and some changes in the rank order over the ten year period, as well as some amendment to union structure through amalgamation and mergers, Clegg's broad conclusions have not been seriously outdated by more recent experience.

Table II:2

Distribution of trade union members by industrial group,
end 1964, and June 1974

Group	Proportion of Employees in Trade Unions (per cent)		
	1964	1974	Rank Order 1974
Coalmining	95	96.2	2
National Government Service	87	90.5	5
Local Government Service	82	85.6a.	6
Gas, Electricity and Water	81	92.0	4
Transport & Communication (excluding railways)	76	95.8b.	3
Railways	73	96.9	1
Footwear	63	79.0	7
Paper, printing and publishing	59	71.6	8
Metals & Engineering	55	69.4	10
All textiles	42	40.9	19
Educational Services	41	—	
Entertainment & media services	41	64.9	11
Timber & Furniture	37	35.2	20
Bricks, Pottery, Glass, Cement, etc.	37	70.9c.	9
Chemicals	36	51.2	14
Insurance, Banking, & Finance	35	44.8	17

Table II:2 (cont.)

Group	Proportion of Employees in Trade Unions (per cent)		
	1964	1974	Rank Order 1974
Other Mining and Quarrying	34	51.8	13
Agriculture, Forestry and Fishing	30	41.4d.	18
Leather, leather goods, and Fur	30	46.6e.	16
Construction	28	27.2	21
Clothing other than Footwear	27	60.0	12
Food, Drink, & Tobacco	27	51.2	14
Professional & Technical Services not elsewhere	27	—	
Other Manufacturing Industries	26	—	
Distributive Trades	12	11.4	22
Catering, hotels, motor repairs, domestic service, and all other miscellaneous services	3	—	

Source: for 1964, H. A. Clegg, *The System of Industrial Relations in Great Britain,* Blackwell, 1970, pages 59-60, quoted from Royal Commission on Trade Unions and Employers' Associations, *Selected Written Evidence,* page 23.

for 1974, R. Price and G. S. Bain, 'Union Growth Re-Visited', *British Journal of Industrial Relations,* Vol. XIV, No. 3, pages 342-343.

a.   includes Education.
b.   average of Road Transport (95.1%), Sea Transport (99.6%), Port and Inland Water Transport (94.7%), and Air Transport (93.6%).
c.   average of Bricks and Building Materials (40.4%), Pottery (93.8%), and Glass (78.5%).
d.   average of Agriculture and Forestry (22.2%), and Fishing (60.5%).
e.   includes only Leather.

Structural Reform

The lack of evidence linking structural form with organisational success may be one reason why efforts to achieve major structural reform and the elimination of multi-unionism have met with mixed fortunes when they have been attemped by the TUC. Periodic dissatisfaction with the current structure has been forcefully expressed on several important occasions in the twentieth century history of the TUC. In 1924, the TUC resolved:

'(a) that the time has arrived when the number of trade unions should be reduced to an absolute minimum, (b) that the aim should be as far as possible organisation by industry, with every worker a member of the appropriate organisation (c) that it is essential that a united front be formed for improving the standards of life of the workers.'

When the TUC General Council reported on its efforts to achieve a complete re-organisation on industrial lines in accordance with this Resolution, in 1927, they concluded that the object was simply not achievable without a serious danger of splitting the movement, because of opposition from craft unions. The only practical method was for the TUC to encourage amalgamation and federation where possible. In 1944, the TUC issued another report on the same theme— *Trade Union Structure and Closer Unity*. This again recognised that whilst industrial unionism was a desirable goal, it could only be achieved by the most patient and cautious measures, which had to respect existing unions' interests. In practice, amalgamations and mergers have continued throughout the history of the trade union movement. The largest number of separate trade unions ever affiliated to the TUC was 266 in 1919. Since then the number has been steadily reduced to 112 in 1979, even though major new affiliations representing employees at professional and managerial levels have taken place throughout the 1960s and into the 1970s.

A particularly strong wave of amalgamation has occurred since the most recent formal enquiry was ordered by the TUC in 1962. On that occasion, the Union of Post Office Workers moved that:

'Congress agrees that it is time the British trade union movement adapted its structure to modern conditions. It instructs the General Council to examine and report to the 1963 Congress on the possibility of reorganising the structure of both the TUC and the British trade union movement with a view to making it better fitted to meet modern industrial conditions.'

In accepting the motion on behalf of the General Council, George Woodcock, TUC General Secretary, made his famous remark: 'Structure . . . is a function of purpose' and went on—'We expect that we shall first of all in our inquiries, inquire into trade union purpose and policy and ask ourselves "What are we here for?" When we know what we are here for, then we can talk about the kind of structure that will enable us to do what we are here for.' He concluded that 'it will be the beginning of a tremendous undertaking.' The mood on that occasion was one of reforming zeal, although it should be noted that Congress did not commit itself to the support of the industrial union principle, as it had on previous occasions.

A year later, George Woodcock reported to Congress on the progress of discussions on the 1962 Resolution. A different note was struck.

'We in the trade union Movement of Great Britain so far have never had a theory of trade unionism. Indeed we have religiously avoided committing ourselves to any theory of trade unionism. So far as the TUC is concerned all unions are equal . . . We have never made any distinction at all inside the TUC between unions on account of their structure . . . this refusal to construct a trade union theory, has been extraordinarily useful in holding together unions of different kinds . . . a very strong case could be made out for asserting that diversity of trade union structure is itself a theory of trade unionism. We have looked at . . . this problem of diversity, this present characteristic. We have come . . . firmly to the conclusion that diversity of structure—that is, unions of different size, of different shape, of different structure—is a characteristic of British trade unionism and always will be . . . We see no real alternative to a continuation for a long time, I would say so far as this Congress is concerned, for ever, of a great degree of diversity.'

Following the 1962 initiative, then, there was to be no dramatic revolution in trade union structure. But the TUC has from that time taken a wider responsibility in calling together groups of unions with similar interests and adjacent areas of recruitment, promoting mergers and amalgamations, where possible; or encouraging closer working arrangements as a less radical alternative.

What has been achieved since 1963, and to what extent does it relate to George Woodcock's concern for the relation between structure and purpose?

Trade unions in the modern world inevitably reach out to include in their purposes the attempt to influence planning at all levels of the economy. Since 1963, this kind of role has received more attention, and been more precisely defined by the development of the industrial democracy debate, the concept of Planning Agreements, the idea of the social audit, and similar developments. Further, in an era of growing unemployment, workers seek membership of unions not only for purposes of wage bargaining, but as a means of pursuing job security. Changes in the composition of large firms through the merger boom of the sixties and seventies, the growing concentration of ownership and control in the boardrooms of British industry, the growth in significance and influence of multi-national companies, and renewed political debate on strategies for achieving social control of the economy, all imply vastly wider roles for trade unions. At the same time, the growth of public sector employment, following postwar nationalisations and the extension of welfare agencies, has produced its own response in the trade union world. 55 per cent of all union members work in the public sector.

As long ago as 1967, John Hughes spelled out what he considered to be the minimum capacities which trade unions needed to develop in the light of these purposes. He argued that they needed to develop:

(i)   their research services
(ii)   their education services
(iii)   their communication networks to their membership
(iv)   the quality and numbers of their full-time staffs.
(v)   their provision for the internal sectional representation of specific occupational and industrial groupings of their members.
(vi)   their technical and advisory services—e.g. on safety, law, organisation and method, and similar questions.
(vii)   their briefing services for their representatives on official Boards.[7]

He added too that they needed to be able to hold out 'the prospect of strengthening and expanding lay participation.' He argued from this that modern trade unions required to have a minimum size and income to fulfil these needs, and that a reasonable minimum size, giving an annual income of £¼ million in the average subscriptions of 1967, was 250,000 members. He drew the conclusions that with this size, unions must develop internal structures which allowed for the articulation of members' interests on a sectional basis; that joint working arrangements between unions should be more positively fostered, that the Bridlington rules should be used more creatively to rationalise structure, that the TUC should expand its system of industrial committees to further inter-union co-ordination, and that an adequate system of TUC servicing of unions required that its real income should increase five-fold. (In fact, between 1967 and 1978, TUC net income from subscriptions has trebled during a period of fierce inflation.) He proposed, as others have done,[8] that dramatic improvement of all these capacities would follow from mergers amongst the very largest group of unions—either the TGWU with the GMWU and the AUEW, or the TGWU with the GMWU and USDAW, or the GMWU with NUPE and other public sector manual unions. He called for multilateral arrangements between unions to exchange members, and for the promotion of dual membership where vertical and horizontal interests of workers required that they have two sets of representatives, as in the case of craftsmen in the steel industry. Such a programme puts some flesh on the rather general and skeletal framework of George Woodcock. In its simplest conclusion, it implies that 'bigger is better'. Let us examine the picture as it concerns those unions with over 250,000 members.

Overall TUC affiliated membership has increased since Mr Woodcock's 1962 speech from 8,312, 875 to 12,128,078 in 1979, a rise of 46.0 per cent. The number of TUC unions has fallen from 182 to 112 in the same period. Thus, the average size of TUC unions has increased from 45,675 to 108,286. In 1962 there were 7 unions with over 250,000 members, representing 55 per cent of TUC membership. In 1979 there were 11 such unions, representing 67 per cent of TUC membership. The list of these unions is presented in the table below.

Table II:3

Unions with over 250,000 members, 1962 and 1977-79

1962			1977	1979
TGWU	1,318,274	TGWU	1,929,834	2,072,818
AEU	982,182	AUEW	1,412,076	1,483,419
GMWU	786,138	GMWU	916,438	964,836
NUM	545,329	NALGO	683,011	729,405
USDAW	351,371	NUPE	650,530	712,000
NUR	308,050	EETPU	420,000	420,000
ETU	252,851	USDAW	412,627	462,178
		ASTMS	396,000	471,000
		UCATT	297,264	320,723
		NUT	289,107	291,239
		NUM	259,966	254,887

Source: TUC *Annual Reports.*

It can be seen that the TGWU has continued to sustain a high rate of growth, partly through take-overs of smaller unions, and partly through net additions to membership. Its growth of 57 per cent in the period compares very favourably with that achieved by the GMWU (22 per cent) and USDAW (31 per cent).

The AUEW's growth is partly explained by the amalgamation of the former Constructional Engineering Union (24,000 members in 1962), the Foundry Workers' Union (72,900 members in 1962), and the Draughtsmen's Association (70,396 members in 1962), with the parent union the Amalgamated Engineering Union. These mergers have been attended by difficulties in the relationship between the sections.

NALGO and the NUT enter the table in 1977 simply because they were not affiliated to the TUC in 1962. Their affiliation has greatly strengthened the TUC's claim to speak for all substantial bodies of trade unionists. The Mineworkers have lost half their members over the period, dropping from 4th to 11th place. (Though this certainly does not imply a necessary loss of bargaining authority within their own industry, as their industrial actions of the early 1970's demonstrated.) The NUR, which fell in numbers to 180,000 in 1979, drops out of the table entirely. The EETPU's growth is partly due to the amalgamation between the electricians and the plumbers (PTU membership was 55,658 in 1962) and partly due to the growth of the electronics industry. NUPE's growth represents mainly its sustained ability to recruit new members amongst lower manual grades, (including part-time workers and women) in local government and the national health service. Its membership in 1962 was 215,000. ASTMS enters the table for similar growth reasons, and also by virtue of a whole series of amalgamations. The original merger which created ASTMS was between the Association of Supervisory Staffs, Executives and Technicians—26,826 in 1962—, and the Association of Scientific Workers—14,256 in 1962. ASTMS's growth is in fact more rapid and spectacular than that of any other union. UCATT appears in the table largely by virtue of amalgamation between former craft and non-craft unions in the building industry.

Table II:4

Number of trade unions analysed by size of union

	1962	1977
Under 100 members	129	74
100–499	156	144
500–999	63	45
1,000–2,499	105	66
2,500–4,999	61	41
5,000–9,999	34	28
10,000–14,999	24	10
15,000–24,999	22	13
25,000–49,999	18	18
50,000–99,999	19	15
100,000–249,999	10	15
250,000 and more	8	11
	649	480

Source: Department of Employment *Gazette.*

Table II:5

Membership of Trade Unions analysed by size of unions (thousands)

	1962	1977
Under 100 members	7	4
100–499	39	37
500–999	44	32
1,000–2,499	173	109
2,500–4,999	203	144
5,000–9,999	229	178
10,000–14,999	289	123
15,000–24,999	410	256
25,000–49,999	637	642
50,000–99,999	1,290	1,015
100,000–249,999	1,609	2,171
250,000 and more	5,085	7,995
	10,015	12,707

Source: Department of Employment *Gazette.*

It is not possible to evaluate the progress made between 1962 and the present time, without consulting the statistics for over-all trade union membership, including non-TUC unions, for the period. These reveal precisely the same trend of growing concentration of membership into a smaller number of unions.

Amalgamation, then, is clearly having a marked impact upon the shape of British trade unionism.

In spite of the spate of union mergers (and still more significant ones are likely in the future), the problem of multi-unionism continues. For this and other reasons workers at shop floor and company level still need to form Joint Shop Steward Committees and Combine Committees. We deal with these organisations in chapter five on shop stewards. At industry-level, the TUC has also sought to meet the need for inter-union collaboration more fully in recent years through its system of industrial committees, which are discussed in chapter 4.

Federations of unions in particular industries, to facilitate collective negotiations were once a significant part of trade union organisation in a number of industries. But of the three most important federations (in building, printing and engineering) only the Confederation of Shipbuilding and Engineering Unions survives, bringing together 23 unions, having its own national conference and negotiating subcommittees. The National Federation of Building Trades Operatives

and the Printing and Kindred Trades Federation have been super-
seded by the more effective and complete reform of structure
represented by union amalgamations, or as their functions were taken
over by TUC Industry Committees.[9]

Federations of unions are in any case not a complete substitute for
amalgamation, particularly because they are less likely to provide for
that 'prospect of strengthening and expanding lay participation'.

Change and Democracy

So, today's trade union movement is dominated by a handful of
mass organisations, the most important of which extend their influence
into a broad cross-section of industries, and assemble the practitioners
of a wide variety of skills and trades. Yet, like flies in amber, we can see
in the roster of affiliates to the TUC, numerous small societies,
restricting their membership to one narrow area, and organising only
the most exclusive trade groups. These associations, with all their local
and specialised distinguishing characteristics, show us something of the
trade union past. Thirty people still belonged to the Sheffield Wool
Shear Workers' Trade Union, in 1979. Nearly ten times that number
remained in the Huddersfield Healders and Twisters Trade and
Friendly Society, or in the Sheffield Sawmakers' Protection Society.[10]
Such survivals have been increasingly squeezed during recent years,
partly because of the concentration and rationalisation of industry,
and partly because as we have just seen, the need for many modern
trade union professional services cannot begin to be met within small
groups, which have to base themselves on a primitive division of
labour. Accordingly, we have seen the disappearance of the London
Jewish Bakers, which for a long time held the record for being the
smallest trade union in the TUC: while distinctive bodies like the
Cardiff, Penarth and Barry Coal Trimmers' Association have amalgamated with larger unions.[11]

But these fossil organisations are interesting, not only because many
of them have a history which is as colourful as their antique silken
banners, but because they have been a veritable laboratory of
democracy. As Sidney and Beatrice Webb pointed out:

'The early trade club was a democracy of the most rudimentary
type, free alike from permanently differentiated officials, executive
council, or representative assembly. The general meeting strove
itself to transact all the business, and grudgingly delegated any of its
functions either to officers or to committees. When this delegation
could no longer be avoided, the expedients of rotation and short
periods of service were used "to prevent imposition" or any undue

influence by particular members. In this earliest type of Trade Union democracy we find, in fact, the most child-like faith not only "all men are equal", but also that "what concerns all should be decided by all".[12]

Even in this simple state, a number of important democratic practices were consolidated: besides the common devices of rotation of office and what would nowadays be called 'the right of recall', a form of separation of powers was sometimes imposed by instituting the office of 'keymaster', or holder of one of the three keys to a triple-locked box in which the funds were kept. As the membership of organisations grew, and the purely local assembly became linked with others, a more complex structure of delegation became inevitable: even where it was jealously resisted. At the same time that unions increased in size, so their functions became more complex. And all the time, they were trying to operate in a hostile environment which itself, as the Webbs clearly understood, compelled them to diverge from their 'simple ideal'. Legal persecution 'made secrecy and promptitude absolutely necessary for successful operations' during the years before the 1824 reform,[13] thus introducing criteria of administrative efficiency as well as democratic accountability into every trade unionist's notion of union organisation. During the subsequent years, trade unions spontaneously discovered or rediscovered almost every axiom of representative government. Students of the political theory of democracy tend to identify particular mechanisms with eminent social philosophers, so that the doctrine of separation of powers, for instance, will commonly be attributed to Locke or Montesquieu, while various notions about accountability or representativity will be given other distinguished attributions. But quite anonymous working people discovered all these principles for themselves, in the struggle to safeguard their organisations from manipulations of various kinds, irregularities in the control of finances, and all the other difficulties with which they were recurrently beset. To be fair, these lessons were only very partly learnt as a result of the need to create a system of controls over responsible functionaries: this need itself very commonly, perhaps normally, arose in response to outside pressures, whether in the form of direct actions by employers, or in the form of governmental restrictions upon trade union activity, or yet in the form of oppressive judgements in the courts. A rich school for democratic responses to these threats was to be found in the institutions of non-conformity, and it was from the rebellious chapels that unions taught themselves the mechanism of the block vote, as well as the courage to resist oppression.

All these issues of democracy are treated in the next chapter.

Meantime, the evidence of this chapter shows that the age of innocence and small primary (community-based) organisations has been ended, not by any greed for power within the unions themselves, but by the inexorable processes of industrial concentration. Unions, like everybody else, have no alternative but that of adapting to these cosmic pressures or becoming irrelevant.

The problem which this poses is, how to change adequately, to respond with sufficient force, without jeopardising that 'childlike faith' of which the Webbs spoke: equality *is* a vital goal, and it remains the more necessary, as power coheres in fewer and more capricious centres, that 'what concerns all should be decided by all.'

NOTES

1. H. A. Turner, *Trade Union Growth, Structure and Policy*, Allen and Unwin, 1962.

2. Even the official Devlin Report (*The Final Report of the Committee of Inquiry under the Rt. Hon. Lord Devlin into Certain Matters Concerning the Port Transport Industry*, HMSO, Cmnd. 2734, August 1965) criticised the TGWU and its officials for their failure adequately to represent the interests of their docks membership.

3. John Hughes, *Trade Union Structure and Government, Part 1*, Donovan Royal Commission Research Paper, No. 5, HMSO 1967.

4. See TUC: *Relations Between Unions*, for a full account of the Bridlington rules.

5. For a perceptive and sympathetic study, see Shirley Lerner, *Breakaway Unions and the Small Trade Union*, Allen and Unwin, 1961.

6. H. A. Clegg, *The System of Industrial Relations in Great Britain*, Blackwell, 1970, pp. 59–60.

7. John Hughes, op. cit.

8. For example, H. A. Turner, 'Trade Union Structure: A New Approach', in *British Journal of Industrial Relations*, Vol. II, No. 2, July 1964.

9. *Trade Union Handbook*, Arthur Marsh, Gower Press 1979.

10. TUC *Report*, 1977.

11. In this case, with the Transport and General Workers' Union in 1968. See TGWU *Report and Balance Sheet*, 1972, facing page 73, for a reproduction of the striking banner of one of this union's branches.

12. *Industrial Democracy*, 1913 edition, WEA, p. 8.

13. Ibid, p. 9.

APPENDIX TO CHAPTER TWO

I

Mergers and attempted mergers of some TUC-affiliated Unions since 1963

We circulated all TUC-affiliated unions in April 1978, and asked them what mergers with other unions they had completed in the last 15 years, and what failed or pending negotiations for mergers they had taken part in over the same period. We also asked them what negotiating committees they sat on in company with other unions. Replies were received from thirty three unions, and these are summarised below. (We wish to thank the unions who co-operated in this enquiry). Only six of the thirty three unions indicated that they had had no discussions on mergers, either successful or unsuccessful. These were the Inland Revenue Staff Federation, the National Union of Agricultural and Allied Workers, the National Union of Mineworkers, the Sheffield Sawmakers' Protection Society, the Health Visitors' Association, and the Professional Footballers Association. Elsewhere, the general picture which emerges is one of fairly considerable, but irregular and unsystematic merger activity, in which the number of failed negotiations for mergers is as noticeable as the numbers which succeed.

Table II:6
Mergers between unions

Union	No. of Members	Successful Mergers/ Takeovers in last 15 years	Failed/Pending merger talks in last 15 years	Negotiating Committees with other unions
1. British Roll-turners Trade Soc.	740	None	With AUEW in 1974 and 1977	Craft unions in steel industry
2. Actors' Equity Association	25,419	Merged with Variety Artists Federation, 1967	None	Performers' Alliance on ITV
3. Nat. Assoc. of Teachers in Further and Higher Education	60,788	NATFHE formed by merger of Assoc. of Teachers in Technical Institutions and Assoc. of Teachers in Colleges and Depts. of Education, 1976	None	—
4. Civil & Public Services Assoc.	226,495	Mergers with 1) Min. of Labour Staff Assoc., 1973, 2) Court Officers' Assoc., 1974	1) Civil Service Union, 1972, 2) Assoc. of Government Supervisors & Radio Operators,	1) Whitley Council 2) Council of Post Office Unions 3) Joint Council— British Airways 4) Joint Council—

5. National Union of Seamen	44,400	None	Failed talks with TGWU, 1970	National Maritime Board
6. Assoc. of Professional, Executive, Clerical & Computer Staff	150,000	Staff Assocs. of General Accident Insurance (1975) & Automobile Assoc., (1978) taken over	Pending merger with Staff Assoc. of Reckitt & Colman Ltd.	Six Joint Industrial Councils
7. Civil Service Union	46,965	None	Discussions with CPSA	Whitley Council & several Joint Industrial Councils
8. Association of Broadcasting Staffs	13,744	None	Merger talks with ACTT. NATTKE declined to participate	
9. Fire Brigades Union	30,000	None	Informal talks with National Assoc. of Fire Officers	National Joint Council
10. National & Local Gov. Officers' Assoc.	709,331	British Gas Staffs Assoc., (1963)	1) GLC Staff Assoc., 2) Thames Water Authority Staff Assoc.	Whitley Councils & several other Joint Councils

Table II:6 (cont.)

Union	No. of Members	Successful Mergers/ Takeovers in last 15 years	Failed/Pending merger talks in last 15 years	Negotiating Committees with other unions
11. Nat. Union of Dyers, Bleachers and Textile Workers	61,416	1) Saddleworth Weavers' Union, 2) Forfar Factory Workers Union	Discussions with 1) Hosiery Union, 2) Tailors & Garment Workers Union, 3) Amalgamated Textile Union, 4) Northern Carpet Union	Several, all in textile industry
12. National Union of Railwaymen	180,000	None	Discussions with TSSA. No response from ASLEF	Thirty-two Nat. Joint Committees
13. Nat. Union of Footwear, Leather, & Allied Trades	68,149	NUFLAT formed (1971) by merger of- 1) Leather Workers' Soc., 2) Nat. Union of Boot & Shoe Operatives, 3) Leather Workers' Union, 4) Nat. Union of Glovers & Leather Workers	Rossendale Union of Boot, Shoe & Slipper Operatives	Some minor participation on Wages Council but principally NUFLAT bargains for whole industry
	Between 1969 and 1975,		Failed talks with	Three National

NUFLAT

...tinghamshire and
Leicestershire

No. Name	Membership	Takeovers/Mergers	Talks	Councils
15. Iron & Steel Trades Confed.	110,636	Took over Corby Foremen's Assoc. 1969	Trying since 1975 to merge with Steel Industry Management Assoc.	TUC Steel Committee
16. National Union of Journalists	29,602	None	Failed talks with Institute of Journalists	Seven Industrial Councils
17. Union of Post Office Workers	197,247	None	'Open door' policy to mergers: POEU shows no interest. Failed talks with Post Office Management Staff Assoc., 1977	Council of Post Office Unions
18. Merchant Navy & Airline Officers Assoc.	42,200	None	Discussions with Mercantile Marine Service Assoc., & with Radio Officers Union	Several National Joint Councils
19. National Union of Public Employees	693,097	Manchester & District Caretakers Assoc.	Preliminary stage of talks with NALGO & COHSE	Whitley Councils and many others

Table II:6 (cont.)

Union	No. of Members	Successful Mergers/ Takeovers in last 15 years	Failed/Pending merger talks in last 15 years	Negotiating Committees with other unions
20. Nat. Assoc. of Schoolmasters/ Union of Women Teachers	102,031	The Union of Women Teachers, and the Scottish School-masters Assoc., merged with the National Assoc. of Schoolmasters to form the NAS/UWT in 1976	None	Burnham Committee for teachers' salaries
21. Rossendale Boot, Shoe, & Slipper Operatives Union	6,325	None	The Union rejected proposed merger with NUFTO (now NUFLAT)	None
22. National Union of Sheetmetal Workers, Coppersmiths, Heating and Domestic Engineers	75,000	Amalgamated with 1) Coppersmiths, (1959) 2) Heating and Domestic Engineers, (1967) 3) Birmingham and Midland Sheetmetal workers (1973) 4) Agreed merge AUEW (1979)	Failed talks with Boilermakers Soc.	Many National Joint Councils
23. Assoc. of Cinematograph, Television &	19,974	None	Pending talks with Assoc. of Broadcasting Staffs	None

ing Workers Engineering Section Constructional Section Foundry Section	1,155,440 25,000 58,888	1) Foundryworkers to become AEF (1969) 2) Construction Engineers and TASS Amalgamated (1971) 3) Sheetmetal Workers voted to amalgamate (1979). Amalgamation expected (1980)	all Engineering-based Unions in CSEU inviting amalgamation discussions (1969). Breakdown of talks with NUVB, which subsequently merged into TGWU. Talks with Boilermakers recurrently, still under consideration. Talks with EEPTU, recurrently 1969, 1978–9. Obstacle is Electricians' insistence on appointment of officers	
25. Electrical, Electronic Telecommunication and Plumbing Union	420,000	Amalgamated with 1) Plumbers' Trade Union 2) BICC Staff Association, AMEE, Lawrence Scott Foreman's Association	Talks with AUEW (1969 and later) GMWU (up to 1974) UCATT	Numerous
26. General and Municipal Workers' Union	945,324	Took over 1) Ulster Transport Union (1963) 2) Salt and General Workers' Union (1968) 3) National Union of Waterworks Employees (1971) 4) Scottish Professional Footballers (1976) 5) Coopers' Federation of GB (1979)	Talks with Chemical Workers' Union (1963)—merged with TGWU, National Society Metal Mechanics (1965), Boilermakers (1978 and continuing), EEPTU (up to 1974 without reaching either Conference)	Numerous

Table II:6 (cont.)

Union	No. of Members	Successful Mergers/ Takeovers in last 15 years	Failed/Pending merger talks in last 15 years	Negotiating Committees with other unions
27. Association of Scientific, Technical and Managerial Staffs.	471,000	ASTMS came into existence in January 1968 as a result of a merger between ASSET (Assoc. of Supervisory Staff, Executives and Technicians) and AScW (Association of Scientific Workers). Since then the following organisations have become part of ASTMS through mergers and amalgamations. Union of Insurance Staffs: 1970; Prudential Clerical Staff Association (District Office): 1970; Prudential Ladies Staff Welfare Association: 1970; Prudential Male Staff Association: 1970; Medical Practitioners Union: 1970; Royal Group Guild: 1971; Midland Bank Staff Association: 1973; Assurance Representatives Organisation (Ireland): 1973;		In the National Health Service, 4 Whitley Councils and 2 other Committees. Joint Committees in the Universities (1), in the Airways (3), in British Rail (1), in Scottish Education (1), in private companies (24). There are also a number of Joint Committees for regulating pensions (5)

Hospital Pharmacists: 1974; Pearl Section—National Union of Insurance Workers: 1974; Forward Trust Staff Association: 1974; Engineering Surveyors Association: 1975; Kodak Senior Staff Association: 1975; London & Manchester Section NUIW: 1975; Midland Bank Technical Services Staff Association: 1975; Union of Speech Therapists: 1975; Health Service Chiropodists Association: 1976; United Commercial Travellers Association: 1976; Liverpool & Victoria Managers Association: 1976; Group 1 Staff Association (Courtaulds): 1977; Excess Insurance Staff Association: 1977; Managers and Over-lookers Society: 1977; Pearl Federation NUIW: 1978; Refuge Section NUIW: 1979; Reckitt & Colman Management Association: 1979; Colonial Mutual Life Assurance Society: 1979

APPENDIX TO CHAPTER TWO
II

Amalgamations which have formed the Transport & General Workers'
Union, 1922–78

The following is an inclusive list of unions which have amalgamated into the TGWU since its foundation in 1922. It illustrates vividly the supreme advantage possessed by a *general*, *open* union, in attracting smaller, national and regional unions of the most diverse kind (quarrymen, builders, mechanics, butchers, textile workers, file grinders, fishermen, hairdressers, Youth Hostel wardens, etc.) into its ranks. The most significant recruits of the 1970's were the Scottish Commercial Motormen's Union, the National Union of Vehicle Builders, and the Chemical Workers' Union.

Amalgamated Society of Watermen, Lightermen and Bargemen ..	1922
Amalgamated Carters, Lorrymen and Motormen's Union..........	
Amalgamated Association of Carters and Motormen................	
Associated Horsemen's Union...	
Dock, Wharf, Riverside and General Workers' Union	
Labour Protection League..	
National Amalgamated Labourers' Union	
National Union of Docks, Wharves and Shipping Staffs	
National Union of Ships' Clerks, Grain Weighers and Coalmeters .	
National Union of Vehicle Workers	
National Amalgamated Coal Workers' Union	
National Union of Dock, Riverside and General Workers	
National Union of British Fishermen	
North of England Trimmers' and Teemers' Association.............	
North of Scotland Horse and Motormen's Association	
United Vehicle Workers...	
Belfast Breadservers' Association	
Greenock Sugar Porters' Association.................................	
Dundee Jute and Flax Stowers' Association..........................	1923
North Wales Craftsmen and General Workers' Union	
North Wales Quarrymen's Union.....................................	
Scottish Union of Dock Labourers....................................	
United Order of General Labourers	1924
Association of Coastwise Masters, Mates and Engineers.............	1925

Weaver Watermen's Association 1926
Irish Mental Hospital Workers' Union ....
National Amalgamated Union of Enginemen, Firemen, Motormen,
    Mechanics and Electrical Workers.............................
Cumberland Enginemen, Boilermen and Electrical Workers' Union 1928
Workers' Union 1929
Belfast Operative Bakers' Union 1930
Northern Ireland Textile Workers' Union ....
London Co-operative Mutuality Club Collectors' Association ......
National Union of Co-operative Insurance Society Employees...... 1933
Portadown Textile Workers' Union.................................
Scottish Farm Servants' Union..
'Altogether' Builders' Labourers' and Constructional Workers'
    Society... 1934
Scottish Busmen's Union ....
National Winding and General Engineers' Society 1935
Electricity Supply Staff Association (Dublin)....................... 1936
Halifax and District Carters' and Motormen's Association..........
Power Loom Tenters' Trade Union of Ireland..................... 1937
Belfast Journeymen Butchers' Association ....
Scottish Seafishers' Union ....
Humber Amalgamated Steam Trawlers' Engineers and Firemen's
    Union... 1938
Imperial War Graves Commission Staff Association ....
Port of London Deal Porters' Union................................ 1939
North of England Engineers' and Firemen's Amalgamation ....
National Glass Workers' Trade Protection Association 1940
Radcliffe and District Enginemen and Boilermen's Provident Society
National Glass Bottle Makers' Society............................. 1940
Liverpool Pilots' Association 1942
Manchester Ship Canal Pilots' Association......................... 1943
Grangemouth Pilots' Association................................... 1944
Leith and Granton Pilots... 1945
Dundee Pilots ....
Methil Pilots ....
Government Civil Employees' Association 1946
Liverpool and District Carters' and Motormen's Union 1947
Lurgan Hemmers', Veiners' and General Workers' Union.......... 1951
United Cut Nail Makers of Great Britain Protection Society ....
Scottish Textile Workers' Union.................................... 1961
Gibraltar Confederation of Labour and the Gibraltar Apprentices
    and Ex-Apprentices Union, Gibraltar Labour Trades Union.. 1963
North of Ireland Operative Butchers' and Allied Workers'
    Association 1965
United Fishermen's Union 1966
Cardiff, Penarth and Barry Coal Trimmers' Union 1967
Scottish Slaters, Tilers, Roofers and Cement Workers' Society 1968

National Association of Operative Plasterers ....
Process and General Workers' Union................................ 1969
Amalgamated Society of Foremen Lightermen of River Thames ...
Irish Union of Hairdressers and Allied Workers ....
Port of Liverpool Staff Association................................
Sheffield Amalgamated Union of File Trades....................... 1970
Scottish Commercial Motormen's Union........................... 1971
Watermen, Lightermen, Tugmen and Bargemen's Union...........
Chemical Workers' Union...
National Union of Vehicle Builders................................. 1972
Scottish Transport and General Workers' Union (Docks)...........
Iron, Steel and Wood Barge Builders and Helpers' Association..... 1973
Union of Bookmakers' Employees.................................... 1974
Union of Kodak Workers...
File Grinders' Society... 1975
Grimsby Steam and Diesel Fishing Vessels' Engineers and Firemen's
    Union... 1976
National Association of Youth Hostel Wardens 1978
Staff Association for Royal Automobile Club Employees............

Chapter Three

Trade Union Government

Problems of Trade Union Democracy

In chapter one we saw how, well over a century ago, it was already understood that the division of labour stultified people's development by compelling them to act out fixed, restrictive roles, often for years on end, without offering them any slightest opportunity to realise a fraction of the wealth of talent which lay within them. A modern study of labour markets in the Midlands shows that 87 per cent of the industrial jobs available require no more skill than is involved in driving to work. Union rulebooks reflect, all too imperfectly, the longing of millions of men and women for a society in which the individual potential of every person may become the most treasured resource of all, and in which all may reach out to the furthest frontiers of their capacities. In chapter two we saw how, as well as mutilating individuals, the changing division of labour also recurrently undermined and broke up their organisations. Trade unions found their structures constantly under pressure, constantly in need of change.

There is a further problem confronting trade unions in the same principle of division of labour, however. The more complex the economy in which they operate, the more unions need their own internal division of labour, to match and pace the organisation and institutions which are ranged against them, and to respond efficiently to opportunities or threats from a whole cluster of specialised agencies. We have already discussed these pressures for increased size, which are all, in themselves, problems for any live democracy.[1]

With all the trends pushing unions to offer more and more qualified specialist assistance, more and more professionalism, it is clear that today more than ever a key element of trade union democracy consists in the struggle for membership control over leaders, and the creation of institutions imposing accountability on representatives and full-time officers.

In itself, although the difficulties it involves are undoubtedly greater nowadays than they were before, this problem is by no means new. Back in 1925, G. D. H. Cole was already writing:

'democratic control, in the large and complex modern unions, becomes a difficult matter. The rank and file feel that both executives and officials are far removed from them, and election is apt to bring to the top only the best man known over a wide area, and not necessarily the best man for the job . . . '[2]

Basic Units of Organisation

It was already beginning to be true in 1925, but today it is generally obvious, that the words 'rank and file' may mean more than one thing. They may be taken to mean the ordinary members as individuals; or perhaps the members at the workplace, involved in the primary levels of workshop organisation; or often in a number of unions, they may refer to the members organised in branches, which are often seen as 'the basic unit in the union' as USDAW has it, or as 'the basic unit of organisation', as is the case in the TGWU, GMWU and AUEW. The two views on organisation, workplace versus branch, are still far from simply compatible. We consider shop steward organisation separately, in chapter five: so here we shall confine our attention to the branch as the primary constituent of union democracy. The theory of the matter is quite simple. USDAW's home study course for union members points it up with a diagram, which 'illustrates the supreme significance of the branch as the basic unit on which the whole of the union's structure is built and depends'.

The same handbook spells it all out verbally:

'Every member of the Union is in one of its 1,300 or more branches. The majority of the Union's branches are organised either on a single employer or trade basis. This means that a branch is either composed of members working for one and the same employer, such as a Co-operative Society or a manufacturing company, e.g. Kellogg's Ltd., in Manchester, or of members working in one particular trade, such as multiple tailoring or multiple grocery. The advantages are obvious inasmuch as members of such branches have similar interests and fairly common work and pay problems. Only in districts or towns where there are too few members to organise branches in this way are there mixed branches comprising members from a number of trades or employers.
In order that branches function effectively, they meet regularly, usually at least once a month and members are informed by notice or know from custom the regular meeting night and place.'[4]

The attempts to constitute branches upon an industrial basis, so that all the members share a common employer and workplace, is by no

Table III:1
The organisation of USDAW[3]

—————— Illustrates the supreme significance of the branch as the basic unit on which the whole of the Union's structure is built and depends.

⋆—The four main levels of the Union's structure.

— — — Represent the downward line of communication and representation ensuring effective consultation on and coordination of the Union policies at all levels.

means confined to USDAW. The ETU (now part of the EEPTU) told the Donovan Commission:

'Although the ETU has had a small number of specialised branches for some time, it is only recently that a determined attempt has been made to make these specialised or industrial branches the rule rather than the exception in our structure. An industrialised branch is one based upon one industrial undertaking or recruiting members from the same section of their trade or industry rather than upon a geographical basis of residence. It is intended that in large industrial concentrations numbers of small branches will be amalgamated and given a full-time branch secretary/treasurer who may also carry out some functions of local negotiations. If this branch is based upon one factory the Union's shop stewards will belong to that branch and will work in close liaison with the full-time secretary. In this way it is hoped that they will be able to deal with aspects of industrial policy and union administration.
In the past one of the main obstacles to efficiency has been the tortuous lines of communication between the various units of the Union. The branch meeting held usually once a fortnight could often not act quickly enough on instructions from Head Office. The large branch with a full-time secretary, particularly based on one undertaking, could considerably improve the speed and effectiveness of communication among the Executive, the branch, the shop stewards and the members. In the same way the member, in close contact with the shop steward, will be able to resolve quickly his industrial problems and will establish a better relationship with his organisation.'[5]

In the GMWU:

'Branches consist of all the members of a given area, or in cases where enough members are concentrated in one branch of industry, it can be industrial or work-place based. Increasingly, the tendency is towards industry, company or work-place branches. In total there are about 2,500 GMW branches.
Each branch has its officers—the secretary (except where there is a branch administrative officer), chairman and auditor. If the branch is more than 50 strong it must have two auditors, in addition it has a committee of not less than seven, including the chairman and secretary. All these are elected by the branch every two years at the last branch meeting in June. Shop Stewards, of whom there are about 30,000 are elected by the membership at the place of work or in the branch, and are subject to the branch and to the regional

committees. The Shop Steward (or Staff Representative) is not a Branch Officer as such.

The branch elects delegates to Congress, Regional Councils and Industrial Conferences, and also elects Regional Officers.

Branch administration is in the hands of either—

    1. The voluntary branch secretary (who holds an ordinary job as well)

or 2. The full-time branch secretary (who lives off commission from branch members)

or 3. The whole-time branch secretary now rapidly being replaced by Branch Administrative Officers (who get a salary based on membership, and who are in the union superannuation scheme, and do not count as lay members of the union)

or 4. District Officers.'[6]

For many years the TGWU has tried to ensure that branch members are all from the same trade group, and increasing numbers of branches are based on a single workplace. Branches must normally have a minimum of 50 members, but may have as many as 5,000 or 6,000: they must meet at least monthly, but may meet more frequently if they wish. 'It is also possible to arrange to hold a branch meeting in two parts, say in a morning and evening session, to enable shift-workers to attend.'[7]

The trend to industrial branches has been resisted by the Engineers, as they explained in their evidence to Donovan:

'Unlike many other Unions, Branches of the A.E.U. are geographically based. This is a conscious decision of the Union: one made in the light of the wider interests of the Labour Movement as a whole. Whilst it could be held to be in the interests of particular workers to base the unit of organisation at factory level, it has always been felt that the A.E.U. is not solely an organisation concerned with sectional interests. It has always been one of the aims of the Union to create the framework within which the ordinary working man could become more aware of his surroundings, his true interests and his responsibility to the community. By providing the meeting place to enable him to discuss not only matters affecting himself and his place of work but also the wider issues of the day—not just within his own locality but nationally and internationally—it was held and is still held today that this makes a far greater contribution to the dignity and well-being of the working class than the more parochial attitudes most probably engendered within Branches based at factory level.'[8]

It would be interesting to see the evidence for his last statement. Many very experienced trade union leaders have argued quite differently. George Woodcock, for instance, claimed that 'branches have ceased to be an important part of trade union structure', and went on to say: 'if I were an active trade unionist again you wouldn't see me anywhere near a branch; there's not enough done there to justify attendance'.[9]

The AEU thinks plenty is done, as it reported to the same Royal Commission

> 'It is at the Branch, which meets fortnightly, that the ordinary member has the closest contact with his Union. It is here he is made a member; pays his contributions; collects benefits; and elects officers. It is at the Branch, too, that any member can raise matters affecting working conditions, union membership and, in fact, all matters concerning "labour interests generally." This means, of course, that, in practice, there is practically no subject that cannot be broached by an interested member . . . The only matters specifically barred by Rule from being discussed are "questions of a religious nature." '[10]

Unfortunately, busy though they undoubtedly are, branches are commonly sparsely attended, and never more than when they are organised on a geographical rather than an industrial basis. A very large number of studies document the poor attendances and low participation ratios which commonly characterise branch meetings.[11] In 1974 the Sociology Department at Warwick University published a far-reaching report which had been commissioned for NUPE, as a basis for that union's thorough-going reform of structure. Speaking of the widespead feelings of isolation and the lack of day-to-day contact which troubled many members, the report went on:

> 'the initial symptoms are equally well known: poor attendance at Branch meetings; little contact with Branch officials and full time Officers alike; difficulty in finding members willing to come forward as Union Stewards and ignorance of the Union both at Branch level and beyond. Our researches provide some evidence of all these features. For example, 67 per cent of Branches said that Branch meetings were attended by only 5 per cent or less of the Branch membership; a quarter of all Union Stewards reported difficulty in contacting some sections they represented; over three-quarters of all

Branch Secretaries said it was difficult, very difficult or impossible to get members to act as Union Stewards and 37 per cent of those attending Area Conference said they did not know what happened to Area Conference resolutions once they had been passed.

Understandably, in these circumstances, frustrated Union activists and beleagured full time officials turn to simple and gratifying explanations of the problems in terms of individual shortcomings, chiefly, of course, "apathy". This was cited by 28 per cent of Branches as the chief reason for poor attendance at Branch meetings, an explanation receiving three times as much support as any other. Apathy and lack of interest usually have some deeper cause. The point was made over 50 years ago by J. J. W. Bradley, President of the Union, when he said:

> It is a deplorable fact that many members do not attend their Branches, some only attend to pay their contributions and take no interest in work, others do not even do this, but send their contributions up. There may be various reasons for this, but I am afraid the main reason is apathy, or because the business of the Branch is not made interesting and attractive, too much time is being taken up and wasted in discussing more details which do not count either way, and more important business is being crowded out.

Confirmation of Bradley's argument is given by the fact that 59 per cent of Branch Secretaries said that their attendance varied according to the issue before the Branch.

We would follow Bradley but, on the basis of our argument above, go even further than him. We suggest that the apparent apathy and lack of interest experienced in some of the ways we have described is also engendered by the difficult environment in which the Union operates rather than being the result of individual members of whole sections simply "not caring" about the Union. In other words, apathy can be understood as a symptom of isolation or remoteness that is caused chiefly by NUPE's environment and partly by NUPE's own structure. But it follows that if this is the case, "apathy" is amenable to structural modification and may be reduced by changes in structure. As one member of the Executive Council put it forcefully, "If our membership really is apathetic, then we in the Union are partly responsible for not overcoming that apathy".[12]

It is very arguable that in such cases it is the ease of accessibility to the structure that counts, rather more than the absolute numbers of people taking part in meetings on one day or another. Where is there a large organisation in which attendances are *not* variable with the subject of the meeting? It seems entirely normal for people to be more interested in some issues than they are in others, and therefore quite proper to arrange trade union structure so as to accommodate this variability. But if ease of access to the union is the key to wider and more relevant participation, it is extremely difficult to justify geographically-based branches in any case where industrially-founded ones are possible.

If branches were *not* 'basic units', this would not matter. But they normally are: and what this rather obscure jargon means is precisely that they are the main electoral foci, usually determining who should attend policy-forming annual conferences, commonly involved at one or another level in electing higher committees, and sometimes making up the direct constituencies in the election of chief officers.

If branches may be structurally unrepresentative, as opposed to being simply poorly attended, this is largely because there is a limit to the percentages of members it is *possible* to involve in a dysfunctional, or irrational, structure. We might be forgiven for thinking that if a TUC General Secretary has advertised his belief that 'there's not enough done there to justify attendance', others might conceivably share his point of view.

The importance of this problem is difficult to overstress, when we take up again G. D. H. Cole's half-century old conundrum, about how this modern rank-and-file is to exercise democratic control over its leaders. Cole was not the first to note that sometimes trade union leaders were not entirely in tune with their followers.

Relations between Members and Organisers

Even earlier, (in 1893) the Webbs recorded their classic description of the social stress under which full-time union officers were alleged to operate:

> 'Whilst the points at issue no longer affect his own earnings or conditions of employment, any disputes between his members and their employers increase his work and add to his worry. The former vivid sense of the privations and subjection of the artisan's life gradually fades from his mind; and he begins more and more to regard all complaints as perverse and unreasonable. With this intellectual change may come a more invidious transformation. Nowadays the salaried officer to a great union is courted and flattered by the middle class. He is asked to dine with them, and will admire their well-appointed houses, their fine carpets, the ease and

luxury of their lives . . . He goes to live in a little villa in a lower-middle-class suburb. The move leads to dropping his workmen friends; and his wife changes her acquaintances. With the habits of his new neighbours he insensibly adopts more and more their ideas . . . His manner to his members . . . undergoes a change . . . A great strike threatens to involve the Society in desperate war. Unconsciously biased by distaste for the hard and unthankful work which a strike entails, he finds himself in small sympathy with the men's demands, and eventually arranges a compromise, on terms distasteful to a large section of his members.'[13]

This is perhaps the clearest statement of the sociological process which has been presented in the theory, set out at length in 1915 by Roberto Michels, that there exists in Labour Movements an 'Iron Law of Oligarchy' based on the progression 'democracy is inconceivable without organisation'[14] but 'organisation is, in fact, the source from which the conservative currents flow over the plain of democracy, occasioning these disastrous floods and rendering the plain unrecognisable'.[15] In less high-flown language, the necessary division of labour within labour organisations is seen as generating, first an elite of labour managers, and then a definite caste of bureaucratic oligarchs. In part, Michels was describing a long past labour movement based upon fairly limited levels of popular literacy. At a time when compulsory schooling to the age of twelve was an innovation, it is clear that the cadre-structure of labour organisations was likely to be set apart by the comparative rarity of its skills. Indeed, Michels made a great deal of the effect of Labour Colleges on the training of the new elite, and wrote at some length about the fostering of 'powerful orators'.[16] Today, with the mass production of a whole variety of intellectual skills, there is likely to be far stiffer competition for office in many labour organisations: oratory being one of the less significant of the requisite talents involved.

At the same time that more qualified candidates are available, the relations between labour professionals and those they serve has been transformed by the vastly increased educational attainments of the new rank and file. The 'Iron Law of Oligarchy' is perhaps a fair description of a bygone division of social labour in which the clerk was a natural aristocrat: but today's skills have certainly modified the landscape with which Michels was familiar, even if there remains a pronounced tendency for labour leaders to find themselves considering, even serving, interests somewhat distinct from some of those felt paramount by their members.[17]

Trade union full-time officers are still a rather small fraternity, in

comparison with the vast armies of voluntary workers upon whom the
day-to-day functions of the unions depend.

In the 1890s, there were already something between six and seven
hundred permanent officials[18] at a time when the TUC counted 225
affiliates with about 1.2 million members.[19] In those days, then, the
average union officer represented or serviced approximately 2,000
people. By 1952, the eighteen largest TUC unions had about 1,600
paid organisers, and this was an average ratio of one organiser to some
3,700 members. Yet this average concealed wide divergencies: the
Amalgamated Union of Building Trade Workers had one full-timer
for each 1,300 members, whilst the National Union of Railwaymen
had one officer for each 19,000.[20]

When the Donovan Commission published its Report, in 1968, the
best guess it could make was that there were about 3,000 full-time
officers, or one for every 3,800 members.[21]

Taken union by union, the ratios of some major organisations were
as follows:

Table III:2
Number of members per full-time union officer in certain trade unions—1966

Union of Shop, Distributive and Allied Workers.	1,978
Transport and General Workers' Union	2,762
General and Municipal Workers' Union	3,868
Electrical Trades Union	4,027
National and Local Government Officers' Association	4,509
Amalgamated Engineering Union	6,807

The fact that some unions were far more intensively and profession-
ally organised than others was high-lighted in a research paper
prepared for the Royal Commission, which is reproduced opposite in
Table III:3.

Yet the intensity of such servicing does not merely vary from one
organisation to the next: it also varies within those organisations.

The most complete picture yet available of developments in a
particular union, since the publication of the Donovan Report, reports
on the trends within the TGWU.[24] During the time in question, the
union had been pioneering in forcing forward new experiments in
productivity bargaining, alongside a systematic drive to extend the
influence of plant bargaining upon which the Royal Commission had
recently reported. Jack Jones, then newly elected General Secretary of
the Union, had always been a partisan of lay participation in and

control over its affairs, and had inherited a series of decisions by the union's delegate conference, which pressed in the same direction. More plant bargaining, more lay control: these pressures can only mean *less* power for full-time officers. And indeed, during the years between 1968 and 1974, that is exactly the tendency of the TGWU's evolution. Not only was the role of full-timers notably modified: the actual numbers of professionals declined very sharply at a time of rapid expansion in membership. This can be seen very plainly in table III:4, which gives the position for each of the union's 11 regions, together with that in its head office. (See page 72.)

Table III:3

Full-time local officers: shop steward responsibilities and contacts

Name of Union	Average No. of Stewards for whom each Officer is responsible	Average No. of Stewards Contacted in last 4 weeks	Proportion of Shop Stewards Contacted in last 4 weeks
Transport & General Workers' Union	120	96	80%
Amalgamated Engineering Union	477	132	28%
General and Municipal Workers' Union	169	65	38%
Electrical Trades Union	232	94	41%
Amalgamated Union of of Building Trade Workers	33	30	91%
All Unions	172	89	52%

Source: Research Paper No. 10 on *Shop Stewards and Workshop Relations* cited in *Report* of the Donovan Commission, p. 189.

If the union had been losing members, this picture might have borne out the complaint that unions are under-professionalised. But since the union was entering a period of phenomenal growth, the reduction of its paid staff can only mean that a vast burden of official work was being undertaken by voluntary workers. It will be seen that this has been a most uneven process: in Region 5, which covers the vast engineering

Table III:4[25]

Ratio of members to full-time officials, Transport & General Workers' Union

Region	Full-Time Officials			Members			Ratios		
	1968	1970	1974	1968	1970	1974	1968	1970	1974
1	132	123	122	352,623	390,285	450,608	2,671-1	3,173-1	3,694-1
2	20	20	19	69,961	81,935	90,237	3,498-1	4,096-1	4,749-1
3	35	34	33	112,243	129,005	137,085	3,207-1	3,794-1	4,154-1
4*	35	28	27	111,618	111,438	110,666	3,189-1	3,980-1	4,098-1
5	45	43	47	246,209	270,610	334,701	5,471-1	6,293-1	7,121-1
6†	78	73	60	177,544	208,391	236,713	2,276-1	2,855-1	3,945-1
7	54	48	60	118,011	129,369	166,559	2,185-1	2,695-1	2,776-1
8	21	21	20	68,112	75,411	82,041	3,243-1	3,591-1	4,102-1
9	27	25	25	71,678	89,465	87,564	2,655-1	3,299-1	3,503-1
10	21	20	15	43,712	52,740	52,851	2,032-1	2,637-1	3,512-1
11	36	35	38	96,220	101,709	99,738	2,673-1	2,906-1	2,625-1
Head Office	26	24	19						
Total	530	494	485	1,472,505	1,638,686	1,857,308	2,780-1	3,317-1	3,834-1

*Region 4 in 1968 is the previous Regions 4 and 13 added together.

†Region 6 in 1968 is the previous Regions 6 and 12 added together.

The above table shows a clear reduction in the number of full time officials and a very marked increase in the ratio of members to officials. Region 5 is clearly outstanding as the region with consistently the highest ratio of members to full time officials between 1968 and 1974.

plants in the Midlands, officer-member ratios had reached the level of 1:7,121 (a figure comparable with traditional levels in the NUM), whilst other regions maintain a fairly constant ratio, as does, most noticeably, Region 11 (from 1:2,673 to 1:2,625 between 1968 and 1974.)

This kind of unevenness is general, throughout the wider trade union movement. Not every group gets equal representation. In 1976, for instance, one estimate claimed that the thirty unions with the largest female memberships had some 2,225 paid organisers, of whom only 98 were women.[26] Ten per cent of NALGO's organisers, and 43 per cent of its members, were women. NALGO had more female organisers than any other organisation and the TGWU, with 16 per cent female membership (289,000 people), had only 3 women organisers to 480 men.

Of course, there is a very great deal more to organising a trade union than appointing a conveniently high ratio of paid officials to members, and we certainly believe that if a union can mobilise adequate voluntary participation, it may be the more democratic for having the less professional administration. Much depends on the nature of the work-force which has to be organised, and the degree to which it is concentrated or dispersed: and it would be unwise to generalise on such matters. Nonetheless, it seems fair to say that there are too few women, and too few black people, in the ranks of the trade union civil service, and it may be that some of the disputed growth areas of trade union recruitment will surrender to those organisations which are quickest to appreciate this fact.

If we are asked 'How representative are union officials?' the question can be answered in the manner already attempted in the last few pages: showing how adequately the membership is covered by union professional services, or, changing the focus of the answer, showing how far the officials as a body reflect the interests, experience and needs of the members. But most people will be seeking yet a third type of answer, which shows exactly in what ways officers are held accountable to their members, and what types of control members can exercise over their collective employees.

Elections

The first and most obvious control which suggests itself is that of election. In fact it is more difficult than might be expected to generalise about the election of trade union leaders in Great Britain: and trade union officers are, of course, a much wider category than the limited number who are called upon to become national leaders. In most unions, but not all, the chief executive officer is the General Secretary.

In some, there is a carefully defined division of responsibilities, separating the powers of a small team of leaders. Among the miners, for instance, the President has a series of duties itemised by rule, while the secretary, again by rule, is also responsible for the union's treasury. But alongside the written rules, there has, by tradition, grown up a body of customs and practices which have still further delimited the job-descriptions of the two chief officers. For many years, the President took charge of political pronouncements, while the Secretary was the leading negotiator.

If we assume that the General Secretary is the most important functionary in most unions, then the first surprise we find is that some of these offices are not filled by elections at all. This has been the case in such different bodies as the National Union of Public Employees, or BISAKTA, the Steelmen's Union, both of whom have had means of appointing their chief officers. In those where elections *are* held, the most common procedure is to ballot either the individual membership directly, or the constituent branches of the organisation. The President and General Secretary of the NUM, for example, are both elected by a pit-head ballot, which ensures a very high percentage poll. The same officers of the AUEW are now elected by a postal ballot of the members, in which approximately one-third of the electorate actually vote.[27] In the shop-workers' union, USDAW, a branch ballot takes place, in which those actually attending the branch meeting are able to cast the entire block vote of the branch's nominal roll. In this manner, a few dozen people may wield hundreds of votes. In some other unions, the Annual Conference elects the principal officers: this happens, for instance, in the TSSA (Railway clerks), the Amalgamated Weavers' Association, and the Dyers' and Bleachers' Union.

However, even where such elections do take place, they are not very often recurrent events. In the AUEW all officers have to submit themselves for re-election (or otherwise) at intervals first of five, and then subsequently of seven, years. But in the other major unions, the TGWU and the GMWU, once elected, General Secretaries will normally continue until they retire. The same rule applies in a whole series of important lesser organisations: the NUM, NUR, TSSA, among those already mentioned.

An obvious curb on the power of such life-long officers is the imposition of fixed terms of office, punctuated by regular ballots. This reform has been actively canvassed, with no success whatever, in the miners' union, in which not only national officials, but also all area professionals, are chosen in a once-for-all poll. Although a vigorous agitation has been carried on for many years, and although many of the miners' local area officers have been chosen on the basis of manifestos committing them personally to the principle of regular five-yearly elections, the proposal has never come anywhere near to gaining approval at the miners' annual conference.

There are thus two main types of criticism of the manner in which unions appoint their officers: on the one side, from those union members who commonly want the chance to bring about greater accountability by imposing an increased frequency of elections: on the other side, from the Conservative Party, which said in 1976:

> '. . . we are ready to help. Public money should be made available for the conduct of postal ballots for union elections where these are requested. Firms should also be encouraged to provide time and facilities for the conduct of union meetings; this should lead to greater participation in union affairs.'[28]

This proposal cuts two ways. Branch meetings during working time, if they could be secured from managerial intervention of any kind, would obviously have a marked beneficial effect on union membership participation. But such branches could obviously not maintain a 'geographical' as opposed to industrial catchment.

A compulsory postal ballot is by no means self-evidently the best means of increasing voting 'turn-out' in the election of officers. Since the institution of such ballots in the engineering section of the AUEW, although the proportion of votes has markedly increased, there has never been any contest without complaints about the working of the system. It is a massive task to mail out 1,168,990 correctly addressed envelopes. Had the AUEW only brought its structure into line with its actual workplace organisation, it would be far simpler to ballot the membership at the workplace, as do the mineworkers, who commonly poll, not one-third, but up to three-quarters, of those eligible to vote. In the EETPU, which also has postal votes, only one-fifth of the members actually participate.[29]

The most commonly heard trade union complaint against postal voting is that it becomes the object of sustained newspaper and media coverage, much of which is a direct and obvious intervention in the union's affairs. It would be difficult to object to this if it were fair, but there is a good deal of evidence that it is not. If one or two mass-circulation newspapers intervene in such an election in favour of the same chosen nominee, it is clearly difficult for his opponents to overcome the disability under which they are consequently placed: they have no means of speaking directly to the millions of people who are reading of the merits of the person against whom they are contending, or even of their own alleged demerits.

As was argued in the TUC education services' manual, *Democracy*

at Work, postal votes are less than perfect reflections of union feeling:

'In a union meeting, decisions are taken in the light of discussion
and debate at the meeting. In a postal ballot many members may
not have full information about candidates, and, so opponents of
postal ballots argue, the press and the media have been able to use
this as an opportunity to interfere in the elections by selectively
publicising certain candidates.
There are also administrative arguments about postal balloting—
that it may be expensive to operate, and that in unions with a high
turnover of membership it would be impossible to operate postal
ballots fairly or effectively. One answer to these dilemmas which is
sometimes put forward is to develop the role of workplace-based
meetings in union elections. These could increase participation in
votes while meeting many of the objections to postal ballots outlined
above.
Another possibility is to improve the standards of *information*
available to voters in union elections.'[30]

This argument has been going on for a long time in the AUEW
engineering section: in 1975 the postal ballot was revoked by a
National Committee decision taken on the chairman's casting vote. It
was restored as a result of a Court action.

Of course, newspaper influences are not confined to postal ballots,
although there are many people who would question whether it would
have been possible for Mr Terry Duffy to triumph over a far more
experienced opponent in the AUEW presidential contest without the
most intelligently co-ordinated press campaign which was waged on
his behalf.[31] During the period running up to the presidential voting in
the NUM, beginning in 1979, long before the incumbent, Mr Joe
Gormley, need retire, a most interesting and sophisticated use was
made of the newspapers. The left-wing candidates for the office were
fairly evidently established: either Mr Scargill, from the union's largest
area, Yorkshire; or, if the ballot were held quickly, before his age made
him ineligible under rule, the Scots Miners' leader, Michael McGahey,
were the obvious choices. There was no very obvious right-wing
contender, however. Such a candidate needed a large area for a
voting-base, and the political geography of the union therefore pointed
towards Nottinghamshire. Yet there existed no-one of the right degree
of seniority to make a remotely plausible candidate from that area.
One new area official had been appointed during the previous year,
and he was of a suitable age, although very much lacking in
experience. To qualify him to run for national office at some time in the

future it was vital to secure his early election to the National Executive Committee, and his rapid promotion within the hierarchy of his own Nottingham Area. At this point, Mr Gormley announced his own premature retirement, triggering a wave of press speculation about his successor. With no evidence whatever to support the thought that this novice official had even contemplated seeking national office, a number of newspapers promptly named him as the favourite 'moderate' nominee. Whatever might be the outcome in the final contest for the NUM's national leadership, this 'news' was obviously useful to the official in question when it came to consolidating his chances of promotion in his own area. Immediately afterwards, Mr Gormley announced that he was reconsidering his early retirement, and could perhaps be persuaded to soldier on.

Obviously, this looks rather like very capable management of the press: but the more that contests of this kind are influenced by newspapers, the more this will become a glaring problem for trade unions as a whole. If all possible candidates in all union elections were entitled to similar coverage, and if the press were equally open to all, no-one should object to the widest possible coverage of union matters, not excluding elections. But when the press comprises a mere handful of million-plus circulation titles, all owned by diversified commercial enterprises (most of which are multinationals), all commonly hostile to many normal objectives of trade unionism, and most partisan for an explicitly Conservative political position, it is not surprising that growing numbers of trade unionists find them biassed, sometimes to an extreme degree.[32]

Separation of Powers

However, whatever the outcome of union elections, and whatever the impact of external influences, in practice once officers have been appointed, the real imposition of accountability and membership control over them turns upon quite other democratic mechanisms than re-election. First, as we have already hinted, many unions develop a separation of powers limiting the scope of influence of particular officers. Probably the most developed instance of this in a major union is the conscious separation of executive, juridical and legislative powers in the AUEW, where a policy-making National Committee legislates, and an elected final appeal court interprets the rules in all contentious disciplinary cases.[33] A separately elected executive administers the union's affairs from day to day.

In effect, separation of powers is an attempt to develop a 'rule of law' within trade union democracy, and so it has been claimed[34] that the same principles should be embodied in union rule books as apply, or are thought to apply, in national government. Supporting this case, Richard Fletcher argues that

'The most important of these are:
(1) the amount of information available to the individual and the power he has to compel notice to be taken of his views.
(2) self-restraint on the part of those who govern, not to exploit every loop-hole in the constitution to the disadvantage of the membership.
(3) The care with which the rules are drafted and their effectiveness as a barrier against autocracy.

It is important that information about the working of the executive should be available to the members to enable them to vote and exercise the other forms of control open to them effectively. Some unions, notably the EETPU, circulate to Branches full minutes of EC decisions giving the voting record of each member. This is an excellent practice and should be more widely adopted.

On the third point, while no rule is self-enforcing, rules which are not stated cannot be enforced. It is, therefore in the interests of the membership that all foreseeable circumstances should as far as possible be covered by rules and simplification should not be undertaken at the expense of completeness.

This is illustrated in the application of the principles of natural justice which have a strong bearing on members' rights, particularly as to procedures to be followed for examples in disciplinary cases.

Rideout[35] considers that detailed lists of offences are preferable to "blanket offences" meriting expulsion, that all disciplinary rules should be brought together and that procedures to be followed should be set out in detail. The NUFTO disciplinary procedure is considered to comply most nearly with the principles of natural justice. It involves the following steps:

Member to be given 14 days notice by registered letter.

Nature of allegation and rule under which charged to be stated in detail to assist preparation of defence.

Member to be entitled to bring not more than 2 witnesses; to submit written statement not less than 7 days before hearing; to question accuser and witnesses; to answer accusation and call own witnesses.

Any member of the General Council (or Branch) may question either side or witnesses and all relevant evidence must be considered.

A similar procedure is to be followed in the conduct of appeals.

Rideout considers that the member should be entitled to be heard separately as to the nature of the penalty to be imposed.'[36]

Even where things are theoretically otherwise checks and balances of various kinds may emerge in practice, by the processes of federation between areas, or alliance between industrial or craft sectors. In many large unions the real power structure involves the balancing of central national powers against regional or sectoral autonomy: all of which means that the union 'kings' have their own problems with their 'barons'. Of course, this analogy is too facile: in contrast with King John, every modern general secretary, and all local, regional and industrial officers, have only one ultimate source of authority, which is in their membership. Even so, some memberships exert greater influence over their affairs than others.

Leadership Succession

It has often been noticed that, throughout the Labour Movement, there exists what has been described as 'the law of Buggins' turn'. Buggins is the man who must, in common justice, be given the opportunity to shine before his (usually long, if sometimes not over-distinguished) career of service comes to an end. Sometimes he has deputised directly for a leader, or even actually carried out a large share of the work of that leader, for a considerable time. Sometimes he has been the longest-established member of a leading committee. Sometimes he has been appointed to a special post by an outgoing leader with the express intention of ensuring continuity of policy by guaranteeing the succession.

More than twenty years ago, V. L. Allen published a detailed study of the effects of Buggins' Law. 'In most cases', he argued 'the position of assistant general secretary is treated as a stepping stone to the chief position in a union, and is regarded as such by ordinary members'.[37] No-one could deny that this happens quite often, although the evidence is not quite as overwhelming as it appeared in Professor Allen's survey: as has been pointed out by Edelstein and Warner:[38]

1. An assistant top officer may be too old to qualify for nomination, under the rules, particularly in Britain, or he may not wish to compete for personal reasons, e.g. ill-health. One should, therefore, also consider top-post elections in which no assistant top officers competed.
2. There may be two or more assistant general secretaries with equal formal standing, and these may compete against each other.
3. The job title of the second-ranking full-time office is not

exclusively 'assistant general secretary', even in Britain, nor is the top office exclusively the 'general secretary'.[39]

4. As Allen himself shows, assistant general secretaries are sometimes defeated for top posts. Allen cites six such instances among twenty-five elections in which such officers competed[40], a proportion which is more than negligible.

5. There may be no full-time next-to-top officer at the national level, especially in smaller unions but even in some larger ones.

What does seem to be important, generally, is that there exist some clearly marked graduations of leadership status, which limit the effective choice in elections to candidates who have gained some real degree of confidence from wide sections of the membership. In unions which are relatively harmoniously administered, this demarcation of status may take the form of a hierarchy of assistants to chief officers, or it may take the form of regional or industrial concentrations of power. In unions which are riven by sharp internal conflicts, it may take the form of the development of clearly perceived oppositional factions, as happened when the Electrical Trades Union was split during the argument about the rigging of its ballots,[41] or when the National Union of Seamen was involved in its major reform struggle during the early 'sixties. Inside the Engineers' Union, both Hugh Scanlon and his successor, Terry Duffy, were not conventional 'runners-up' or Bugginses: both having been relative newcomers to their Union's small Executive Committee before they became chosen contenders for the Union's Presidency, each representing a different faction in the Union's sharply fought and continuous political contest.

Opposition

Very often the most effective membership sanction for controlling a remote leadership arises precisely in the growth of this kind of factionalism, which sometimes reaches the point of creating a structural opposition. A classic case of this is to be found in the upheaval in the National Union of Seamen, during the years following 1960. Here an oligarchy of the purest water had evolved, dominating the whole union and imposing policies of blatant subordination to the employers' needs. Pyramidic appointment structures enabled the union's leaders to 'fix' most of their opponents, year after year. No marked fastidiousness was shown during this process, as was later reported, after rebellion finally broke out:

'There was from the start of the conflict a feeling that coercion might be used, for it had acquired almost the quality of a tradition within the NUS and was perhaps more acceptable than might be the case in other unions. Hence the officials had closely watched the disruptive members. Lists of names had been compiled and records checked. Personal files and reports on some members without doubt were obtained from Special Branch policemen. A smear campaign was launched. One rank and file leader had been away from the sea and had paid no union dues since 1957, a fact publicised by the officials only too readily. The Reformers were alleged to be totally self-interested communist plotters and disrupters, and this angered the men.

> "There was an attack by the union on the seamen, they said we were communists, we were bandits, we were bloody rogues . . . They said I'd been highly trained in Australia, which was just bloody ridiculous . . . And this built up the anti-union feeling."

Jim Slater, the leader of the Reformers on the north-east coast suffered attempts by local officials to force him out to sea as bosun on a trader, and others suffered equivalent harassment. Although the members expected such behaviour from the leaders, the conflict did now begin to move towards outright coercive strategies by both parties, as the bargaining assumed less-preferred forms . . .'[42]

The dramatic struggle in the NUS generated some pretty tough in-fighting, and John Hemingway has documented some questionable practices on both sides. But the NUS was, in British terms, a quite exceptionally undemocratic organisation until the final, belated, victory of the reformers. Most unions are more tolerantly conducted, and contain oppositional groupings with far better grace. A close observer of the trade union scene, Richard Fletcher, has offered the following short charter which, he feels, ought to apply to trade union oppositional rights:

> 'For internal opposition to be effective, members must have the right to organise into factions and must have a real opportunity of taking power.
> Here the criteria are similar to those usually accepted for democracy in national government as set out in the Universal Declaration of Human Rights and the declarations of the International Commission of Jurists. They include the following:
> Freedom of peaceful assembly and association.
> Freedom of expression and the press.
> The right to take part in government.
> The right to form opposition parties.
> The right to stand for election and the vote.
> Representative government and free elections.'[43]

Without being over-sanguine ('Few . . . British unions actually encourage the formation of opposition parties') Richard Fletcher believes that, in most cases, 'they are tolerated with more or less goodwill'.[44]

This was not always the case. Following a split in the international trade union movement, and a fierce development of the cold war in the domestic labour movement, in 1949 the Biennial Delegate Conference of the TGWU modified its rules to bar communists or fascists from either holding office or attending Conference. The onslaught on communists was to some extent acceptable to parts of the TGWU membership in the late 'forties, although within a decade it had become an object of sustained criticism (It was repealed in 1968). But its effect during the early years of its imposition was greatly to reinforce the arbitrary powers of Arthur Deakin, one of the last great hierarchs of British Trade Unionism.

> 'Deakin would openly boast of his power and as openly use it. Only those he could trust to follow his line had the backing of his union when they sought election to the General Council of the TUC or the National Executive of the Labour Party. Leaders of unions who held their seats on either body with his support were frankly told that unless they could persuade their unions to support his policies he would switch his vote to some more reliable candidate.'[45]

Naturally, this kind of influence was deployed not against communists, but against Deakin's opponents (notably, Aneurin Bevan) in the Labour Party. Yet it is questionable whether, if communists' factional rights had been maintained uninterruptedly, Deakin could ever have maintained such unchallenged sway: not that communists would necessarily have supported his Labour opponents (in fact, they did not), but that they would have created an imbalance which could from time to time have opened the general secretary to effective question.[46]

The NUR still proscribes the election of communists to its highest offices, because its rules require both of those holding these posts to serve as Labour Party Conference delegates. The old Boot and Shoe Union, NUBSO (now merged into NUFLAT) had rules proscribing communist *opinions*. Aspirants to office had to complete a form saying 'I am opposed to the principles of communism and agree that my appointment is made on that understanding'.

On the other side, Communist office-holders in the ETU were tried in the Courts and found guilty of an elaborate conspiracy to rig ballots in the elections of that union, thus depriving of office duly elected opponents who had fallen foul of the dominant party machine. Having learnt from this lesson, democrats of whatever political persuasion will seek to ensure the widest possible rights of assembly, communication, and access to relevant information and opinion-forming organs. Trade union rules can be designed to establish and safeguard these rights, and where necessary they should be reformed to ensure that they do.

At the same time, constitutional guarantees for democratic principles are only part of the battle to enforce genuinely democratic working practices. Rules are one thing: behaviour, often enough, is another.

Lay Government versus Professionalism

During the public employees' strikes of early 1979, towards the end of February the unions' negotiators reached what they obviously regarded as the basis for a settlement. Leaders of the GMW and the TGWU were promptly empowered to commend the employers' offer to their members. To the great surprise of the media, the national executive of the third major union involved, NUPE, then voted unanimously to recommend their balloting members to reject the proposed settlement, even though their general secretary had been actively involved in negotiating it. The lay executive felt that insufficient progress had been registered in the pursuit of their original £60 weekly minimum claim. Questioned about this, Alan Fisher had to explain his union's structure, and insist that his executive, which had appointed him, had the right to determine the policies within which he worked. When pressed by a radio interviewer who wished to know whether Mr Fisher 'had lost control of his members', the NUPE spokesman quite rightly replied that it was no part of his job to 'control' his executive, but that his executive, on the contrary, had every right to 'control' its general secretary.

A similarly strong statement was made by Moss Evans during 1978, during the time when he was taking over the responsibility of his new office. Fulltime officers, said Mr Evans, should be on hand 'to service the members, rather than to tell them what to do.' As we have seen already the TGWU is perhaps classically the union in which to study lay influence. Theoretically lay members have for a time long held ultimate power, not only over the Biennial Delegate Conference (1,000 strong), and the regional and industrial sections in which they are organised, but over the central councils of the entire organisation. The Union's General Executive consists entirely of working members, each of whom has been chosen for a period of two years by his relevant region or industrial group. An inner cabinet, or Finance and General Purposes Committee, is chosen by this Executive, and this ensures that working busmen or dockers can arrive at a greater degree of actual power than any professional functionary of the union other than the

General Secretary himself. All the signs are that this lay power is gathering strength and self-confidence. As Roger Undy reports, in his important study on the devolution of bargaining in the union:

> 'Official national encouragement, and indeed promotion, of lay involvement in bargaining was a radical departure from past practice in the traditionally full-time officer dominated T & GWU. The majority of centrally or regionally appointed full-time officers were traditionally more dependent on central, rather than lay members, support for legitimisation of their bargaining decisions. Thus, the use by J. Jones of the 'unique authority' vested in the position of General Secretary to reverse the past pattern of responsibilities in the bargaining field appeared to some of the Union's more long serving full-time officials to be a near revolutionary act. For this group of officials it was somewhat contradictory, to say the least, that the centralised power of the General Secretary should be used in the late 1960s and early 1970s to devolve bargaining responsibilities which were traditionally their prerogative.
>
> Finally, it can be reasonably suggested that the recent (July 1977) defeat of the now retired General Secretary. J. Jones, at the T & GWU's BDC on the question of wage restraint, was not unconnected with his previous sponsorship of the procedural changes identified above. From 1945 to 1977 the platform of the Conference, helped by the "unique authority" of the General Secretary, had only previously been defeated on two comparatively minor issues, both concerned with the formation of new trade groups. Apart from these defeats, successive general secretaries had carried the conference. No doubt the lay delegates in 1977, in rejecting the platform's proposals, felt disinclined to accept further nationally imposed restrictions over their relatively new-found freedom to bargain locally. Hence, paradoxically, it can be argued that defeat for the General Secretary in 1977 was the final, if ironic, tribute to the success of his previous policy of devolving bargaining responsibilities.'[47]

It is because lay government reaches right up to the top in the TGWU that occasional working representatives may appear on the General Council of the TUC: Bill Jones, the London busman, or Stan Pemberton, the Liverpool steward from Dunlop Speke, or Walt Greendale, the Hull docker would not at present, without taking up full-time work as organisers, have stood any chance of joining the General Council as representatives from any other union than the TGWU. No other section of the General Council contains men and women whose diaries include long slabs of time spent on the shop floor, leading substantially the same lives as the people they represent.

The members of the policy-making National Committee of the AUEW are prevented from discharging a similar role to the lay leadership of the TGWU by the fact that they normally confer only once a year, even though their deliberations continue for a longer time than do most union annual conferences. Fifty people constitute this Committee, so that they lack the authority of a major delegate conference. But the gap between their sessions is too long to allow the Committee to hold any careful watching brief over the doings of the very small, and completely professional Executive, which thus constantly strays into policymaking rather than implementing policies made for it. In fact, from time to time, AEU National Committees have tried to reinforce their admitted constitutional role, by approving resolutions which have included a provision for their own recall in the event of something happening, or failing to happen.[48] The constraints which such recall might place upon the freedom of action of the executive of the union have ensured that this kind of proposal has met with small executive enthusiasm. A celebrated dispute in 1966 resulted in a decision by the union's Final Appeal Court to censure the executive for failing to act upon such a recall motion: but union elections changed the composition of the leadership, still leaving the issue potentially liable to recur. Indeed, it seems entirely possible that this kind of argument may continue, unless the union's structure is modified to prevent it doing so.

Sometimes lay representation is conspicuous by its absence. Executive Committees of the NUM, for instance, do not normally include many working miners, since the union's federal origins guarantee a built-in tendency by most areas to field, at executive level, their best known professional agents. Yet various problems in the history of the NUM might have been solved differently if more lay members had access to top leadership committees. Even so, NUM members have long insisted on ultimate control over the results of national bargaining, which are nowadays invariably referred to the membership.

Communications

The trade union press faces an onerous responsibility, because, in general, the established media are by no means over-friendly to the Labour Movement. This leaves a considerable task of explanation to trade union journalists who are often amateurs, and commonly without any great resources. Quite a lot of money is spent on trade union publications, but few are distributed through any conventional channels. The NUR publication *Transport Review*, and the Teachers' weekly newspaper, are both sold through newsagents. All the other major unions produce either a regular magazine, or a tabloid magazine, or both: and almost all of these are distributed free of charge.

In certain professional unions the journal is obviously seen as a key instrument of communication with the members, and this is reflected in appropriately high circulation figures. NALGO, for instance, with 710 thousand members, prints 740 thousand copies of its most informative monthly-journal, *Public Service*. ASTMS print one copy of their bimonthly for each of their 450 thousand members, who receive it by post. British Actors' Equity *Journal* prints 32,000 copies for 24,000 members; the Journalist 30,000 for 28 and a half thousand members; and most civil service unions also provide enough copies for all their members.

On the other hand, the biggest unions make no attempt to reach all their membership with their journals. The TGWU, which produces a bright tabloid newspaper, *The Record*, prints something over 400 thousand copies for 2 million members. This compares rather well with the much stodgier *Journal* of the AUEW, which only prints 145 thousand for more than one million people, or the General and Municipal Workers' *Journal*, which prints 70 thousand for a membership of 950 thousand. Since distribution is free in each case, there is no way of telling what proportion of these print orders is actually distributed, leave alone read.

Most unions publish their journals monthly and since many do not sell much advertisng space, this can be a costly business. The SLADE *Journal*, with a circulation of 22,000, almost covers its costs through advertising receipts, but this appears to be an exceptional case. Some unions are reticent about their publishing costs, but those prepared to disclose an annual outlay of £20,000 or more are listed in Table III:5.

Intelligent guesses at the printing costs of the Engineers' and GMWU *Journals* would put them at £170,000 and £35,000 per annum respectively. This gives a joint expenditure, by 16 trade unions, of £1,422,000 a year on the subsidisation of union newspapers and journals.

As to whether this produces value for money, there might be room for some argument. Some journals are briskly conducted, and punchy in their style. Others are unbelievably bad. (*The Boilermaker*, for instance, gives over numerous pages in each issue to recording the names of members who have fallen into arrears.) Sometimes a professional journalist is engaged to edit the union newspaper, but quite commonly the job is taken on by a responsible official, especially when control of the journal may contribute to some advantage in the internal political struggles of the organisation. The AUEW *Journal*, for

Table III:5
Union journals, costs and advertising revenue

Union	Cost of Journal 1978–9	Advertising Revenue
APEX	£33,000	£1,000
COHSE	£70,000	£8,000
CPSA	£165,000*	
Musicians' Union	£20,000*	
NALGO	£249,000	£56,000
NATFHE	£72,000	£18,000
NUAAW	£24,000*	little
NUBE	£51,000*	£12,000
NUJ	£22,000	£1,500
SCPS	£73,000	£33,000
SOGAT	£48,000	£6,000
SPOE	£40,000*	some
TGWU	£250,000	12½%
USDAW	£100,000	

(Part of this information comes from a survey taken in Summer 1978, and part from a different investigation made in March 1979. At a time of rising inflation, it is necessary to distinguish the later information with a *.)

instance, is edited by John Boyd, the General Secretary. A lesser publication, for the union's women and youth members (*The Way*) is traditionally conducted by an assistant General Secretary. Complaints about the allocation of space and photographs in such journals are a common feature of union electoral contests. On the whole, it may be doubted whether such complaints are all that well-founded, since it is an open question how many potential voters ever read the disputed material.

A far more serious question is posed if one sets aside the union press as it is, and considers it as it might be. With modern printing technology, bright, flexible, effective publicity is cheaply available, and if it is rationally employed it can make a considerable impact. Yet the trade unions, which controlled a daily newspaper all through the 'twenties, 'thirties, 'forties and 'fifties, have been totally without any national voice in the press during two decades, through which time they have fought off more than one political offensive aimed at reducing their rights and social influence. Can the TUC remain satisfied with this unbalanced, even menacing position?

Table III:6

Union journals—circulation and distribution

Union	Member-ship 000s	Journal (format)	Circulation (000s)	Distribution Method	Price	Cost (000s)
TGWU	2,000	Record (Tabloid)	400+	Demand: to shop stewards' homes	Free	£250 12½% advertising
AUEW (Eng. Section)	1,193	Journal (Magazine)	145	Branches/Convenors	Free	£170+(est)
GMWU	950	Journal (Magazine)	70	Direct mail/bulk (50:50)	Free	£35+ (est)
NALGO	710	Public Service (Tabloid)	740	Post/roadline: to 1,200 branches	Free	£169
NUPE	693	Public Employees (Tabloid)			Free	
EETPU	420	Contact (Tabloid)				
USDAW	450	Dawn (Magazine)	140	Post/rail/vans	Free	£100
ASTMS	450	Journal (Tabloid)	450	Post to home	Free	
UCATT	320	Viewpoint (Tabloid)	80	Bulk via regional offices	Free	
NUT	265	The Teacher (Tabloid)	52	Newsagents/copy to each school		
NUM	259	The Miner (Tabloid)				

NOTES

1. Small is beautiful, and there is no doubt that Dr Schumacher discovered the power of this truth because he was so long working for the vast bureaucracy of the National Coal Board. But competition is the force which centralises vast monopoly power, and no-one has ever discovered how to run that motor backwards. Unions have to square the circle: to be big enough to exercise counter-power, and accessible enough to allow democracy to flourish in their internal affairs.

2. G. D. H. Cole: *British Trade Unionism: Problems and Policy*, L.R.D. 1925, p. 19.

3. USDAW: *Introducing USDAW: The Structure Government and Administration of the Union*. Home Study Course, Part III, USDAW, 1972? p. 30.

4. Ibid, p. 31.

5. ETU: *Submission of Evidence to the Royal Commission on Trade Unions and Employers' Associations*, ETU n.d. p. 4.

6. GMWU; *The General and Municipal Workers' Union—its History, Structure, Policies, Benefits and Services*, GMWU 1975, p. 5.

7. TGWU: *Training Manual* Part 2, 1960, pp. 4–5.

8. AEU: *Trade Unions and The Contemporary Scene*. Evidence to Royal Commission on Trade Unions and Employers' Associations, 1965.

9. Cited in Jim Gardner: *Key Questions for Trade Unionists*, Lawrence and Wishart, 1960, p. 34.

10. AEU, op. cit.

11. Cf. J. Goldstein: *The Government of British Trade Unions*, Allen and Unwin, 1952. This offers an estimate that TGWU branch attendance never rose above 15 per cent. Controversial within the TGWU at the time of its publication, this study attempts to probe reasons for non-involvement. B. C. Roberts: *Trade Union Government and Administration in Great Britain* claims figures as low as 4 per cent and 7 per cent, but up to 15 per cent. London School of Economics/Bell, 1956, cf. pp. 95 et seq. PEP: *British Trade Unionism* 1948 put them between 15 per cent and 20 per cent. J. H. Goldthorpe et al: *The Affluent Worker*. Cambridge University Press, 1968, 1969, found that 60 per cent of car workers never attended. This and other evidence is summarised in Robert Taylor: *The Fifth Estate—Britain's Unions in the Seventies*, Routledge & Kegan Paul, 1978, pp. 106–9.

12. Bob Fryer, Andy Fairclough and Tom Manson: *Organization and Change in the National Union of Public Employees*. University of Warwick, 1974, pp. 21–3.

13. Sidney and Beatrice Webb: *History of Trade Unionism*, WEA, 1920, pp. 466–70.

14. Roberto Michels: *Political Parties*, Constable/Dover, 1950, p. 21.
15. Ibid, p. 22.
16. Ibid, pp. 70 et seq.
17. There is an interesting discussion of these questions in Richard Hyman: *Marxism and the Sociology of Trade Unionism*, Pluto Press, 1971.
18. Brian Pearce: *Some Rank-and-File Movements*, Labour Review, 1959, p. 13.
19. TUC Annual Report, 1978: *Details of past Congresses*.
20. B. C. Roberts, op. cit, pp. 288–9. A corrective to these figures is to be found in H. A. Clegg, A. J. Killick and R. Adams: *Trade Union Officers*, Blackwell, 1960, pp. 37 et seq., especially p. 40.
21. The Donovan Report (Cmnd. 5623) insisted that this ratio was on the high side: in the USA comparable figures were 'of the order of' 1:1,400, whilst in Federal Germany they were 1:1,800. 'Both Italy and France appear to have twice as many officers per member as we do.'
22. Ibid, p. 188.
23. Cited in the Donovan Report, p. 189.
24. Roger Undy: 'The Devolution of Bargaining Levels and Responsibilities in the T & GWU 1965–75'. *Industrial Relations Journal* 9, 3 pp. 44 et seq.
25. Ibid, p. 49.
26. The Equal Pay and Opportunity Campaign, Canonbury Park North, London N1: figures for 1976.
27. The most useful account of recent electoral struggles in both the NUM and the AEU/AUEW is to be found in J. D. Edelstein and M. Warner: *Comparative Union Democracy*, Allen and Unwin, 1975, Chapters 8 and 9.
28. The Conservative Party: *The Right Approach*, October 1976.
29. Cf. Robert Taylor, op. cit, p. 110.
30. For instance, in 1968, under the branch voting system, only 11 per cent of the AUEW's membership voted in the election for General Secretary. In 1975 38 per cent of the membership voted in postal ballots for national officials. Postal ballots may also reduce the chances of abuse of electoral procedures, and since voting is secret, are likely to reduce the amount of 'pressure' on the voter from fellow union members. *Democracy at Work*, *Trade Union Studies*, BBC, p. 155.
31. The mechanics of similar previous contests are very fully described in Edelstein and Warner, op. cit.
32. For a summary of trade union attitudes to these questions, see *Workers' Control*, the Bulletin of the IWC, No. 3 and 4, 1979.
33. AEF: *Structure and Function of the Union*, 1969, p. 6: 'branches are grouped in eleven electoral divisions for the election of eleven delegates'.
34. R. W. Rideout: 'Responsible Self-Government in British Trade Unions', *British Journal of Industrial Relations*, 5 (1967) p. 74.
35. R. W. Rideout: 'The Content of Trade Union Disciplinary Rules', *B.J.I.R.*, 3 (1965) p. 153.
36. Richard Fletcher: 'Trade Union Democracy: the Case of the AUEW Rule Book', *Trade Union Register 3*. Spokesman, 1973, pp. 125–49.
37. Cf. V. L. Allen: *Power in Trade Unions*, Longmans, 1954, pp. 184 et seq. 271 et seq. This quotation is p. 206.

38. Op. cit, pp. 91-2.
39. B. C. Roberts, op. cit, pp. 263 et seq.
40. V. L. Allen, op. cit, pp. 203-4.
41. Cf. C. H. Rolph: *All Those in Favour—The ETU Trial*, Andre Deutsch, 1962.
42. J. Hemingway: *Conflict and Democracy—Studies in Trade Union Government*, OUP, 1978, p. 52.
43. Richard Fletcher: 'Trade Union Democracy—Structural Factors' in *Trade Union Register, 2*, Spokesman, 1970, p. 78.
44. Ibid. See also the same author's *Case of the AUEW Rule Book* in *Trade Union Register 3*, Spokesman, 1973.
45. R. Hunter: *The Road to Brighton Pier*, cited in Gardner, op. cit, p. 43.
46. The important study by Mark Jenkins: *Bevanism; Labour's High Tide*, published by Spokesman in 1979, throws much light on this question.
47. Roger Undy, op. cit, p. 56.
48. Cf. Edelstein and Warner, Ch. 9.

APPENDIX TO CHAPTER 3

This check list, prepared by Richard Fletcher for the third number of the *Trade Union Register*, provides a convenient list of criteria for the evaluation of Trade Union Democracy.

HOW DEMOCRATIC IS *YOUR* UNION?

CHECK LIST*
Some criteria for comparison of formal democracy in union constitutions.

Structure

Are top officials elected?	Frequently.....	Occasionally...
	Once only	Never ....
Are other officials elected?	Frequently.....	Occasionally...
	Once only	Never ....
Are Executive members elected?	Frequently.....	Occasionally...
Is Executive Council	Lay?	Full time?......

Is some authority devolved to:

Elected lay area committees?	Yes........	No ....
Elected lay trade committees?	Yes........	No ....

If so do these include direct representation of

shop stewards?	Yes........	No ....
Is policy determined by delegate conference?	Yes........	No ....

Members' Rights (of Opposition)

Freedom to meet outside union structure	Yes........	No ....
Freedom to criticise leadership	Yes........	No ....

Independent appeal against disciplinary

action	Yes........	No ....
Is internal opposition harrassed or persecuted?	No	Yes........

Elections

Balloting	Individual members' vote in branches by post?...........	
	Branch vote cast in block	....
Can E.C. suspend members from election?	No	Yes........

If yes above, is there effective independent

appeals machinery?	Yes........	No ....

Are ballots reasonably proof against fraud? Yes........ No ....
Most successful candidate secure majority of
   votes cast? Yes........ No ....

Communications
Are full minutes and voting record of E.C.
   published Yes........ No ....
Are verbatim reports of conferences
   published? Yes........ No ....
Does union journal publish impartially letters
   from members? Yes........ No ....
Does union journal publish impartially
   articles from members? Yes........ No ....
Is information about all members seeking
   election published? Yes........ No ....
Do members have right to visit branches
   other than their own? Yes........ No ....
Do members have right to circulate branches
   without E.C. permission? Yes........ No ....
Do members have right to write to press about
   union affairs? Yes........ No ....
If not are penalties for infringement? Mild ...... Severe ....
Do union leaders use national media to attack
   opposition? Little...... Much.....

Policy-making
Is policy determined by delegate conference? Yes........ No ....
Does basis of delegation give equal weight to
   all members? Yes........ No ....
Is conference managed by independently
   elected committee? Yes........ No ....
Does conference decide its own meeting
   place? Yes........ No ....

Rule Change
Are changes of rule decided by: Rules revision or delegate conference .....
                           General ballot of members ......

   * Respondents should attach their own weightings to alternatives. Left-hand column, or first alternative, in the writer's opinion, denotes higher level of democracy. (Trade union members' attitudes to the questions would make an interesting further study.)

Chapter Four

The TUC

The Origins and Development of the TUC

The TUC dates its inception to the year 1868, when the Manchester and Salford Trades Council convened what turned out to be the first of a continuous series of trade union conferences.[1] There had been earlier attempts to form an all-embracing forum of trade unionism, notably the Grand National Consolidated Trade Union of the 1830's, associated with the name and ideas of Robert Owen, and the National Association of United Trades for the Protection of Labour, of 1845. The early years of the TUC were dominated by the need to ensure that parliamentary legislation on trade union affairs was favourably influenced. To this end, the TUC set up its Parliamentary Committee in 1871, to lobby MPs, send deputations to Ministers, and organise publicity campaigns. The work of the Parliamentary Committee, which was manned by six leading secretaries of the unions of the day, was conducted on a voluntary basis, with no full-time staff. By 1900, the TUC had progressed to the appointment of a Secretary, assisted by a clerk and a part-time advisory barrister. In 1902, the salary of the secretary was fixed at £250, and in 1905 the post was made into a full-time one. The first generation of TUC leaders had been craft-oriented, cautious and even hostile to industrial action, and concerned above all to win a respected and respectable place for their version of trade unionism within a liberal capitalist society whose fundamental norms they did not seek to challenge. This search for an alliance with the liberals even led prominent members of the trade union establishment into secret dealings with the Liberal Party and with individual employers.[2]

A new wave of trade union affiliations enlarged the TUC in the 1890s, following the growth of organisation amongst unskilled manual workers, and they brought with them more aggressive policies based on explicitly socialist beliefs; the younger generation of craft unionists sometimes shared these ideas.[3]

The old guard of the TUC leadership succeeded in avoiding direct involvement in socialist methods and policies, but were forced to convene the conferences out of which arose in 1899, the General

Federation of Trade Unions, and in 1900 the Labour Representation Committee, which converted itself into the Labour Party in 1906. The GFTU was intended to provide a much more co-ordinated approach to industrial action, with a common strike fund. But only a minority of trade unions joined it, and it deteriorated into a fund holder for the purely defensive mutual insurance of unions, having most significance for the smaller organisations.

Syndicalists looked forward to the time when the GFTU would supercede the TUC as the more suitable body to effect central co-ordination of trade union policies, but their hopes were never realised, and by creating a separate Labour Party, the trade unions also saw to it that the TUC was not directly involved in the alternative, parliamentary road to emancipation. The Parliamentary Committee retained its role as a purely lobbying body, even though, between 1905 and 1919, it was formally associated with the Labour Party and the GFTU through a Joint Board.[4]

As the scope of social legislation widened in the first two decades of the 20th century, so the role of the Parliamentary Committee increased, and in 1917 the TUC added an assistant secretary to its staff, and reinforced its clerical assistance. In 1920, under the prevailing influences of syndicalism, industrial unionism, and guild socialism, the TUC organisation underwent a substantial structural reform. In place of the limited Parliamentary Committee, a General Council was created which was elected from affiliated unions divided into 17 Trade Groups, corresponding roughly to industrial divisions. (An eighteenth element on the General Council was added in the form of special representation for women workers). Whilst by 1919 the Parliamentary Committee had totalled 16 members, the General Council numbered 32. Nomination for election to represent each Group on the General Council was confined to unions within each Group, but voting for the seats was by the whole affiliated membership. The General Council was conceived as a much more dynamic, industrially active general staff of the labour movement than the old Parliamentary Committee, and the Trade Groups were intended to foreshadow structural reform leading to industrial unionism. To initiate this trend, G. D. H. Cole, who drafted the new constitution, proposed that a start be made by establishing five industrial sub-committees within the TUC. During this period, moves to unite the TUC and the Labour Party went no further than the setting up of the National Joint Council of Labour, a consultative body comprising representatives of the Parliamentary Labour Party, the Party's National Executive Committee, and the TUC General Council.

Ambitious schemes were proposed by the radical reformers of the movement, and common departments between the Labour Party and the TUC were established for research, international affairs, and publicity. Their staff in 1925 was larger by five than the whole administrative staff of the TUC, and the TUC contributed £6,500 out of its total income of £18,500 to the joint departments. In 1926, after recording their disenchantment with the first Labour Government's indifference to the TUC, the latter withdrew from the departments, which ceased to function.[5]

The new constitution for the TUC, which was adopted when the General Council was formed, and which still forms the basis of the TUC Rules and Standing Orders, did contain overt political objectives. For example, in Rule 2, 'Objects', it is declared that Congress 'shall endeavour to establish the following measures . . . Public Ownership and control of natural resources and of services—Nationalisation of land, mines and minerals, nationalisation of railways, the extension of State and municipal enterprise for the provision of social necessities and services, proper provision for the adequate participation of the workers in the control and management of public services and industries.'

The advocates of the TUC as co-ordinator of industrial action achieved some success in inserting provisions in Rule 8 'Duties of the General Council' which required the Council to 'co-ordinate industrial action' to 'promote common action . . . on general questions' and 'to assist any union which is attacked on any vital question of trade union principle.' Another interesting General Council duty which reflects the post-1918 climate of opinion is the following extract from Rule 8:

> 'In order that the Trade Union Movement may do everything which lies in its power to prevent future wars, the General Council shall, in the event of there being a danger of an outbreak of war, call a Special Congress to decide on industrial action, such Congress to be called, if possible, before war is declared.'

A further provision within Rule 11, 'Industrial Disputes', states that the General Council should, where its advice and assistance is accepted by a union which is in dispute with an employer but which nevertheless finds itself in continued dispute because of the policy of the employers, 'take steps to organise on behalf of the organisation or organisations concerned all such moral and material support as the circumstances of the dispute may appear to justify.'

Thus the new constitution did give the TUC powers of co-ordination, but did not fundamentally threaten the autonomy of individual unions. No central strike fund was established, and the General

Council could only act with the consent of the affiliated unions. These contradictory elements in the constitution were fully exposed in the General Strike of 1926, the first and only occasion when the powers of the TUC to lead industrial action on behalf of the whole movement were tested. This is not the place for a full survey of that potent episode. It is enough to note that 'constitutionalist' opinion within the TUC became firmly established after the General Strike, resolving that such an action would 'never again' be undertaken. (There were angry scenes at the General Council in 1958, when Frank Cousins—a new and 'junior' left-wing General Secretary at the time—sought to invoke the active industrial assistance of the TUC on behalf of his striking London busmen, and shades of the General Strike were present in the room.[6] The Council advised Cousins to seek a settlement and not to count on their aid.* But in 1971, the TUC came close to sanctioning strike action against the Industrial Relations Bill, and came within a few days of a general stoppage over the case of the imprisoned London dockworkers the following year. 'Never' is an injudicious word to employ in this kind of context, and it is possible to imagine circumstances, such as the threat of unjustified war, or of a fascist take-over of power in Britain, when the TUC might be under the strongest moral obligation to consider leading industrial action.)

Under the leadership of Walter Citrine, (General Secretary) and of Ernest Bevin of the TGWU, the TUC in the inter-war and war years pursued a constitutional role, and continued the historical trend to-wards a wider involvement in consultations with governments, and participation in the affairs of state as a very junior partner. This was particularly so during the war, and during the Labour administration from 1945-51. (Earlier, the first Labour Prime Minister Ramsay MacDonald had kept the TUC very much at arm's length, and hardly deigned to consult them at all.[7]) Moreover, in the war and post-war years, the TUC recovered and surpassed the numerical affiliated strength which had declined so drastically after 1926, and for this reason alone could claim an increasingly representative nature. For the most part, the Conservative Governments of the 1950s continued the tradition of 'consulting' the TUC, but of regarding it as of limited significance for its overall policies and postures, and the TUC, under a succession of right-of-centre alliances amongst its leadership, conformed to the role assigned to it. As the economic circumstances of Britain went into relative decline, and as the hegemony of right-wing leadership in the TUC became challenged after the succession of Frank Cousins to the leadership of the TGWU, the climate changed.

*See Chapter 7.

The period since about 1962 has seen such large-scale and far-reaching changes in the role of the TUC that a more extended treatment of those decades is needed. A dramatic process, which is by no means completed in 1979, was set in train, in which the TUC at first was compelled to respond to initiatives of Government leading to greater and greater encroachment of the state in industrial relations and trade union affairs, whilst at a later stage, the TUC itself took the initiative in claiming and achieving a far wider role for itself and its affiliates.

Wages Policy and the TUC

In 1962, the Conservative Government set up two organisations, the National Economic Development Council (NEDC) and the National Incomes Commission (NIC). NEDC was the first major organisation to embody the concept of 'tripartite' representation in a threefold state body, being comprised of representatives of the Government, the employers, and the TUC, which nominated its six most senior General Council members to represent it. George Woodcock, the TUC General Secretary, declared that 'NEDC is to us a serious undertaking indeed'. 'We go in *as a side* . . . we are linked together all the time.' (Italics added).[8] Consequently, NEDC has survived, although not without its trade union critics, and we shall discuss it again when we consider the general issue of tripartism.

The different TUC response to the NIC was equally sharp, clear, and unequivocal. Its purpose was seen as the enforcement of a Government policy of wage restraint, and its form, (it was a body entirely appointed by Government, with no representative element, and with no clear accountability) made it repugnant to the TUC, which accused the Government of trying to shift the opprobrium of wage restraint away from itself onto an entirely inappropriate organisation. The TUC had not been invited to participate in the NIC, and indeed were only informed of its formation some hours before the announcement in the House of Commons. Any attempt to impose wage restraint by an external body would be resisted by the TUC, although the General Secretary was at pains to point out that he and the General Council were not averse to discussing wages within a wider context of economic planning such as might be achieved within the NEDC. The TUC advised unions to boycott all NIC investigations and hearings, and the organisation did not survive the downfall of the Conservative Government in 1974.

The General Council's willingness to admit wages as an item on the NEDC agenda was itself too much for the TUC as a whole at this stage. Led by the TGWU under Frank Cousins, the 1963 annual Congress rejected General Council policy, and approved a motion expressing 'complete opposition to any form of wages restraint.' In the debate, Woodcock was taken to task by Cousins and others for claiming that the TUC was now wholly concerned with Committee work in 'the corridors of power' and that 'we left Trafalgar Square a long time ago.' Yet Woodcock in one sense may have had the last word; in a remarkable anticipation of the social contract which was to emerge a decade later, he remarked, 'If you want in a democracy . . . to get restraint . . . you must seek to create, to have accepted, what Rousseau called a general will.'[9]

In subsequent years and phases of Government incomes and wage restraint policies, TUC opposition rarely took the absolute form of 1963, and there are important periods when it accommodated such policies within its own strategy. This ambivalent attitude to wage restraint contrasts strongly, as we shall see, with the unequivocal and successful resistance mounted by the TUC against Government attempts to legislate to control and limit trade union organisations and methods. It may be that the TUC has regarded incomes policy as a lesser threat to its role, because it has been regarded as a temporary measure and because in the later 'social contract' version of incomes restraint, the terms have been to some extent bargainable with Government and there have been compensatory gains for the unions. Chapter 6 below is devoted to the detailed questions of collective bargaining and some aspects of incomes policy.

Periodic attempts by government to control wages have led to a situation in which the TUC has been, in effect, conducting collective bargaining on behalf of the whole trade union movement, and this has profound implications for its role and authority. It has meant amongst other things that the TUC has begun to evolve bargaining targets and strategies which it has then urged on the trade unions. This adaptation to incomes policies stands in contrast to the unequivocal *opposition* which the TUC has led when the basic organisational freedoms of trade unionism were under threat.[10]

One element in the TUC's bargaining strategy has been the sucessive target figures for minimum earnings which have been adopted by Congress. It was in 1967, at the height of the Wilson government's statutory incomes policy, that the TUC passed a TGWU resolution establishing a minimum earnings target of £15. By 1970 this had been raised to £20, and in subsequent years up to 1974 it was raised to £30. It may be significant that when the most recent attempt to increase the figure to £50 in 1977, in line with cost-of-living increases since 1974, the union moving the motion was NUPE, entirely confined within the public sector, and that the General Council set its face against this upward revision for the first time, arguing that such an increase (of some 30 per cent) was incompatible with an 'orderly' return to free collective bargaining. The NUPE motion was lost, and thus the moral authority of the TUC was withdrawn from the struggle against low pay.

The TUC has not confined its thinking on collective bargaining strategies to the minimum earnings target. Since 1968 it has published an annual *Economic Review*, a major strategic document linking economic analysis and forecast with collective bargaining strategy, which has often enabled it to adopt an independent and critical stance in relation to government forecasts and targets. The *Review*, which takes into account successful resolutions of the previous year's Congress, has consistently stood for expansionist and interventionist economic policies. Associated with the *Review*, the TUC introduced the practice of calling a conference of union Executive committees to debate and ratify it, thus giving a further reinforcement to General Council policies. In the 1969 *Annual Report*, the General Council affirmed that the purposes of the *Review* were to recast incomes policy along TUC policy lines, to point up the divergence between its thinking on economic policy and that of the government, to provide it with a new basis for consulting with and influencing government, and to give a policy foundation for all its participation in tripartite activities, independent of the thinking emanating from the NEDC office.

In a major review of TUC Structure and Development in 1970, the TUC devoted considerable further attention to collective bargaining strategy.[11] They argued that the TUC should be concerned not just with wages, but the total economic environment of its affiliates, including the factors which contributed to success in strike actions. The document also discussed ways and means of developing an information service for unions, through promotion of discussions with trade union research officers, through more frequent publication of TUC bulletins on economic indicators, and through a TUC initiative to pool, store, and analyse economic data and collective agreements. It was in 1970 too that the TUC renamed its Incomes Policy Committee as a Collective Bargaining Committee, with representation from each TUC Trade Group plus the General Secretary. Its objects were declared to be the discussion of collective bargaining targets, to review collective bargaining developments, and to promote common objectives amongst its affiliates. However, the Committee ceased to function after 1974, presumably because the General Council itself assumed more central authority in this field in the context of the social contract.

In 1972, the TUC produced a follow-up report on its structure and development, which continued to stress the need for co-ordination of unions' collective bargaining objectives. Wages Council industries needed co-ordination particularly, and the demand for Equal Pay should be speeded up. Non-wage benefits such as job security and redundancy agreements, shorter hours, longer holidays, sick-pay schemes and pensions schemes could be adopted as common targets. It spoke of annual holidays of three weeks as an immediate goal, and the 35 hour week, the four week holiday, the four day week, and more public holidays, as longer-term goals, and reported that the TUC Collective Bargaining Committee had discussed these goals with trade union negotiators in large companies. It expressed strong demands for the disclosure of information from employers, and foreshadowed later legislation to deal with employers who refused requests for disclosure of information.[12]

All this story provides strong evidence of the TUC's growing involvement in collective bargaining; the continuous battering on the door of trade union autonomy by successive Government wage policies has led the movement to use its central organisation more and more, both as co-ordinator and policy maker in this field. The process is incomplete—we shall refer to its further development through TUC Industry Committees later—and has encountered a persistent weakness and indecision in the key area of public sector bargaining.

When we turn to review the period from 1965 onwards, in respect of Government programmes to legislate on trade union organisation and rights, we find a more forthright determination by the TUC to defend union autonomy, but a similar outcome to that of incomes policy history—the TUC acquires, through the battles over legislative programmes, more authority and power.

The TUC and Legislative Onslaughts

The largely voluntary reforms in collective bargaining proposed by the Donovan Royal Commission in 1968 caused no profound crisis in the TUC, and in fact stimulated the early stages of TUC initiative in the collective bargaining field which we have reviewed above; six 'Post-Donovan' conferences of unions in different sectors were summoned by the TUC to consider the reform of bargaining practice and trade union organisation.[13] But Donovan's voluntarism was soon overtaken by tougher government measures.

The Labour government's White Paper, *In Place of Strife*, which was published in 1969, proposed that legislation should be enacted to give governments power to order a strike ballot before a major strike, and to order 'cooling off' periods in the case particularly of unofficial and unconstitutional strikes. It also proposed to empower a newly formed Commission for Industrial Relations to enforce its decisions in cases of inter-union disputes over recognition. These proposed measures were firmly resisted by the TUC. Other proposals, including the registration of procedure agreements, the guaranteeing of workers' rights to join trade unions, and to trade unions of the right to recognition, the protection of individuals against unfair dismissal, the provision of better information for collective bargaining purposes, and the extensions of the jurisdiction of Industrial Tribunals, were in principle acceptable to the TUC. A major political crisis for the Government developed around the TUC resistance to the 'penal clauses', and the government was forced to withdraw them. But a very important outcome was that the TUC, in undertaking to police inter-union disputes and unconstitutional stoppages more fully, assumed wider authority over its affiliated unions. In the TUC's published response to *In Place of Strife*, the *Programme for Action*, it was proposed that TUC Rules 11 and 12 should be amended to give effect to these increased central powers. On unconstitutional strikes, unions would in future be required to inform the General Council of 'unauthorised and unconstitutional stoppages of work' and to follow TUC advice as to how to deal with them. Concerning inter-union disputes, unions would be required to inform the General Council whenever an official stoppage was contemplated in an inter-union dispute, and to desist from authorised strike action until the TUC had considered the case. If an unauthorised stoppage took place in an inter-union conflict, the union concerned was to have a duty to strive for a recommencement of work by its members.

A special Congress summoned at Croydon on June 5th 1969 approved the TUC's counter-proposals by very large majorities. The General Council held ten meetings with the Prime Minister, and a sub-committee of the Council held four meetings with him; at the end of this lengthy process, the Government withdrew its proposals for penal sanctions and strike ballots, in return for a 'solemn and binding undertaking' to operate the amendments to Rules 11 and 12.

The opposition of the trade unions to the Conservative government's Industrial Relations Act of 1971 provides one of the most remarkable demonstrations of the exercise of TUC authority. The details of the Act are dealt with in our chapter on Law; at this stage it is only necessary to remind ourselves that the Act carried much further the concept of legal penalties for trade unionists committing specified 'unfair practices' and introduced an elaborate system of legal regulation of trade unions, including a specification of requirements for union rule books. The Act represented the most systematic and radical attempt ever made by modern governments to control trade unionism within a tight legal strait-jacket.

The trade union movement was in no doubt that it should resist the legislation, and seek to render it inoperable. To achieve this end they required a united and common programme, and a sustained public campaign; these could not be achieved without a massive concentration of effort through their central organisation, the TUC. Whilst the legislation was before parliament, the TUC organised its campaign. A conference of union officers was called in November 1970, the education department of the TUC produced a training kit which was used to train thousands of union officials and lay representatives in regional programmes, TUC regional conferences were held, 118 Trades Councils organised meetings on the Bill, and the TUC called two national demonstrations against it, the larger one summoning 140,000 trade unionists to Hyde Park and Trafalgar Square. A national petition to parliament contained ½ million signatures, and TUC press advertisements cost £51,000. TUC publications on the Bill included a film and a special gramophone record with a message from the General Secretary.

TUC policy on the Bill included; a call for its early repeal, (a necessity which did much to draw the TUC and Labour Party into closer alliance), advice to unions to insist that new clauses in collective agreements should specifically opt against their legal enforceability, an insistence that unions should continue to observe the TUC's Bridlington rules rather than use the new legal procedures for recognition in inter-union conflicts, a boycott of the statutory bodies—Commission on Industrial Relations, and National Industrial Relations Court—set up by the Act, a withdrawal of union nominees from service on Industrial Tribunals, a rejection of the Code of Industrial Relations Practice issued under the Act and the publication of an independent TUC *Guide to Good Industrial Relations*, and above all, a campaign to ensure that no trade unions sought registered status under the Act. In debating this latter policy at the 1971 Congress, the movement was involved in an important debate about the extent of TUC authority, and about the defence of trade union autonomy against legal interference. The device of registration in the Act embodied an attempt by the government to bring trade union rule-making under the control of the law and of a state registrar of unions. The Act contained a long list of union rule requirements which had to appear in the rule book of a union before it was eligible for registration, which in its turn, conferred apparent advantages on unions, including tax relief on provident income.

So strong was the unions' feeling on this subject however, that the TUC decided that unions ought not to register under these terms, deliberately choosing instead to remain outside the law, even though de-registration would cost the unions £5 million per annum in tax relief. In their policy recommendation to the Congress, the General Council stated that unions were 'strongly advised' not to register. Hugh Scanlon, President of the engineering union, led a move to substitute the word 'instructs' for 'strongly advise'—the TUC should *instruct* its affiliates not to register. Despite the pleas of General Secretary Vic Feather, the Congress passed this amendment, and the General Council then vigorously applied this compulsory policy; in 1972, Congress suspended twenty-five unions for failing to de-register, and in 1973 Congress confirmed the expulsion of twenty unions, with a membership of 370,000. Two other unions resigned from the TUC. After the repeal of the Act in 1974, Congress re-admitted most of these unions, although it also exacted affiliation fees from them for the period of their expulsion. The strong exercise of TUC authority had been effective in rendering much of the Act quite inoperable, and had dissuaded many faint hearts amongst the unions from collaborating with its various mechanisms. This confounded much 'informed' newspaper opinion at the time, which claimed that the de-registration policy would surely fail, as one union after another would break the line and seek its own sectional salvation within the framework of the Act. No such collapse took place. It is difficult to exaggerate the effect that this episode had on the self-confidence and moral strength of the TUC in the labour movement.

The Social Contract

During the period of Conservative government, the TUC was not only leading the fight against the Industrial Relations Act, but was actively preparing the political ground for its repeal and replacement, by building a more intimate alliance with the Labour Party than had been conceived at any time since the Party's foundation. The TUC-Labour Party Liaison Committee, comprising representatives of the General Council, the leadership of the Parliamentary Party and the Party's National Executive Committee, was formed in 1972. This body gave the TUC a formidable influence on the policy-making process whilst Labour was in opposition, and its published policy documents largely comprised the election manifesto which took Labour to office in 1974. The drafts of laws to repeal the Industrial Relations Act, and to provide an Employment Protection Act, were passed through this committee during 1972–3, and the key policy document, *Economic Policy and the Cost of Living*, was jointly launched by the leader of the

Labour Party and the TUC General Secretary. The TUC followed this with its own publication, *Collective Bargaining and the Social Contract*, in June 1974, after the Labour government's election. The essence of the 'contract' was the promise by the Labour Party of legislation favourable to trade unionism, in return for voluntary pay restraint by the trade unions.

In assessing the balance sheet of this grand package deal, it is necessary to bear in mind what *Economic Policy and the Cost of Living* contained. In the field of industrial legislation, it laid down a three-stage programme. First the Industrial Relations Act would be repealed and a new Trade Union and Labour Relations Act would take its place. Second, legislation on Employment Protection would be enacted. And third, an Industrial Democracy law would be passed. The first two items were delivered by the Labour government in the first two years of its life and the TUC was constantly consulted, and frequently prevailed in such consultations, over the details of these Acts. For good measure there was an important *Health and Safety at Work Act*, which contained the vital provision, which the TUC had requested, for the appointment of trade union safety representatives, and a *Sex Discrimination Act*, which again reflected TUC policy. But the third item, the Industrial Democracy legislation, was postponed more than once by the government, and the original TUC proposals, for 50 per cent of directors' boards in large private companies to be elected by trade union employees in those companies, had been seriously watered down. These matters concern us in a separate chapter on Industrial Democracy, but their relevance here is to demonstrate the limits of TUC influence on government policy through the social contract—limits which were clearly marked out when the CBI led a virulent opposition to the modest industrial democracy proposals in the Bullock Report.

In the passage of the *Trade Union and Labour Relations Act* and the *Employment Protection Act*, we have seen that the TUC enjoyed considerable influence. Many details of this could be cited; as an example, we may take the case of day release with pay to enable trade union representatives to undertake trade union training courses in working time. The original drafts of the Employment Protection Bill provided that the Advisory, Conciliation and Arbitration Service should have the power to approve courses which trade unionists could attend under this provision. The TUC successfully pressed for the exclusion of this clause, and for a new clause which established the right of the TUC, or of an individual trade union, to approve the training courses. Thus the TUC got itself written into an Act of Parliament, as a body enjoying statutory rights in this field.

In one area, the debate around the new legislation led to the TUC acquiring a new quasi-judicial function. In the original version of the *Trade Union and Labour Relations Act*, passed during the minority administration of Labour between the February and October elections of 1974, there was provision for legal machinery to be used by an individual who considered that he had been arbitrarily or unreasonably expelled or excluded from membership of a union. The TUC disliked this intensely, arguing that trade union internal appeals machinery was the appropriate method of ensuring that justice was done to individuals with this kind of grievance. The Government however, felt that there should be additional machinery, and suggested that an alternative to a statutory provision could be voluntary machinery established by the TUC. The TUC accepted this suggestion, and established for this purpose an Independent Review Committee, in return for which the Government repealed the offending section of the law in its *Trade Union and Labour Relations (Amendment) Act* of 1976.

The Review Committee considers appeals from individuals who have been dismissed from their jobs as a consequence of being expelled from, or having been refused admission to, a union in a situation where union membership is a condition of employment. The Committee has an independent chairman with legal qualifications, and two other members. All three are appointed by the TUC General Council in consultation with the Secretary of Employment and with the chairman of ACAS. The first three appointments were of Professor K. W. Wedderburn, (as the chairman), George Doughty, a retired union general secretary, and Lord McCarthy, university teacher of industrial relations and scholar. The Review Committee in its proceedings must first satisfy itself that internal union appeals machinery has been exhausted, must discuss the case with the union and attempt to resolve the matter by agreement, and if this process fails, make a recommendation that the union should either accept or re-instate the individual into membership, or that the union's action was justified. There is a clear, TUC-imposed, responsibility on the part of the union to act on the Committee's recommendation. The Committee is now a functioning part of the TUC machinery, and in its first sixteen months it received some twenty complaints and held five formal hearings.

This is perhaps not the place to review the whole record of the Labour Government over the period 1974-8, but it is clear that TUC influence on that Government was at its height in 1974-5, when the initial stages of social contract legislation were being passed. Following this, the TUC, despite regular and sustained pronouncements, was unable to dissuade the Government from its chosen course of toleration for very high levels of unemployment, substantial cuts in public spending, and a generally deflationary economic policy largely dictated by the requirements of the International Monetary Fund. Nevertheless, through this later period, the TUC-Liaison Committee continued to meet regularly and frequently, and published a further general statement in 1976, *The Next Three Years and the Problem of Priorities*, (up-dated the following year as *The Next Three Years and Into the Eighties*) intended to serve the same strategic purpose as the 1973 statement on *Economic Policy and the Cost of Living*.

Both these documents are less specific, more muted, on the details of future Labour programmes than was the statement of 1973, and both concentrate much more on the purely economic goals of higher growth, reduced unemployment, and the control of inflation. They also record the failure of Government to implement the commitment to planning agreements, and the consequent vacuum in economic planning which exists at the level of the large companies. Both documents, moreover, reiterate the Government's pledge to legislate for 'parity representation' of trade unionists on the top boards of large companies; although it became apparent from the White Paper on Industrial Democracy finally published in 1978[14] that this objective had been indefinitely postponed by the Government. Reference to incomes policy in the documents is very guarded and vague. The Social Contract had run out of steam, and the powerful influence of the TUC on Governments over the period 1973–6 had run out with it. This fact was dramatically emphasised with the advent of the Conservative administration of 1979.

Throughout the past two decades, a strong tide has been running in favour of what has become known as 'tripartism', the system of conducting government and quasi-governmental functions through the agency of bodies drawing representation from Government, employers, and trade unions. As the central representative body for trade unions, the TUC has played a major role in nominating its representatives on to these bodies, and through them, is potentially in a strong position to co-ordinate trade union influence on policies by developing a system of briefing and reporting back. A list of some agencies on which the TUC has representation may be found on page 127, but here we may mention some of the more significant. As we have already said, amongst the oldest of the post-war generation of tripartite bodies is the National Economic Development Council, which is supposed to deal with long-term planning objectives, and which has in membership representatives of the CBI, ministers of the government, chairmen of the nationalised industry corporations, and six senior members of the TUC General Council. It is chaired by either the Chancellor of the Exchequer, or the Prime Minister. It is backed by a servicing Office.

Whilst the TUC takes the business of tripartite planning very seriously, it is hard to detect a similar commitment on the part of Governments or the CBI. When Economic Development Committees for particular industries were established, in 1963, in an attempt to take the planning process down the line from the central NEDC, the TUC sought nominations for the trade union seats on these bodies from unions with large interests in the particular industries, and the TUC was responsible for the final selection of representatives. In 1967, the TUC demonstrated its concern to make planning a serious process, by proposing on the NEDC that a National Planning College should be founded. This admirable suggestion has been completely ignored. Already by 1968 the TUC was expressing concern that genuine tripartite planning on the NEDC was being replaced by the use to which government was putting the Committee—as a mere sounding board for its own policies. In 1976, the NEDC machinery was given a new look by the setting up of 37 Sector Working Parties to cover various branches of the economy, and to implement what the Labour Government has called its Industrial Strategy, although this strategy was, to be polite, never defined with any precision. The TUC called on the unions in these sectors to nominate lay union officials to occupy seats on them wherever possible, and it called for the discussion of Working Party recommendations to be carried down to the company and major plant levels within the sectors. This is in line with the TUC's consistent view that planning should be conceived as a total process, which operates at all levels, from the economy, to the sector, the industry, the company and the plant. In fact there is no real authority in this structure at any level. In particular, the sector working parties lack any means of controlling the decisions of the major multi-national companies within their orbits, and at company level itself, there has been an almost total failure to implement the practice of planning agreements as envisaged in the 1975 *Industry Act*, despite the TUC (and TUC-Labour Party Liaison Committee) constantly calling on the government to speed up this process. When the government decided in 1975 to dilute the original concept of compulsory planning agreements between government, unions, and the largest companies, and to make such agreements voluntary, they effectively removed a key element in any over-all tripartite approach to economic planning.

The Growth of Quangos

A new kind of tripartite agency was brought into existence in the first wave of social contract legislation, and the TUC nominate one-third or more seats on these bodies; the Manpower Services Commission, the Council of the Advisory, Conciliation, and Arbitration Service, the Health and Safety Commission, and the Equal Opportunities Commission. More recently in 1976-7, the TUC secured two seats on the new Commission for Racial Equality, and one-third of the seats on an Energy Commission, the existence of which was the direct outcome of a TUC proposal to the Minister.

Some of these new agencies, which were hived off from the direct control of the civil service in the Department of Employment, such as the MSC and ACAS, have acquired a policy-making role as well as a purely executive function; the MSC was successful in persuading government to allocate substantial funds for job creation, and ACAS is felt by the employers to be too much an arm of the TUC. The sharp growth of these kinds of agencies in numbers and complexity has transformed the kinds of response which the TUC has been required to make. Before the second world war, the TUC General Council only nominated members to one dozen government appointed committees or statutory bodies. By 1948 TUC nominees were present on 60 such bodies. In origin all of these were seen as utilitarian institutions: but in practice, some of them became sinecures, which commonly carried either a fee or a regular income, which was a valuable supplement to the retirement pension of an outgoing General Councillor.

Robert Taylor reports that Sir John Hare, the Minister of Agriculture during the '50s, actually complained to the TUC 'about the lack of effort being put in by union nominees serving at that time on the marketing boards'. 'At this time' he cites George Woodcock as commenting:

'There was no reporting back. We never knew what they were doing. In fact, they did damn all . . .'

Taylor goes on to report that when Vincent Tewson, an earlier TUC General Secretary, served on the (now defunct) National Economic Planning Board for the TUC 'he did not even tell Woodcock what was happening'.[15]

Undoubtedly, the TUC nowadays regards it nominees on these bodies much more strictly, as trade union *representatives*; it arranges for briefings to be provided for its members of the MSC, the NEDCs, and the Health and Safety Commission, and in doing so, it works in co-operation with research officers of individual unions. In its 1977 *Annual Report*, the General Council pointed out that the TUC's own resources were too limited to effect a complete briefing service and a reporting back progress for all these agencies, and urged individual unions to come into this field much more; very few unions, it was reported, actually undertake such work. This is a serious deficiency; tripartism as a strategy for advancing independent trade union controls in the economy and in social and welfare matters is a mask which can cover an actual corporatism unless the unions retain their autonomy, and ensure effective briefing (or better, mandating) and reporting back procedures.

The TUC is heavily involved in nominating trade union representatives on the various judicial organs which now surround industrial relations. It nominates 12 trade unionists for the workers' side panel of the Employment Appeal Tribunal, it fills places on the Central Arbitration Committee, and oversees nomination to over 700 trade union places on the workers' sides of Industrial Tribunals. Royal Commissions, and *ad hoc* Committees and Commissions on particular subjects have long been incomplete without their TUC nominees; recent examples include four TUC representatives on Sir Harold Wilson's Committee on Financial Institutions, and three representatives on the Bullock Committee on Industrial Democracy. Additionally, of course, the TUC rarely omits to submit carefully prepared and researched evidence to official Committees and Enquiries, on a very wide range of subjects, from broadcasting, the legal profession, the National Health Service, to metrication. We provide a list charting the main participation by General Councillors in such organisations, nowadays commonly described as QUANGOs, in an Appendix to this chapter.

It is interesting to note however, that the TUC does not regard every aspect of its work as suitable for tripartite or joint treatment. In the early 1960s, the TUC *did* draw up a joint statement with the employers' organisations recognising that employers should be allowed a say in syllabuses, where they granted day release for trade unionists to attend educational courses. In the 1970s, however, the TUC has firmly rejected this approach, and has successfully insisted on its sole right to endorse courses of study which trade unionists should attend. On another issue, the TUC is insistent that trade unions which are seeking recognition from employers in a context where there is any element of inter-union rivalry, should settle such questions by reference to the TUC Disputes machinery, and not by going to ACAS or the courts. In general, the TUC has a clear view that trade unions' own internal affairs should be dealt with by trade unions.

The Functioning of Congress

The TUC is primarily a policy-making, rather than an executive, body, and its main functions are to provide a federal umbrella under which the trade unions can gather to develop common policies, to administer rules governing inter-union relations, and to provide various services for its affiliated organisations. In determining policy, the TUC is not a power in itself: it depends on achieving consensus between the general secretaries of member unions. The significance of its policies depends primarily on the degree to which it represents the whole trade union movement, and also on the extent to which it can represent the working population. The accompanying table indicates the growth of TUC affiliated membership since its inception in 1868 up to 1979. It shows a continuous record of significant growth, until the point has now been reached where the TUC represents about half the working population of Britain; in fact its affiliated unions negotiate wages and conditions for at least 70 per cent of that population. Only half a million trade unionists remain outside the TUC.

Table IV:1
TUC growth, 1868–1979

Year	No. of Unions affiliated	No. of members affiliated	Year	No. of Unions affiliated	No. of members affiliated
1868	—	118,367	1969	155	8,875,381
1878	114	623,957	1970	150	9,402,170
1888	138	816,944	1971	142	10,002,204
1898	188	1,093,191	1972	132	9,894,881
1908	214	1,777,000	1973	126	10,001,419
1918	262	4,532,085	1974	109	10,002,224
1928	196	3,874,842	1975	111	10,363,724
1938	216	4,460,617	1976	113	11,036,326
1948	188	7,791,470	1977	115	11,515,920
1958	185	8,337,325	1978	112	11,865,390
1968	160	8,725,604	1979	112	12,128,078

Source: TUC *Annual Report*, 1979.

In the early 1960s there was a momentary threat to the unity of British trade unionism; in the 1962 TUC Congress, the Bank Employees' Union drew attention to the formation of a 'Conference of Public and Professional Service Organisations' and warned that this represented a dangerous initiative which could lead to the emergence of a rival white-collar, non-party political TUC. At that moment, with white-collar and public sector trade unionism poised before its major growth of the '60s and '70s, there was no guarantee that some of the major unions in this sector, notably NALGO and the NUT, would join the TUC. It is significant that both these unions, and after them others with a similarly middle-class professional approach to collective organisation, such as the Association of University Teachers and the higher Civil Servants, finally chose to join the TUC. Undoubtedly one reason for this choice was the evident wish of governments not to have to consult with more than one trade union centre, and the wage and salary problems posed in the public sector during government wage restraint policies was a further compelling reason. (It is ironic that this problem has regularly proved too difficult for the TUC to tackle effectively!) It can now be said that there are no large or influential trade unions outside the TUC, which can therefore claim to be more representative of British workers than at any time in its history.

The TUC is governed broadly by two elements in its constitution; the annual Congress, and the General Council. Congress is convened annually, when about 1,000 delegates assemble, now invariably at either Brighton or Blackpool, from Monday to Friday of the first week of September. It has three functions: to receive and consider the annual Report of the General Council, to debate and vote on motions submitted by unions, and to elect the General Council for the coming year. Congress has become, particularly in the age of television, an important set-piece occasion in the political year, and its proceedings enjoy wide coverage in the media. From time to time, proposals are made to alter its timing or its procedures, and occasionally the complaint is heard that it is dominated by the will of the General Council, or that too much time at the rostrum is occupied by the general secretaries of the largest unions. But all attempts at reform have met with opposition from the General Council. In fact, Congress gets through a large amount of business during the week, and resolutions passed and motions remitted to the General Council do receive careful attention by the Council during the ensuing year. And there have been significant (if infrequent) occasions when the General Council's policy has been overturned by Congress. This happened notably in 1950, over the maintenance of wage-restraint, and in 1971 on the issue of de-registration under the Industrial Relations Act. It is certain that proceedings are dominated by the leading full-time officials of unions, but reform here may be as much to do with the internal control of union delegations as with the TUC itself.

'. . . some General Council members who have been chairmen of delegation meetings have used their authority over procedural matters to question the competency of delegations to determine or revise policy. When everything else has failed, the opinion of delegation meetings has been flouted and union block votes have been cast to meet General Council requirements. Because the policy-making functions of delegation meetings are rarely formulated in union constitutions, their authority is frequently determined by the need of immediate situations. Where the rules are vague, the delegation chairmen have the authority to interpret them. The Amalgamated Engineering Union has a history of procedural wrangles about the policy-making rights of delegations which has been marked by bitterness and legal action. At the 1966 TUC lay members in two unions sought legal injunctions to restrain the leaders of their union delegations from voting for General Council policies. The problem is a perennial one.'[16]

The governing body of the TUC between annual Congresses is the 41-person General Council, elected annually by the bloc votes of unions at Congress. For electoral purposes the affiliated unions are grouped into Trade Groups roughly delineating an industry or sector. Each Trade Group is allocated a number of seats on the General Council, and only unions within each Group may nominate candidates for seats within the Group. If there are more candidates than seats for the Group, a ballot vote is taken, at which all the unions are entitled to vote. So that although the nominations are confined to the Group, the whole Congress votes where a contest occurs. The results of this unique process for 1978 are shown in the accompanying table.

It will be seen that in the case of Groups 4 (shipbuilding), 7 (electricity), 10 (paper and printing), 14 (agriculture), and 18 (general workers), there was no contest and that in all these cases except printing and paper, the Group contains only one union.

This means that for some unions, their general secretary is guaranteed a seat on the General Council; indeed this applies to far more unions than to those in the 'no contest' category, since it would be unthinkable for Congress not to elect the General Secretaries of say the TGWU and the USDAW, or the President of the AUEW. The system however means that the candidates (almost invariably their general secretaries) of some unions have to enter an election, where the choice is made by all the affiliated unions voting with their affiliated membership strengths. Success in these elections does not always go to the larger (and therefore more representative) unions in the Group; in Group 15 for example, Mr Casey of the Schoolmasters and Women Teachers Union, and Mr Broadbridge, of the Teachers in Further and Higher Education, (who were unsuccessful candidates) both have more than twice as many members as Mr Parry, of the Fire Brigades Union, who was elected.

Table IV:2
Elections to the General Council

Group	No. of Unions	No. of members	General Council Seats	Members per Seat	1978 Election Result
1. Mining & Quarrying	3	295,187	2	147,594	L. Daly NUM (elected) J. Gormley, NUM (elected) N. Schofield, BACM (not elected) AE Simpson, NACODS (not elected)
2. Railways	3	280,449	2	140,225	R. Buckton, ASLEF (elected) S. Weighell, NUR (elected) T. Jenkins, TSSA (not elected)
3. Transport other than railways	6	2,141,927	5	428,385	A. M. Evans, TGWU (elected) W. Greendale, TGWU (elected) S. Pemberton, TGWU (elected) C. H. Urwin, TGWU (elected) J. H. Slater, NUS (elected) J. Moore, URTU (not elected) E. Nevin, MNAOA (not elected)
4. Shipbuilding	1	129,956	1	129,956	J. Chalmers, ASBSBSW (no contest)
5. Engineering Founding and vehicle building	10	1,389,411	4	347,353	R. Birch, AUEW (elected) J. Boyd, AUEW (elected) T. Duffy, AUEW (elected) L. G. Guy, SMW (elected) G. Eastwood, APAC (not elected) J. H. Wood, NSMM (not elected)
6. Technical engineering and scientific	5	679,758	2	339,879	K. Gill, TASS (elected) C. Jenkins, ASTMS (elected) J. Lyons, BMA (not elected)
7. Electricity	1	420,000	1	420,000	F. Chapple, EEPTU (no contest)
8. Iron & Steel & Minor	9	146,745	1	146,745	W. Sirs, ISTC (elected) H. C. Smith, NUB (not elected) [illegible] UCATT (elected)

	Trade Group		Membership		Membership per seat	Candidates
11.	(continued)	15	125,617	1	125,617	W. H. Keys, SOGAT (no contest) F. Dyson, NUDBTW (elected) J. Brown, ATWU (not elected)
12.	Clothing, Leather, boot & shoe	6	267,679	1	267,679	D. T. Carter, PLCWTWA (not elected) J. Macgougan, NUTGW (elected) H. L. Gibson, NUHKW (not elected)
13.	Glass, Ceramics, Chemicals, Food, Drink, Tobacco, Brushmaking & Distribution	9	596,782	2	298,391	S. F. Clapham, NUFLAT (not elected) Lord Allen, USDAW (elected) C. D. Grieve, TWU (elected) S. Maddox, Bakers (not elected) L, R, Sillitoe, Ceramics (not elected)
14.	Agriculture	1	85,000	1	85,000	J. R. Boddy (no contest)
15.	Public Employees	11	2,197,175	5	439,435	G. A. Drain, NALGO (elected) A. W. Fisher, NUPE (elected) F. F. Jarvis, NUT (elected) T. Parry, FBU (elected) E. A. G. Spanswick, COHSE (elected) S. R. Broadbridge, NATFHE (not elected)
16.	Civil Servants & Post Office	12	949,073	3	316,358	T. A. Casey, NAS (not elected) A. M. Christopher, IRSF (no contest) T. Jackson, UPW (no contest)
17.	Professional, Clerical and Entertainment	10	404,220	2	202,110	K. R. Thomas, CPSA (no contest) J. Morton, MU (elected) A. Sapper, ACTT (elected) R. A. Grantham, APEX (not elected)
18.	General Workers	1	945,324	3	315,108	L. A. Mills, NUBE (not elected) F. A. Baker, NUGMW (no contest) D. Basnett, NUGMW (no contest) J. F. Eccles, NUGMW (no contest)
19.	Women workers. There are two General Council seats for women workers' representatives; any union with female members may nominate for these seats, but as in other groups, the whole Congress votes if there is a contest. In 1978, there were five candidates, and Miss M. Patterson (TGWU) and Miss A. Maddocks (NALGO) were successful.					
	TOTAL (excluding women's seats)	112	11,865,390	39	304,241	

Source: TUC Annual Report, 1978.

The distribution of seats between the Groups is a frequent source of criticism and it is clear that this does not correspond very precisely to their relative arithmetical strengths. Excluding the special women's seats, 39 members of the General Council represent 11,865,390 members, an average of 304,241 members per seat. It is clear from the Table that several Groups are heavily over-represented on the Council, notably Mining, Railways, Shipbuilding, Iron and Steel, Textiles, and Agriculture. It is significant that these Groups are amongst the oldest constitutents of the TUC, and all represent industries which have declined from former positions of numerical superiority. It is not surprising therefore that some of the younger and more virile unions complain about the weight of tradition and the influence of the past, in the composition of the Council. But this argument, according to the established view of the General Council, is to miss the point of the electoral system, which is not designed to ensure precise mathematical representation of Groups, but rather aims to achieve a broadly representative sample of unions on the Council, who should be regarded as *all* being accountable to the whole Congress, and not just to their Groups.

It is significant of the movement's approach to selection, that where contests operate, there are rarely any close-run affairs. The average vote for successful candidates in 1978 was 10 million, and for unsuccessful candidates it was $1\frac{1}{2}$ million. These figures emphasise important tendencies. Once elected, a Council member can almost invariably expect solid support for his continuous re-election; respect for continuity and seniority are powerful factors in the electoral process. Politics do play a part; but they are usually the internal politics of the trade union leadership. For example, Bryn Roberts, general secretary of NUPE in the forties and fifties, and clearly at the time the most representative trade union leader in the Public Employees Trade Group, stood as a candidate for the General Council for many years; he was never elected. This was certainly due to the fact that his union's aggressive recruitment policies, which sometimes paid scant regard to the Bridlington Rules, incurred the permanent displeasure of the leadership of the two large general unions.

The TUC does of course revise the number and distribution of Council seats from time to time, and has been compelled to do so more frequently in recent times, because of the major changes in the distribution of membership between the Groups. As recently as 1977, three additional seats were created, one for the Transport (other than Railways) Group, one for the Public Employees, and one for the Civil Service and Post Office Group. In 1977–8, the then 41 members of the Council came from 30 unions, six unions having more than one member, and seventeen Councillors coming from unions with less than 200,000 members.

Proposals for the radical reform of the General Council arise from time to time from within the TUC. It has been suggested that the Council should be replaced by a smaller, full-time executive committee, supplemented by regular meetings of the unions' General Secretaries. The General Council reject this with the argument that a full-time executive would be more out of touch with the membership than the present Council, which is almost entirely composed of union General Secretaries. (There are only two lay members of the Council at present, both from the TGWU). Alternately, it has been proposed that the Council be much increased in size, to allow for more of the unrepresented unions in the TUC to compete for places, and to share out the Committee work of the Council amongst a wider number. This too has been rejected by the Council. In 1976 it was proposed that unions over a certain size, say 100,000 or 200,000, should automatically be represented, with proportionate increases in representation for larger unions, and another group of seats for smaller unions, to be filled by election. But the only regular reform which the Council appears willing to contemplate is the periodic re-distribution of seats between the Groups, and even here, in deference to the values attached to seniority and experience, it will not usually take away a seat from a Group which is declining in membership until the sitting Councillor has retired from his General Secretaryship!

But the TUC has recently become more sensitive to internal criticism that it is less representative than it should be of its affiliated unions, and has sought to meet this criticism by the calling of special ad hoc conferences and Congresses, and by the development of its committee structure, particularly through the formation of Industrial Committees on which non-General Council representatives sit alongside General Councillors.

The practice of conducting most of its business through sub-Committees is in fact a longstanding one in the TUC, which behaves similarly in this respect to a Local Government authority. Chairmanship of the key General Council Committees is keenly contested, since it confers considerable influence on the persons chosen. The Standing Committees include Finance and General Purposes, International, Education, Social Insurance and Industrial Welfare, Employment Policy and Organisation, Economic, and Equal Rights. These are all manned by members of the General Council. Joint Committees, which include members of the General Council and other trade union representatives, or third parties, include the Women's Advisory Committee, the Race Relations Advisory Committee, the Trades

Councils' Joint Consultative Committee, the National Economic Development Council, the Trades Union Congress and Confederation of British Industry, the Standing Advisory Committee to the TUC Centenary Institute of Occupational Health, and the TUC-Labour Party Liaison Committee. This Committee structure is under fairly regular revision, as new needs arise, or as old ones disappear.

Committees which have been wound up in the past decade include the Commonwealth Advisory Committee, the Non-Manual Workers' Advisory Committee, the Wages Council Advisory Committee, the National Advisory Committee for Local Government Service, and the Nursing Advisory Committee.

The TUC's regular and extensive committee work, supported by serious 'back-room' secretariats, which in their departmentalised organisation develop considerable expertise in their own fields, receives very little publicity, either in the labour movement, or in the outside world. All this work is at present, as it has been traditionally, devoted almost exclusively to the business of lobbying the Government in power. This, according to George Woodcock, is what the TUC is most qualified to do. 'We left Trafalgar Square a long time ago' he once said, when claiming that the TUC did its best work in committee.

Thus, if we take just one TUC committee, and examine its work over a year, the Education Committee during 1978–9 held debates, and approved papers, on Nursery Education for under 5s, the education of the 16–18-year olds, higher education and the universities, corporal punishment in schools, the role of the WEA in trade union education, the future of Fircroft College (a residential adult education college in Birmingham), Government education bills, education for handicapped children, school meals and milk, the reform of school examinations, the education of children from ethnic minorities, links between school and industry, public lending rights for authors, the arts, entertainment, and sport. The overwhelming weight of TUC opinion on these questions was humane, reforming, civilised and progressive. Most of these subjects became the basis of correspondence and meetings with the Governmental Department of Education and Science, and lengthy and carefully prepared papers were submitted by the TUC, and answered by the Department. Whilst it is true that on some of these issues, the TUC made efforts to publicise its views to its affiliated unions by the production of pamphlets, the main direction of its efforts was upwards, through the 'corridors of power' towards Government ministers. The same story is repeated across the whole spectrum of TUC standing committees. It would be untrue to say that all this effort was wasted; Governments from time to time make concessions as a result of this lobbying activity. But in recent history, after the initial honeymoon period of 1974-5, the Labour government's policies bore less and less relationship to those of the TUC, as ministers accepted the constraints imposed by orthodox treasury opinion and the dictat of the International Monetary Fund. Clearly the Conservative Government elected in 1979 pays even less attention to the TUC. What the TUC's method has lacked, historically, has been any mobilising drive to enlist the mass support of its affiliated membership behind all this staid committee work; yet the issues it takes up are commonly potentially popular and vital ones for the whole of our society. When the Labour Movement had its own newspaper, in the *Daily Herald*, there was at least a possibility of feeding out to the membership the often superbly documented case material which the TUC prepares and which nowadays reaches only the most limited audience, and often the least sympathetic ears.

In 1970-71, as we have noted, the TUC, through its education department, did mount an educational campaign amongst its membership which had a marked effect on the successful resistance to the Industrial Relations Act. In 1979, it appeared to be prepared to enter the arena of mass compaigning again, against the effects of the Conservative Government's public spending cuts. These models perhaps need generalising, in the harsh economic and political climate which now confronts the TUC, so that its back-room studies may become the basis of an outward-facing effort of economic and political education, rather than the restricted raw material of an increasingly ingrown and frustrating lobby in the corridors of power, where the TUC's views are decreasingly welcome.

A new structure of Industry Committees, was instituted in 1970, following the experience of the Steel Industry Committee set up to co-ordinate policies after the 1967 nationalisation of steel. The idea of Industry Committees, on which General Council members sit with representatives of the main unions in the industry concerned, is a development which has its roots in the original concept of Trade Groups which the TUC of the 1920s saw as a precursor of industrial unionism and the co-ordination of union policies in the major sectors of the economy. The only significance of the Trade Group system now is that it forms the basis of the electoral system for the General Council. The new Industry Committees do have the same potential for generating common trade union policies and overcoming the problems of multi-unionism, as the original concept. At present there are nine of them; Construction, Fuel and Power, Health Services, Hotel and Catering, Local Government, Printing, Steel, Textile Clothing and Footwear, and Transport. The steel committee has already reached the stage of bargaining directly with the British Steel

Corporation, and has served as the forum where complex problems of multi-union recognition claims in the white-collar field have been dealt with. Others of the Committees have dealt with inter-union relations, with government planning of their industry (as in the case of Transport), and in general have aimed to generate common union policies in their areas. The fact that they are linked to the General Council, and are serviced by the departments and staff of the TUC, represents a considerable advance in central TUC influence over its unions. There is considerable scope in the system for the growth of union policy-making and intervention in industrial policies. The Construction Committee for example has devoted much time to the problem of the Lump and the decasualisation of the industry, Fuel and Power was concerned with the setting up of the Energy Commission in consultation with the Minister Tony Benn, the Hotel and Catering Committee has set up a joint study with the English Tourist Board on travel facilities for the disabled, the Printing Committee operates its own disputes procedure when unions are engaged in disputes with employers, and the Steel Committee was involved in setting up the Shotton Works Steel Committee, the only example of a multi-union work-based committee involved with the TUC machinery. Jack Jones (*Tribune*, April 25th 1978) has proposed that there should be systematic links between TUC, Industry Committees, and Shop Stewards' Combine Committees.

All these matters and many more, are fully reported in the TUC Annual Report, and help to shed light on and generate thinking about, the normally unseen processes of policy-making and industrial negotiations, other than those directly concerned with pay. Apart from their direct functional role, the Industry Committees are seen by the TUC as an important means of meeting the criticism made by smaller unions and those without General Council representation, that the TUC does not provide a channel for them to exercise influence.

The work of the TUC's Education Department as a provider of facilities has expanded dramatically since it took over the former National Council of Labour Colleges and the Workers' Educational Trade Union Committee in 1964. The Education Department has been, until recently, the only part of the TUC structure which employs full-time staff, (the Regional Education Officers) in the regions and outside Congress House.

A highly significant development in recent years has been the provision of grant-aid jointly by the Department of Education and Science and the Department of Employment, towards the cost of TUC educational services, amounting to £650,000 in 1977–8. Amongst other things, this grant helps to pay the day-release course fees charged to the TUC by public educational bodies—the technical colleges, the WEA, and University Extra-mural Departments. These day-release courses, (the core of the TUC's educational work), enrolled 27,500 students in 1977–8, an increase of 28.5 per cent on the previous year. The students are shop stewards and trade union safety representatives.

The regional machinery of the TUC has always been a threadbare and under-serviced aspect of its work. It was re-organised after 1973, and now comprises eight Regional TUC Councils, on which full-time officers from unions in the regions sit, alongside representatives of the County Associations of Trade Councils, which hold 25 per cent of the seats. The Scottish unions have long held their own public Congress, and now Wales has been accorded the status of its own Annual Conference of 300 delegates, and a Welsh General Council of 45, of which 30 come from union representatives in the principality, and 15 from Welsh Trades Councils. If regionalism ever became a serious political reality in England, the TUC would have to look seriously at its weakness in this field. The Regional Councils have potentially important functions in the field of regional economic planning, but they have until now had no full-time staff—apart from the Education Officers, who are answerable to Congress House and to a Regional Education Advisory Committee. There are signs that the TUC would like to strengthen regional organisation by appointing full-time regional secretaries. The purely local link in the chain, the country's 441 Trades Councils, have suffered a drastic eclipse of influence since their hey-day in the 19th century. As the officially recognised representatives of the TUC in the localities, they are regarded rather paternalistically by the central body, and have periodically been a source of TUC-Establishment anxieties over the presence in their ranks of left-wing influence. Their relationship with head office has often therefore been stultifying, and although they have worthy functions such as nominating trade union representatives on a variety of local committees and institutions, (e.g. the governing bodies of local educational establishments) they are so frequently disregarded by local trade unionists that only 25 per cent of the country's trade union branches actually affiliate to them. A separate chapter deals with the international trade union activity of the British trade union movement; we record here merely the remarkable fact that it consumes a larger share of TUC revenues than does any other aspect of its affairs.

The second largest item in the TUC accounts is the cost of running Congress House, at £500,000, largely devoted to salaries. The TUC education service costs £300,000, mainly devoted to the TUC regional education service. The TUC's modest income of just under £2 million in 1977 was largely raised by the 18p per member affiliation fee from its constituent unions. (The fee was raised to 20p in 1978). Income from investments amounts to a mere £60,000. With such small resources, it is not surprising that the TUC can maintain only a small full-time staff—some hundred people constitute the strength of Congress House's administrative staff.[17] It is clear that the trade unions prefer to maintain their central organisation on modest, non-bureaucratic lines. The TUC itself argues that, as a policy-making rather than an executive body, this is the best arrangement, and accordingly urges individual unions to compensate for the low level of TUC resources by stepping up their own expenditure on services. Yet not every union can afford expensive modern aids to effective trade unionism, such as research and education staff. Small unions, which it might be thought could have benefited from a wider TUC servicing role, lack the muscle to insist on its provision: while some, indeed undoubtedly lack any ambition to see education and research developed effectively. Rationalisation and centralisation of trade union services would seem sensible on economic grounds, but in the past few years, the TUC has turned down proposals to provide a centralised Legal Department, a Research Bureau, and a central computer service for the unions.

NOTES

1. B. C. Roberts, *The Trades Union Congress, 1868-1921*, is a standard source on the early history of the TUC, although it has been seriously criticised by V. L. Allen, in *The Sociology of Industrial Relations*, (Longmans, 1971), which itself contains a series of valuable essays on key moments in TUC history. The relative dearth of literature on the TUC as an institution is possibly due to the peripheral role it has played, until the last two decades, in industrial relations. H. A. Clegg argued that most of the work of the TUC (and of the CBI) 'belongs to a study of political pressure groups rather than to a book on industrial relations.' (*The System of Industrial Relations in Great Britain*, Blackwell, 1970).
2. See V. L. Allen, 'The Establishment of the TUC, 1868-1875', op. cit.
3. V. L. Allen, 'The TUC Before Socialism, 1875-1886', op. cit.
4. V. L. Allen, 'The Re-organisation of the TUC, 1918-1927', op. cit.
5. V. L. Allen, op. cit.
6. Richard Clements, *Glory Without Power*, Barker, 1959.
7. Fred Bramley, the TUC General Secretary from 1923 to 1925, said that he did not have more than five minutes conversation with Ramsay McDonald during his first premiership in 1924.

8. TUC *Annual Report*, 1962.

9. TUC *Annual Report*, 1962.

10. But note that the TUC, in entering into its so-called 'Concordat' with the Labour Government in February 1979, offered its support to the notion that 'reforms' were needed (albeit voluntary) in picketing, strike decisions, and the closed shop. These were to become the subject of proposals for legislative intervention by the Thatcher administration.

11. TUC *Annual Report*, 1970.

12. TUC *Annual Report*, 1972.

13. The proceedings of these conferences were published in six booklets by the TUC in 1969.

14. *Industrial Democracy*, HMSO, Cmnd. 7231, May 1978.

15. Robert Taylor: *The Fifth Estate—Britain's Unions in the 'Seventies*, Routledge, 1978.

16. V. L. Allen, 'The Centenary of the TUC, 1868-1968' op. cit., 1971. This essay, written at the end of the 1960s, rightly stresses the over-all historical weakness of the TUC's central authority, its conservatism, and its opposition to the election of left-wing General Councillors. In the light of subsequent experience, however, particularly the period of the ascendancy of Jack Jones and Hugh Scanlon between 1970 and 1975, some revision of these conclusions seems reasonable, even though the ultimate evolution of the two leaders after the latter date reaffirms the historical trend.

17. 'most of the officers . . . are university graduates. They constitute by far the largest group of specialists in the trade union movement'. H. A. Clegg: *The Changing System of Industrial Relations in Great Britain*, Blackwell, 1979, p. 336.

APPENDIX TO CHAPTER 4

The General Council Involvement in Public Bodies

The participation of Trade Unions, and above all of the TUC, in various Governmental and Quasi-Governmental consultative and planning bodies, has markedly increased during the postwar period. Governmental patronage has grown rapidly during that time, and such Quangos (in America: Quasi-autonomous *Non*-Governmental Organisations; in English *National* Governmental) have become more and more common, and it would not be possible for a serious representative to sleep through the sessions of at any rate the more important ones.

Nonetheless, such bodies are often less effective than they might be, because they depend largely upon patronage for their existence, and lack either the legal powers or the democratic clout to compel attention. When the Health and Safety Executive goes to work, it does dispose of certain clearly defined powers which it applies within a clearly defined set of responsibilities. This is less true when we consider the work of some other bodies.

Ideally, representative forms of democratic alliance could be evolved to discharge such functions of these bodies as are necessary, in the context of as much legislative support as might be needed. As things are, members of such quangos often do not have much muscle, mainly *because* they remain largely unaccountable to their wider constituencies.

In 1978 the Civil Service Department produced its second directory of paid public appointments made by ministers. This revealed that ministers currently disposed of 5,600 such jobs: and it also showed that 19 quasi-autonomous governmental bodies (11 of which had been disbanded) had been taken off the previous (1976) list, whilst 25 new ones had been added.

The consolidated official lists are tabulated below in table IV:3.

It is not possible to calculate the full part played by trade unions in this multiplicity of organisations. At its peak the Quango boom saw 17 ministers in control of 8,411 paid appointments and some 25,000 unpaid ones, at a cost to public funds of £5m+.

Table IV:3
Public appointments in the gift of ministers[1]

	Salaries	Fee-paid	Unpaid	Cost
Agriculture	107	281	1,037	£143,000
Defence	26	644	1,872	n.a.
Education	11	127	594	£185,000
Employment	76	2,456	5,661	£306,102
Environment	313	856	1,102	£509,636
Energy	148	1	73	£911,000
FCO/ODM	20	12	313	£54,738
Home	54	117	2,115	£310,000
Industry	78	14	403	£727,102
N. Ireland	30	61	148	£122,810
Prices and Consumer	26	49	989	£253,750
Scotland		422	n.a.	£380,000
Social Services	140	1,949	8,700	n.a.
Trade	52	9	244	£345,264
Transport	206	—	289	£488,876
Wales	69	57	412	£175,158

After the return of the Labour Governments of 1974, some 50 such bodies were established. The most costly bodies were the following:

Table IV:4
Quango costs, staff memberships

	Acronym	Cost 1978–9	Staff
Arbitration, Conciliation and Advisory Service	ACAS	£10.3m	819
Price Commission		£7.2m	587
Commission for Racial Equality	CRE	£4.7m	200
Scottish Development Agency		£4.5m	543
Welsh Development Agency		£2.4m	391
Equal Opportunities Commission	EOC	£1.9m	400

Upon the election of the Conservative (Thatcher) administration, some Quangos were dissolved, including the Price Commission which figures on this list. New ones were also created.

The TUC maintains a list of its General Council's appointments to Government Committees and outside bodies, on which there are named 57 major and subsidiary bodies outside the education field, of which 10 are subsidiary organisations. These appointments include memberships of the Royal Commission on the Distribution of Income and Wealth (G. Doughty, former General Secretary of the Draughtsmen's Union, and D. E. Lea, of the TUC's own Economic Department); social advisory committees on disablement or industrial health; and economic organisations across a huge range, from the White Fish Authority to the Construction Industry Manpower Board.

This list does not include a very large number of appointments which do not involve either nomination by the General Council or some process of formal consultation: from Lord Allen's Governorship of the BBC to Hugh Scanlon's chairmanship of the Engineering Industry Training Board. If we consult the lists in *Whitaker's Almanack*, or the (sometimes self-effacing) entries in *Who's Who*, we find an extraordinary concentration of responsibility. At the beginning of the alphabet, Lord Allen of Fallowfield was, at the point of his 1979 retirement from union office, as we have said already, a BBC Governor, and also a Crown Estate Commissioner, a member of the Equal Opportunities Commission, one of the TUC six members of NEDC, an ACAS member, and, lest we forget, General Secretary of his union, USDAW. At the other end of the alphabet, Harry Urwin, recently appointed to the Standing Commission on Pay Comparability (under the chairmanship of Hugh Clegg), was, until the time of this decision, also a member of the National Freight Corporation, the Manpower Services Committee, the National Enterprise Board, the Industrial Development Advisory Board, the Energy Commission, and the Health and Safety Commission's Advisory Committee on Dangerous Substances. Unlike some of his colleagues on the General Council, Harry Urwin will not accept this kind of responsibility without a prior agreement with his union, the TGWU. Even so, such a serious spread of responsibility must be taxing, even for someone who is both energetic and well-assisted by adequate services.

Table IV:5
List of members of the TUC General Council who participate in various
QUANGOS

Members	Union	Government Appointments/ Membership of Quangos
Tom Jackson [Chairman]	UPW	— Member of Commission for Racial Equality — Government Director British Petroleum Co. Ltd.
David Basnett [Vice-Chairman]	GMWU	— Member of National Enterprise Board — Member of NEDC
Lord Allen, CBE	USDAW	— Member of Equal Opportunities Commission — Member NEDC — Member of BBC Board of Governors — Chairman of Chemicals Economic Development Committee — Member of British Airports Authority — Member Central Lancashire Development Corporation — Director of Industrial Training Service — Member of Committee to Review the Functioning of Financial Institutions
F. A. Baker, CBE	GMWU	— Member of Energy Commission — Member, BBC Group on Industrial & Business Affairs — Member of British Shipbuilders
R. Birch	AUEW [Engineering Section]	— Member of Energy Commission
J. R. Boddy, MBE	NUAAW	—

Members	Union	Government Appointments/ Membership of Quangos
J. M. Boyd, CBE	AUEW [Engineering Section]	— Member of ACAS Council
Ray Buckton	ASLEF	— Member of IBA General Advisory Council — Member of Occupational Pensions Board — Member of Health Services Board — Member of CIT Council — Member of National Advisory Council on Employment of Disabled People — Member of Remploy Ltd Board — Member of Industrial Injuries Advisory Council — Member of Advisory Committee on Alcoholism — Member of Dangerous Substances Advisory Committee
J. Chalmers, CBE	ASBSBSW	— Member Central Arbitration Committee (CAC)
Frank Chapple	EETPU	— Member of National Electronics Council — Member of Prison Industries Joint Committee — Member of Energy Commission — Member of Horserace Totalisator Board — Member Construction Industry Manpower Board
A. M. G. Christopher	Inland Revenue Staff Association	— Member of Royal Commission on Distribution of Income and Wealth [now wound up] — Member of Independent Broadcasting Authority
L. Daly	NUM	—

Members	Union	Government Appointments/ Membership of Quangos
G. A. Drain	NALGO	— Member NEDO Section Working Party for Paper and Board Industry — Chairman of Insolvency Law Review Committee — Member of Energy Commission — Member of NEDC — Member of CAC — Trustee of Community Projects Foundation — Member of Board of Volunteer Centre
Terence Duffy	AUEW [Engineering Section]	— Member NEDC
Fred Dyson	National Union of Dyers, Bleachers and Textile Workers	— Member of Industrial Injuries Advisory Council — Member of the Garments and Allied Industries Requirements Board — Member, Toxic Substances Committee, Health and Safety Commission
J. F. Eccles	GMWU	— Member of Remploy Board — Member, Toxic Substances Committee, Health and Safety Commission — Part-time Commissioner of Equal Opportunities Commission (EOC) — Member of English Industrial Estates Corp.
A. M. Evans	TGWU	— Member of National Bus Company — Member of British Overseas Trade Board — Member of NEDC
Alan Fisher	NUPE	— Member of London Area Electricity Board — Member Radiological Protection Board — Member of British Airways Board

Members	Union	Government Appointments/ Membership of Quangos
Kenneth Gill	AUEW (TASS)	— Member of Medical Advisory Committee, Health and Safety Commission — Member of D of E Tripartite Steering Group on Job Satisfaction — Member Medical Advisory Committee, Health and Safety Executive
J. Gormley, OBE	NUM	— Member of National Research Development Corporation (NRDC) — Member of Energy Commission — Member British Overseas Trade Board
W. Greendale	TGWU	— Member Dangerous Substances Advisory Committee, Health and Safety Commission
C. D. Grieve	Tobacco Workers' Union	— Member D of E Tripartite Steering Group on Job Satisfaction
L. G. Guy	National Union of Sheet Metal Workers, Coppersmiths, Heating and Domestic Engineers	—
F. F. Jarvis	NUT	— Member of Design Council — Member UK National Commission for UNESCO
Clive Jenkins	ASTMS	— Member of NRDC — Member of Committee to Review the Functioning of Financial Institutions
W. H. Keys	SOGAT	— Member of CAC — Part-time Commissioner of Commission for Racial Equality — Member of Advisory Council on Race Relations — Member, Manpower Services Commission

Members	Union	Government Appointments/ Membership of Quangos
G. Lloyd	UCATT	— Member of Health and Safety Commission — Member of Building Economic Development Committee — Member of Noise Advisory Council — Member of Occupational Pensions Board
J. Macgougan	National Union of Tailors and Garment Workers	— Member of Manpower Services Commission — Member of CAC
Miss A. W. Maddocks	NALGO	— Member Medical Advisory Committee, Health and Safety Executive
J. M. Morton	Musicians' Union	— Member of Cinematograph Films Council
T. Parry	FBU	— Member of Health and Safety Commission — Member of Industrial Injuries Advisory Council
Mrs C. M. Patterson, CBE	TGWU	— Member of CAC — Member, Women's National Commission — Part-time Commissioner of EOC — Member, Women's Employment Advisory Committee (D. of Emp.) — Member of Hotel and Catering Industrial Training Board — Member of Food, Drink and Tobacco Industrial Training Board — Member, Dental Estimates Board — Director of Remploy Ltd.
S. Pemberton	TGWU	— Member, BBC Group on Industrial and Business Affairs — Member, Territorial Army Advisory Committee

Members	Union	Government Appointments/ Membership of Quangos
A. L. Sapper	Assn. of Cinematograph, Television and Allied Technicians	— Member of Cinematograph Films Council — Member of Interim Action Committee on the Film Industry Governor British Film Institute
W. Sirs	Iron and Steel Trades Confederation	— Member of Employment Appeal Tribunal
J. H. Slater	NUS	—
Les Wood	UCATT	—
[Replaces Sir George Smith, CBE, who died in November 1978]		
E. A. G. Spanswick	COHSE	— Member, Health Education Council
K. R. Thomas	CPSA	—
Harry Urwin	TGWU	— Member of Manpower Services Commission — Member of Machine Tools Economic Development Committee — Member of Industrial Development Advisory Board — Member of National Enterprise Board — Member of Committee on Finance for Investment — Member of Energy Commission — Member of Industrial Tribunals Panel — Member of Central Arbitration Committee — Board member, National Freight Corporation
Sidney Weighell	NUR	—

From the point of view of trade union representation, the key question remains one upon which we touched in Chapter 2. Who briefs these representatives? More important, perhaps, who debriefs them? In 1971 the Belgian equivalent of the TUC, the FGTB, published a careful programme for workers' control,[2] in which they pointed out that current union involvement in a whole plethora of industrial planning bodies could, if information flows were adequately pooled, secure a great increase in bargaining efficiency and alternative planning capacity on a wide range of issues. Only when such a network of exchanges and reports begins to extend across all the distinct union research offices, and to merge the access to relevant knowledge thus obtained, will trade unions begin to reap real benefit from the quango growth industry, whether or not, by that time, steps have been taken to make it all more open and more democratically accountable. Meantime, some unions may wonder whether they might institute rule changes to give them greater control over their officials' extramural activities (or, perhaps, their external earnings), so that they could ensure adequate consultation about which public appointments should be approved and encouraged and which not.

Membership of these bodies may be paid or unpaid, according to their constitutions. Different forms of renumeration apply in some, which pay fees, while others fix part-time salaries. Many of the offices listed above are voluntary.

In addition to the bodies listed, TUC General Councillors and full-time officers serve on 33 educational bodies, and a number of international ones. The table above does not list the bodies in which heads of TUC Departments are serving, nor does it list the nominations, by the TUC, of non-General Councillors, or retired General Councillors.

NOTES TO APPENDIX

1. Official Report, June 28th and 29th, 1978, reproduced in *Financial Weekly*, March 23rd 1979.
2. Translated as *A Trade Union Strategy in the Common Market*, Spokesman, 1971, see pp. 67 et seq.

Chapter Five

Shop Stewards and Workplace Trade Unionism

The Development of Workplace Representation

For all the recent national prominence given to full-time general secretaries of trade unions, and the role of the TUC, the trade union movement remains heavily dependent on the work of voluntary, part-time trade union representatives. In an earlier time, the base of trade unionism was the local branch, and the key officers were the branch secretary and chairman. Today, the focus of organisation and activity is the work-place, and the key figure is the workplace representative of the membership, usually termed the shop steward, whose functions are to represent the interests of trade union members at plant level.

Not all industries and unions apply the term shop steward to their workplace representatives; in printing they speak of the 'Father of the Chapel', amongst draughtsmen of the 'corresponding member', and in white-collar occupations of 'staff representatives'. In some few industries, (for example agriculture) the shop steward system has not appeared, whilst in large areas of non-manual employment, (for example amongst local government officers) the system is still in its fledgling stage. Across employment as a whole however, the appointment of working employees to represent trade union members in the workplace is almost universal, covering for example 95 per cent of employees in metal manufacture, 88 per cent of office workers, and 78 per cent of distributive workers.[1] An estimate in 1971 put the total number of stewards in Britain at between 250,000 and 300,000.[2] In 1973, it was found that shop stewards existed in four-fifths of unionised establishments.[3]

It was not always so. Whilst we may suppose that from an early period in the industrial revolution work groups often threw up informal and unrecognised spokesmen, there is no evidence that shop stewards achieved any widespread significance much before the first world war. Work-place representation certainly did exist in some 19th century industries. Legislation in 1860 provided for workers' representatives (checkweighmen) to be appointed in coal mines, and representatives were recognised in the North-East coast steel industry conciliation machinery from 1869. Engineering shop stewards had achieved a presence for some years before the turn of the century, collecting stewards with a bargaining role appeared in the gas industry in 1889, and the collectors of the old Workers' Union were acting as spokesmen before 1914.[4] Undoubtedly however, the first major manifestation of steward organisation came with the first world war, when both their numbers and their powers expanded considerably, particularly in engineering and munitions.

After the war, in the inter-war period of mass unemployment, the steward system went into decline, although not before it had been partially recognised in the formal procedures of industrial relations in some industries, such as engineering. In the later 1930s stewards re-emerged, significantly in industries such as aircraft manufacture which first felt the resurgence of demand associated with re-armament. In the second world war, they again became prominent in the major manufacturing industries, often associated with the spread of Joint Production Committees in the plants, to promote war production. After the war, the continuation of full-employment conditions meant that there was no collapse of shop-floor trade unionism, which went from strength to strength.

The growth of informal plant level bargaining activity by shop stewards in the 1950s and early 1960s gave rise to much concern and hostility from employers, trade union leaders and the mass media, who commonly identified them with the twin 'problems' of 'wage-drift' (the tendency for total earnings to rise above the rate of growth of officially determined wage rates negotiated by national industry-wide bargaining) and the rising incidence of plant-level unofficial strikes. These concerns were largely responsible for the setting-up of Lord Donovan's Royal Commission on Trade Unions and Employers' Associations in 1964. From some of the research work carried out for this Commission[5] and from an earlier survey of 1960[6] statistical evidence began to accumulate about the nature, functions and activities of shop stewards. The moderating influence of this work (which showed that stewards were normally 'lubricants, not irritants' in work-place industrial relations, and that plant managers usually preferred to deal with shop stewards rather than full-time trade union officials) was ignored by the more extreme advocates of penal sanctions to deal with the shop steward 'problem'. The Commission in its Report nevertheless expressed a central anxiety about the gulf which had developed between the formal and informal systems of industrial relations, and recommended that employers and trade unions should close this by evolving more formal systems of procedural agreements at plant and company level, and by incorporating stewards more fully into trade union machinery. Although there has been an expansion of formal written procedures in industry since then, and although trade unions have given greatly more attention to the shop steward's role, more recent research continues to emphasise the element of informality and custom and practice in work-place industrial relations. An authoritative survey of the period from 1966 to 1972 found that 'of the Donovan Commission's enthusiasm for the formalisation of factory-wide agreements there was remarkably little evidence'.[7]

In the meantime, the wave of productivity bargaining which accompanied the Labour government's incomes policies in the late 1960s, whilst being part of the managerial strategy for incorporating shop stewards in more formal procedures, served in part to stimulate further growth in steward numbers and to diversify their functions.[8] The method of penal sanctions to curb plant-level initiative and to reduce the shop steward to a subordinate and dependent role was successively frustrated (with the 1969 withdrawal of Labour's legislative proposals in the White Paper *In Place of Strife*) and then tried and repealed (in the case of the Conservative Goverment's *Industrial Relations Act* of 1971–4). More recently, the legislation of the 1974–9 Labour Government included measures which provided some legal protection for shop stewards and which promoted a widening of their representative role,[9] whilst at the same time the pay restraint policies of these same governments have restricted the influence of plant-bargaining by shop stewards on their members' earnings. New fields of concern for stewards have simultaneously opened out, as unemployment and company mergers have made issues such as job security and company investment policy much more important. Thus as the economic, political and legal environments have undergone a series of changes in recent decades, the shop steward system has successfully adapted to them, showing remarkable resilience and capacity for growth. Stewards also continue to retain the confidence of the members whom they represent—three-quarters of them are elected to office without opposition.[10] In a Sheffield enquiry of 1977, it was found that only 16 per cent of AUEW stewards were opposed in their first election to office, and only 10 per cent in subsequent elections.[11]

The office of shop steward was incorporated into trade union rule books often after they had spontaneously proliferated, and exercised varying degrees of influence for some time, and consequently the rules are often vague as to their functions and mode of appointment. An exception to this is the EETPU whose rules stipulate that shop stewards are under the control of the area full-time official and of the Executive Committee. The GMWU rules specify that the shop steward has no authority to call strikes (in fact this is universally true, but most rule books do not incude such a specific restriction)[12] and in unions with craft traditions, such as the AUEW, stewards are subject to the formal control of the union's District Committees. Most rule books simply provide that shop stewards 'shall be appointed', without indicating the method. In practice a shop-floor show of hands is the most common method, and shop-floor appointments are five times as common as appointments at branch meetings. In fact whilst regular re-appointment of stewards is general, its method is controlled largely by local custom and practice. Most union rule books are similarly vague about the stewards' functions, usually referring only to their role in recruiting and retaining members. Nor do they lay down how many shop stewards there should be. In fact, most of the surveys from the late 1950s onwards reveal a remarkable consistency in the average size of shop stewards' constituencies, of between 50 and 60 members.[13] The relationship between work-place democracy and the formal organs of trade union authority from the branch upwards are seldom defined in rules; the widespread practice of shop-floor members' meetings (convened by stewards outside the formality of the branch meeting) is ignored.[14] It is true that in recent years some unions (such as the EETPU and NUPE) have instituted official national meetings of stewards in particular industries or sectors, but these have only consultative status; they are not part of the union's policy-making machinery.

In some unions, the branch secretary or chairman undertakes the representative and negotiating functions normally discharged by shop stewards. This happens in the civil service, bus transport, the railways and nationalised sections of the port industry, in each of which these officers *are* much more fully integrated into the formal structures of the unions.

It is quite commonly found that shop stewards are 'pushed' into taking up office by members' pressure; only a minority actively seek the job. One study has distinguished several reasons for the occupancy of the role. Amongst those who were 'pushed', some arrive because of a crisis in the plant, some because of their popularity, and some simply by accident. Amongst those who actively seek the job some are motivated by the need to solve work-shop problems, some by ideological considerations, and some by personal ambition.[15]

Most generalisations about shop stewards have been based on studies of the engineering industry where, as we have seen, the system developed early. In engineering, and also in printing, shop stewards developed naturally because the industry was characterised by a multitude of separate firms, exercising strong local management control, and where scope for work-place bargaining was correspond-ingly wide. Following these precedents, the system spread to the other manufacturing industries, and to the bulk of the private sector manual work-force, in the 1940s and 1950s. An exception is building, where stewards were only recognised by employers in 1964. In important sectors of public employment, the system is of much more recent origin. The NUPE only introduced shop stewards in the 1960s, winning recognition for them in local government in 1969, and in the National Health Service in 1971. There are now some 9,500 manual workers' shop stewards in local government, and their growth appears to be re-lated to the spread of productivity bargaining in that sector—some 70 per cent of local government male members of NUPE were covered by incentive schemes in 1975.[16] NALGO, the white-collar union in local government pioneered a shop steward system as recently as 1973; a study of a 6,000-strong NALGO city branch found that the system had begun to stimulate a more active trade union membership than hitherto.[17] One of the problems of plant-level organisation in such sectors as local government is the geographical dispersion of the work-force in small groups, which tends to inhibit the growth of the more sophisticated internal steward organisations common in manufactur-ing.[18] Elsewhere in the public sector, institutions such as the Post Office and British Rail have long traditions of centralised management which have also acted to limit shop steward functions in those industries.

Shop stewards obviously function more effectively if they have access to certain facilities. In recent years, trade unions and the TUC have mounted a campaign to induce employers to grant extended facilities, and the *Employment Protection Act (1975)*, and the *Health and Safety at Work Act (1974)*, have given statutory backing to this drive in some respects. The TUC advocates that employers should provide stewards with lists of new entrants to the plant, facilities on the premises for stewards to explain to each new worker about trade union membership and the terms of collective agreements, facilities for collecting union contributions or a check-off system, a desk and adequate facilities for storing papers, access to telephones and typing and duplicating services, a notice board and use of an internal post system, a suitable room for consulting and reporting to members during working hours and for meetings of shop steward committees, and sufficient time off with pay for performing union duties, and attending training courses and conferences.[19] Rights to time off with pay for training and for performing shop steward duties are now provided for in legislation. The evidence shows that such facilities are becoming more widely available in most kinds of employment, and that they are common in well-organised work-places. A survey in 1972 found that 82 per cent of the shop steward sample claimed that they had the right to hold work-place meetings with members, 53 per cent of them in working hours.[20] Nevertheless, one-third of stewards remained dissatisfied with their facilities.[21]

One of the earliest functions of the stewards historically was the recruitment of members and the collection of union subscriptions. The spread of the closed shop, (more recently the 'union membership agreement' under the *Trade Union and Labour Relations Act*, 1974 and 1976) and of the check-off system, have reduced the burden on stewards in both these areas. The check-off, whereby union contributions are deducted from pay by the employer and paid over to the union, is now well-nigh universal in the public sector, and one regional organisation of the TGWU, with most of its members in the private sector, collects three-quarters of its members' subscriptions in this way.[22]

The Functions of Shop Stewards

The wider modern functions of shop stewards can be classified into (1) bargaining and representative functions on behalf of the membership and (2) communicative functions on behalf of the union. A more complex classification is offered in a recent article, where it is suggested that shop stewards evolve the following pattern of activities: (1) spokesman for the work-group (2) disseminator of information between the organisation and the group, (3) minor bargaining over grievances, (4) monitoring of information, (5) liaison, with other groups and with managers, (6) exercising leadership, to strengthen the cohesion and therefore the bargaining power of the group, (7) decision-making, (8) formal negotiation with senior management.[23]

In the research conducted for the Donovan Royal Commission it was found that over half the steward sample negotiated regularly on wage issues and hours of work, and that a further quarter did so sometimes, that two-thirds negotiated regularly on overtime, and that between 20 per cent and 30 per cent negotiated regularly on redundancy, suspensions, dismissals, manning, new machinery and new jobs, and on the pace and quality of work, and that many more did so sometimes.[24]

In manufacturing industry and the private sector generally, the post-war growth of shop steward influence has undoubtedly been based on their ability to negotiate on plant-level wage issues. In a 1976 survey, it was found that in manufacturing, 90 per cent of wage negotiators were part-timers (i.e. shop stewards or the like) and that for 53 per cent of firms the plant was the most significant level for wage-fixing. (This figure was as high as 71 per cent in engineering and 73 per cent in metal manufacture).[25] National wage bargaining, is more dominant in the public sector, where it is less amenable to stewards' influence, remaining in the hands of full-time trade union officials. But even here, whilst stewards may lack such a power base on the wages issue, the range of their activities is currently widening; moreover the plant-based wages activity of stewards in the private sector may itself have been reduced by Labour Government wage restraint policies between 1975 and 1978. But new issues are being taken up. A 1973 survey found that 50 per cent of the steward sample wanted to widen the scope of bargaining, and 19 per cent wanted to discuss 'the organisation of the firm'.[26] Redundancy and job security are being brought within the scope of stewards' bargaining functions, as are such matters as disclosure of information, (stimulated, although in a limited way, by the requirements of the *Employment Protection Act (1975)*), the environment, health and safety (again with recent legislative encouragement), and company pension plans. The even wider issue of workers' representation in company policy-making has at least appeared on the agenda in the debate on industrial democracy, and in some large companies experimental and limited forms of workers' participation are engaging shop stewards' attention. Engineering stewards in Sheffield were recently found to be discussing takeovers, redundancies, investment policies, meetings with bankers and heads of nationalised industries, MPs and Government ministers.[27]

Increased knowledge gained during the 1970s, on shop stewards' internal plant organisation, their motives, power bases and methods, has filled out and elaborated the stereotype presented by the earlier researches of the Donovan Commission. In this generalised portrait the 'typical' steward emerged as aged 45, a skilled worker, who had left school for an apprenticeship at the statutory school leaving age, was not interested in promotion in the firm or the union, who was an active member of the Labour Party, devoting six hours a week to the union (a part of them in his own time), had been elected unopposed and would normally give it up after six years through a change of employment inside or outside the firm. Sociologists have objected that this picture fails to explain the motives and dynamics of shop steward performance, that it provides no framework in which to study the stewards' role, and no testing of the relations between stewards and members, a vital relationship in view of the members' right of instant recall of their representatives.[28] It may be significant, for instance, that the average age of shop stewards appears to be declining since the 1960s; the recent Sheffield research found that half their sample of engineering stewards was under 40, that 39 per cent were under 35, and that 30 per cent were over 50. The 35–50 age group was under-represented, probably because of its greater family commitments.

Shop stewards do not all see their job in the same light. One writer distinguishes four different functions amongst stewards; those of a mediator, of a welfare officer, of a problem solver, and of a representative of trade union principles. The welfare concept was most common, and the embodiment of principles the least common.[30] The day-to-day initiatives of shop stewards give us examples of these roles. A welfare function may arise whenever members have domestic problems, particularly those which infringe upon life at work. For example, a tacit agreement between unions and management stipulates that the week's holiday due during the winter period shall not be taken in Christmas week, since everyone would want to be off work at that time. A member has a sick wife, and he desperately needs to ensure that at least some Christmas shopping is done for his family. The shop steward takes this case to management and persuades them to treat this as a special and deserving case. They thus waive the agreement.

A mediating role is common where shop stewards represent more than one work-group whose interests over such things as overtime working or grading may conflict and require reconciliation. Some stewards also believe that their role includes that of liaising with management over the maintenance of production. Problem-solvers amongst stewards seek out and tackle a whole range of plant-level issues and 'attempt to establish general precedents from individual cases'. And trade union principles are upheld when a steward calls for solidarity action, such as refraining from undertaking any work normally done by other workers who are in dispute with management, or blacking the products of another company where a strike is in progress. Stewards in the docks industry are particularly noted for this kind of action, yet they are also—and this is far less well-known—amongst the most advanced practicioners of an extended 'welfare' function, reaching well beyond their own members. The Hull docks shop stewards' committee regularly purchases and presents TV sets for hospital wards and Old People's Homes, and in 1979, they won their members' agreement to hand over all the back-pay to which they were entitled with the award of a new wage increase, to a fund for purchasing an expensive item of equipment for brain surgery for a local hospital.

A minority of shop stewards are consciously and actively political. In 1968, 17 per cent belonged to a political party, and in the GMWU, only 54 per cent pay the political levy to the Labour Party.[31] But amongst the Sheffield engineering stewards a trade union and labour-socialist family background appeared to be important for many, although the commonly-shared work experience of the whole sample tended to produce similar attitudes regardless of family background. The shop stewards' trade union role was often supplemented by wider leadership roles in the local community.[32]

Different types of stewards have been observed in a number of studies. Some, usually the least experienced, confine themselves to a 'spokesman' role merely expressing the grievances of their members as they are defined by the group; others are more active, shaping a conscious strategy and taking much more initiative. The longer the tenure of a steward in office, the more likely he is to evolve towards a leadership role of this last kind. One analysis[33] classifies stewards as 'leaders', 'nascent leaders', 'populists', and 'cowboys'. The leaders, usually though not always the convenors and senior stewards, are those with the most extensive networks and shop-floor organisations, who build 'strong bargaining relations' with managers, and who occupy the top of the shop steward hierarchy. They tend to take a long-term view of the interests of the members and the union, are cautious but tough negotiators, and are the most successful stewards. The 'populists' are those who are content simply to reflect members' immediate wishes, whilst the 'cowboys' are erratic and unpredictable personalities, who come and go quickly. Naturally these types are not altogether exclusive.

The 'leaders' are most successful when achievement is measured by their members' earnings, and most conscious and effective in protecting the 'frontier of control' against managemet encroachments. They tend to have a lower level of recourse both to strike action and to the use of the formal rules of procedure. But at the same time 'leaders' may become so involved with management that they become divorced from their members. The result may be member revolt and the demise of 'leadership'.[34] The fact that 'member revolt' in these circumstances remains a possibility represents an important safeguard against the entrenchment of a permanent and invulnerable bureaucracy amongst senior stewards. It has been shown that already in 1966 about one-fifth of stewards were 'senior stewards' with a convening or chairmanship role among groups of stewards in the same plant. The average constituency of senior stewards was 350 members, and there were some 2,000 of them (compared with about 3,000 full-time trade union officials) in all areas of employment in the early 1960s.[35] By 1976, the number of full-time convenors of shop stewards in private manufacturing industry alone had risen from 1,000 in 1966 to 5,000, outnumbering all trade union full-time officials.[36]

The effectiveness of shop stewards depends not only on their personalities and the degree of leadership they exercise, but also on the work environment in which they operate. Important factors here include the mobility which his job allows to a steward—e.g. an inspector can move about more freely than a machine operator, the presence or absence of piece-work pressure, the relative isolation of the shop or bay in which the shop steward works, the degree of craftsmanship in the job, the sex and colour of the work-force, the facilities provided by management, the level of labour turnover, and even the availability of public transport to and from the plant, which affects the possibility of holding mass meetings of members and stewards' committee meetings.[37]

Continuity of office is important for the effectiveness of shop steward representation, and the relatively high rate of turnover amongst stewards has been a source of concern to trade unions. The Donovan Commission's research found an average turnover rate amongst stewards of 15 per cent per annum. Recent attention has focused on the factors affecting turnover. It has been shown that this is lower where stewards exist in groups in the larger plants, providing each other with mutual reinforcement. This effect is strengthened where stewards share a common ideology. Amongst other factors, longer tenure is associated with large plants, larger numbers of shop stewards per plant, higher skills, co-operative management and good shop steward facilities, good relations between the stewards and the outside unions, a leadership rather than a populist role, and commitment of the steward to the wider political goals of the labour movement.[38] Stability in office was measured in a survey covering 453 work-places employing 330,000 manual workers across a wide range of industries. It was found that the proportion of stewards with more than four years experience ranged from 40 per cent in engineering to only 29 per cent in local authorities. Plants with under 500 employees and under 10 shop stewards showed much the greatest instability.[39] As with hierarchy and leadership amongst shop stewards, it may perhaps be feared that *too* great a stability amongst stewards would reinforce bureaucratic tendencies. But Batstone and his colleagues found that there was no inevitable tendency for a particular pattern of shop steward power to become permanently stabilised; 'random shocks' could lead to changes amongst stewards, and whilst 'leader' stewards were more stable than 'populists', their continuity in office was still conditional on member satisfaction and success. 'Shocks', of course, might not be altogether 'random', in that they might follow major policy changes, or crises in the plant.

What methods do shop stewards use to achieve their aims? They rely heavily in argument with management upon the use of comparisons of rates and conditions between work-groups and plants, they build up case-law, establish precedents, and insist on fairness of treatment for their constituents. They flourish on the informality and unwritten nature of many of the procedural arrangements with management. They frequently by-pass first-line management (the supervisors) and approach higher management directly.[40] They exercise unilateral controls in some areas, particularly on overtime, mobility of labour, and lay-offs, and in the case of craftsmen, they police the unilateral trade union rules on apprenticeship and demarcation. They are the guardians of custom and practice, the unwritten rules which grow up from precedent to precedent at plant level.[41]

Shop stewards have an ambivalent attitude to the use of formal written procedures for negotiation and the handling of grievances. Until the reforming wave of the past decade these procedures, drawn up between employers' associations and unions in an earlier period when unions were much weaker, were often extremely unsatisfactory, involving lengthy delay in settling issues, often excluding the shop steward after the initial stage, preserving management rights to initiate changes unilaterally, and being confined to a narrow range of subjects. In the wake of the Donovan Commission, the TUC and the unions put their weight behind a drive to reform these characteristics, so that shop stewards should be involved at all stages of procedure, to cut out delays, to introduce *status quo* clauses, and to widen the scope of procedure. Considerable progress has been made in many industries along these lines.

Joint Consultation

The practice of joint consultation, once a favourite device of management to provide a semblance of worker participation separate from trade union bargaining, and retaining all decision-making authority in management hands, has declined or been transformed under the impact of shop steward development since the war.

'Two propositions can be advanced about the relationship between shop steward bargaining and joint consultative machinery . . . First, plant consultative committees . . . cannot survive the development of effective shop floor organisation. Either they must become . . . negotiating committees . . . or they are boycotted by shop stewards and . . . fall into disuse. Secondly, shop stewards . . . do not [agree with] . . . separate institutional arrangements for . . . dealing with so-called 'conflicting' and 'common interest' questions, and any committee on which they serve which cannot reach decisions . . . they regard as . . . an inferior . . . substitute for . . . negotiating machinery.'[42]

Where joint consultation survives it tends to be taken over on the workers' side by shop steward representation. A recent survey found that in plants with over 500 employees, 80 per cent of the joint consultative committees were staffed on the workers' side exclusively by shop stewards. This incidentally strengthens the trade union case, accepted by the Bullock enquiry on industrial democracy in 1976, that all representation in industrial relations and industrial democracy should be through the single channel of trade union machinery.[43]

Steward Organisation in the Plant

The power bases which shop stewards build up vary from plant to plant. Except in very small plants with fewer than 3 stewards, some form of shop steward organisation and hierarchy develops, with full-time stewards, steward committees, and the election of steward executive committees by the stewards themselves. Half the stewards surveys in 1973 had regular meetings amongst themselves.[44] Hierarchical organisation tends to appear where there are 10 or more stewards in a plant, and 50 per cent of work-places with over 500 employees had full-time stewards, although the presence of full-time stewards is more marked in private manufacturing than in the public service.[45] 'Leader' stewards built up resources and sanctions largely though their network of relations with other stewards, and a major resource in this respect is the existence of shop steward committees.[46]

Although some slight decline has been noticed in plant-level multi-unionism since 1966[47] it remains a very common phenomenon. In 1973, it was found that 50 per cent of manual workers' establishments had more than one union, and 30 per cent of non-manual establishments.[48] In the earlier post-war years unions were critical of inter-union joint shop steward committees for developing 'private' unions, and for becoming self-governing organisations despite the formal allegiance of stewards to individual unions. At plant-level, unions have become much more tolerant of joint committees of stewards on multi-union lines—we refer to the wider phenomenon of company-level combine committees later. At plant level, multi-union steward organisation is frequently of a more developed and hierarchical character than in the single-union plant; union heterogeneity seems to encourage stronger steward organisation, which in turn makes inter-union co-operation more manageable.[49] Conversely, poor inter-union relations are to be found in plants with low levels of steward organisation.

The most obvious base of shop steward authority is the membership —the work-force as organised into trade unions. Ever since the 'human relations' school of industrial psychology in America in the 1920s 'discovered' the informal work-group, it has been recognised that the work force in modern industry is not an undifferentiated mass of physical atoms, but a complex social organisation. The original American research studied the work-group in isolation from trade unionism; in Britain more attention has been given to the relationship between work-groups and shop stewards, and it is clear that there is no single, universal type of group. Task groups, human relations groups, friendship cliques and interest groups co-exist and over-lap on the shop floor.[50] Work groups have been classified as (a) apathetic—a condition found amongst low paid, unskilled workers with individual jobs, such as cleaners and lavatory attendants, (b) erratic—amongst low status groups with identical, physically demanding jobs, such as assembly-line work, (c) strategic—skilled, relatively well-paid, individual jobs such as metal finishers and process workers in iron and steel, and (d) conservative—the most skilled elite of maintenance craftsmen.[51]

This type of analysis emphasises the influence of technology and occupation on the relative powers of work-groups and stewards, but technology by no means explains the observable differences in shop-floor power; groups need to be aware of their power and prepared to use it and these aspects of consciousness derive from the nature of their trade unionism. Growing experience of collective action in response to grievances and claims builds up something which is stronger than a loose coalition, and develops a group commitment to continued reliance on collective methods.[52] Moreover, there is no simple one-to-one relationship between stewards and work-groups. In a case study of 19 stewards in 6 factories, it was found that the average number of distinct groups represented by each shop steward was 5.[53]

Work-groups are thus autonomous with respect to shop-floor trade union organisation; they are not necessarily co-terminous with shop steward constituencies. This implies that stewards must consciously strive to retain the confidence and support of the groups they represent. They are not always successful in this; an important study of industrial relations in the car industry identified the phenomenon of the 'unofficial-unofficial' strike, in which workers strike in defiance not only of the outside union, but of their own shop stewards.[54] Clearly, the recent tendencies for numbers of stewards to increase, and for improved facilities to hold meetings with their members, enhance the possibility for stewards accurately to represent their groups' feelings, and the existence of autonomous group pressure constitutes a permanent check on the growth of shop steward bureaucracy. However prominent the role of the 'leader' stewards, decision-making must ultimately be shared with the work-group; only a small minority of shop stewards can 'always' get their own way with the members.[55]

The shop steward power bases and methods which we have

surveyed—the informality of work-place relations, custom and practice, the use of procedure and sanctions, joint consultation, shop steward committees, multi-unionism, technology and group pressure —are conditioned by two further factors; the role of management and the system of collective bargaining. Several surveys have established that plant management prefers to deal with shop stewards rather than with full-time union officials, where trade union organisation exists. The evidence suggests strongly that the post-war growth of shop stewards has in part been fostered by a management keen to settle issues and disputes where they arise, on the shop-floor. As with the stewards themselves, a degree of informality seems to bring the advantages of flexibility for managers; it is certain that the traditional formal industrial relations structure of employers, such as Employers' Associations have little influence at plant level, nor do managers usually encourage them to intervene.[56] Managers' attitudes to shop stewards at least amongst manual workers however, do not appear to be decisive in large plants; a history of management opposition is as likely to produce strong steward organisation, as is a history of encouragement. (In work-places below 500 workers, past management opposition seems to have stimulated steward strength, encouragement to have inhibited it).[57]

Managers of manual workers appear on the whole keen to build 'strong bargaining relations' with the more influential 'leader' stewards, and derive strength from these relations in their own power struggles with other managers. But where stewards limit their goals to the control of purely plant level issues (and this is still the most common practice) then although they successfully constrain management prerogative at that level, and enforce joint regulation of those issues, their lack of influence over wider issues of company policy means that 'it can hardly be claimed that workers were as powerful as management'.[58]

Where collective bargaining over wages is centralised at national, industry level, there is no scope for shop steward initiative on this subject at plant level. At the opposite extreme comes purely plant level wage fixing, where the stewards' role is obviously central. Between these lies a whole range of wage-systems, with varying degrees of nationally and locally determined elements in the wage-packet. The 'tightness' of nationally determined wages, and the 'looseness' of plant bargaining, is largely a difference between the public and private sectors of the economy, and these differences help to account for the lower level of steward organisation in the public sector.[59]

The method of wage payment also influences the shop steward role. It is well established that the post-war growth of shop stewards in manufacturing industry rested initially on their ability constantly to re-negotiate rates in a system of payment-by-results. From the late 1960s onwards, management has striven in many industries to replace payment-by-results with measured day work, in order precisely to cut down shop stewards' control over wages by reducing opportunities to bargain. Although this drive has made progress, half the stewards surveyed in 1973 were still operating on payment-by-results.[60] Where measured day work has been introduced, it has caused difficulties for some steward organisations, as for example at British Leyland.[61] But bargaining about rates under payment-by-result may be replaced by bargaining over effort under measured day work. Just as work-groups regulate output and impose informal norms under payment-by-result, in order to stabilise earnings, they can apply similar methods under measured day work. In any case, recent research shows that strong, sophisticated steward organisation can exist even where there is no work-place bargaining over wages[62] and this has encouraging implications for the development of public sector shop stewards, and for the survival of the shop steward's task generally in an era in which imposed incomes policies alternate with attempts to impede bargaining by establishing 'cash limits' in the public sector, and general deflation outside it. High rates of unemployment obviously reinforce such adverse pressures.

Relations with the Unions

The relationship between shop stewards and their trade union organisation, though not easy to define, is of fundamental importance. Union support for and endorsement of the stewards' office, and protection against victimisation, is essential. Unions also offer practical advice and guidance for stewards, provide training courses on an increasing scale, and facilities for forming policy. Trade union principles provide powerful reinforcement at the ideological level, for shop stewards. In turn, without stewards, trade union administration and cohesion, as we know it, would collapse. Yet the links between the shop stewards and union branches and higher committees is (with some exceptions such as the AUEW and NUPE) based more on the personal commitment of stewards than on constitutions. It is usually the hard core of active stewards who keep branch life going, and who serve on the unions' higher committees. The trend towards plant-based branches, (as distinct from branches which cover a geographical area) is helping towards a closer relationship between stewards and union structures. At present, the branch serves as a much more important forum and meeting place for stewards in the public service than in manufacturing, as it does generally for smaller and dispersed work-forces.[63] District Committees vary in influence over the plant; in the AUEW they are very important but elsewhere the full-time official is more significant. Industry or trade conferences of stewards at regional and natinal level are held by the GMWU, USDAW, and the EETPU, but their impact is limited and they have no authority in the unions' constitutions.

All the published studies tend to show that for stewards their relation with full-time union officials is more important than are those with the branch or higher union committees.

Despite this, and despite the urgings of the Donovan Commission in 1968, the ratio between trade union members and full-time officials did not improve between 1966 and 1972, and one-third of stewards in 1972 reported difficulties in contacting their local official.[64] However, there has been a considerable qualitative change in the shop steward-full-time official relationship since the 1950s; the extra-plant authority of the official has declined and his relations with stewards have in many cases become more democratic. This is partly the result of the growth of the stewards' autonomy, but also partly the result of deliberate policy decisions by union leaderships. (Jack Jones in the TGWU, for example, insisted on the need for his full-time officials to become more responsive to steward needs. His successor, Moss Evans, has expressed himself forcefully on the same lines: 'All we are, the national officials, is bloody professionals. We ought to be there to offer some help to the lay people if they need it. Nothing more.'[65]) Clearly the politics of trade union leaderships, and their attitudes to democracy, can either foster or restrict shop stewards influence.

There remain wide variations across industry in the relationships between shop stewards and their full-time officials, ranging from complete steward dependence on the full-time official, to almost complete independence. There are inevitable strains within the relationship, but stewards do use their full-time official, informally, as a resource and support, and at least in the 1960s, four-fifths of full-time officials were reportedly satisfied with the degree of their influence over stewards.[66] At a later date, only one-third of stewards thought that their official played an important role in negotiations[67] and two-thirds of stewards wanted more contact than they had with their full-time official.[68]

Amongst stewards in the GMWU, 45 per cent in manufacturing, but only 33 per cent in public service, met their full-time officials at least once a month. When asked who they would contact if they had a problem, 39 per cent of public service stewards, but only 19 per cent of manufacturing stewards, said they would go to the full-time official. It is clear from this and other evidence that stewards in public services are more dependent on full-time officials than they are in manufacturing.[69] A greater degree of dependence is also to be found among stewards of white-collar staff.[70] Wherever steward organisation is weak, and national wage agreements central, full-time officials find it more difficult to satisfy the demand for servicing from shop stewards. One of the few unions which has attempted to make formal arrangements to respond to this problem is a public service union, NUPE. It has put great emphasis on formal training for all new stewards, and its rules now require that stewards should serve on branch and district committees. The inherited geographical structure of older trade unions may mean that full-time official services are very unevenly spread across the country; in the AUEW the number of members per full-time official varied in different districts from 7,000 to 30,000.[71]

But the principal influence on the relationship between stewards and full-time officials is that of plant size. The large plant develops its own resources, convenors, steward committees, and facilities. In this context, the convenor may easily come to rival the full-time official in skill and experience. Size of plant outweighs other variables, but within this limitation, full-time officials can influence the growth of steward organisation, by encouraging or hindering styles of bargaining which foster the independence of the plant stewards.[72] Beyond the attitudes taken up towards steward initiatives by individual unions, there is the policy of the TUC as a whole, which from the 1950s onwards has reflected a shift from authoritarian to permissive responses, and then, in the 1970s, towards democratic attitudes to steward organisation. The TUC's most recent official training manuals even encourage stewards to strengthen links with their fellows in other plants, by forming combine committees: something which would have been unthinkable to the draftsmen of the famous 1960 statement on 'disputes and workshop representation', which condemned such initiatives.

Combine Organisation

So far, we have considered shop stewards as operating purely at plant level. A further dimension of their activity, which has been important at key moments in shop steward history, and receiving renewed attention today, is the association of workplace representatives in multi-plant companies. Given the trend towards take-overs and mergers leading to the current concentration of ownership which we discussed in chapter 1 (in which a hundred companies account for half the UK's manufacturing output and employment, most of which is in multi-plant, multi-union enterprises), the growth of Combine Committees of stewards in these companies was inevitable, (the 50th largest company had 6 plants in 1958; in 1968 it had 20, and the number must be even larger today).[73] Today, stewards from half of all manufacturing companies hold at least some meetings with stewards from other work-places of the same employer.

In the multi-plant firm, bargaining at plant level alone leaves most of the key decisions in the hands of top management. They may therefore positively seek to confine their stewards to operation at the plant level. However, leap-frogging claims between plants may in some cases (as happened in British Leyland) force management to consider company-level bargaining as an alternative. Some companies have indeed favoured company bargaining from the outset, hoping thereby to negotiate only with national full-time union officials. This was the strategy of Fords, in particular. But the internal union reforms of the last two decades led in that case to the eventual involvement of shop stewards in the national company-level negotiations. The whole logic of such company bargaining tends to call forth company-level shop steward organisation. Combine Committees have in fact been quite common throughout the post-war years in engineering and in the motor industry; prominent contemporary examples of such Combines include those at British Leyland, Fords, Dunlop–Pirelli, Lucas Aerospace, and Vickers.[74]

The Lucas organisation is a particularly interesting example. Set up in the 1960's in response to fears of rationalisation and redundancies the Combine Committee took over four years to develop its mature functions and structure. It has set up a number of advisory services for stewards and workers in the company, including one on company pensions, and another on science and technology. It publishes a four-page bi-monthly newspaper of which it distributes 10,000 copies to workers. Its principal achievement, which has made it widely known far beyond the boundaries of company industrial relations, is the researching and publication of an 'Alternative Corporate Plan' which advocates the adoption of a whole range of new company products, selected after canvassing the work-force and after detailed technical and commercial studies, and based on considerations of social usefulness (e.g. kidney machines, and new forms of energy generation). For this work the Committee has been proposed for a Nobel Peace Prize. Recently the Combine has set up, jointly with the North-East London Polytechnic, a Centre for Alternative Industrial and Technological Systems. Other Combine Committees which have developed alternative product plans to combat rationalisation and redundancy include those at Vickers, Parsons, and Chryslers.[75]

Unfortunately, Combine Committees are constantly threatened by plant sectionalism; often arising in response to a job crisis in the company, they may find it hard to consolidate their organisation and to ensure its continuity. Failing recognition by the company, the combine's role may become limited to one of exchanging information between plants, though it should be said that this in itself can be a very useful function. This poses the question of whether combine committees should seek company recognition and a formal collective bargaining role. For some committees this has been a dilemma, since they have been wary of undermining the strength and independence of their constituent plant steward organisations. Yet recognition, and a bargaining function may well overcome the organisational difficulties which beset them. Two students of combine committees have gone so far as to claim that 'the future effectiveness of collective bargaining rests on whether combine committees can cope.' They conclude that 'we can expect to see officially recognised combine committees becoming more common and consequently increasingly effective as bargaining agents'.[76]

For those whose persistent efforts have failed to secure from their employers any modicum of recognition, these words may seem slightly optimistic.

Combine Committees, of course, carry with them their own problems, as well as opportunities for the extension of the trade union role. Obviously, by concentrating attention upon company affairs, they risk neglecting the wider, industry and class loyalties and unities which lie beyond that level. In this sense, they may substitute new sectionalisms for older (e.g. craft) loyalties. Yet considering the still predominantly plant-level nature of shop steward organisation, and the overwhelming corporate power which is embodied at company level, in the large, conglomerate corporations, an increase in these 'problems' would mark a substantial advance from lower to higher and more effective levels of shop steward organisation. The aim to meet, bargain with, and control the corporate decision-makers of Fords, with its 23 plants in the United Kingdom alone, represents something more than narrow sectionalism. A high level of strategic thinking can be provoked in the striving for wider and wider forms of shop steward association in a major company, including the need for international and multi-company links. This is illustrated by the experience of leading convenors in Fords UK factories.[77] *Multi-*company participation in the evolution of shop stewards' alternative planning about the whole motor industry is exemplified in the Motors' Group of the Institute for Workers' Control, whose published deliberations involved representatives from Chrysler, Vauxhall, Ford, British Leyland and Wilmott Breedon.[78] In another industry, the Coventry Machine-Tool Workers' Committee, with shop steward and convenor representation from five major companies in the industry, commissioned their own report on the economics of their industry.[79] The possibilities for organising joint trade union initiatives of this kind, across a group of companies, or of embracing a whole industry or sector, are enormously strengthened by the prior existence of company-level Combine Committees. Yet the tendencies towards co-ordination of shop steward activity—in the plant, with the growth of full-time convenors, and in the company, with the growth of Combine Committees—has led some writers to reflect on the dangers of the 'bureaucratisation of the rank and file',[80] and to resurrect a modified version of Michel's 'iron law of oligarchy'. Whilst Hyman, for example, acknowledges the desirability and inevitability of some degree of 'centralisation' of workplace organisation, he also advocates that 'the types of strategy long associated with 'unofficial' struggles must now be re-interpreted and re-applied within shop steward organisation.'

The aspirations of workers and their stewards organisations, embarked as they are in the early stages of a sustained and difficult evolution to create working trade union structures which can face up to the powers of multi-national companies may well bring them into conflict with such proposals. To pose the possibility, or desirability, of constructing unofficial rank and file organisation in opposition to convenors and Combine Committees is to conjure up an infinite regression of reactive organisations. There could be little reasonable doubt that if such a movement developed, it too would in its turn become 'bureaucratised' in the eyes of such critics, and so on, as it says in the poem: big fleas have little fleas, upon their backs to bite 'em; and little fleas have lesser fleas, and so ad infinitum. This is not to say that the time-honoured trade union controls of election, report-back, and recall, should not be applied to shop stewards, convenors, and Combine Committees, and indeed to all other representatives. It is, however, to argue that recent developments in the field of Combine and multi-company stewards' initiatives require a positive response from trade unions and perhaps even from commentators upon trade unionism.

NOTES

1. S. R. Parker, *Workplace Industrial Relations, 1972*, HMSO, 1974.
2. Commission on Industrial Relations, *Study no.2. Industrial Relations at Establishment Level: A Statistical Survey*, HMSO, 1973.
3. S. R. Parker, *Workplace Industrial Relations 1973*, HMSO, 1975.
4. H. A. Clegg, *The System of Industrial Relations in Great Britain*, Blackwell, 1970, and H. A. Clegg, A. Fox, and E. F. Thompson, *A History of British Trade Unions since 1889, vol 1: 1889-1910*. Clarendon, 1964.
5. W. E. J. McCarthy, *The Role of Shop Stewards in British Industrial Relations*, Research Paper 1, Donovan Royal Commission, HMSO 1966, and W. E. J. McCarthy and S. R. Parker, *Shop Stewards and Workshop Relations*, Research Paper 10, Donovan Royal Commission, HMSO, 1968.
6. H. A. Clegg, A. J. Killick and Rex Adams, *Trade Union Officers*, Blackwell, 1960.
7. M. G. Wilders and S. R. Parker, 'Changes in Workplace Industrial Relations, 1966-72', *British Journal of Industrial Relations, vol. 13*, 1975.
8. In an unpublished Sheffield University research report, (by R. Jones, J. Halstead, and M. Barratt Brown, 1977) it was recorded that amongst plants surveyed in the local engineering industry, the number of shop stewards doubled in 1968-9 with the emergence of productivity bargaining.
9. In the *Employment Protection Act*, 1975, and in the *Health and Safety at Work Act*, 1974.
10. M. G. Wilders and S. R. Parker, loc. cit.
11. R. Jones, J. Halstead, and M. Barratt Brown, loc. cit.
12. Robert Taylor, *The Fifth Estate*, Routledge, Kegan, Paul, 1978.
13. In R. Jones, J. Halstead and M. Barratt Brown (loc. cit) the average was 60, in H. A. Clegg, A. J. Killick, and Rex Adams, (loc. cit) the average was 51, in W. E. J. McCarthy and S. R. Parker (op. cit) the average was 60, and in W. Brown, R. Ebsworth and M. Terry, 'Factors Shaping Shop Steward Organisation in Britain,' *British Journal of Industrial Relations, vol. XVI, no. 2*, July 1978, the average was 51.
14. W. E. J. McCarthy, op. cit.
15. N. Nicholson, 'The Role of the Shop Steward: an Empirical Case Study', *Industrial Relations Journal*, vol. 7, no. 1, 1976.
16. M. Somerton, *Trade Unions and Industrial Relations in Local Government*, WEA 1978.
17. N. Nicholson and G. Ursell, 'The NALGO Activists', *New Society*, 15th December 1977.
18. W. Brown, R. Ebsworth and M. Terry, loc. cit.
19. TUC, *Good Industrial Relations: A Guide for Negotiators*, 1971.
20. M. G. Wilders and S. R. Parker, loc. cit.
21. S. R. Parker, op. cit. 1975.
22. Data supplied by the Transport & General Workers' Union Region 10, for the second quarter of 1978.

23. B. Partridge, 'The Activities of Shop Stewards', *Industrial Relations Journal, vol. 8, no. 4*, 1977-8.
24. W. E. J. McCarthy and S. R. Parker, op. cit.
25. W. Daniel, *Wage Determination in Industry*, PEP, 1976.
26. S. R. Parker, op. cit., 1975.
27. R. Jones, J. Halstead, and M. Barratt Brown, loc. cit. To keep matters in perspective it should be added that the report found that two-thirds of the stewards still placed wage rates as their top priority.
28. B. Partridge, loc. cit.
29. R. Jones, J. Halstead and M. Barratt Brown, loc. cit.
30. N. Nicholson, loc. cit.
31. R. Taylor, op. cit.
32. R. Jones, J. Halstead and M. Barratt Brown, loc. cit.
33. E. Batstone, I. Boraston, and S. Frenkel, *Shop Stewards in Action*, Blackwell, 1977.
34. E. Batstone, I. Boraston, and S. Frenkel, op. cit.
35. H. A. Clegg, op. cit.
36. W. Brown and M. Terry, 'The Future of Collective Bargaining', *New Society*, 23rd March 1978.
37. R. Jones, J. Halstead and M. Barratt Brown, loc. cit.
38. R. Jones, J. Halstead, and M. Barratt Brown, loc. cit. See also Graham Winch, 'Shop Steward Turnover and Workplace Relations' *Industrial Relations Journal*, forthcoming.
39. W. Brown, R. Ebsworth and M. Terry, loc. cit.
40. Three-quarters of shop stewards practiced this in 1973. S. R. Parker, op. cit, 1975.
41. W. Brown, 'A Consideration of Custom and Practice', *British Journal of Industrial Relations, vol. X, no. 1*, March 1972.
42. W. E. J. McCarthy, op. cit.
43. W. Brown, R. Ebsworth and M. Terry, loc. cit.
44. S. R. Parker, op. cit, 1975.
45. W. Brown, R. Ebsworth and M. Terry, loc. cit.
46. E. Batstone, I. Boraston and S. Frenkel, op. cit.
47. M. G. Wilders and S. R. Parker, loc. cit.
48. Commission on Industrial Relations, op. cit. In W. Brown, R. Ebsworth and M. Terry, (loc. cit.) it is reported that two-thirds of stewards were in multi-union workplaces.
49. W. Brown, R. Ebsworth and M. Terry, loc. cit.
50. B. Partridge, *Towards on Action Theory of Workplace Industrial Relations*, University of Aston Management Centre, Working Paper no. 50, 1976.
51. L. R. Sayles, *Behaviour of Industrial Work Groups: Prediction and Control*, Chapman and Hall, 1958.
52. B. Partridge, op. cit. 1976.
53. J. F. B. Goodman and T. G. Whittingham, *Shop Stewards in British Industry*, McGraw-Hill, 1969.
54. H. A. Turner, G. Clack, and G. Roberts, *Labour Relations in the Motor Industry*, Allen and Unwin, 1967.

55. S. R. Parker, op. cit. 1975.
56. W. E. J. McCarthy and S. R. Parker, op. cit.
57. W. Brown, R. Ebsworth and M. Terry, loc. cit.
58. E. Batstone, I. Boraston, and S. Frenkel, op. cit.
59. I. Boraston, H. A. Clegg, and M. Rimmer, *Workplace and Union*, Heinemann, 1975.
60. S. R. Parker, op. cit., 1975.
61. H. Friedman, *Multi-Plant Working and Trade Union Organisation*, WEA 1976.
62. I. Boraston, H. A. Clegg, and M. Rimmer, op. cit., and W. Brown, R. Ebsworth and M. Terry, loc. cit.
63. W. Brown, R. Ebsworth and M. Terry, loc. cit.
64. M. G. Wilders and S. R. Parker, loc. cit.
65. Quoted in Huw Beynon, *Working for Ford*, Penguin, 1973.
66. W. E. J. McCarthy and S. R. Parker, op. cit.
67. S. R. Parker, op. cit., 1975.
68. W. Brown, R. Ebsworth and M. Terry, loc. cit.
69. W. Brown, R. Ebsworth and M. Terry, loc. cit.
70. E. Batstone, I. Boraston, and S. Frenkel, op. cit.
71. I. Boraston, H. A. Clegg, and M. Rimmer, op. cit.
72. I. Boraston, H. A. Clegg and M. Rimmer, op. cit.
73. W. Brown and M. Terry, loc. cit.
74. Case studies of these and other committees are provided in H. Friedman, op. cit.
75. For an account of the Lucas Combine Committee see K. Coates (ed.), *The Right to Useful Work*, Spokesman Books 1978.
76. W. Brown and M. Terry, loc. cit.
77. See Bernie Passingham and Danny Connor, (TGWU convenors at Ford Dagenham), *Ford Shop Stewards on Industrial Democracy*, IWC Pamphlet no. 54, 1977.
78. See IWC Motors' Group, *A Workers' Enquiry into the Motor Industry*, IWC 1978.
79. See *Crisis in Engineering: Machine Tool Workers Fight for Jobs*, Coventry Workshop and the IWC, June 1979.
80. Richard Hyman, 'The Politics of Workplace Trade Unionism: Recent Tendencies and some Problems for Theory', in *Capital and Class*, vol. 8, Summer 1979.

Chapter Six

Collective Bargaining

The Range of Trade Union Methods
In their study of trade unionism, Sidney and Beatrice Webb had
already distinguished three approaches by which trade unions sought
to achieve their aims: the method of Mutual Insurance, the method of
Legal Enactment, and the method of Collective Bargaining.[1]

Even while the Webbs were describing it, it was clear that the first of
these was withering considerably: it belongs classically to the period of
craft unionism, and a time when collective bargaining was far from
widespread. The method of Mutual Insurance, (apart from its formal
insurance aspect in the provision of cash benefits for sickness, industrial
injury, retirement and death) involved the use of trade union funds to
provide 'out-of-work' benefit, and travelling allowances, to individual
workers to enable them to refuse jobs offered at below the rate agreed
amongst the union members; the Webbs christened this technique the
'strike in detail'. That it was a time-honoured method of trade
unionism, designed to maintain labour's prices against the employers'
market power, is attested by Fred Knee, an old militant who, also
writing in the early years of this century, complained bitterly about its
supercession by collective bargaining, which he regarded as a distinct
compromise, and a compromise for the worse.

> 'It surprises me when I hear "collective bargaining" spoken of . . .
> as the first principle of trade unionism. You may search the
> "objects" of the older unions for this precious "first principle" but
> you will not find it. The object of trade unionism used to be to
> uphold the price of labour *against* the encroachments of the
> employers, not in agreement with them. "Collective bargaining" is
> an afterthought forced on Capital and Labour alike because of this
> straining after "industrial peace" . . .'[2]

Obviously the method of Mutual Insurance, which required no
formal recognition of trade unions by employers, and indeed no necessity for a bargaining process, was a response to a time when industrial
relations were rudimentary and undeveloped, when employers insisted
successfully on their prerogatives, and when trade unions were small
and confined to defined crafts and particular occupational skills. Yet

such unions were not necessarily impotent. Another method, not separately categorised by the Webbs, which is suited to such circumstances, survives strongly today in the era of mass unionism: that of unilateral workers' regulation. When groups of workers place unwritten and informal, but effective, limits on their earnings under systems of payment-by-result, when they administer the fair distribution of overtime amongst themselves, or when road haulage drivers place limits on the scheduling of their vehicles, or when a thousand and one informal 'norms' established by custom and practice are observed in industry, then no bargaining, and no recognition of unions, is required.

But, whatever Fred Knee thought about it, it is hardly possible to conceive of a *mass* trade union movement, enrolling people of diverse skills and people of no specific skill, exerting its present-day level of influence on labour's terms and conditions of employment without the widespread use of the method of Collective Bargaining. Moreover the supplementary function of Mutual Insurance, the provision of welfare cash benefits, was also most appropriately associated with a system of craft unions with relatively high subscriptions, in a pre-welfare state society, and has consequently declined with the historical evolution (which is itself largely attributable to the trade union method of Legal Enactment) of state provision for unemployment, sickness, accidents, and retirement. We are left inevitably with collective bargaining as the classic function of a trade unionism which, inheriting some of the liberal suspicions of legislative 'interference', and strong on the doctrine of self-reliance, turned to Legal Enactment only in respect of specific areas of weakness and dependence, such as the protection of women and child labour. More recently, of course, the balance of emphasis in trade union methods between collective bargaining and legal enactment has shifted somewhat in favour of the law, but even today the British trade union movement as a whole (unlike some European unions) rejects the notion of legally enforceable minimum wages *except* in industries where collective bargaining has failed to develop, and is also indifferent to the legal enforcement of standard working hours. There are some unions (notably NUPE) which have strenuously argued for a legal minimum wage, but they are in a minority.

Wages and hours have in fact provided the staple diet for orthodox collective bargaining; for long periods, these have been the only subjects (along with 'conditions of work' rather narrowly defined) on which bargaining rights have been ceded by employers, or demanded by trade unions. One of the most dynamic and significant changes in trade unionism over the past two decades has been the drive to expand the areas of managerial control which are subject to the joint regulation of collective bargaining. At the same time, the traditional claim to legitimacy for wage bargaining has itself been increasingly challenged by the state in its pursuit of incomes policy, thus signalling an end to the prevailing assumption of the past two hundred years, that the state should leave wage regulation to the market, or to the bilateral regulation of employers and unions.

At a much earlier period of history, Government regulation of wages both centrally and through its local Justices of the Peace, goes back to the 16th century and earlier. The grounds for a challenge to this State paternalism were prepared earlier in this country than elsewhere, with the rise of capitalist employment relations in agriculture from the 16th century onwards; the rising industrial capitalist class of the 18th century took up the struggle against the regulatory and paternalist State, and won the argument to the point where state control of wages was allowed first to deteriorate through neglect, and then was formally abolished.[3] During the transitional period, workers were to be found in the late 18th century petitioning governments for the enforcement of the old laws on minimum wages and other working conditions. When they found these approaches treated first with indifference and then with official hostility, they were thrown back on their own resources in their struggle to control the dominant new force of the labour market. By a painful and prolonged process of struggle, workers evolved over the next hundred years the means (trade union organisation), they compelled the concession from employers (trade union recognition), and they elaborated the method (collective bargaining), by which to bring the labour market closer towards their own interests.

The Development of Collective Bargaining

Over the two-hundred years history of trade unionism, collective bargaining has evolved from (a) 'primitive' work-place bargaining, reinforced by the method of mutual insurance, to (b) district or local agreements in particular industries, (the majority situation before 1914), to (c) national-level, industry-wide agreements (the traditional aim of trade unionism, laying down a 'common rule' on wages and hours, and resting 'on the capacity of the two parties to make an agreement which will apply to the whole industry'),[4] to (d) the post-1945 situation, in which national agreements, particularly in the private sector of the economy, have been supplemented by widespread plant bargaining by local managers and shop stewards. Into this last pattern has been sketched a further level of proto-bargaining by (e) TUC negotiations with the state over the content of government incomes policies. While this has been developing, there has also been a growth of separate negotiations at company-level. This system of company bargaining applies, for instance, at Fords, ICI and Metal Box; and also within the nationalised industries.

Trade unions during much of the 19th century were too weak to enforce their rights to negotiate. Their demands to do so would be met with the kind of statement issued by the engineering employers during their lock-out of the members of the newly-formed Associated Society of Engineers in 1852: 'We alone are the competent judges of our own business, that we are respectively the masters of our own establishments, and it is our firm intention to remain so.'[5] This attitude was gradually broken down as the unions grew in strength, the engineering industry making its first agreement on negotiating procedure in 1897, and by 1914 many skilled workers' unions had achieved recognition and established some national agreements. Before the first world war, however, the majority of workers were still either unorganised, or were conducting their negotiations with individual employers or groups of employers at local level only, which led to great variety of rates throughout the country in each industry. In 1910, only one-quarter of all industrial workers were covered by negotiated agreements of any kind, and the period from 1910-14 was characterised by many national-level strikes and disputes revolving round the issue of national-level recognition and national wage bargaining. The first world war greatly accelerated the trend towards national level industry-wide bargaining, as a result of four main factors. First, the labour shortage tempted employers to bid up wages competitively: to prevent this happening, some employers were willing to overcome their objections to national negotiations and national rates, since these would prevent such competition. Second, the increased cost of living led to many claims of a similar kind pouring into the arbitration bodies, so that to simplify settlement there was a tendency to award industry-wide flat rate increases in wages. Third, there had been increasing intervention by government in industrial relations: industries such as mining and the railways were administered by the state at a national level. Lastly, growing unofficial labour unrest, led by the shop stewards' movement, led government to set up a wide-ranging enquiry under the chairmanship of Mr J. H. Whitley, M.P., deputy speaker of the House of Commons, 'on the relations between employers and employed'.

The Whitley Reports in particular have, ever since, been identified as the founding charter for the subsequent evolution of the British system of industrial relations, which later generations have continued to inherit until the present-day. The Whitley Reports (1916-17) recommended: (i) the establishment of Joint Industrial Councils, representative of employers and trade unions, to make formal national, industry-wide agreements in particular industries, (ii) subordinate District Committees below the JICs, (iii) works committees for consultative purposes in particular companies and plants, (iv) the extension of the Trades Boards system of statutory wage regulation in industries where collective organisation was inadequate to sustain collective bargaining, (v) a permanent arbitration board available for voluntary settlement of disputes, and (vi) recourse to government-appointed Courts of Inquiry to aid the understanding and settlement of major, intractable disputes. The principle on which the Whitley enquiry based its recommendations was 'the advisability of a continuance, as far as possible, of the present system whereby industries make their own agreements and settle their differences themselves.'

The advance towards a uniform system of national negotiations industry by industry was not uniform during the inter-war years. Some, such as building and railways, concluded agreements on national machinery, whilst others, which had achieved national rates during the war, such as the coal industry, reverted to district rates. Some others such as cotton, experienced a complete break-down in an established system of negotiated rates, and had to be helped out of their difficulties by state intervention. At the same time, the creation by mergers of the two large general unions in the 1920s added weight to the pressure on employers to concede the principle of national machinery; the TGWU and GMWU became the most active propagandists for Joint Industrial Council machinery in the trade union world. The changing character of industrial organisation assisted the growth of national agreements,—the appearance of large combines in such industries as Chemicals, Flour Milling, and Cement was one sign of a general shift away from small family business towards large-scale enterprise, managed along professional lines. Trade union professionalism, concentrated at national level, became the counterpart, the two sides converging on national agreements. In the aftermath of the failed General Strike of 1926, employers and union officials found common ground in their search for 'constitutional' forms of joint regulation.

The second world war gave a further impetus to the setting up of national negotiating machinery, fifty-six new Joint Industrial Councils being created during 1939–45. At the end of the war, the Acts which established the nationalised industries all contained clauses compelling the newly created authorities to set up negotiating machinery with the appropriate trade unions. By 1946 already, some $15\frac{1}{2}$ million workers in industrial and service occupations were covered by collective machinery, or by statutory Wages Councils. Since the war, some 70 per cent of the working population has had its wages and working conditions regulated by these means.

The forms taken by collective bargaining vary widely as we shall see, but at the national level they all require an adequate degree of organisation and representation on the part of unions and employers. Since multi-unionism is the norm in British industry, then at national, company, and even at plant level, it is usually necessary for unions to 'recognise' each other's claims to represent a part of the work-force, and to form joint teams of negotiators to engage in bargaining. Sometimes these joint arrangement are formalised into Federations, (the Confederation of Shipbuilding and Engineering Unions comprises twenty-three unions with 2.4 million members), or into joint councils of unions, as is the case in the Post Office. TUC co-ordination of unions for bargaining purposes is embryonic although the TUC Steel Committee has some bargaining functions with British Steel. In other cases, unions simply negotiate amongst themselves about their relative share of seats on Joint Industrial Councils or Whitley Councils. Inter-union rivalries are sometimes manifest in this process, for example between NUPE and the general unions on Local Government and Health Service Committees, but there is a surprising degree of co-operation and mutual tolerance within many of these arrangements. Differences of policy on the same negotiating body between unions can emerge, as was the case between the TGWU and AUEW and the GMWU and EEPTU, over whether support should be given to shop steward opposition to settlement of Ford wage claims in 1969.[6] Only rarely do such disputes reach the stage of threatening the disruption of the bargaining machinery itself, and by the spread of their membership across many industries, the large general unions in particular acquire vast experience and expertise in operating joint union representation in literally hundreds of negotiating bodies.

Joint employers' organisation is necessary where the bargaining structure embraces more than a single firm, as is the case with the major national bargains in the private sector. Like trade unions, employers' associations have undergone a process of rationalistion and mergers: in 1936 there were 270 national federations of employers, whereas today the number is 172. In the past and particularly before the first world war, employers' associations were major innovators in the field of industrial relations, particularly in developing conciliation machinery and district agreements. Since the Reports of the Whitley Committee, government and unions have been more likely to initiate changes in bargaining practice, at least until the Report of the Donovan Royal Commission in 1968, since when individual companies, rather than associations of employers, have assumed a greater role in reforming structures and procedures, and the introduction of such things as 'fringe benefits' has been developed at company, rather than association, level. Of course, some associations retain over-all control in major national bargains, such as the Engineering Employers' Federation, whose negotiations with the CSEU cover $3\frac{1}{2}$ million workers. But the Donovan Report concluded that the most useful functions retained by employers' organisations were their provision of access to an industry-wide disputes procedure, and their symbolic representation of their members' commitment to the formalities of collective bargaining.[7]

Collective Bargaining Institutions

Collective bargaining takes place through a wide variety of institutions, and at several different levels. It is usual to distinguish between national, industry-wide bargains conducted either through a Joint Industrial Council or through more ad hoc meetings of the two parties, through public sector machinery arranged according to JIC (or Whitley) principles, through centralised bargaining in each nationalised industry, through independent ('non-federated') private sector company bargains, and through Wages Councils. These constitute what the Donovan Commission called the 'formal' institutions of the industrial relations system. In addition, though varying in significance between sectors and industries, there is widespread supplementary bargaining activity between shop stewards and local managers, at the level of the individual plant or work-place,—what Donovan called the 'informal' aspects of the system.

As we have already pointed out, Joint Industrial Councils were originally set up in response to the Whitley Committee's recommendations, with formal constitutions and a representative composition of employers, their associations, and the appropriate unions. Between 1918 and 1921, 73 Councils were formed; between the wars the numbers declined to a total of 45 in 1938. The second war saw a revival of the form, and in post-war Britain there have been around 200 Councils.[8] Some large private sector industries rely on purely ad hoc meetings for bargaining, and avoid the setting up of elaborate constitutional machinery. This is the case in engineering, where either the CSEU or the EEF can request a meeting of the two sides whenever necessary

The civil service and the National Health Service have elaborate structures of national bargaining committees going under the generic name of Whitley Councils divided into separate Councils for particular branches and grades of employees. Local government has a similar

structure of National bargaining committees, and each of the nationalised industries conducts its own separate national bargains with the
recognised unions. A feature of many of these formal structures is that
separate machinery, and separate bargains, are maintained for
craftworkers, semi- and un-skilled workers, and for non-manual employees.

Wages Councils are statutory bodies established to provide a means
of settlement of wages and certain basic conditions in industries where
voluntary collective bargaining has not evolved; they too are composed of employer and union representatives, but in their case with a
third element of independent members appointed by government.
Unlike the voluntary system, minimum wages determined by Wages
Councils have the force of law, though enforcement in practice is often
a difficult matter in back-street industries policed by an inadequate
number of government wages inspectors.

Broadly speaking, the distribution of the various forms of collective
bargaining amongst the working population is as follows:

1. Industry-wide agreements with important supplementary earnings from company/plant bargains (mainly private sector): 8
   million workers
2. Industry-wide agreements closely followed (mainly public
   sector): 6 million workers
3. Wages Council agreements (private sector): 3 million workers
4. No collective bargaining machinery (mainly white-collar in
   private sector): 4 million workers.[9]

These figures date from 1970. An alternative form of breakdown of
similar, but not directly comparable, figures for 1973 was derived from
the Third Report of the Pay Board as follows:

1. Public Sector Agreements: 4,442,000 workers
2. Wages Councils: 3,363,000 workers
3. Other national agreements: 4,871,000 workers
4. Company agreements: 4,797,000 workers.[10]

A third, and particularly revealing measure of the coverage of different form of agreement is provided in table VI:1, the figures again
relating to 1973.

From the table, it is possible to derive the following seven
conclusions. First, the majority of male workers are covered by
collective agreements, whether they be manual or non-manual. In the
case of male manual workers, the proportion is over 80 per cent.
Second, a majority of female workers are also covered by collective
agreements, and the proportion of female non-manual employees

Bargaining structure in 1973[17]

Percentages of full-time adults reported to be affected by various types of collective agreement

Agreement Coverage			National plus Supplementary Agreements	National Agreement only	Company District or Local Agreement only	No Agreement
Sample Group	Industry Group	All Agreements				
Manual Males	Manufacturing (n=31693)	83.9	45.0	24.1	14.8	16.1
	Non-manufacturing (n=31275)	82.6	19.3	57.3	6.0	17.4
	Private sector (n=43718)	77.4	33.8	31.5	12.1	22.6
	Public sector (n=19250)	93.3	25.2	62.2	5.9	6.7
	All (n=62968)	83.2	32.2	40.6	10.4	16.8
Non-manual males	Manufacturing (n=10670)	46.2	18.1	12.5	15.6	53.8
	Non-manufacturing (n=23343)	67.0	8.4	52.0	6.6	33.0
	Private sector (n=19741)	42.4	12.8	15.5	14.2	57.6
	Public Sector (n=14272)	85.0	9.3	72.9	2.7	15.0
	All (n=34013)	60.4	11.4	39.6	9.5	39.6
Manual females	Manufacturing (n=9021)	73.7	32.0	29.4	12.3	26.3
	Non-manufacturing (n=5232)	68.3	13.4	48.5	6.4	31.7
	Private sector (n=11424)	65.3	25.9	27.4	12.0	34.7
	Public sector (n=2829)	90.3	17.4	70.5	2.5	9.7
	All (n=14253)	71.7	25.2	36.4	10.1	28.3
Non-manual females	Manufacturing (n=4666)	47.0	16.7	13.5	16.8	53.0
	Non-manufacturing (n=21053)	68.8	7.5	55.7	5.5	31.2
	Private sector (n=13380)	43.6	11.8	19.3	12.5	56.4
	Public Sector (n=12339)	87.3	6.3	79.0	2.0	12.7
	All (n=25719)	64.8	9.2	48.1	7.6	35.2

Note: The public sector, for the purposes of this table, is made up of S.I.C. Nos. II, VI, XXI, XXII, XXV, XXVII. The public private sector division is thus only an approximation, since several of these S.I.C.'s contain private sector companies.

covered is actually greater than that of non-manual males. Thirdly, the public sector proves a higher proportion of coverage in all four groups (manual and non-manual males, manual and non-manual females) than does the private sector. Next, in no group does the proportion covered by 'national agreements plus supplementary agreements' reach 50 per cent, the highest being among manual males in manufacturing, where it reaches 45 per cent. Fifthly, in the category 'national agreement only' the public sector covers a majority in all four groups. Sixth, in no group does the coverage provided by 'company, district or local agreement only' reach 20 per cent. Lastly, only in the four categories of non-manual male and female workers in manufacturing and the private sector, do we find more than half the employees outside any kind of agreement. These findings illustrate both the wide-ranging coverage of collective bargaining, which is seen to be very much the norm throughout industry, and its relative strengths in different sectors of the labour force. They help towards an appraisal of the dominant analysis of the Donovan Royal Commission in 1968, which highlighted what it called the conflict between the 'formal' and the 'informal' systems of industrial relations in Britain.

> 'Britain has two systems of industrial relations . . . the formal system embodied in the official institutions [and] the informal system created by the actual behaviour of trade union and employers' associations, of managers, shop stewards and workers . . . The keystone of the formal system is the industry-wide collective agreement . . . The central defect in British industrial relations is the disorder . . . promoted by the conflict between the formal and the informal systems . . .'[12]

Later writers, commenting on this diagnosis, have argued that the Donovan dichotomy relies too much upon research evidence derived from the engineering industry, which does of course fall into the category 'national bargaining plus supplementary agreements' and which therefore lends itself to the support of theories of 'wages drift', claims of 'disorder' in bargaining, and the lament about the loss of official control over wages and industrial disputes. But it can be seen from table VI:1 that this kind of arrangement is not so dominant as the Donovan Report assumed.

Local and Plant Bargaining

Yet certainly it would be wrong now to belittle the role of local and plant bargaining. It has been the base on which trade union strength and influence has grown, ever since the war.

Plant bargaining by shop stewards cover a wide range of methods for raising the total earnings of their members, including; production/ shift bonuses, piece-work allowances and the price of jobs, special allowances for dirt, danger, and responsibility, comparability claims, merit money, general or flat rate increases, upgrading and overtime. Stewards deploy a whole arsenal of arguments in pressing these claims: changes in conditions of work, changes in the nature of the job, or abnormal working conditions; improvements in the amount of work produced, or the quality of labour and occupational knowledge; comparisons with other workers, low job evaluation ratings, or low piece-rates; the levels of company profits, are among some of those heard more frequently.

Some of these practices were regularised and formalised during the spate of productivity bargains which followed the recommendations of the Donovan Report and the pressures of Incomes Policy during the period from 1966 to 1970.[13] Whilst, for some shop stewards, productivity bargaining and the formalisation of company and plant agreements along the lines sketched out by Donovan may have represented a new constraint on their activities, for many others it meant a new involvement in bargaining in new areas of management decision-making, and a more active role vis-a-vis their full-time officials.[14] At the same time, as we have already shown in chapter five, their numbers have grown under the impact of this more sophisticated form of bargaining, as greater demands have been placed on them. Moreover, as the unions have democratised their internal government and bargaining procedures (admittedly unevenly, with more or less enthusiasm in the different head offices) stewards have in some cases penetrated to the levels at which national, company level, bargains are made,[15] and have obtained reporting-back rights in some industry-level bargains. Most significantly, pay disputes have commonly moved up from the plant to the industry level since the Donovan analysis was presented. This trend can be measured in the incidence of major national strikes during the 1970s. (This is discussed in chapter seven, below.)

In this context, it is not surprising that recent research has re-emphasised the importance of national agreements[16] and has stressed 'the extent to which the coverage of national agreements has grown in the post-war period'. Thus, basic pay, (largely negotiated at national level) rose as a percentage of standard weekly earnings from 80.8 per cent in 1968 to 83.5 per cent in 1973, for full-time males over 21. This is explained by a decline in the proportion of workers on payment-by-result schemes which have characteristically been negotiated at plant level. This proportion is volatile however; more recent evidence suggests a swing back to PBR systems of payment.

Whilst the balance of significance between industry and plant bargaining is important, a further level—that of company bargaining in what Stuart Holland called the meso-sector[17]—poses an unsolved structural problem for trade unions. As we emphasised in chapter five, the growth of the large, multi-plant and often multi-national company has removed managerial decision-making on major aspects of policy from the reach of plant-based shop stewards' committees; this has only been marginally rectified by the development of trade union combine committees with a bargaining role. Only 14 out of 150 of the largest British companies officially recognise Combine Committees.[18] At this level, the need to reform bargaining structures in order to confront the decision-makers, merges with the wider recent concern for the development of industrial democracy.

> 'Arguably the most substantial consequence of implementing the Bullock committee report would have been the strengthening of collective bargaining through building up combine committees. The report proposed to link employee directors and the employees through a Joint Representation Committee of (in most cases) shop stewards appointed by all the workplaces in the company. Given legal support and ample time and facilities, these JRCs would have made the combine committees of the present look amateurish.[19]

Traditionally, the subjects regarded as 'suitable' for collective bargaining have been largely restricted to wages, hours, and working conditions, although the pattern and location of such bargaining has varied widely. For instance in the engineering industry, central negotiations have determined minimum time rates for skilled, semi-skilled, and unskilled grades; these have been subject to supplementary District rates, and plant bargaining over piece-work times and prices. In JIC-type bargaining generally, it is customary at national level to determine minimum time rates, hours of work, paid holidays, overtime rates, and shift premia, and sometimes a minimum fall-back rate for piece-workers. National bargaining in Britain only rarely fixes a terminal date for an agreement; some industries experimented with two or three-year package deals in the 1960s, but they have fallen from favour since then. The most common practice, of course, is to revise agreements annually,—a post-war pattern which has been made almost inevitable by the pressures of inflation.

At plant level, in addition to the detailed determination of payment-by-result, there is frequent recourse to the payment of lieu rates, various forms of bonus payment, and merit pay, and it is here too that a range of working rules and practices are agreed. During the wave of productivity bargains of the late '60s and early '70s, management often succeeded in introducing job evaluated wage structures, and either introduced or extended the use of work-study, thus providing further subjects around which bargaining might take place.

The complicated make-up of the wage packets which emerge from these varied processes defies any standard description. Some occupations, such as teachers and nurses, rely almost entirely upon their basic pay determined nationally; some others, such as road haulage drivers and passenger transport workers (on both road and rail) depend for as much as 25 or 30 per cent of their earnings on overtime pay; still others, including manual workers in steel, engineering and the docks find that payment-by-result earnings account for between a fifth and a third of their actual earnings.

The managerial drive to replace payment-by-result systems, during the productivity bargaining phase, has recently been reversed for all groups except female manual workers. (see table VI:2).

Table VI:2

Workers receiving payments by results (percentages)

	1973	1978
Manual males: All industries and services	39.3	42.3
All manufacturing	43.3	45.0
Manual females: All industries and services	32.8	31.5
All manufacturing	45.2	43.0
Non-Manual males: All industries and services	7.9	10.6
All manufacturing	8.1	15.3
Non Manual females: All industries and services	3.3	6.2
All manufacturing	3.6	11.8

Source: New Earnings Survey, 1973 and 1978.

Within these aggregate figures are concealed some large changes: in coal-mining, the percentage of workers on payment-by-result rose from 8 per cent in 1973 to 86.8 per cent in 1978, as a consequence of the re-introduction of productivity bonuses after the major national strikes over national time-wages in 1972 and 1974. In the same period, the proportion on PBR in shipbuilding declined from 56.6 per cent to 36.2 per cent. For most industrial categories, the changes between the two years were much more marginal. But the range of coverage of PBR runs from only 1.3 per cent of postal and telecommunication workers to 93.7 per cent of workers in electricity supply. There does appear to have been a check to the spread of measured-day-work systems of payment (a high day wage with specified performance levels) which management was seeking to introduce a decade ago. (In 1973, about 9 per cent of manual workers were on MDW, but 13 per cent of all firms, employing 24 per cent of all workers, were planning to introduce it at that time.)[20]

The Subjects of Bargaining

In 1965, the Ministry of Labour reported that 'While collective bargaining has established itself firmly throughout the economy so that the wages, hours and holidays of the great majority of workers are settled by such bargaining, the scope of its subject matter is relatively narrow by comparison with some other countries like the USA . . .'[21] It went on to note that

'One area which has been relatively neglected may be described broadly as "security of employment". Such matters as the period of notice of dismissals, arrangements for dealing with possible redundancies, sick pay, pension schemes, and the circumstances justifying individual dismissal have not been the subject of collective bargaining for workers generally.'[22]

Since that report was written, trade union policy has developed a much wider ambition, which is to bring virtually the whole territory of management decision-making into the process of collective bargaining. Progress towards this goal is varied and many times removed from completion, but the trend is evident. In 1971, as part of its campaign against statutory regulation of industrial relations under the *Industrial Relations Act*, the TUC published a guide for negotiators which stressed the need for trade unions to bargain for (i) improved shop steward facilities (ii) manpower planning (iii) job and income security (including guaranteed weeks, pensions, sick pay and injury pay, discipline and dismissals) and (iv) disclosure of information.[23] Legislation carried between 1974 and 1976 encouraged such trends by providing some statutory reinforcement to the demands for bargaining over redundancies, information disclosure, and health and safety (see our chapter on the Law and Trade Unions). A steady trickle of newly signed 'Information Agreements' have been signed between individual companies and trade unions, which provide for regular flows of information from companies to unions on specified items of company affairs, even if the unions are often disappointed with the results of such negotiations. ICI has set up Central and Divisional Business Investment Committees, on which sit shop steward representatives. These committees receive hitherto secret company information. Fords have received (and partially responded to) a lengthy shopping list of items of information requested by the unions from the company.[24] At one stage in the lifetime of the Labour government of 1974-9, it seemed that unions would become involved in the negotiation of company Planning Agreements with the government and major companies, but after 1975 the concept was heavily diluted in the wording of the final version of the *Industry Act 1975*; planning agreements were made optional rather than compulsory, and trade unions were accorded only a consultative role. In the event only one such agreement was made in the private sector, at the time when Chryslers were on the point of withdrawing from motor manufacture.

In the debate on the proposals of the Bullock Committee (see chapter eight, below) some unions took the view that it was a mistake to demand statutory and mandatory re-structuring of company Boards to include trade union representatives; they preferred the approach followed in Sweden, where statutory obligations are placed on companies to negotiate with unions across the whole field of decision-making. (It should be added that the Swedes do place two worker-directors on company boards, to obtain information for the collective bargaining process.) This would represent the ultimate development of the method of collective bargaining. Whilst it is too early to quantify the progress into new territories of bargaining, the direction of change, from the base of wage bargaining upwards into corporate decision-making, is manifest. Most recently, in the face of the silicon-chip revolution in industrial technology, the TUC is urging its affiliates to bargain about the use of new technologies.

'Companies should be asked by trade unions to set up study teams to prepare an assessment of the potentialities of introducing micro-processors into their production processes as a basis for new or improved products. The teams, which should include trade union representation, should present a set of proposals to both management and unions. The aim then should be for both sides to agree a plan which should include the changes to be introduced and a timescale for action. A manpower and social plan should also be produced covering matters such as retraining, future requirements for labour differentiated by type, the scope for reducing working time, and improvements in the quality of working life. If there is a forecast that some workers will be displaced, then the company and trade unions should study the prospects for successfully diversifying and developing new products with the objective of avoiding redundancies and expanding the company's labour force.'[25]

In the business of proposing new products, based on criteria of social usefulness, the Alternative Corporate Plan of the Lucas Combine Shop Stewards Committee has of course been the pioneer.[26]

A variant on this method has also been proposed by the TUC.

'One approach which could combine the development of collective bargaining with a response to technological change would be the pursuit of New Technology Agreements. These might incorporate initially various aspects of existing agreements such as status-quo and mutuality clauses but would seek to turn them into more positive provisions. The first principle of such an approach would be that no new technology which has major effects on the workforce should be introduced unilaterally. Full agreement on the range of negotiating issues should be a precondition of technological change.'[27]

An example of this kind of New Technology Agreement is that between the ACTT (cine technicians) and the Independent Television Contractors Association. Operative from July 1978, it states:

'When a company is contemplating the introduction of any automated and/or new equipment, discussions shall take place locally between the accredited representatives of the Union and representatives of the company *prior* to the ordering of the new equipment.'[28]

The Results of Collective Agreements

Returning to the time-honoured themes of wages and hours, we should record that the forty-hour week, established in Britain by collective bargaining in the early 1960s, now stands, in the trade union view, in need of further reduction, in the face of mass unemployment and the prospects offered by new technology. The 35-hour week is now the official policy goal of the TUC and individual unions, as well as of the European TUC. In fact a whole series of bargaining options is available to reduce working time, including longer holidays, sabbatical leave, educational leave, early retirement, the four day week, and the raising of the school-leaving age. What choices the unions in Britain will make, and whether they will rely entirely upon collective bargaining, or turn to the method of Legal Enactment in pursuit of this aim, remains to be seen. A legislative initiative has been widely canvassed in Belgium, linking provision for a reduction to a 38 hour week, with a requirement to expand manning levels as hours are reduced.[29]

Finally on wages, the key queston remains: how effective is collective bargaining in producing results for union members? This question involves two aspects: first, how far does collective bargaining advance wages beyond those which would be paid; and second, how far the sector of wage-incomes has encroached historically upon that of profits and property income during the development of trade unionism. This last question we will examine below, in our discussion of incomes policies and their implications. To the first question, it can be demonstrated that collective agreements made by trade unions do indeed influence relative wages.

Table VI:3
Average gross hourly earnings by all agreements and no agreement
(Adults in Great Britain in April, 1973)[30]

Agreement coverage	Industry group	1 All agreements	2 Differential	3 No agreement
Sample Group				
		£	%	£
Manual males	Manufacturing	0.87	+ 8.8	0.80
	Non-manufacturing	0.79	+16.2	0.68
	Public sector	0.81	+12.5	0.72
	Private sector	0.84	+12.0	0.75
	All	0.83	+12.2	0.74
Manual females	Manufacturing	0.52	+13.0	0.46
	Non-manufacturing	0.49	+28.9	0.38
	Public sector	0.50	+31.6	0.38
	Private sector	0.51	+18.6	0.43
	All	0.51	+18.6	0.43
Non-manual males	Manufacturing	1.13	−14.4	1.32
	Non-manufacturing	1.25	0.0	1.25
	Public sector	1.28	+ 6.7	1.20
	Private sector	1.13	−11.7	1.28
	All	1.21	− 4.7	1.27
Non-manual females	Manufacturing	0.57	− 1.7	0.58
	Non-manufacturing	0.76	+33.3	0.57
	Public sector	0.83	+36.1	0.61
	Private sector	0.58	+ 3.6	0.56
	All	0.73	+28.1	0.57

It appears from this table that all sections of the labour force, except non-manual males and non-manual females in the manufacturing and private sectors, benefit from the operation of collective bargaining. It is interesting to note that in these two exceptional cases, it seems that men working in private industry cost more to 'buy off' from the lure of trade unionism than do their female counter-parts! Other findings by the authors of this table are worth looking at. As we have just seen, they find an earnings differential which favours groups covered by collective agreement over those not covered. This favourable differential is lower when the collective agreement in question includes a high proportion of the total group, than it is in agreements involving more restricted groupings. Wide-coverage agreements seem to exact greater indirect influence through the use of so-called 'coercive comparisons': though we might add that legislative encouragement to use the collectively agreed rate to bring non-covered employers into line (the Schedule 11 procedure of the Employment Protection Act— which is discussed in chapter nine) could have begun to have an effect in this area. They found a positive wage differential for those covered by decentralised, over those covered only by centralised, bargaining. Thomson and his colleagues found that supplementary components in the wage packet weighed heavier in those covered by decentralised bargaining, and they found that the dispersion of earnings (the gap between higher and lower incomes) was lower in groups covered by collective agreements, than in those not covered. This finding supports the view that trade unionism exerts an equalising pressure on earning differentials.

Procedures

Collective bargaining, the joint regulation of industrial relations, includes procedural rules as well as the substantive matters with which we have so far been concerned in this chapter.

In outline, the pattern looks like this:

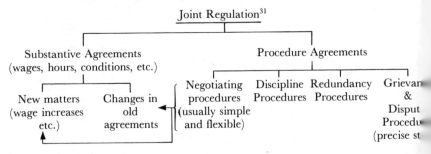

Many disputes procedures in the pre-Donovan era were rightly criticised by trade unions and by the Donovan Commission itself, for their employer-bias, the delays built into them, and for the narrowness of their scope. The classic case was that of the 1922 Engineering National Agreement. This contained the well-known affirmation of 'employers' prerogatives', and gave employers great freedom to innovate without negotiating. At the same time it involved months of delay in 'processing' a worker's grievance or dispute through a number of stages to a national conference in York, where employers sat in judgement.[32] Major disagreements arose over the revision of this procedure. The unions wanted a commitment that employers would talk *before* bringing changes, rather than after the event. This became known as the issue of the 'status quo': in which a formula was sought to require an employer to 'go through' the disputes procedure before innovating against the wishes of union members. The 1922 agreement was terminated in 1971. Until 1976, when a new agreement was at last made, there was no national disputes procedure in engineering, and the ensuing dependence on purely local or plant procedures for the resolution of disputes was admitted by the employers to have forced them to give greater attention to local settlement of disputes.[33]

In 1976 a new national engineering disputes agreement was signed between the EEF and the CSEU. There is no longer any reference to employer prerogatives in this document. It sets out a simple procedure outside the plant, limiting the scope for delay to a joint conference which must be held within seven days of an application (and which can in fact be held in the works concerned). In this agreement there is now a comprehensive status quo clause, which reads:

'Where any party wishes to raise a matter for resolution, there shall be discussion at domestic or national level as appropriate. It is agreed that in the event of any difference arising which cannot immediately be disposed of, then whatever practice or agreement existed prior to the difference shall continue to operate pending a settlement or until the agreed procedure is exhausted.'

Here the emphasis placed by trade union and TUC policy, upon brevity, local settlement, and the status quo, have all been achieved. Engineering is by no means an exception, since similar reforms of disputes procedures have been widely adopted, largely through union pressure, in the past decade. Of course, JIC, industry-level disputes procedures still survive and are used—for example in the chemical industry, whose JIC, embracing 296 companies through the Chemical Industry Association, provides a comprehensive procedure for 'dealing with grievances of all kinds'.[34] But in the complicated and overlapping mixture of plant and national procedures, described below, the recent emphasis is on speedy, domestic resolution of grievances and disputes.

> Many grievance procedures are purely domestic, being concerned essentially with laying down a recognised method of bringing a grievance to attention and securing further consideration of the issue if it is not settled when first raised. This is normally achieved through a staged procedure of progressive reference to higher authority . . .
>
> The final stage of domestic procedure may be the end of the road for both small and large firms but both may have recourse to outside help through the external stages of an industry-wide procedure. Of the industry procedures studied 98 per cent contained provisions for resolving disputes at industry level, the large majority being incorporated in jointly-negotiated agreements. 78 per cent of the agreements also contained provisions for dispute resolution at domestic level and 44 per cent at intermediate level. The commonest provision for dispute resolution at industry level was some form of joint disputes committee but 17 per cent of the agreements provided for a joint arbitration body drawn from within the industry with the power to make an award.
>
> Both management and unions normally prefer to settle at domestic level rather than commit an issue to external procedures.'[35]

A model example of a domestic procedure, emphasising status quo, speed, and the key role of the shop steward, is provided by the TGWU.

> '(a) any grievance arising in a department shall be raised with the shop steward by the employee or employees . . . and the matter shall be dealt with by the steward and appropriate foreman.
>
> (b) if the matter is not satisfactorily settled the shop steward shall seek to resolve the matter with the departmental head.
>
> (c) if the grievance is still unresolved a meeting shall be arranged between the senior stewards and the management who shall endeavour to satisfactorily settle the matter. In the event of continuing difficulty the senior stewards may call in the appropriate full-time union officer to assist.
>
> (d) until all the above stages have been exhausted the conditions applying immediately before the action leading to the dispute shall apply.
>
> (e) it shall be the spirit and intention of both company and union that there will be no undue delay in progressing issues through the above procedure.'[36]

Shop stewards have won more control in recent years not only over disputes procedures, but, as we have noticed earlier, in *negotiating* procedures as well. In the post-Donovan era, the TUC first tentatively invited unions' views on this desirability of this trend—

' . . . Comment is invited from unions as to whether there should generally be the opportunity for joint negotiators to put major agreements to shop stewards' committees so that questions can be raised and answered before an agreement is signed.'[37]

Five years on, this caution gave way to a wholehearted welcome:

'A feature . . . in the private sector, and also parts of the public sector, has been the increasing paticipation by lay members in vital negotiations . . . Coupled with the extension of the areas of collective bargaining and improvement of procedures at all levels, it represents a major increase in collective bargaining.'[38]

Collective bargaining, unless constrained by statutory limitations, always implies a possibility of 'failure to agree', between the parties. During the process of negotiation, whether through the disputes or negotiating procedures, it is usual for the parties to accept formally that no strike or lock-out should be declared. (Of course this undertaking is not always observed; 'unconstitutional' strikes are a feature of the industrial relations scene, and we discuss this contentious issue in chapter seven). But what happens when the formal procedure is 'exhausted'—that is, when all stages have been used, without agreement having been reached? The answer varies from industry to industry. In some cases, the parties are immediately free to take industrial action, whilst in others, provision is made for recourse to either internal or external conciliation, mediation, and/or arbitration.

Arbitration and Conciliation

Some industries, notably in the public sector (such as railways and the civil service) have their own specific arbitration tribunals to which disputes are finally referred. Others—the vast majority—use the government-financed but independent services of the Advisory, Conciliation and Arbitration Service (ACAS) and the Central Arbitration Committee (CAC). The origins of these services dates back to the late 19th century when government, impressed by what it observed of private arrangements for conciliation operating in a number of industries (such as steel, and the boot and shoe industry) assumed powers under the *Conciliation Act* 1896 to provide arbitration and conciliation services where these were requested voluntarily by both parties to a dispute. Thus the principle was established that government would offer a service, but would not impose any obligation to use it. Following this precedent, a permanent arbitration court, adhering to the same principles, was set up in 1919 (the *Industrial Court Act*). An element of compulsory, unilateral arbitration was introduced during both world wars, when strikes were illegal. This became a permanent feature after the second war, enabling first the Industrial Disputes Tribunal, and later the Industrial Court to make legally binding awards to apply where employers were judged not to be observing minimum standards of pay established by collective bargaining. The former Industrial Court has undergone several changes in title, and has now been succeeded by the CAC established under the *Employment Protection Act* 1975. The CAC provides traditional voluntary, mutually acceptable arbitration in single industrial disputes, and also compulsory unilateral judgements on minimum wage questions, (under Schedule 11 of the *Employment Protection Act*), union recognition, and disclosure of information. The conciliation services formerly provided successively by the Board of Trade, the Ministry of Labour, and the Department of Employment, have now been hived off to the independent, tripartitely administered ACAS. The creation of such a service, independent of government and the civil service, was felt to be necessary to restore confidence in the whole method, following long periods in the post-war years when unions felt that government was influencing arbitration awards and its conciliation officers in the interests of state wage restraint policies. The ACAS governing body, its Council, has declared that it will not be an 'interpreter, monitor, or enforcement agent of an incomes policy.'[39]

Conciliation is a process in which a third party assists the two sides to resume talks after a breakdown or deadlock in negotiations. It is a voluntary procedure, and conciliators make neither awards nor pronouncements concerning the issues at stake. Their diplomatic skills are deployed to bring about renewed discussion, and once talks reopen, the conciliators' role is at an end.

During the 1960s, ministry conciliators were handling some 2-300 disputes a year, 40-50 per cent of which were about pay, 30 per cent about trade union recognition, and 10 per cent about redundancy and dismissals.[40] Their successor, ACAS, with a staff of 819, (660 of them based in regional offices) conciliated in 2,706 disputes in 1978, 1,997 of which were successfully brought to settlement. The usual subjects of dispute were again wages, union recognition, dismissal and discipline, and redundancy. Trade unions asked for conciliation services in 56 per cent of cases, employers in 18 per cent, 22 per cent were joint requests, and in 3 per cent, ACAS took the initiative itself.

In addition to collective conciliation cases, ACAS has a duty to conciliate in cases where individuals complain of loss of rights to an Industrial Tribunal. The service handled 44,713 such cases in 1978, of which 39,289 were cases of unfair dismissal. 34 per cent of these cases were settled by conciliation, 4 per cent were settled privately, and 25 per cent were withdrawn. This left 37 per cent which went forward to hearings of Industrial Tribunals.

ACAS also provides an arbitration, investigation, and mediation service. In the case of arbitration (which differs from conciliation in that the arbitration body makes a definite decision, or award, to settle the dispute) ACAS may appoint a single arbitrator, or an ad hoc arbitration board, or may refer the case to the Central Arbitration Committee. Mediation may be defined as a more formal type of conciliation, and is a variant on the services offered by ACAS. In 1978, ACAS appointed 346 single arbitrators in disputes, set up 39 ad hoc boards, refereed 5 cases to the CAC, and appointed outside mediators in 29 cases. Government pay policy, which left little room for disputes, reduced the number of general wage claims requiring arbitration in 1978 to 4 per cent of all arbitration cases, whereas in 1975, when no incomes policy was operating during the first six months, they had comprised 29 per cent. A measure of the range of the ACAS conciliation service can be obtained from table VI:4.

Table VI:4

Completed conciliation cases analysed by cause of dispute[41]

| | 1977 | | 1978 | |
	No. of cases	%	No. of cases	%
Pay and terms and conditions	1,601	55.4	1,652	61.0
Recognition	635	22.0	451	16.7
Demarcation	32	1.1	26	1.0
Other trade union matters	143	4.9	130	4.8
Redundancy	134	4.6	91	3.4
Dismissal and discipline	239	8.3	218	8.0
Others	107	3.7	138	5.1
Total	2,891	100	2,706	100

The CAC is made up of a chairman, a panel of deputy chairmen, and panels of members with experience as representatives of employers and of workers. For any one case, the Committee will comprise a chairman and one representative each from the employers' and unions' panel. Its function as arbitrator in voluntary cases arising from orthodox industrial disputes is now a small part of its total workload; out of a total of 836 awards made in 1978, only 3 were voluntary arbitration cases.[42] 519 cases were brought in that year under Schedule 11 (Terms and conditions of Employment) of the *Employment Protection Act*, 7 cases involved trade union recognition, and 10 were disputes about disclosure of information. Awards made under Fair Wages Resolutions totalled 271, and the rest of the cases concerned CAC powers to arbitrate under specific pieces of legislation applying to particular industries, (like the *Road Traffic Act* 1960, or the *Road Haulage Wages Act* 1938), or to particular groups (like the *Equal Pay Act* 1970.

In outline, then, we have the British collective bargaining system: based on trade union rights to organise and negotiate, on employers' recognition of these rights, covering wages and conditions for the vast majority of the labour force, but expanding into new areas of decision-making, embracing both substantive agreements and voluntary procedural rules, and supported by officially-sponsored, statutory, but independent conciliation and arbitration services. Up to this point, we have chosen to ignore a major anomaly, which in most years since the second world war, has challenged the assumptions of voluntarism and independence on which this system has rested. We have passed over Government wages and incomes policies. We must now put this right.

Incomes Policy

Our chief concern in looking at incomes policy is to appraise its implications for the traditional, and indeed for any alternative, role for trade unions. Before attempting this however, a brief summary of incomes policy experience is necessary. The traditional role of the state in wage-fixing, since the repeal of the Combination Laws in 1824–5, up until the second world war, has usually been assumed to have been one of 'non-intervention'. In fact this has only been true in so far as market forces in the labour market, and trade union weakness and immaturity, were in such a condition that wage movements did not threaten the stability of the capitalist market system. In both world wars, when there was a great shortage of labour, the government did not hesitate to impose compulsory arbitration. This was clearly intended to prevent trade union bargaining power from 'pushing up wages too far'. And in 1925–6, at the climax of half-a-decade of conflict generated by employers' attempted wage cuts, the Prime Minister, Mr Baldwin, explicitly embraced a 'wages policy' when, following the return to the gold standard at the pre-1914 parity, he told the TUC leaders that 'we must all accept wage cuts to put the country on its feet'.

But it is of course with the post-1945 experience of much more overtly interventionist Government policy on wages that trade unions must now be most concerned. That experience has moved through a number of phases. The 'Stafford Cripps policy' of 1948–50 consisted of official Government pronouncements and appeals calling for wage restraint, rising to a call for a wages freeze in 1949. Although the Government took no direct powers to enforce wage limits, it applied its policy in the public sector, and won the support of the TUC for its general policy for a period of eighteen months. Rising inflation provoked by the devaluation of the pound, and the Korean war, led to increasing opposition from the trade unions, and to the defeat of the TUC General Council's commitment to the continuation of the policy, at the 1950 TUC Congress.

During the 1950s, Conservative Governments tried to obtain agreement for a policy of voluntary wage restraint. These met with little trade union sympathy. Government influence on statutory wage fixing bodies was resented by the unions, who rejected the policies advocated by a government-established Council on Prices, Productivity and Incomes (the Cohen Council).

In 1961, the Government went further towards direct wage restraint by imposing a 'Pay Pause'; again no statutory powers were invoked, but the Government used its influence in the public sector and amongst arbitrators, to ensure a measure of adherence to the policy. The Pause was followed in 1962 by an attempt to establish a long-term incomes policy, and a 'norm' of $2-2\frac{1}{2}$ per cent wage increases was proposed. A National Incomes Commission was established to police the policy, which the TUC opposed and boycotted.

The returning Labour Government in 1964 abolished the Conservative's NIC, and initially operated a voluntary policy on incomes, prices, and productivity, based on a Joint Statement of Intent signed by government, the TUC, and the employers. A new body, the National Board for Prices and Incomes, was set up to examine particular cases of wage claims. A White Paper in 1965 laid down the criteria on which the Board would judge both proposed price and wage increases, and a norm of $3-3\frac{1}{2}$ per cent for wage increases was announced. Increases above that amount were only to be justified by acceptance of 'improved working practices' leading to higher productivity.

The TUC, still anxious to make the policy work voluntarily, set up its own 'early warning' system for vetting pay claims by their affiliated unions; the Government created a statutory early warning system of its own, requiring companies and unions to notify it of proposed wage and price increases. In 1966, the Government decreed a statutory freeze on wages and prices which lasted six months. Orders preventing increases had the force of law, and striking against them was illegal. A 'nil norm' followed during 1967, only exceptional cases for increases based on stringent productivity criteria being allowed. The Government retained its statutory authority to enforce this degree of restraint. In 1968 a $3\frac{1}{2}$ per cent norm of wage increases was introduced, and the Government continued to foster productivity deals. During these years these became a widespread method of obtaining the wage increases demanded by union members, since the cost of living was specifically ruled out as a criterion on which extra pay increases might be conceded. Such policies persisted through 1969; in 1970 a new norm of $2\frac{1}{2}$–$4\frac{1}{2}$ per cent was decreed, and the policy was relaxed to accept claims based not only on productivity, but on the general ground of low pay, public sector pay, and equal pay for women. By the end of the Labour government's period in office, the policy was visibly breaking down. It went out in the tumult of an unprecedented wave of major strikes.

The Conservative Government of 1970–4 began by abolishing the NBPI and the Government's wage restraint powers. Following substantial pay settlements in the public sector in 1970–1, a government policy of reducing each subsequent settlement by 1 per cent was enforced in that sector. This provoked several major official strikes. Following the failure of Downing Street talks in 1972 between the Prime Minister and TUC and employer representatives, which were aimed at achieving a voluntary code of co-operation on restraint, the Government imposed a ninety-day statutory pay and prices freeze—Phase 1 of its Counter-Inflationary Policy.[43] This was succeeded by Phase 2,[44] which set up a Pay Board and propounded a norm of £1 a week increase plus 4 per cent on the average pay bill per head up to a ceiling of a £250 annual increase for any individual. The statutory Phase 3[45] extended the role of the Pay Board and created a norm for increases of £2.25 or 7 per cent (whichever was greater) in the average pay bill per head, plus 1 per cent flexibility margin, plus threshold payments geared to the rise in the cost of living, up to a maximum of £4.80. There was also a maximum of £350 per annum for individual increases.

The assault on these policies was led by the miners, in 1972 and 1973–4, and the subsequent General Election in February 1974, called at the height of a miners' strike, led to the defeat of the Government.

The Labour Government of 1974–9 commenced its period in office with a voluntary policy, agreed with the TUC, and based on TUC guidelines calling for wage increases simply to keep pace with increases in the cost of living.[46] In July 1975, the Government, after difficult bargaining with the TUC, again obtained endorsement for a limit on wage increases, of a flat rate supplement of up to £6. The TUC's guidelines were actually reproduced in the appropriate Government White Paper.[47] A person earning more than £8,500 was denied any wage increase. On the insistence of the TUC, and especially of Jack Jones, this phase was the first which had created a flat rate, as opposed to a percentage, norm. In 1976-7, (the Government and the TUC having by now succeeded in adopting an agreed annual wage round running from July to July,) the TUC again bargained with Government to establish guidelines subsequently endorsed in a White Paper.[48] On this occasion, a further supplement on earnings was agreed: it was fixed at up to £2.50 per week for those earnings under £50 a week, up to 5 per cent for those earning between £50 and £80 a week. A £4 flat rate was applied to those earning more than £80 a week By 1977, the strains of these successive policies within the trade union movement were beginning to make themselves felt; differentials had been seriously distorted and the call for a return to free collective bargaining was strongly pressed at TUC meetings. Between 1977 and 1978, the Government's unilateral creation of a 10 per cent norm[49] fared badly in some major private sector settlements and provoked strikes in the public sector—notable amongst which was an official strike of firemen. In 1978-9, Government was again faced with determined trade union requirements for an end to norms, and a return to unfettered collective bargaining. It persisted however in seeking to impose a 5 per cent norm,[50] (substantially below the rise in the cost of living) and had to face a winter of severe strike action, involving lorry drivers, and many groups in the public service. The Government's powers to penalise private firms which settled above the norm, (by denying them contracts or financial supports) were removed by the House of Commons, and the 5 per cent policy was commonly held to have been an important factor in the defeat of the Labour administration in the election of May 1979.

The policy of the restored Conservative Government disavowed any interest in incomes policy, and it seemed to be the intention of the main leaders of this administration to rely upon monetary policies and increased unemployment to secure the dampening effect upon wage claims which had previously been obtained by direct State intervention.

This account has necessarily been brief, and has not spelt out the detailed effects of incomes policies on Governments and trade unions at any stage. In fact it can be said that wage restraint has been a rock on which successive Governments have foundered in the post-war years, and it has been a factor introducing great uncertainty in the minds of trade unionists. It is now necessary to appraise this experience, and to ask what it implies for the future of trade unionism.

The Experience of State Intervention

Upon what principle should wages be allocated? The question, which is involved in any attempt at incomes policy, poses greater difficulties than are commonly admitted in newspapers, although some informed people have always been willing to confess that it has perplexed them. Speaking a hundred years ago, for instance, Judge Ellison, who had been invited to umpire a mining dispute in Yorkshire, allowed himself to be recorded as saying:

> 'It is (he said) for (the employers' advocate) to put the men's wages as high as he can. It is for (the men's advocate) to put them as low as he can. And when you have done that it is for me to deal with the question as well as I can; but on what principle I have to deal with it I have not the slightest idea. There is no principle of law involved in it. There is no principle of political economy in it. Both masters and men are arguing and standing upon what is completely within their rights. The master is not bound to employ labor except at a price which he thinks will pay him. The man is not bound to work for wages that won't assist (subsist) him and his family sufficiently, and so forth. So that you are both within your rights; and that's the difficulty I see in dealing with the question.'[51]

Almost certainly the judge was at that time unaware that an identical point had been made by Karl Marx, in *Capital*, which had been published in German twelve years earlier. 'There is here', he had written, 'an antinomy, right against right, both equally bearing the seal of the law of exchanges. Between equal rights, force decides'.[52] In this tradition, there grew up a long-term socialist opposition to what became known as 'the bondage of wagery', in which the whole relationship of employees to employers, or, as it was described, the system of wage-labour was exposed to powerful criticism.

In modern England this may seem strange, since 'free collective bargaining' is nowadays commonly perceived to be a war-cry of militant trade unionists, and leftwing *opposition* to such bargaining may not be easily understood. Yet such opposition was at one time widely argued.

Judge Ellison was, of course, speaking when there was a comparatively free market in operation, as compared with today's multi-nationally cartelised economy. If Labour markets have always been less 'free' than many economists have believed, today we stand on the brink of major technological changes which could radically worsen the bargaining position of Labour. At the same time, the concentration of ownership and the growth of industrial scale have produced recurrent and persistent pressures for incomes policies in order to 'plan' the distribution of pay, and thus limit the force of labour market pressures on companies.

Here it is important to distinguish between the relatively profitable meso-sector of giant transnational companies, which can commonly afford high wages and remain viable, and a growing slum sector of the economy in which dire market pressures might squeeze out employment altogether if what many would regard as minimal conditions of work and reward were established. Both these sectors are privately controlled. Under public control there is a similar mix, with a greater concentration of ailing industries, and the perennial problem of welfare services which are never adequately funded to meet the need they have uncovered.

This dual economy poses problems for any Government which wishes to tax industrial concerns, since it positively needs an elastic measure if it is not to choke life out of the uncompetitive sector at one extreme, or to feather-bed the great quasi-monopolistic concerns at the other. The same issue already applies to trade unions, and is likely immeasurably to complicate the discussion on any future incomes policies unless the manufacturing basis of the British economy can be miraculously resuscitated.

Economic laws will increasingly allow that rewards in the two sectors remain different, whilst their members will continue to shop in the same supermarkets. Free collective bargaining, if it is not prevented, may well expose the limits of these differences, but it will provide no machinery for passing over them. Legislative enactment (for shorter hours or longer holidays, or for minimum wages) could have some limited impact, but in the mid-term this would only be effective if it were backed by entrepreneurial intervention (possibly by the State or workers' co-operatives as well as or instead of the current directorship) to overcome the capital and planning starvation of the weak enterprises.

The traditional argument for incomes policies was summed up by Harold Wilson, speaking at the 1964 TUC:

'We have the right to ask for an incomes policy because we are prepared to contribute the three necessary conditions. First, an assurance of rising production and rising incomes, so that the sacrifice, the restraint, for which we ask is matched by an assurance that it will result in increased production and increased rewards. Second, an assurance of equity and social justice, in that our policies will be directed to the benefit of the nation as a whole and not to the advantage of a sectional interest. Third, an assurance that what we ask for in wages and salaries will apply equally to profits and dividends—and rents.'[53]

Table VI:5

Income shares as a percentage of gross national product at factor cost: United Kingdom 1860-9 to 1976[54]

Years	Employee compensation	Income from self-employment Farmers	Income from self-employment Others	Corporate profits	Rent	Total domestic profits	Net property income from abroad	Gross national product
1860-9	45.2	6.4	30.6		14.8		3.0	100
1870-9	45.2	4.5	32.1		13.7		4.5	100
1880-9	46.2	2.7	31.4		13.9		5.8	100
1890-9	48.0	2.4	30.8		12.5		6.2	100
1900-9	47.7	2.3	31.3		12.1		6.6	100
1910-14	47.3	2.5	13.7	17.1	11.0	28.1	8.4	100
1921-4	58.5	2.1	15.1	13.0	6.8	19.8	4.5	100
1925-9	58.1	1.3	14.8	12.5	7.5	20.0	5.8	100
1930-4	59.3	1.6	13.4	12.5	9.0	21.5	4.2	100
1935-8	58.9	1.6	11.6	15.0	8.8	23.8	4.1	100
1946-9	65.3	2.9	9.4	16.8	4.0	20.8	1.7	100
1950-4	65.3	2.8	7.8	18.0	3.9	21.9	2.1	100
1955-9	67.0	2.3	6.9	18.0	4.5	22.5	1.3	100
1960-3	67.4	2.1	6.3	17.9	5.1	23.0	1.2	100
1964-8	67.6		8.0	16.8	6.4	23.2	1.2	100
1969-73	68.9		9.0	13.2	7.6	20.8	1.3	100
1974	70.6		9.3	10.0	7.5	17.5	1.7	100
1975	73.5		8.8	9.3	7.4	16.7	1.0	100
1976	71.5		8.5	10.6	7.3	17.9	1.1	100
1977	69.7		9.4	13.0	7.5	20.5	0.4	100
1978	69.5		9.2	13.2	7.6	20.8	0.5	100

It is, to say the very least, difficult to apply these assurances during a prolonged slump with stagnant production and falling real incomes, in which it is clear that supernatural efforts will be required to enable any prospect of recovery to be maintained.

In fact, even in times of relatively rapid growth, the mechanisms of incomes policy did not secure the kind of redistribution of the social product which was commonly advanced as their purpose. In fact, the sector of wages and salary incomes improved by 0.2 per cent of the Gross National Product during the four years of this policy. In the next four years, after the collapse of the policy it further improved, in the course of a veritable tidal wave of strikes and industrial unrest, by 1.3 per cent. During the cataclysm in which the Heath administration was carried off, it improved in one single year by 1.7 per cent. In the first and only deliberately redistributive year of the social contract, 1975, it improved by 2.9 per cent. Thereafter it declined, and in 1978 it was once again below the 1974 level.

Profits, by 1978, were restored to the same level (20.8 per cent) at which they had been in 1969–73. Incomes policy during the majority of these years had registered rather limited direct gains for the whole sector of wages and salaries, when compared to the effects of its indirect impact, through the strikes and unrest which it invariably provoked. Only in 1975 was there a conspicuous exception to this pattern.

But although the sector of wages, taken in relation to other broad sectors, went through a cycle during the second half of the 'seventies, in which at the end it arrived back close to its starting point, there was nonetheless a certain tendency inside that sector for differentials to be reduced.

This appears quite markedly when we examine the gross weekly earnings of full-time workers. A certain equalitarian movement has taken place among manual workers, between non-manual and manual workers, within the limits we have already discussed between men and women, and last, but very important, between private and public sectors. This can be clearly seen in table VI:6.

However, this modest degree of levelling had not at all taken place in the context described by Mr Wilson, but rather at a time of severely restricted growth or actual decline, during unrelenting inflation, with rising unemployment and heightened social tension. Hardly surprisingly, it has not therefore been seen as an unmitigated or universal benefit. Indeed, as insecurity has become widespread, there has been a considerable increase of resentment at the erosion of these time-honoured differentials, and many people would ascribe to this fact the main reason for Mrs Thatcher's remarkable success in winning votes from trade unionists during the 1979 election. If economic growth

Table VI:6

Gross weekly earnings of full-time workers: differentials 1970-77[55]

Workers	1970	1974	1975	1976	1977
Male Manual Workers					
Top decile % of Median	149.6	145.3	145.8	145.9	145.6
Top decile % of Bottom	230	219	216	214	212
Male Non-manual Workers					
Top decile % of Median	178.8	173.9	168.2	169.7	166.0
Top decile % of Bottom	309	293	282	282	274
Non-manual Median					
% of Manual Median	123	115	116	118	119
Women Median % of Men Median					
Manual	51	55.5	59.5	62.5	64
Non-manual	52	55	59	61.5	62
Public % of Private					
Men Manual	93	97	105	102	100
Non-manual	103	102	106	110	106
Women Manual	100	106	112	108	105
Non-manual	140	132	140	137	130

certainly gives no guarantee of redistribution of income, lack of such growth most assuredly does not make it any easier. We arrive once again at a truism, that questions of income are intimately connected with degrees of effective social power, and that without a significant shift in the balance of power, no serious change in distribution of income is possible.

Even if it is temporarily eclipsed during the upsurge of monetarist policy which accompanied the political rise of Mrs Thatcher, the argument on incomes policy will probably continue as long as the capitalist form of industrial enterprise survives. What it shows no signs of doing is finding any more solid basis for answering Judge Ellison's question than he himself could discover a hundred years ago.

NOTES

1. Sydney and Beatrice Webb, *Industrial Democracy*, first published 1897, Longman Green edition 1926.
2. Fred Knee, 'The Revolt of Labour' in *Social Democrat* 1910, re-printed in K. Coates and T. Topham (eds), *Industrial Democracy in Great Britain*, 3rd edition, vol 1, Spokesman Books 1975.
3. Alan Fox, 'The Social Origins of Present Forms and Methods in Britain and Germany', in *Industrial Democracy; International Views*, SSRC 1978.
4. *Trade Unionism*, TUC 1966.
5. For the history of the engineers' union, see J. B. Jefferys, *The Story of the Engineers 1800–1945*, published by the union, 1945.
6. For the story of trade unionism in Fords, See H. Beynon, *Working For Fords*, Penguin, 1973.
7. Royal Commission on Trade Unions and Employers' Associations, 1965–68, *Report*, Cmnd. 3623, HMSO 1968, paras 81–82.
8. Ministry of Labour, *Industrial Relations Handbook*, 1964. This useful compendium, long out-of-date, is to be succeeded by a new volume under preparation by ACAS.
9. Figures from NEDO Wall-Chart, 1970
10. Figures from Incomes Data Services *Focus*, July 1976.
11. Table from W. J. Thomson, C. Mulvey, and M. Farbman, 'Bargaining Structure and Relative Earnings in Great Britain', *British Journal of Industrial Relations*, July 1977.
12. Donovan Royal Commission *Report*, paras 1007, 1008 and 1019.
13. For a summary of the pros and cons of productivity bargaining from a trade union point of view see Tony Topham, *The Organised Worker*, Arrow-Hutchinsons in association with the Society of Industrial Tutors, 1975, page 77.
14. See Tony Topham, 'New Types of Bargaining,' in *The Incompatibles: Trade Union Militancy and the Consensus*, Penguin, 1967.
15. See Tony Topham, *The Organised Worker*, op. cit., pp.72–74, for an account of the way in which Ford shop stewards obtained representation on their NJNC.
16. R. Elliott and R. Steele, 'The Importance of National Wage Agreements' in *British Journal of Industrial Relations*, Vol. XIV, no. 1, 1976.
17. 'Meso-sector' is a phrase coined by Stuart Holland to describe the area of the economy dominated by large, multi-plant and multi-national companies, neither 'micro-' nor 'macro-' sector.
18. Doug Gowan, 'The Bargaining System' in *Industrial Studies 2: The Bargaining Context*, ed. Ed Coker and Geoffrey Stuttard, Arrow-Hutchinsons, in association with the Society of Industrial Tutors, 1976.
19. William Brown and Michael Terry, 'The Future of Collective Bargaining,' in *New Society*, 23rd March 1978.
20. Bill Conboy, *Pay at Work*, Arrow-Hutchinsons, in association with the Society of Industrial Tutors, 1976.
21. Ministry of Labour, *Written Evidence* to the Donovan Royal Commission, HMSO, 1965.

22. Ministry of Labour, ibid.
23. *Good Industrial Relations: A Guide for Negotiators*, TUC 1971.
24. *The Ford Wage Claim*, Transport & General Workers' Union, 1977.
25. *Trades Union Congress Economic Review 1979*, TUC 1979.
26. *Lucas, An Alternative Plan*, IWC, 1977.
27. *Technology and Jobs*, TUC 1979.
28. '*Micro-Electronics: The Trade Union Response*,' in *Labour Research* June 1979.
29. See Incomes Data Service: International Report 95, April 1979.
30. W. J. Thomson, C. Mulvey and M. Farbman, loc. cit.
31. Diagram taken from Tony Topham, *The Organised Worker*, op. cit.
32. For a detailed study of the old engineering procedure, see Richard Hyman, *Disputes Procedure in Action*, Heinemann, 1972.
33. Norman Singleton, *Industrial Relations Procedures*, Department of Employment Manpower Paper no. 14, HMSO, 1975.
34. See C. Gill, R. Morris, and J. Eaton, *Industrial Relations in the Chemical Industry*, Saxon House, 1978.
35. Norman Singleton, op. cit.
36. Harry Urwin, *Plant and Productivity Bargaining*, TGWU, 3rd edition 1972.
37. *Post-Donovan Conferences: Collective Bargaining and Trade Union Development in the Private Sector*, TUC 1969.
38. *Industrial Democracy*, TUC 1974.
39. *Annual Report, ACAS 1978*, 1979.
40. Ministry of Labour *Industrial Relations Handbook*, HMSO 1964.
41. From *ACAS Annual Report, 1978*.
42. See *Annual Report 1978, CAC*, 1979.
43. Cmnd. 5125, November 1972, HMSO, 1972.
44. Cmnd. 5205, 5206 (January 1973), and 5267 (March 1973), HMSO, 1973.
45. Cmnd. 5444 and 5446 (October 1973), HMSO 1973.
46. *Collective Bargaining and the Social Contract* TUC June 1974.
47. Cmnd. 6151 (July 1975) HMSO 1975.
48. Cmnd. 6507 (July 1976) HMSO 1976.
49. Cmnd. 6882 (July 1977) HMSO 1977.
50. Cmnd. 7293 (July 1978) HMSO 1978.
51. Quoted by the Webbs in *Industrial Democracy* (WEA, London, 1913) p. 229.
52. *Capital*, Volume 1.
53. TUC *Annual Report, 1964*, pp. 384-5.
54. Cf Michael Barratt Brown: The Growth and Distribution of the National Income, in Ken Coates: *What Went Wrong?* Spokesman, 1979, pp. 60-1. Source of figures in this table: 1860-9 to 1960-3: C. H. Feinstein, *The Distribution of National Income* (MacMillan, 1968), Table 1, pp. 116-17, as adapted by J. King and T. Regan, *Relative Income Shares* (MacMillan, 1978), Table 1, p. 19. 1964-8 and 1969-73: King and Reagan, op. cit., Table 1, p 19. 1974-78 Michael Barratt Brown, from National Income and Expenditure Data.
55. Ibid, p. 64 Source of figures in this table: *Social Trends* 1979, and NIESR *Economic Review*, February 1979.

APPENDIX TO CHAPTER 6

A Procedural Agreement

The Procedural Agreement between the Confederation of Ship-building and Engineering Unions and the Engineering Employers' Federation, concluded in March 1976, followed some years of difficult bargaining.[1] Because it covers such a very large labour force in both the Engineering and Shipbuilding Industries, it makes sense to reproduce it here. This Agreement sets out the agreed stages through which disputes should be processed. Domestic stages are the subject of separate agreements, plant by plant, within the terms of reference laid down below. External stages are spelt out in this document. Enshrined within this agreement is the extremely important principle of 'status quo', which insists that 'whatever practice . . . existed prior to the difference shall continue to operate pending a settlement or until the agreed procedure has been exhausted.'

I. *PARTIES*

1. This Agreement is between the Engineering Employers' Federation on the one hand, and the Confederation of Shipbuilding and Engineering Unions and the signatory Unions on the other. It is made on behalf of the Federation and federated engineering employers, and the Confederation of Shipbuilding and Engineering Unions and the signatory Unions and their members employed as manual workers in federated establishments.

II. *FRAMEWORK OF COLLECTIVE BARGAINING*

2. The signatory Unions are confirmed as the only Unions to have collective bargaining rights for manual workers employed in federated establishments.

3. In order that negotiations at all levels can be conducted on a fully representative and authoritative basis, the employers recognise that it is desirable that all manual workers should be members of an appropriate signatory Union.

4. Consultation and collective bargaining in the engineering industry takes place at different levels. Certain matters are reserved by agreement for determination at national level, and any variation in

such matters should be by negotiation and agreement nationally and not at domestic level. It is for the parties, nationally, to determine from time to time which matters shall be subject to negotiation and agreement at national level.

5.   Where any party wishes to raise a matter for resolution, there shall be discussion at domestic or national level, as appropriate. It is agreed that in the event of any difference arising which cannot immediately be disposed of, then whatever practice or agreement existed prior to the difference shall continue to operate pending a settlement or until the agreed procedure has been exhausted. In order to allow for the peaceful resolution of any matter raised by any party, there shall be no stoppage of work, either of a partial or general character, such as a strike, lock-out, go-slow, work-to-rule, overtime ban or any other restrictions, before the stages of procedure provided for in this Agreement have been exhausted.

Note to Agreement
Instant Dismissal
(a)   In any case of gross industrial misconduct which necessitates instant dismissal, then it is open to the dismissed person to contest that dismissal, but the person will no longer be an employee of the company as from the time of dismissal.

Dismissal with due notice
(b)   Where notice of dismissal is given (other than instant dismissal), it is open to the dismissed person to contest that dismissal, and if necessary to call through the Union for an EXTERNAL Conference, and in such a case the person will remain an employee of the company until such time as either agreement is reached or the procedure is exhausted.

6.   The resolution of inter-Union or internal Union disputes is primarily the responsibility of Unions themselves. The signatory Unions undertake to seek the peaceful resolution of any such disputes through the appropriate available machinery, and shall not, therefore, make them the subject of any industrial or other coercive action.

7.   The Federation and the Unions will use their best endeavours to ensure that their respective members honour their obligations and to this end they will not give any support, financial or otherwise, to their respective members if acting in breach of the obligations arising from Clauses 5 and 6 above.

III. *PROCEDURE FOR DEALING WITH MATTERS ARISING AT DOMESTIC LEVEL*
8.   Where any party has a matter to raise, it shall first be discussed

within the DOMESTIC STAGES of procedure. If the matter is not resolved at that level the matter may be referred to the EXTERNAL STAGES.

Domestic Stages
9. The domestic stages of procedure shall be agreed in the establishment concerned and should be incorporated within a written procedure. This should cover such matters as the number of stages, the stage at which the shop stewards and, where recognised, the chief shop steward shall be involved, the level of management to be involved at each stage, the procedural level at which matters (whether individual, sectional or general) shall be raised by the party concerned, and the time limits within which different types of questions shall be discussed.
10. Where it is decided to establish a Works Committee as a procedural stage, its constitution and terms of reference are matters for discussion and agreement in the establishment concerned. However, the following provisions shall be incorporated within its constitution and terms of reference:

(i) it shall be the final stage in domestic procedure.
(ii) Where a sectional issue is discussed at the Works Committee and there is no representative from that section on the Committee, then a representative of the section shall be co-opted for that discussion.
(iii) the decision of a Works Committee on an issue shall not prevent a Union from referring the issue to an EXTERNAL Conference for further discussion.

Any difficulties in the setting up or operation of such a Committee shall be discussed in accordance with Clauses 15–17 of this Agreement.

Shop Stewards
11. Shop stewards shall be elected from Union members employed in the establishment, in conformity with the rules of their Union, and shall act in accordance with the terms of this Agreement.
12. Shop stewards shall be afforded reasonable facilities to deal with matters appropriate to be dealt with by them. In all other respects they shall conform to the same working conditions as their fellow employees, and shall act in accordance with the terms of this or any other relevant agreement, national, local, or domestic.
13. The numbers of shop stewards and their constituencies shall be clearly defined. No employee shall be eligible to act as a shop steward unless employed in the agreed constituency. Any difficulty concerning such matters shall, if necessary, be discussed at local and subsequently at national level.

14. On appointment, or replacement, the name of each shop steward, and the constituency represented, shall be notified to the management, in writing, by the Union office concerned. When such an appointment is taken up, management shall ensure that the shop steward has a copy of the domestic procedure and is fully aware of its terms. Management shall keep shop stewards notified of the names of management representatives involved at the various stages.

External Stages

15. Failing settlement at the final DOMESTIC STAGE, and where the party concerned wishes to pursue the reference further, the question at issue shall be referred on behalf of either party directly concerned to an EXTERNAL Conference. An EXTERNAL Conference shall involve representatives of the employers' association and local officials of the Trade Union(s) concerned, as well as the management representative(s) and the shop steward(s) concerned. An EXTERNAL Conference shall be held within seven working days (unless otherwise mutually agreed) of receipt of written application from the party wishing to pursue the reference.

Note to Agreement

This Agreement does not lay down the detailed arrangements for an EXTERNAL Conference, but it is expected that it would normally be held off the premises of the establishment concerned. However, there is nothing to stop an EXTERNAL Conference being held on the premises where this is mutually desired. Neither is there anything within the terms of this Agreement to prevent the holding, before an EXTERNAL Conference, of an informal discussion within the works with the local officials of the employers' association and Trade Unions where this was mutually agreed in an effort to clarify and resolve an outstanding issue.

16. Matters which concern the interpretation or application of this or any other National Agreement shall be referred for discussion at national level between the parties to the agreement. Such discussion at national level shall be held within 7 working days of receipt of written application, unless otherwise mutually agreed.

17. Failing settlement at EXTERNAL Conference of questions other than those concerning the interpretation or application of a National Agreement, the procedure shall be regarded as exhausted. Notwithstanding this, a special meeting involving national representatives of the Federation and of the Union or Unions concerned shall be arranged as required by either party.

IV. *JOINT CONSULTATIVE AND ADVISORY*
ARRANGEMENTS AT NATIONAL LEVEL

18.   There shall be an agreed forum with representatives of the Federation and the Confederation which will meet from time to time as required to consider matters of mutual concern to the parties.

V. *DATE OF OPERATION*

19.   This Agreement will be operative as from Monday, 5th April 1976.

NOTE

1.   See Michael Somerton: 'The Proposals for Changes in the Engineering Procedural Agreement'. *Trade Union Register 2*, Spokesman 1970, p. 205 et seq.

Chapter Seven

Strikes

The Occurrence of Strikes

The author of the classic book on strikes offers us the following definition: a strike is, he tells us: 'a temporary stoppage of work by a group of employees in order to express a grievance or enforce a demand.'[1] This formula draws attention to the central features of a strike—its temporary nature (the strikers intend to return to work eventually), the fact that it is an action by employed persons (not self-employed or employers), and the fact that it is purposeful, that there exists an objective to be achieved. It is noticeable that there is no reference to trade unions. Strikes by unorganised groups of workpeople can and do take place without the presence or engagement of a union. At the same time, strikes have a most intimate relationship with trade unionism, and it is one of the purposes of this chapter to explore this.

Strikes are simply the most visible and measurable manifestation of conflict between the owners and/or managers of industry, and their employees. There are many other forms which this conflict may take, including lock-outs, autocratic forms of supervision, speed-up of work, disciplinary sackings, output restriction, labour turnover, sickness and accident rates, absenteeism, overtime bans, working-to-rule, sit-ins, work-ins, and sabotage. Some of these forms are deliberate and organised, some spontaneous and unplanned, some are initiated by workers, some by managers.[2]

If strikes are only one expression of industrial conflict, they are themselves a complex phenomenon; they cannot be regarded as 'a simple category of social action' since the social conditions which stimulate some kinds of strike, can lead to the diminution of other kinds.[3] For some thinkers, the continued presence of discontent among workers, as expressed in the post-war records of strikes, must be a puzzling affair, difficult to explain rationally. For instance, Talcott Parsons believes that:

> 'Through industrial development under democratic auspices, the most importantly legitimately-to-be-expected aspirations of the "working class" have, in fact, been realised.'[4]

This kind of thinking leads in the direction of a 'unitary' theory of industrial relations, which claims that within the employment relationship employers and employees share common goals and mutual interests, which should normally produce a state of industrial harmony. If working people are indeed satisfied in their aspirations, and employed in socially harmonious conditions, then only two possible explanations of strikes appear credible: either workers are ignorant of their true situation, and therefore act irrationally when they strike, or they are deliberately misled by 'trouble-makers' and political extremists. The remedies for strikes which follow from these theories then vary between attempts at the improvement of 'communications' between management and workers on the one side: and the disciplining and dismissal of strike leaders, or political or legal constraints on strikers and trade unions, on the other. These remedies have been tried from time to time, with none but a temporary effect; indeed they have sometimes led to an increase in strike action. A considerable body of academic literature on strikes has shown that the conspiracy theory is to say the least implausible:[5] while there is no evidence that an improved flow of information from management to workers will dissipate workers' grievances. On the contrary, there are times when it may well augment them.

Strikes are best understood by combining a study of the social and economic circumstances in which they occur, with studies of the beliefs and attitudes of strikers; including, of course, their interpretation and understanding of their place in industry and society, which in turn are influenced by specific experiences of industrial relations in particular countries, industries, companies, and plants, and by the forms of collective organisation (trade unionism) which have developed there. In the Western World at least, the alienation of the worker which generates conflict is certainly attributable to capitalism's treatment of labour as a commodity—a thing to be bought and sold in the pursuit of profit. Whether this conflict expresses itself in strikes will depend on a complex of factors: Talcott Parsons notwithstanding, one of the main achievements of industrial capitalism is that it has created 'legitimately-to-be-expected' aspirations even larger in volume and richer in cost, whilst not always slaking them. It is entirely reasonable to claim that:

'Strike action shows every sign of being endemic to capitalism. It is an historical phenomenon which has persisted through radical changes in living standards. It is a spreading phenomenon which is overcoming all manner of social barriers . . . It has defied all prescribed solutions, both prophylactic and punitive.'[6]

Industrial conflict and strikes occur also in the socialised economies of Eastern Europe and Soviet Russia[7] sometimes as in Poland accompanied by considerable violence. Whilst strikes may be 'endemic' to capitalism, they are not unique to it; alienation may also be produced by bureaucratic, undemocratic administration of large-scale industrialised societies under public ownership. Even in the worker self-management system of Yugoslavia strikes are fairly common, and have been intelligently acknowledged by the authorities in that country as symptoms and indicators of the malfunctioning of that system.[8]

Measuring Strikes

An important aspect of the study of strikes is the analysis of strike statistics.

The official source of this information in Britain is the Department of Employment's monthly *Gazette* which together with its predecessors from the Board of Trade and the Ministry of Labour, has been collecting and publishing information on strikes since the last decade of the 19th century. Most western industrial countries have a similar central source of information, and international strike statistics are collected and published by the International Labour Organisation in its *Year Book of Labour Statistics*. British statistics are limited as follows:

> 'The official series of statistics of stoppages of work due to industrial disputes in the UK relates to disputes connected with terms and conditions of employment. Stoppages involving fewer than ten workers or lasting less than one day are excluded except where the aggregate of working days lost exceeded 100. Workers involved are those directly involved and indirectly involved (thrown out of work although not parties to the dispute) *at the establishment where the dispute occurred*. The number of working days lost is the aggregate of days lost by workers both directly and indirectly involved (as defined). It follows that the statistics do *not* reflect repercussions elsewhere, that is, *at establishments other than those at which the disputes occurred.*'[9]

Notice that these limitations mean that political strikes are excluded, and whilst these have normally been of the most negligible significance, they have, since 1970, become more important, as we shall see. Very small and short-lived strikes are also excluded, and Professor Turner has estimated that 30 per cent of mining strikes, and 80 per cent of strikes in the car industry, have been excluded from the official statistics for this reason.[10]

Whilst this represents a deficiency in the official statistics, it is important that it should not be exaggerated, as the *Sunday Times* has attempted to do.[11] For instance, the privately collected car manu-facturers' statistics which are the basis of Turner's comparisons with those of the Department of Employment, included such minor 'stoppages' as 'shop stewards coming back late from lunch-hour committee meetings' and another of a strike costing a mere 17 man-hours.[12]

The Department of Employment relies for the collection of its figures upon information supplied by managers, supplemented by the monitoring of the press both local and national. The role of management in this process gives rise to some concern, since 'manage-ment often have the power to define a situation as a strike or not' and there is some evidence that where management feel themselves to have been in the wrong, they may not always notify the authorities fully about what has happened.[13]

This may lead to the under-representation of strikes on issues such as safety and working conditions, and a consequent exaggeration of strikes about wages, in the official statistics. A further omission from the information is the level at which strike action occurs—work-group, section, plant, company, industry,—a dimension which has major sociological interest.[14]

These reservations do not invalidate the use of official statistics; the omissions of the smallest and shortest strikes does not amount to the neglect of anything of serious economic consequence—these brief affairs are best considered as part of the unquantifiable but socio-logically significant underworld of endemic industrial unrest—and the official series are consistent in their criteria, thus enabling us properly to use them to identify *trends* in strikes. The same things may be said about comparative international strike statistics; although different countries have different criteria for their statistical series, so that there is legitimate controversy about their absolute position in the inter-national league table,[15] the internal consistency of the multiple series makes possible, as we shall see, a valid comparison of relative trends between countries.

Three key measures are available in the British figures; the number of strikes, the number of workers involved, and the number of 'working days lost'. The latter official terminology has been rightly criticised as emotive and questionable; a more neutral description which we shall use is 'number of striker-days'. From these statistics can be derived also the average duration of stoppages, and the average number of workers per strike. The Department of Employment also publishes tables indicating the causes of strikes as reported to it, on the number of strikes of varying duration, disaggregated figures for the major industries and regions, and figures of strikes 'known to be official' as compared with what are assumed to be unofficial strikes.

Beyond these bare figures of strike incidence lies the question as to how much economic disruption is caused by strikes. What do strikes cost and who bears the cost? We shall deal later with the cost of strikes to strikers themselves and to their unions. At this stage we are concerned with the cost to the employer and the economy. In fact there is little or no statistical evidence about this aspect of strikes, but what there is suggests that the economic effects of strikes are frequently exaggerated and that they are in general of a minimal nature. For example one of the few case studies available, of an official strike in printing in 1959, showed that the $2\frac{1}{2}$ per cent pay rise which was conceded by the employers to settle the issue would, if not passed on, have reduced employers' profits by $1\frac{1}{4}$ *per cent of total turnover.*[16] There have been some spectacular cases of employers making a profit from a strike. This happened in the major national dispute in the Post Office in 1971, when the loss-making postal service closed down, whilst the profit-making telephone side of the organisation's services expanded. In other instances, notably in the car industry, strikes are sometimes provoked and 'used' by employers as a substitute for lay-offs during periods of slack demand, or during re-tooling for a new model.[17]

Of course, it is true that some strikes, which take on the aspect of a major trial of strength in strategically key areas of the economy, may inflict economic damage. In the first half of the 1920s, and the early 1970s, such contests have assumed significance; industries in this category include coal, rail, steel, the ports, the merchant service, gas, water and electricity. But even here, the economic effect is likely to be temporary.

An important controversy arose around the conclusions of the Donovan Royal Commission in 1968 that the short, small, unofficial and unconstitutional strikes (which dominated the strike statistics at the time) were peculiarly damaging because they were unpredictable, and inhibiting of management initiative. Apart from the consideration that it is unlikely that this type of strike was a particularly British phenomenon, the comment of Dr W. E. J. McCarthy is apposite:

'. . . I have always thought that the Donovan Report grossly oversold the psychological deterrent effect of strikes; it has always seemed to me a managerial excuse, the first refuge of the lazy and the last ditch of the cowardly.'[18]

In most strikes, there is an increase in the solidarity of the workforce, which often carries over after the dispute, in increased collective willingness to work overtime, or to raise output under incentive payment schemes. The workers may be additionally motivated to do this by their need to recoup lost wages. All this minimises the economic loss of the strike. This effect was powerfully demonstrated, not just for short plant-level stoppages, but on a national scale, in the three-day week (which was tantamount to a partial national lock-out) during the coal dispute of 1973–4; because managers and workers had a common interest in maintaining production, much co-operative ingenuity was applied to the problem, and the result was a remarkably sustained level of total output. Evans and Creigh concluded their essay on the economic costs of strikes by saying that 'many of the charges levelled against strikes on economic grounds seem to rest on rather dubious evidence.'[19]

This conclusion, it may be argued, may apply to allegations about the 'loss of production' but is surely invalid if we consider the effect of strikes upon wage-price inflation?

The same authors maintain the same scepticism in this matter also, citing in support the evidence of other specialist research, which concluded that 'the role of strikes (in money-wage inflation) was a minor one',[20] and that 'the direct effect of strikes in pushing up wages, or arresting their fall does not seem to have been very great'.[21] By itself, the single year of 1974, which saw a large strike incidence and a wage explosion of unprecedented proportions, cannot offer evidence to refute the much longer-term studies of the earlier years. That year merits careful analysis, not because it was typical, but because it shows us a window onto the limits of our present system of industrial relations.

It is worth-while also to point to the figures of other causes of lost production in weighing these controversies; in 1970 for example, whilst 10 million days were 'lost' through strikes, industrial accidents accounted for 20 million days, unemployment (at 1 million workers) for 200 million days, and certified sickness for 300 million days.[22] Another calculation, in 1973, showed that 'the average union member goes on strike once (and sometimes more) every twelve years, for a period of about two and a half days at a time'.[23]

Of course, average figures may conceal major variations in the experience of different industries (we return to this subject later) and between different establishments within an industry. The peculiarly strike-prone *plant* is a well-known phenomenon and in these cases economic loss may be real enough. In engineering, an apparently strike-prone industry, it has been shown that, in the period from 1960 to 1966, only 9 per cent of the 1000 federated firms investigated experienced any unconstitutional stoppages (a category of strike which accounted for 96 per cent of all stoppages by manual workers)[24]. In another study, it was shown that of 432 engineering establishments

Table VII:1

Number of strikes, number of workers involved, and striker-days in the U.K. 1889–1978

	Number of strikes	Number of workers involved (000s)	Striker days (000,000s)
1889–91*	1050	340	7.1
1892–96	760	360	13.3
1897–01	720	210	7.1
1902–06	410	160	2.6
1907–11	570	440	7.2
1912–16	890	660	13.2
1917–21	1120	1660	31.8
1922–26	570	950	41.8
1927–31	380	310	4.4
1932–36	520	250	2.5
1937–41	1020	370	1.6
1942–46	1960	580	2.4
1947–51	1590	430	1.9
1952–56	2100	680	2.5
1957–61	2630	830	4.6
1962	2449	4420	5.8
1963	2068	590	1.8
1964	2524	872	2.3
1965	2354	868	2.9
1966	1937	530	2.4
1967	2116	731	2.8
1968	2378	2255	4.7
1969	3116	1654	6.8
1970	3906	1793	11.0
1971	2228	1171	13.6
1972	2497	1722	24.0
1973	2873	1513	7.2
1974	2922	1622	14.8
1975	2282	789	6.0
1976	2016	666	3.3
1977	2703	1155	10.1
1978	2471	1001	9.4
1979	—	—	23.0**

Source: Department of Employment.

*Figures for the years 1889–1961 have been given as five-yearly annual averages, except for 1889–91, which is a three year annual average.

**first nine months only.

surveyed, 38 per cent had been free of strikes (even including brief stoppages down to a half-hour duration), that under 1 per cent (just three establishments) had over 40 per cent of the strikes; and 5 per cent had 65 per cent of them. Almost 80 per cent of the managements 'would think of themselves as strike free'.[25]

Table VII:1 presents the historical record of British strikes in the 20th century, derived from the official statistics. With its aid we can trace the main trends and delineate the different phases into which this history falls. Col. 1 of the table measures the number of separate occasions per annum on which some group of workers took action. Col. 2 indicates the number of workers involved in action during the year, and col. 3 the number of striker-days. Thus columns 2 and 3 provide different measures of the scale and severity of the strikes recorded in col. 1.

Historical Patterns

The 1890s were marked by some severe contests as trade unions came under attack from anti-union employers who were determined to reverse the gains made by the 'new unions' in the 1880s. The older craft unions were also subject to a prolonged rearguard action in 1897 in the engineering industry. After a lull in the first decade of the 20th century, the first wave of modern, large-scale, industry-level strikes occurred during the syndicalist period of 1910–14, involving notably the mining, inland road transport, docks, and railway industries, in which a new generation of militants fought with considerable success for recognition, negotiating rights, and wage increases.

During the first world war, strikes were made illegal, and the official national strike almost disappeared, to be replaced by an escalating number of short, localised, unofficial disputes associated with the rise of the shop stewards' movement. After the war, the militants resumed their large aggressive actions but were soon, after the short post-war boom of 1919–20, driven on to the defensive, from which position they sustained what was historically the highest ever level of strike action (particularly as measured by the scale of the strikes, rather than their number) against wage cuts and a mounting offensive by employers against union encroachment on their prerogatives. This phase culminated in the General Strike of 1926, in which year, it should be noted that of the 162 million striker-days, only 15 million were caused by the General Strike itself; 146 million were the result of the prolonged lock-out of the miners which lasted from May to November.

The General Strike and the miners' lock-out represent the most severe defeat ever suffered by the British trade union movement, and the ensuing demoralisation, decline in union membership, and the onset of the world slump in 1929 which persisted through most of the 'thirties, combined with a new mood of subservience and respectability amongst trade union leaders to produce through the 1930s the lowest records of 20th century strike activity. However, during the second world war, when strikes were again made illegal, the number of strikes rose sharply, yet because these strikes were of a different character from the 1920s, being short, small, and unofficial, the number of striker days remained at its low levels of the 1930s.

The war-time experience is instructive; the legal ban on strikes and the institution of compulsory arbitration in disputes were totally effective in dissuading unions from supporting strikes, but were clearly ineffective in preventing unofficial stoppages. One, then youthful, strike leader has testified to the casual and disrespectful attitude which he and his fellows harboured towards the law.

> 'Six of us, apprentices at Metro-Vickers and other factories in Manchester, were dragged into court in 1941, probably one of the prosecutions under the new regulations which Ernie Bevin had introduced at the Ministry of Labour during the war. You were supposed to give twenty-one days notice of disputes, but we were only kids, between 16 and 20, and we didn't know about niceties like that . . . Eventually they found us guilty and bound us over not to do it again. Platts Mills in court tried to hold things up by trying to get them to make Ernie Bevin come up from London and give evidence that he hadn't been notified of the strike. And there were hilarious scenes in court when they tried to prove that we were out on strike.'[26]

By October 1941 there had been over 1000 illegal strikes, but only six such prosecutions. Another of these was the famous affair of the strike by 1,000 miners at the Betteshanger colliery in Kent, whose mass summons was made the occasion for a carnival procession by the local mining community, complete with brass bands, the results of which was to ridicule the Regulation.[27] Despite this, in 1944, Bevin's Department forged a new weapon in the Defence Regulation 1AA, which made even incitement to strike an offence; the Regulation was never used and was hastily revoked the following year.[28]

It is useful to compare the strike record of the war years for another reason. This concerns the common assumptions made in newspapers (and elsewhere) about the relation between agitators, particularly communists, and the incidence of strikes. Between 1939 and 1945 the figures were as follows:

Table VII:2

Number of strikes, number of workers involved and number of striker-days, 1939–45, Great Britain

Year	Number of strikes	Number of work-people directly and indirectly involved (000s)	Striker-days (000s)
1939	940	337	1,356
1940	922	299	940
1941	1,251	360	1,079
1942	1,303	456	1,527
1943	1,785	557	1,808
1944	2,194	821	3,714
1945	2,293	531	2,835

At the beginning of the Second World War, the Communist Party policy was to support strikes. The result was that in 1940 there were 18 *less* strikes, involving 416,000 less workdays than had been the case in 1939. When Russia was attacked in mid-1941, the Communist Party adopted a policy of strong opposition to strikes, and worked hard to make a success of joint production committees. Its wartime conferences of shop stewards were thenceforward widely and sympathetically reported in the press. The result? Strikes increased to 1,251 in 1941, and then, each year, to 1,303; 1,785; 2,194 and 2,293, while striker-days rose to a peak of over 3,700,000 by 1944.

(This number of strikes was the highest hitherto recorded, yet the number of striker-days is not high by either the standards of the 'twenties or the 'seventies.) All this evidence casts doubt on the assumptions of those who think they can reduce industrial discord by hunting for witches. A post-war triumvirate of Will Lawther (NUM), Arthur Deakin (TGWU), and Tom Williamson (GMWU), controlled TUC policy and held together a firm anti-strike policy, in keeping with their uncritical loyalty to the Labour Government. This included a continuing tolerance of the wartime Order 1305 banning strikes, into peace-time circumstances. Between 1945 and 1950, there were nevertheless 10,000 strikes—all of them illegal.[29] There were no post-war prosecutions, and in 1951 the Order was repealed. Between 1933 and 1953 there had not been one single official national strike.

After resuming their legality, the characteristic strike of the 1950s and 1960s continued to be the short, small, unofficial dispute, although official strikes began to make their re-appearance—on the railways, the docks, and in printing, in 1955, in ship-building and engineering in 1957,[30] and on the London buses in 1958. In the last two cases at least, a new factor was to emerge as central to an understanding of post-war trends: namely Government wage restraint policies.

In the London bus strike the TGWU, led by Frank Cousins, the more militant successor to Arthur Deakin, gave official support to its members, whose pay claim was resisted by the government (the ultimate sources of finance for the London Passenger Transport Board) in the name of its declared policy of wage restraint.

As the strike became more and more prolonged, and was clearly being undermined by private car transport and the London underground, Cousins approached the TUC for support, citing Rule 11 of the TUC's constitution. The initial response of the TUC was to declare its support for the strike, and its conviction that its cause was to be laid at the government's door.

> 'Government policy has brought London's buses to a standstill. Having mismanaged the economy the Government has chosen the pay claim of London's busmen to put pressure on a public employer to conform to its policy of holding down wages and to bolster the resistance of private employers . . . This strike has been made unavoidable by the Government's determination to hold down wages in publicly-owned industries and services, which, in times of rising prices, can only be done by cutting the living standards of the workers concerned.'

The TUC General Council participated in negotiations with the government, including meetings with the Prime Minister, during which the TGWU accepted the initiatives of the TUC and collaborated with them. These negotiations collapsed, and Frank Cousins was faced with the question, which he posed to the TUC General Council, as to 'how soon was this strike going to be developed into something that somebody was going to take notice of?'. He proposed an extension of the action, to call out TGWU members who drove petrol bowsers into London, and who worked in London's power stations. The government responded by cancelling week-end leave for troops in the London area, and affirmed that it would ensure supplies of petrol and electricity to the capital. Cousins then asked the General Council whether they would follow 'normal trade union practice' by treating energy and fuel supplied by troops as 'black'. A positive response to this request would have seemed almost mandatory for the General Council, bearing in mind the wording of Rule 11(d) of its constitution, under which its participation in the dispute was taking place. The clause reads:

> Where the Council intervenes [in a dispute] as herein provided, and the organisation or organisations concerned accept the assistance and advice of the Council, and where despite the efforts of the Council, the policy of the employers enforces a stoppage of work by strike or lock-out, the Council shall forthwith take all steps to organise on behalf of the organisation or organisations concerned all such moral and material support as the circumstances of the dispute may appear to justify.'

This clause, (which still exists today) appears almost tailormade for the 1958 London bus strike. Yet the General Council members beat a hasty retreat from its previous stand of verbal and financial solidarity with the strike, and in an angry debate with Cousins, in which there were many references to the dangers of a 1926 type of conflict with government, told him that they would not support the proposed extension of the strike, and even threatened that any such extension would result in the withdrawal of the TUC's earlier appeal for financial support from other unions for the strikers. The Council bluntly advised Cousins to resume negotiations; the busmen were thus effectively isolated and compelled to accept a compromise settlement. The implications of this episode which highlights the self-imposed limitations on solidarity action by the TUC, are of permanent significance during the whole subsequent period to the present day; public service pay claims have constantly posed the same questions for the TUC as Frank Cousins did in 1958, and the TUC has constantly avoided the issue.[31]

During the '50s and '60s, a significant trend was at work which was concealed within the aggregate figures of numbers of strikes. The mining industry in the 1950s dominated the strike field. This predominance came to a peak in 1957, when mining accounted for 2,224 strikes out of a total of 2,859. These miners' strikes were overwhelmingly local affairs, caused either by disputes over rate-fixing in the decentralised system of incentive payments then in operation, or by disagreements on the interpretation of such contracts. Yet by 1968 a remarkable reversal of the situation was completed; in that year there were a mere 219 mining strikes, following a steady fall over the previous ten years. The decline was the result of the reduced bargaining power of the miners in a multi-fuel market in which oil and gas competed more and more lethally, and a consequent large-scale reduction in the mining labour force. This was complemented in 1966 by the conclusion of a new National Power Loading Agreement between the NCB and the NUM, which effectively centralised wage bargaining and ended local tonnage rates.[32]

Remarkably, outside the mining industry, there was a five-fold increase in numbers of strikes during the very years of the decline in mining strikes. The credit for uncovering this trend belongs to Professor H. A. Turner[33] but the phenomenon was soon the focus of less dispassionate attention, and the examination of the rise of non-mining strikes, most evident in engineering and the car industry, but spreading to other manufacturing, came to dominate the literature and the political debate about Britain's 'strike problem' in the 1960s. It received much attention from the Donovan Royal Commission and provided the rationale behind the proposals of the Labour Government's White Paper *In Place of Strife*, of 1969, and of the Conservative Party's policy document *Fair Deal at Work*, of 1968, both of which set out to create legal penalties for certain types of strike.

But hardly was the ink dry on these proposed remedies, than the nature and scale of strike incidence began to change. Whilst during the furore over the unofficial strikes of the early and middle 'sixties the number of striker-days increased hardly at all compared with the whole previous period back to the 1920s, it did grow with remorseless regularity thereafter. In 1966 there were 2.4 million days involved: this had risen to 24 million days in 1972, a figure which had not been remotely approached since the 1920s. Clearly this provides yet another distinct phase in the recent history. This new period was characterised by the re-establishment of a pattern of long, official national strikes. Only a few of these are required in any year to send the number of striker-days rocketing: for example, the 45 day strike by the UPW in 1971 accounted for 6.3 million days out of the year's total of 13.6 million. Whilst, during the early 'sixties, only five really large strikes per year had been occurring there were twenty of this type in the years 1969–70.[34] During the years following 1969, strikes spread to previously strike-free groups, especially amongst public employees such as dustmen, teachers, hospital workers, and postmen. Trade union membership was growing rapidly at this time (after its long post-war plateau at around 8 million) and an increasing number of strikes involved groups seeking recognition and negotiating rights. Long-quiescent groups and long-unionised industries in clothing, steel and glass[35] took up the strike weapon, and there were revivals of strikes amongst car workers and above all by the miners.[36]

This last case is instructive. We have shown that the NCB and NUM had previously, in 1966, brought wage-bargaining in the industry under central direction. Undoubtedly at the time this reflected a managerial strategy to regain control of wages, to check wage-drift and reduce pit-level strikes. But the effect on the miners and their union was to re-create the much earlier tradition of concern for the *industry* wage-level, to make them aware of their declining position in the national wages league[37] and to eliminate their bargaining power at any level lower than that of the *whole* union. The oil price explosion was a late contributor to the rediscovery of the miners' power, and together these causes issued into the two great national mining strikes of 1972 and 1974.

The increasingly political character of the large strikes of the 70s is clearly evident, and the role of Government wage restraint policies was central, so that the collapse of the Conservative Goverment after the second miners' strike was predictable. Yet Mr Heath was defeated in a General Election, not an insurrection: and he lost votes whilst his opponents failed to win them. Not only incomes policy, but the whole trend of legislative intervention from the Industrial Relations Act in 1971, to the Social Contract legislation of 1974-6, was bound to involve the state more actively in the strike scene. And the changing nature of trade union leadership, (as evidenced by the initiative of two new leaders, Jack Jones and Hugh Scanlon, who early in their tenure of office took decisive steps to recognise and support the unconstitutional strike at Fords in 1969) combined with the increasing militancy and frustration of the membership under successive incomes policies ensured that official strikes became much more common. However, in no year since 1972 has the level of strikes reached that recorded in that year (although 1979 promises to do so), and whilst it remains consistently higher than in the post-war years up to 1968, the most noticeable feature of the 1970s is the volatility of the figures. In certain years, particularly 1973 and 1975-6, workers and unions appear to accept the wage norms imposed by incomes policy. At other times the dam bursts and strike action rises again. This happened most recently between 1977 and 1979. Of course there was undoubtedly a political element in the explanation of the lull of 1975-6, when Labour in office was delivering some of the most important parts of the promised social contract legislation, for the unions; we shall return to this question in considering the causes of strikes.

We can summarise the trends we have been discussing as follows: before the 1940s, there was usually less than 1,000 strikes per annum. the average being 700, whilst after 1941 there has always been more than 1,000 per annum, the average being over 2,000. In terms of striker-days, up to 1933 the average annual figure was 15 million, between 1933 and 1967 it was under 3 million, and since 1968 has been over 10 million.[38] Those who desire 'industrial peace' must, on this record, long also for the total defeat of the trade unions, as in 1926, and the

Table VII:3

International comparisons of statistics relating to stoppages due to industrial disputes in mining, manufacturing, construction and transport.

Name of country	Average annual figures for the three years 1964–66 inclusive			
	No. of stoppages per 100,000 workers	Av. No. of persons per stoppage	Av. duration of each stoppage: days	No. of working days struck per 1000 workers
United Kingdom	16.8	340	3.4	190
Australia	63.8(1)	350(1)	1.8(1)	400(1)
Belgium	7.0	680	9.2	200
Canada	15.8	430	14.0	970
Denmark	5.5(2)	370(2)	7.3(2)	160(2)
Finland	10.8	360	2.1	80
France	21.8	1,090	0.8	200
Federal Germany	(3)	(3)	3.6	(4)
Ireland	25.6	450	15.2	1,620
Italy	32.9	720	5.3	1,170
Japan	7.6	1,040	2.9	240
Netherlands	2.2	370	2.4	20
New Zealand	26.8	250	2.1	150
Norway	0.6	100	26.0	(4)
Sweden	0.5(5)	570(5)	15.4(5)	40(5)
United States	13.2(6)	470(6)	14.2(6)	870(6)

Source: Donovan Royal Commission on Trade Unions and Employers Associations, *Report*, HMSO 1968, page 95, based on information supplied by the International Labour Office.

(1) Including electricity and gas
(2) Manufacturing only
(3) Figures not available
(4) Fewer than 10 working days lost
(5) All industries
(6) Including electricity, gas, water, sanitary services

thorough demoralisation of trade unionists which accompanied the mass unemployment of the 1930s.

International Comparisons

International comparison of strike statistics is not a straightforward exercise:

'Because countries adopt different statistical practices, the figures are not strictly comparable in every respect. The most important variation is in the level below which strikes are regarded as too small to be included; some other countries adopt levels lower than the United Kingdom, notably Australia, Canada, Japan, Norway and the United States. Some countries, unlike the United Kingdom, exclude from their statistics workers laid off as a result of stoppages at their place of work.'[39]

Nevertheless we can assume that each country's collection of information remains internally consistent, and we can therefore use the ILO's statistics to analyse comparative trends in strikes. Judged by the record

Table VII:4

Index of striker-days per thousand workers (industrial sector only); for each country, the annual average for 1953-68 = 100

Country	Index of annual average days lost per thousand workers, 1969-74
Australia	319
Belgium	116
Canada	240
Denmark	243
Finland	461
France(a)	74
Federal Germany	149
Ireland	148
Italy	241
Japan	79
Netherlands	254
New Zealand	270
Norway	52
Sweden	190
United Kingdom	402
United States	129
All countries(inc. USA)(b)	200

Source: T. G. Sweet and Dudley Jackson, *The World Strike Wave 1969-7?*, Aston University Management Centre: Working Paper Series no. 63, January 1977, based on ILO data.

Table VII:5

Measures of industrial disputes in OECD countries for the years 1969–1974 relative to the years 1951–68

Index for 1969–74 annual average, with annual average
for 1951–68 = 100

Country	Striker-days	No. of strikes	No. of workers involved
Australia	387	192	304
Belgium	117	206	74
Canada	309	221	328
Denmark	331	311	483
Finland	179	1,304	610
France(c)	110	179	114
Federal Germany	158	(d)	184
Ireland	187	192	· 210
Italy	273	182	228
Japan	109	294	167
Netherlands	263	57	193
New Zealand	170	381	358
Norway	55	58	69
Sweden	186	366	384
United Kingdom	387	128	157
United States	145	136	135
Average	185	175	176

Source: as Table VII:4
Notes: In Table VII:4 (a) The base value of 100 for France is calculated from the annual average for the years 1953–1967
                (b) All countries' index excluding USA is 215.
  In Table VII:5 (c) 1951–68 indices for France exclude 1968 as no figures are available for that year.

at the time of the Donovan *Report*, in the period 1964–6 Britain's position in the table VII:3 was 'about average', being sixth out of the sixteen countries in terms of stoppages per 1,000 employees, and ninth out of the sixteen in terms of number of striker-days per 1,000 employees. Britain's strikes were the ninth longest in average duration, and only the thirteenth largest in average number of workers involved. What happened subsequently can be summarised by relating that the UK was 5th in numbers of disputes for the period 1965–9, and fell to seventh in 1970–4, recording only the fourteenth largest percentage rise between the two latter periods. In terms of striker-days the UK rose to sixth in 1965–9, and to fifth in 1970–4, recording the sixth highest percentage rise over the two periods. Table VII:4 measures relative changes in striker days per 1,000 employees over a longer period, from 1953–68, to 1969–74; it can be seen that only Finland recorded a larger growth than Britain between the two periods. Finally table VII:5 indicates that Britain and Australia shared top place for the growth in striker-days between the periods 1951–68 and 1969–74, but occupied only the thirteenth and twelfth place respectively in terms of growth in number of strikes and number of workers involved. We can conclude (a) that Britain has shared fully in the world's escalating incidence of strikes in recent years, (b) that starting from an average position in the mid-sixties, Britain has experienced a lower increase than most countries in numbers of strikes and numbers of workers involved, but a larger increase than all save one country in striker-days (c) that these relative increases reflect the changing pattern of Britain's strike incidence, from a predominance of small disputes to large ones.

Quite apart from the position of Britain, tables VII:4 and VII:5 reveal the 'remarkable international uniformity of the strike wave'.[40] For the industrial OECD countries excluding the USA, there were 31.7 million striker-days per annum in the period 1946–50, 25.4 million in the period 1951–67, but 58.8 million in the period 1969–74.[41] Moreover:

'When we consider the data already available to us for 1975, which by now is nearly complete, it is unquestionably the case that the strike wave continues through 1975; and moreover even the scanty figures at hand for 1976 do not suggest that the strike wave has yet faltered. We must remember that the improved performance of the UK in 1975 and 1976 is a result primarily of the special circumstances of the Social Contract; these circumstances do not yet appear in other countries, it seems.'[42]

General Explanations of Strikes

This evidence for the existence of a current world strike wave adds new interest to the literature on strikes which seeks for general explanations of the causes of strikes. One of the earliest modern enquiries is that of K. G. J. C. Knowles.[43] His work inevitably suffers from being out-dated, but remains a valuable general discussion of the subject. In particular, he suggested a three-fold classification of strikes according to different causes, as follows: (a) Basic issues, including wages increases and decreases, other wage questions, and hours of labour, (b) Frictional issues, including the employment of certain classes of persons, other working arrangements, rules and discipline, (c) Solidarity issues, including trade union principles and sympathetic action. The sub-categories are derived from the original official statistics of the Ministry of Labour, and the use of 'single-cause' classification is subject to the reservation that most strikes are 'multi-causal'. The results of the analysis, based on the years 1927-36, show for example that the mining industry was high on solidarity strikes, but low on basic strikes, which serves to illustrate the limitations of an investigation confined to a few years, since in the years both before and after these, miners' strikes were overwhelmingly about basic issues. But Knowles' work does draw attention to the important category of 'frictional' issues, to which we shall return.

Ross and Hartman conducted a famous enquiry on an international basis.[44] They explained strikes as the products of industrial relations 'systems' in which key influences included the age of the labour movement and the stability of trade union membership, factionalism and the presence of a Communist Party influence in the trade unions, the degree of employer recognition of trade unions, and a consolidated bargaining structure, the role of Labour Parties and Labour Governments, and the role of the state in industrial relations. They found in the British case a low level of trade union member involvement in strikes, which were mainly of short duration. The proportion of British trade union members engaging in strikes had fallen from 16.1 per cent in 1900-29, to 5.9 per cent in 1948-56, and the average duration of strikes from 23 days to 4.3 days. They found this to be part of a general 'withering away of the strike' internationally, which they explained by reference to the ending of the historical struggle for trade union recognition, the evolution of a mature trade union-management relationship, and an organised labour market which 'institutionalised' industrial conflict, together wth the turning of labour's attention to the political sphere and the election of Labour governments. This analysis may offer a partial explanation of the period studied, but has clearly proved, in the light of subsequent experience, to be hopelessly lacking in predictive value. Above all it ignores the fact that the balance of class power established in the slump years of the 1930s and carried over for a time into the early post-war period, was disadvantageous to labour, which would seek to redress the balance, given the opportunity.

Kerr and Siegel were responsible for another well-known attempt at a global analysis of strike records.[45] They studied the comparative strike levels of different industries in eleven countries, and concluded that the high strike- proneness of mining, merchant service, the docks, lumber and textiles was due to their characteristics as single-industry communities, with little occupational differentiation, the geographical or social isolation of their communities, and strong group cohesion. Low strike-proneness in agriculture, trade, railways, clothing, gas, electricity and water, and in services like hotels and restaurants, they attributed to the opposite characteristics; these industries are located in multi-industry communities, with considerable occupational dif-ferentiation, integrated into the general society, or experiencing individual isolation, as on farms. In this interpretation, group cohesion is treated as crucial, and it clearly contributes to an explanation in the case of *some* groups such as, perhaps, dockers and miners. Even there it should be used with caution: some of the most close-knit mining communities have been among the least strike-prone, for instance. But it certainly does not apply consistently across all countries to other industries, and is a contributory factor anyway in so much of mass-employment manufacturing industry that it loses its edge as a specific casual influence in particular industries. Further, the spread of strikes to wider and wider sectors of employment, which has been a feature of the 'sixties and 'seventies, occurring after the Kerr and Siegel work, is hard to explain in their terms.

Certainly, strike-proneness is a feature of some industries in Britain. Apart from mining, which as we have seen has been through a peculiar and unique evolution in post-war years, the top British industries for strikes are docks, motors, shipbuilding, iron and steel, aircraft and general engineering. Lowest strike figures are usually recorded for agriculture, distribution, finance and administration, gas, water, electricity and clothing. Several studies have however drawn attention to the increased spread of strikes in recent years, to industries previously immune.[46] Whilst the *level* of strikes remains uneven between industries (from 5 minutes per worker per year in distribution, to $6\frac{1}{2}$ days per worker per year in docks, in 1973) the *trend* towards increased strikes has been *even*, across industries.[47] Hyman, following Goodman, notes that the top five industries accounted for 69 per cent of strikes in 1952, 52 per cent in 1965, and 47 per cent in 1970. (The trend has been slightly reversed since then; the figure for 1977 is 52 per cent). In the light of this kind of evidence, theories which concentrate on explaining the situation in especially strike-prone industries will ignore much that is significant in the recent scene.

G. K. Ingham has subjected the Ross-Hartman thesis to searching criticism in the course of his comparative study of British and Scandinavian patterns of industrial conflict.[48] He finds that, far from belonging to a common 'North European' pattern of industrial relations, Britain and Scandinavia diverged in many respects, and the differences help to explain the higher strike figures in Britain. His thesis is that industrial concentration and a simple, specialised industrial structure in the small Scandinavian economies have led to centralisation of industrial relations there, and a high level of 'institutionalisation' of industrial conflict, and that the reverse is true of Britain. He contrasts, for example, the British TUC, 'which has displayed chronic constitutional and *de facto* weakness throughout its entire history' with its counterpart in the authoritative Swedish LO. The British economy he finds to be characterised by 'complexity, product differentiation, and relatively low industrial concentration' the results of being the first country to industrialise, so that craft workshop, mass production and automation technologies all co-exist and overlap. The employers' associations in the contrasted economies reflect the same features— there were 1350 such associations in Britain in 1968, but only 44 in Sweden in 1961. British employers only succeeded in forming a unified central body (the Confederation of British Industry) in 1965, almost a hundred years after the foundation of the TUC. The structural complexity of British trade unionism contrasts with the simple industrial union structure of the Scandinavians. Hence the abiding character of British industrial relations, with its fragmented and decentralised collective bargaining and the strength of custom which survives at plant level, which contribute potently as sources of conflict and strikes. Britain's 'failure' to achieve the transition from customary to formal industrial relations lies at the heart of Britain's strike 'problem'. As a contribution to the debate, Ingham's thesis is certainly fruitful, but probably remains content with too great a dependence on the study of institutional superstructures. Surely the deeper reasons for the relative strike-proneness of Britain as compared with Scandinavia lie buried in the fundamental class divisions, historically and continually sharper and more antagonistic in Britain than in Northern Europe.

There is something in common between Ingham's thesis and that of the Donovan Royal Commission, which found Britain's industrial relations problem to consist of a lack of formality in collective bargaining. A recent study of a sample of 45 plants chosen from amongst both strike-prone and strike-free establishments in six different industries, throws some interesting light on this influential theory.[49] The strike records of the plants were examined for 1966-70, and correlated with various characteristics of management and it was found that:

'. . . so far from declining with the establishment and development of formal collective agreements, conciliation procedures and consultative arrangements, or with increasing provision for regular trade union activities and representation within the enterprise, the incidence of labour unrest appears, if anything, to increase.[50]

Was the formalisation of industrial relations a cause or an effect of labour unrest? The authors incline to the view that it was a cause. 'At the least, the proposition that formal arrangements for bargaining and union activity at the enterprise level necessarily encourage industrial peace must be highly suspect'.[51]

High and rising levels of trade union membership and high levels of strikes have often been correlated in British history, from the time of the Owenite movement in the 1830s, through the syndicalist period of 1910–14 and its succeeding phase up to 1926, and in the recent period of the late 1960s to 1977. The casual relationship between the two quantities is complex; it can as well be argued on the evidence that strikes stimulate trade union recruitment as that trade unions cause strikes. Certainly some of the most central features of British trade union structure and organisation, such as the general unions, were born and expanded in the context of strike actions. But equally, the minimal commitment to collective action implied in *joining* a trade union is commonly required before workers will contemplate going on strike. Non-union strikers, where this precondition does not apply, invariably have as one of their purposes, the formation of a union organisation and the obtaining of employer recognition for this: although of course this demand may be elaborated in the course of the dispute itself.

The relationship between strikes and the level of employment also deserves attention. The one durable period of full employment in our history, from 1940 to 1967, was characterised by relatively large numbers of small, short, unofficial strikes. These had no economic significance, though they were heavy with social and political meaning. The most severe and prolonged period of unemployment, from 1929 to 1937, was the nearest to 'industrial peace' which has been experienced in the 20th century, and it has usually been assumed that experience of unemployment is a deterrent to strike action. Yet the period from 1967 to the present was one of rising unemployment associated with a rising incidence of strike activity. This coincides most closely with the period from 1919–26, and we might conclude that severe, large, prolonged strikes are associated with periods of economic dislocation and nascent slump, a time when workers' organisations are still strong, undefeated in major conflicts, and when workers are most conscious of what they have to lose, in terms of living standards and job security. Insecurity caused by slump conditions and technological change is undoubtedly one of the factors driving more workers to join trade unions, and we have argued that rising trade union membership at least coincides historically with rising strike action.

Moreover, the recent period has a further disturbing element absent from the 1919–26 phase, that of inflation. Dislocation and disturbance of established norms, expectations and income differentials are some of the consequences of inflation which, like job insecurity, can be expected to turn workers towards trade unionism and the collective defence of living standards. The severe inflation of the 1970s has 'weakened the hold of traditional frames of reference for judging pay'.[52] This is a profoundly disruptive trend, since it implies the destabilisation of that delicate balance of expectations which has, in the past, related one reference group to another. And this has been associated, in the British case at least, with the increasing tendency for the state to impose wage restraint policies, which bite with particular effectiveness in the public sector, and it is clear that the pincers of inflation and wage control go far to explain the recent outbreaks of strikes in this sector. Indeed, in the light of the evidence for a world-wide strike wave in the 1970s, it is feasible to discover a common, global causation in the universality of inflation, technical change, and dislocation caused by rising unemployment.

Causes of Unrest in Britain

We may turn now from general theories of strike causation to examine the evidence on causes as provided in official British statistics. These figures must be treated with some care, since (a) the stated cause of a strike may not be its 'real' cause; discontent on a whole range of grievances may finally surface in a strike which is ostensibly about wage arrangements (b) the source of information for the stated cause is usually management, rather than the strikers themselves, and (c) strikes are usually (one source believes 'invariably')[53] multi-causal. The official classification on strikes by cause was altered in the Department of Employment in 1973, but a re-working of the old series was provided in the Department's *Gazette* back to 1966. Table VII:6 gives percentage figures of numbers of strike by cause for selected years between 1938 and 1966, using the old classification, table VII:7 provides similar percentages for the period 1966–78, and table VII:8 gives percentages of striker-days by cause for the same period. Comparing the number of strikes due to wages, across the two tables VII:6 and VII:7, we can see that this has tended to rise over the whole post-war period, and to have been particularly high in the years of greatest strike incidence in the late 1960s and 1970s. This effect is even more marked in table VII:8, showing striker-days due to wages rising to 88.5 per cent, 90.4 per cent and 85 per cent, in the years of

Table VII:6

*No. of strikes, by cause, in selected years, 1938–66, as percentages of all strikes
(old classification)*

Cause	1938	1942	1946	1950	1954	1958	1962	1966
Wages	39	62	43	44	47	46	46	45
Hours of work	5	4	3	3	2	2	—	1
Demarcation, disputes on employment & discharge (inc. redundancy & other personnel questions)	29	13	13	15	12	13	19	21
Other working arrangements, rules and discipline	15	19	36	34	37	36	29	29
Trade union status	11	1	4	2	2	2	4	3
Sympathetic	1	1	1	2	—	1	2	1
Strikes in year (number)	875	1,303	2,205	1,339	1,989	2,629	2,449	1,937

Source: Ministry of Labour *Gazette*, Employment and Productivity *Gazette*.

heaviest strikes in 1971, 1972 and 1974. The heavier the strike incidence, the more likely it is to be about wages.

The old series category of 'other working arrangements, rules and discipline' corresponds roughly with the new classifications of 'working conditions', 'manning and work allocations' and 'dismissals and other disciplinary matters'. It can be seen in table VII:6 that this category rose from its 1938 level of 15 per cent of all strikes, to an average of over one-third in the post-war years. Examining this trend in 1963, Professor Turner argued that:

> 'One could say that these disputes all involve attempts to submit managerial discretion and authority to agreed—or failing that customary—rules: alternatively that they reflect an implicit pressure for more democracy and individual rights in industry . . . it seems clear that here one is dealing with a strong contemporary current of feeling, which has not so far been satisfied by the limited development of joint consultation.'[54]

In the subsequent years, the three relevant catagories in the new series

Table VII:7

No. of strikes, by cause, 1966–78, as percentages of all strikes (new classification)

Cause	1966	1967	1968	1969	1970	1971	1972	1973	1974	1975	1976	1977	1978
Wage rates and earnings levels	43.0	44.8	51.8	56.6	62.0	51.0	57.0	47.1	61.5	55.3	39.2	52.4	58.2
Extra-wage and fringe benefits	2.8	2.0	2.0	2.8	2.0	1.8	2.4	3.2	4.3	2.5	4.2	5.2	3.4
ALL PAY	45.8	46.8	53.8	59.4	64.0	52.8	59.4	50.3	65.8	57.8	43.4	57.6	61.6
Duration and pattern of hours worked	2.1	3.2	2.1	2.0	1.4	1.9	2.2	2.5	1.8	1.1	3.3	1.7	2.0
Redundancy questions	3.6	3.5	3.3	2.7	3.1	6.9	12.6	3.0	2.9	5.1	4.3	2.8	2.5
Trade union matters	7.7	8.5	9.5	8.5	8.1	7.9	6.6	8.2	6.3	6.2	8.2	7.0	4.5
Working conditions	7.8	8.4	5.5	5.0	5.7	5.7	5.2	8.2	5.3	6.8	10.7	9.3	7.7
Manning and work allocation	18.7	15.0	12.0	11.0	7.4	10.3	10.5	13.4	9.0	12.1	19.8	13.1	12.5
Dismissals and other disciplinary measures	13.1	13.8	13.2	10.5	7.4	14.2	10.4	13.4	8.9	10.9	10.4	8.5	9.2
Miscellaneous	0.4	0.7	0.4	0.7	0.6	0.3	0.4	0.4	—	—	—	—	—
Strike in year (number)	1,937	2,116	2,378	3,116	3,906	2,228	2,497	2,873	2,922	2,282	2,016	2,703	2,349

Source: Department of Employment *Gazette.*

Table VII:8

No. of striker-days, by cause, 1966–78, as percentages of all striker-days (new classification)

Cause	1966	1967	1968	1969	1970	1971	1972	1973	1974	1975	1976	1977	1978
Wage-rates and earnings levels	65.7	58.6	76.0	57.4	82.0	88.5	90.4	69.4	85.0	74.4	47.3	73.5	77.3
Extra wage and fringe benefits	3.0	1.1	1.0	2.0	3.0	2.0	0.3	2.6	3.3	0.8	4.8	5.7	1.7
ALL PAY	68.7	59.7	77.0	59.4	85.0	90.5	90.7	72.0	88.3	75.2	52.1	79.2	78.9
Duration and pattern of hours worked	2.7	2.7	0.5	15.2	0.3	0.8	0.3	0.8	1.4	0.4	1.1	0.3	2.5
Redundancy questions	5.6	2.0	1.8	1.3	2.0	2.3	4.1	2.0	0.7	3.6	5.7	1.6	1.2
Trade Unions matters	7.6	6.9	9.8	6.5	4.9	1.5	1.7	8.0	3.4	8.0	10.8	3.0	3.1
Working conditions	2.4	3.3	1.7	0.8	1.2	0.4	0.3	2.7	0.8	1.9	5.8	2.0	2.7
Manning and work allocation	5.8	15.8	3.8	5.0	2.5	1.6	1.0	6.2	2.8	6.8	11.4	8.7	8.1
Dismissals and other disciplinary measures	7.2	9.3	5.1	11.5	4.0	2.9	2.0	8.3	2.8	4.0	13.0	5.1	3.5
Miscellaneous	0.2	0.3	0.04	0.4	—	—	—	—	—	—	—	—	—
Striker-days in year (number/millions)	2,395	2,783	4,719	6,925	10,908	13,589	23,923	7,145	14,845	5,914	3,509	10,378	9,391

Source: Department of Employment Gazette.

have maintained this 'current of feeling' right through the period of steadily rising strike incidence, at an average of 30 per cent of all strikes, from 1966 to 1977, although as a proportion of striker-days they account only for an annual average of 14 per cent, showing that strikes on these issues are smaller and shorter, than those on wages and other matters.

Of the other categories of strike, it is noteworthy that hours of work, trade union 'status' or trade union 'matters' (which include recognition and closed shop disputes) and 'extra-wage and fringe benefits' are all quite minor causes, and contrary to popular opinion, more detailed enquiries have revealed that demarcation alone accounted for only 2–3 per cent of strikes during the 1960s,[55] and that multi-unionism is a factor in not more than 5 per cent of strikes.[56]

It is interesting, after this examination of causes according to official statistics, to look at what workers have had to say about their reasons for striking. In an extensive case-study of a large engineering plant, Batstone *et al* found that 'the most dominant vocabularies attribute blame to management' and that amongst management behaviour which provoked strikes were the breaking of agreements, 'conning', 'adopting a hard line', ignoring men's efforts, goodwill, or intentions, and adopting an aggressive approach. Security of earnings and loss of money appear twice as often amongst reasons for striking, as a desire to increase earnings, and 'an average of five types of reason existed for each strike or near-strike which we observed'.[57]

A very specific and potent cause of recent increases in strike figures in Britain has, we have argued, been the juxtaposition of high inflation rates with statutory or near-statutory incomes policies. These circumstances have borne particularly heavily on public sector workers, especially since incomes policies have been tightened up to exclude the traditional public service unions' claims for 'fair comparisons' with outside industries. Along with the imposition of cash limits on public expenditure, monetarist economists, whose self-destructive influence has spread deep into the Treasury and into the front benches of both major political parties, have called for the deliberate abandonment of the concept of a 'going-rate' of wages, so that the claim for parity by public service workers can be removed from the collective bargaining scene. Since the wide public debate of incomes policies has the effect of making everyone more conscious of their relative pay, it is small wonder that the public sector has been driven more and more frequently into intransigent collective action. The persistent failure of the public service unions and the TUC to co-ordinate this action has meant that it has frequently been less effective than it might have been. We wrote at some length about this in 1972, and everything we said then is still relevant.[58]

Strikes with an overtly political motive have usually been a very small proportion of total stoppages, and are indeed excluded from the official statistics. During the perid from 1910 to 1926, and particularly in the pre-war years of 1910–14, syndicalist philosophy, which regards strikes as a training ground for social revolution, and the General Strike as the ultimate political weapon, had some influence in British trade unionism[59] but it is impossible to ascribe political motives to the mass of strikers, and the General Strike when it came in 1926 seems to have been regarded by most trade unionists largely as a defensive action of solidarity with the miners. The aspirations of those who saw the strike as a political offensive against the state were rudely over-ridden by the behaviour of the TUC leaders, who backed away rapidly when the political implications of their actions became evident to them. A few years earlier, the militants of the Triple Alliance had called unsuccessfully for a general strike to force an end to the government's physical intervention against Soviet Russia, but in 1920 the Council of Action set up by the TUC, the parliamentary Labour Party, and the Labour Party, did in fact contemplate such action, and may well have influenced the government in its withdrawal of support for the anti-Soviet Poles.

Much more recently, industrial action on a considerable scale was directed against the Industrial Relations Bill in 1971. There were four one-day unofficial strikes against the Bill, accounting for 350,000, 180,000, 1,250,000 and 1,250,000 striker days. Between 1970 and 1974, official estimates record that there were 3,300,000 striker days against the Bill and the Act, 1,000,000 striker days against decisions of the National Industrial Relations Court, 1,600,000 striker days against incomes policies, 100,000 striker-days of postmen against the sacking of their chairman, 200,000 striker-days against the government's decision to let Upper Clyde Shipbuilders go bankrupt, and 85,000 days in protest against unemployment, a total of political or near-political striker days of 6,285,000.[60] Ingham's study, already cited, includes this apposite statement:

'. . . if this "politicisation" of industrial conflict continues, govern-ments in Britain are likely to change the pattern of industrial conflict from that which we witnessed in the last decade. The existence of a clearly identifiable and coercive source of grievance in the form of the state will almost inevitably increase the size and scope of industrial disputes.'[61]

Implicit in our discussion so far have been certain distinctions between different types of strike—long, large stoppages and short, small strikes, official and unofficial strikes. To these classes we should add also so-called 'constitutional' and 'unconstitutional' strikes. The long, large strike, intended by both sides as a serious trial of strength, is a quite different kind of social action from the small, short strike intended by workers mainly as a demonstration of feeling.[62] The major trials of strength occur, as we have seen, mainly around national industry-level wage claims, whilst the short, local demonstration strike may have a hundred and one different causes in local grievances.

Unofficial Stoppages

Most of the latter strikes are unofficial, which is to say that they lack the authority of the strikers' union behind them. This may mean that the union disapproves in an active sense, or it may mean that it maintains a largely benevolent neutrality. Whilst the right to strike appertains to individuals, to persons, there is no legal ground for such distinctions as 'official' or 'unofficial', since all strikes equally involve people, whilst only some involve organisations.

The censure of unofficial strikers in the press is almost entirely unhelpful and inappropriate. Trade union leaders can rarely act in advance of their members[63] and hence official support is often a matter of policy, late in being declared, by which time many strikes will have already finished. In other cases, union funds may be too low to allow the union to risk recognising the strike. Even where the trade union definitely opposes the strike, the degree of discipline which it can exert is strictly limited by the very nature of trade unions, and by most union rule books. (Only three union rule books of a large sample investigated give specific authority to discipline unofficial strikers, and only one gives the authority for the executive to expel members in these circumstances.[64]) It is in any case a dubious proposition to suggest that any union ought to have this kind of power over its members; the only legitimate control which unions should enjoy over members is that which comes from the expression of members' grievances and aspirations, *not* from suppressing them.

In practice then, unofficial strikes present a complex phenomenon. One writer has distinguished as many of five different categories:[65] (a) those in which the union executive supports the strike but does not wish to finance it, (b) those in which the union gives tacit support, to shift the employers' position, (c) those to which the union would have given recognition had the strike not been too short, (d) those which have the support of the District union organisation, but not of the national centre, (e) those which the union fully opposed, which probably means that they were at least partially directed *against* the union. That these latter two categories are a small proportion of the whole is indicated by the evidence of the TUC which found (in 1959–60) that 'in about half the cases reported to the General Council where strikes began without official sanction, the union paid dispute benefit.'[66] Even were their numbers greater, it would be at some risk to liberty that they were ever prevented. If a union is out of favour with its members, they may have arguments on their side.

Table VII:9

The percentage of strikes, and striker-days, accounted for by official strikes, 1961–77

	No. of strikes %	No. of striker-days %
1961	2.2	28.3
1962	3.2	70.9
1963	2.4	30.0
1964	2.8	30.3
1965	4.1	20.8
1966	3.1	48.9
1967	5.1	14.1
1968	3.8	46.9
1969	3.1	23.6
1970	4.1	30.2
1971	7.2	74.2
1972	6.4	76.2
1973	4.6	27.9
1974	4.3	47.9
1975	6.1	19.1
1976	3.4	14.4
1977	2.9	24.8
1978	3.6	42.5

Source: Department of Employment *Gazette.*

Table VII:9 gives the official record of the proportion of strikes ana striker-days due to official strikes, for 1961–77. It can be seen that the vast majority (always over 90 per cent) of strikes are classified as unofficial, but that striker-days in official disputes are always a much more significant proportion as we should expect, since it is the longer and larger strikes which are most likely to receive official backing. There was a noticeable increase in the proportion of official striker-days between the 1960s and 1970s. For the years 1961–8, omitting 1962 (which was distorted by a one-day strike of the whole engineering industry) the annual average of official striker-days was 31.3 per cent of all striker-days, but in the strike-wave years of 1969–74 the proportion rose to an annual average of 46.6 per cent. It is noteworthy that this proportion fell sharply in the 'social contract years' of 1975 and 1976.

The distinction between 'constitutional' and 'unconstitutional' strikes is between those which are called only after the appropriate disputes procedure is fully exhausted, and those which are called 'in breach of procedure'. We have very little statistical evidence about their relative significance, but we should expect that some unofficial strikes were also unconstitutional. The annual reports of the Engineering Employers' Federation claim that for 1961–71, three-quarters of all staff strikes in their industry, and 96 per cent of manual workers' strikes, were unconstitutional.[67] But this evidence may be atypical, since the procedure agreement in engineering at that time was outrageously cumbersome, slow, flagrantly biassed in favour of the employers, and out-dated. Perhaps we might *expect* unconstitutional stoppages to be common in the absence of effective, fair and speedy disputes procedures. These particular rituals had been imposed in the 1922 lockout, and remained unchanged until the middle '70s, only because it had been possible to ignore them for such a long time. The remedy is clearly not to bewail the lack of constitutionality, but to create honest and practicable procedures.

Recognition Strikes

There is a further type of strike which deserves a special category to itself and which looms large at least in the consciousness of the active trade unionists; what we may call the 'intransigent recognition strike'. These occur at company level (usually a small company which yet has powerful backers or a strong parent company which remains in the background) when an anti-union employer digs in his heels and refuses recognition to his employees' trade union. These have often proved to be the most testing type of strike for the whole trade union movement, being frequently prolonged for months or years, involving major hardship for the strikers, and sometimes exposing the inability of the trade union movement to act with effective solidarity. Amongst these famous affairs we may list the Roberts-Arundel strike,[68] the Fine Tubes strike,[69] the Jersey Mills strike,[70] the Grunwick strike,[71] and the Sanderson fork-lift factory strike of 1977–8.

Financing Strikes

The financing of strikes has been the subject of a recent authoritative study from which most of the facts in the following paragraphs are derived; the whole book merits thorough study.[72]

Strike pay as a proportion of average earnings did rise between 1950 and 1970; in the AUEW from 15.5 per cent to 24.7 per cent, in the TGWU from 15.5 per cent to 20.6 per cent, in the GMWU from 23.3 per cent to 24.7 per cent, and in NUPE from 15.5 per cent to 16.5 per cent.

Trade unions clearly only contribute financially in the case of official strikes, the general level of strike benefit paid out by unions is very low, and has quite failed in recent years to match the rate of inflation. Thus 60 per cent of male trade unionists were entitled to union strike pay of between £5 and £6 a week in 1971. (In 1978, the AUEW was paying £9 a week, and the TGWU £6 a week, to their striking members at Fords). Strike benefit is low largely because trade union subscriptions are low; most union subscriptions were 10p a week or less in 1971, and have not kept pace with inflation since then. There is enormous variation between unions in the levels of their strike benefits, from SLADE's £15 a week to the female rate in the Bleachers and Dyers' union which was 70p a week. (A considerable number of unions have no specific rule providing for strike funds and strike benefits, including major unions in the public sector.)

Trade unions often have discretion as to whether or not to pay strike benefit even in official disputes; the UPW in 1971 paid benefit only to members ineligible for state Supplementary Benefit, and the NUM in 1972 used its strike funds only to pay members on picket duty. The reference to State benefit takes us to a lively recent controversy around what has been called the 'state subsidy theory of strikes' with which Gennard deals most thoroughly.[73] He shows that public assistance to strikers' families was widespread in the big, long, strikes of the 1920s, but that this did not give rise to the anti-benefit outcry such as is heard today. He speculates wisely that this was because 'it was considered so degrading to be on relief that few people could seriously characterise the Poor Laws as a prop for industrial action'. He finds that Supplementary Benefit *has* grown as a proportion of total finance of strikes since 1967, but that (a) it is paid only in a minority of strikes (mainly the long, official strikes) and (b) it is paid only to a minority of strikers in those strikes. To be valid, the state subsidy theory, which holds that strikes are encouraged and sustained by payment of Supplementary Benefit to strikers' families and by Income Tax rebate, must establish certain assumptions about strikers' knowledge of benefits, about their response to receiving benefit, and about benefit being a substantial share of strikers' incomes. In an investigation into the UPW strike of 1971, and a strike of Coventry electricians at Chrysler in 1973, Gennard and Lasko found (a) that strikers were ignorant about the timing and amount of benefit to which they were entitled, and that most were unpleasantly surprised by the amount they received (b) that they had made no previous calculations about entitlement to benefit, (c) in the Chrysler case, that one-third of the strikers received Supplementary Benefit for some part of the strike, but that it accounted for only 1.4 per cent of the income of the average striker, (d) that in the UPW case, benefit accounted for only 14.5 per cent of strikers' incomes, and that (e) in both cases most strikers expected to live on their wife's earnings, holiday savings, wages owing to them, and help from friends and relatives. The first three of these were *in fact* the main sources of strikers' incomes. In a *Guardian* article reviewing Gennard's book, John Torode concluded: 'The truth of the matter is that the state does not finance strikes and neither do the unions. It is the families who bear overwhelmingly the greatest burden. To cut off all state aid would have little more than symbolic importance. And the political repercussions would be enormous'.[74]

Finally, we may ask the question, 'how far do strikes succeed in achieving their aims?' To this there is no glib statistical answer, although investigations that have been undertaken in mining[75] and in a multi-industry study[76] have found a positive correlation between militancy and relative wage-rates. Over the historical period of the 20th century, we can identify the 1910–14 period as one of successful strikes; the 1919–26 period as one of major defeats, the 1950s and 1960s as a period when the small, short unofficial strikes were usually successful; and the period since 1969 as one of major official strikes, requiring more detailed scrutiny.

Even on a most cursory view, however, these have included some spectacular victories (the miners particularly, in 1972 and 1974) together with some tough 'draws' (perhaps the Firemen in 1977–8) and some unambiguously lost strikes (for example the Post Office in 1971). Whilst we should not be understood as enthusing over strike action, since in any given situation there may be very cogent reasons for avoiding it,[76] in the broad sweep of social history there is little doubt that strikes have contributed positively to the nurturing and sustainance of trade union organisation, to advance wages, and to wrest more democratic controls over working conditions and managerial decision-making, throughout industry.

NOTES

1. K. G. J. C. Knowles, *Strikes: A Study in Industrial Conflict*, Blackwell, 1952.
2. See M. P. Jackson, *Industrial Relations*, Croom Helm, 1977. Also Geoff Brown, *Sabotage* Spokesman, 1977.

3. J. E. T. Eldridge, *Industrial Disputes*, Routledge, Kegan, and Paul, 1968.
4. Talcott Parsons, 'Communism and the West', in *Social Change*, (eds. A. and E. Etzioni,) Glencoe, Ill., 1964, quoted in G. K. Ingham, *Strikes and Industrial Conflict*, Macmillan 1974.
5. J. Hemingway, *Conflict and Democracy: Studies in Trade Union Government*, Clarendon, 1978, describes Harold Wilson's allegations that the 1966 seamen's strike was led by 'a tightly knit group of politically motivated men' as 'quite implausible'.
6. V. L. Allen, *Trade Union Militancy*, Merlin Press, 1966.
7. See for example Mary McAuley, *Labour Disputes in Soviet Russia, 1957-65*, Clarendon, 1969.
8. Milojko Drulovic: *Self-management on Trial*: Spokesman Books 1978.
9. Department of Employment *Gazette*. Italics in original.
10. H. A. Turner, *Is Britain Really Strike-Prone?* Cambridge, 1969.
11. 'The Truth about Britain's Strikes', *Sunday Times*, October 29th 1978, and 'The Awful Truth about Strife in our Factories', *Sunday Times*, November 12th, 1978.
12. H. A. Turner, op. cit.
13. E. Batstone, I. Boraston, and S. Frenkel, *The Social Organisation of Strikes*, Blackwell, 1978.
14. E. Batstone *et al.*, op. cit.
15. See W. E. J. McCarthy, 'The Nature of Britain's Strike Problem', in *British Journal of Industrial Relations*, vol.VIII, 1970, wherein the author challenges the interpetation of international strike statistics to be found in H. A. Turner, op. cit.
16. Ministry of Labour *Gazette*, vol. LXVIII, 1960, cited in E. W. Evans and S. Creigh, 'Introduction' in their *Industrial Conflict in Britain*, Frank Cass, 1977.
17. H. A. Turner, G. Clack, and G. Roberts, *Labour Relations in the Motor Industry*, Allen and Unwin, 1967.
18. W. E. J. McCarthy, loc. cit.
19. E. W. Evans and S. Creigh, op. cit.
20. K. G. Knight, 'Strikes and Wage Inflation in British Manufacturing Industry, 1950-68', *Bulletin of the Oxford Institute of Economics and Statistics*, vol. 34, 1972.
21. K. G. J. C. Knowles, op. cit.
22. R. Hyman, *Strikes*, Fontana, 2nd edition 1977.
23. M. Silver, 'Recent British Strike Trends: A Factual Analysis', *British Journal of Industrial Relations*, vol. XI, no. 1, 1973.
24. A. I. Marsh and W. E. J. McCarthy, *Disputes Procedures in British Industry*, Research Paper no. 2, Part 2, Donovan Royal Commission on Trade Unions and Employers' Associaton, HMSO, 1966.
25. A. I. Marsh, E. O. Evans, and P. Garcia, *Workplace Industrial Relations in Engineering*, Federation Research Paper 4, Engineering Employers' Federation, 1971.
26. Dick Nettleton, former apprentices' leader, in R. A. Leeson (ed), *Strike: A Live History, 1887-1971*, Allen and Unwin, 1973.

27. A full account of the Betteshanger prosecution, factual yet ironic, is given by the war-time Ministry of Labour's Chief Industrial Commission, Sir Harold Emmerson, in Appendix 6 of the *Report* of the Donovan Royal Commission, HMSO, Cmnd. 3623, 1968.
28. E. Wigham, *Strikes and the Government, 1893–1974*, McMillan 1976.
29. E. Wigham, op. cit.
30. See H. A. Clegg and R. Adams, *The Employers' Challenge*, Blackwell, 1957.
31. TUC Annual Report, 1958, which contains a detailed 10 page report on the whole history of the strike and the TUC's involvement.
32. See R. H. Heath, 'The National Power-Loading Agreement in the Coal Industry and some aspects of Workers' Control,' in Michael Barratt Brown, K. Coates, and T. Topham, (eds)., *Trade Union Register 1969*, Merlin Press, 1969.
33. H. A. Turner, *The Trend of Strikes*, Leeds University Press, 1963.
34. R. Hyman, op. cit.
35. See T. Lane, and K. Roberts, *Strike at Pilkingtons*, Fontana, 1971.
36. R. Hyman, op. cit.
37. See J. Hughes and R. Moore, *A Special Case?* Penguin, 1972.
38. R. Hyman, op. cit.
39. The Donovan Royal Commission *Report*, HMSO 1968, Cmnd. 3623.
40. T. G. Sweet and D. Jackson, *The World Strike Wave, 1969–7?* University of Aston Management Centre; Working Paper Series no. 63, January 1977.
41. T. G. Sweet and D. Jackson, op. cit.
42. T. G. Sweet and D. Jackson, op. cit. The latest available figures from the ILO published in the January 1979 issue of the Department of Employment *Gazette*, give provisional statistics for 1977. In that year, strike days per 1,000 employees in Mining, Manufacturing, Construction and Transport rose above the 1976 levels in six countries, and fell below in eight countries. This suggests at least a pause in the strike wave detected by Sweet and Jackson. But the 5 year average figures for 1973–7 show increases in thirteen countries, over the 5 year average for 1968–72, and a decrease in only five countries (the UK, USA, West Germany, Ireland and Sweden).
43. K. G. J. C. Knowles, 'Strike Proneness and its Determinants', in W. Galenson and S. M. Wiley, (eds), *Labor and Trade Unionism*, Wiley 1960.
44. A. M. Ross and P. T. Hartman, *Changing Patterns of Industrial Conflict*, Wiley, 1960.
45. Clark Kerr and A. Siegel, 'The Inter-Industry Propensity to Strike—an International Comparison' in A. Kornhauser, R. Dubin and A. Ross (eds), *Industrial Conflict*, McGraw-Hill, 1954.
46. J. F. B. Goodman, 'Strikes in the U.K.' *International Labour Review*, vol. 95, 1967, and H. A. Clegg, *The System of Industrial Relations in Great Britain*, Blackwell, 1970, for the 1960s, and R. Hyman, op. cit, for the period up to 1975.
47. M. Silver, loc. cit.
48. G. K. Ingham, op. cit.

49. H. A. Turner, G. Roberts, and D. Roberts, *Management Characteristics and Labour Conflict*, Cambridge, 1977.
50. H. A. Turner, G. Roberts and D. Roberts, op. cit.
51. H. A. Turner, G. Roberts and D. Roberts, op. cit.
52. R. Hyman, op. cit.
53. E. Batstone, I. Boraston, and S. Frenkel, op. cit.
54. H. A. Turner, op. cit, Leeds University Press 1963.
55. J. F. B. Goodman, loc. cit.
56. H. A. Clegg, op. cit.
57. E. Batstone, I. Boraston, and S. Frenkel, op. cit.
58. *The New Unionism*, Penguin Books, 1972.
59. Bob Holton, *British Syndicalism*, Pluto Press, 1977.
60. E. Wigham, op. cit.
61. G. K. Ingham, op. cit.
62. R. Hyman, op. cit.
63. R. Hyman, op. cit.
64. J. Gennard, *Financing Strikers*, McMillan, 1977.
65. M. P. Jackson, op. cit.
66. TUC annual *Report*, 1961.
67. M. Silver, loc. cit.
68. See J. Arnison, *The Million Pound Strike*, Lawrence and Wishart, 1970.
69. See Tony Beck, *The Fine Tubes Strike*, Stage 1, 1974.
70. See Mike Taylor, 'The Machine-Minder' in Roland Fraser (ed) *Work 2*, Penguin, 1969.
71. See Tom Durkin, *Grunwick: Bravery and Betrayal*, Brent Trades Council, 1978.
72. J. Gennard, op. cit.
73. See also J. W. Durcan and W. E. J. McCarthy, 'The State Subsidy Theory of Strikes: an examination of the statistical data for the period 1956-70' *British Journal of Industrial Relations*, vol. XII, no. 1, March 1974, L. C. Hunter, 'The State Subsidy Theory of Strikes: A Reconsideration' *British Journal of Industrial Relations*, vol. XII, no. 3, November 1974, and J. Gennard and R. J. Lasko, 'The Individual and the Strike' *British Journal of Industrial Relations*, vol. XIII, no. 3, November 1975.
74. *The Guardian*, October 18th, 1978.
75. John Hughes *The Rise of the Militants*. Trade Union Affairs, No. 1, 1960-1.
76. H. A. Turner, G. Roberts and D. Roberts, op. cit.
77. A fascinating account of *workers'* reasons for *not* striking is contained in E. Batstone, I. Boraston, and E. Frenkel, op. cit.

Chapter Eight

Industrial Democracy

'The very discovery of improved industrial methods, by leading to specialisation, makes manual labourer and brain-worker alike dependent on the rest of the community for the means of subsistence, and subordinates them, even in their own crafts, to the action of others. In the world of civilisation and progress, no man can be his own master. But the very fact that, in modern society, the individual thus necessarily loses control over his own life, makes him desire to regain collectively what has become individually impossible. Hence the irresistible tendency to popular government, in spite of all its difficulties and dangers.'[1]

It was in 1897 that the Webbs drafted this conclusion to their work on *Industrial Democracy*. Undoubtedly their recognition that 'no man can be his own master' was tempered by the earlier defiant insistence, by their contemporary, William Morris, that 'no man is good enough to be another man's master'.

However, the 'desire to regain collectively what has become individually impossible' has moved through many troubled phases during the civil tumults of the twentieth century. There have been times when it has been a bold and captivating demand, loudly upheld by vast numbers of people. There have been other times when it has survived as a whispered memory, while mass unemployment has intimidated millions of trade unionists into silent conformity. Whilst these phases have continued, they have commonly during that time seemed to be permanent. Commenting upon this very same peroration by the Webbs, the author of a later work on trade unions, Allan Flanders, writing in the mid-'fifties, captured the dominant mood of the immediate post-war years:

'Unfortunately it seems also to be true that modern society tends to destroy the individual's confidence in his capacity to control his own life and thus to weaken any feeling of personal responsibility for his social environment.'[2]

This opinion adequately reflects the official climate of the years after 1945, which, in retrospect, now appear to have been the end of an interlude in British Labour Politics.

Three Periods of Concern: A Historical Background

The history of this century seems to have been characterised by a vast discontent which has recurrently created widespread interest in the ideas of industrial democracy and workers' control.[3] The first third of the century, culminating in the General Strike of 1926, was characterised by the rise of the Labour Party, the prewar 'great unrest', and a proliferation of syndicalist, guild socialist and industrial unionist agitations. After the 1926 defeat, trade unionism was put on the defensive, shop steward organisation was disrupted and smashed in large parts of industry, and the unions only began to recover some of their former powers with the onset of re-armament and the war itself. Up to 1940 unemployment remained over the million mark, and it took trade unionists some years to recover their old self-assurance with the conquest of full employment.

When the Labour Party came to power in 1945, the call for industrial democracy was commonly equated with and reduced to the nationalisation programme, even though many far-sighted trade unionists complained at the time that this was a mistaken policy. Writing while this disappointment was already becoming articulate, Allan Flanders recognised the historical commitment of the trade union movement:

'The growth of trade unionism . . . had undoubtedly contributed to the awakening among employees of a fuller awareness of their own dignity and importance, and this has found expression in demands to more than a larger pay packet and greater leisure. There is a long tradition among British trade unions in favour of the workers having some share in the management and control of the industries in which they are employed, as well as in the determination of their wages and working conditions.'[4]

In the years since the fall of the 1951 Labour Government, there has been a constant strengthening of trade union shop floor responsibility and power, and from the late '50s onwards, a marked renewal of interest in a wide range of prescriptions for democracy in industry.

The Historical Perspective

At its strongest, this call has always been revolutionary in its implications. From near the beginning of the century, James Connolly expressed it very clearly in his work *Socialism Made Easy*,[5] a classic which has frequently been reprinted by the Irish Transport and General Workers' Union. Connolly took the dictum, 'Political institutions are not adapted to the administration of industry', and turned it against those who used it as a conservative defence of the power of property. He developed the argument for an industrial franchise, replacing the territorial division of power upon which rests the foundation of modern states.

'The delegation of the function of government into the hands of representatives elected from certain districts, States, or territories,' he wrote, 'represents no real natural division suited to the requirements of modern society, but is a survival from a time when territorial influences were more potent in the world than industrial influences, and for that reason is totally unsuited to the needs of the new social order, which must be based upon industry . . . What the Socialist does realise is that under a social democratic form of society the administration of affairs will be in the hands of representatives of the various industries of the nation; that the workers in the shops and factories will organise themselves into unions, each union comprising all the workers at a given industry; that said union will democratically control the workshop life of its own industry, electing all foremen, etc., and regulating the routine of labour in that industry in subordination to the needs of society in general, to the needs of its allied trades, and to the departments of industry to which it belongs; that representatives elected from these various departments of industry will meet and form the industrial administration or national government of the country.'

This, said Connolly, would constitute a true social democracy 'from the bottom upward', in place of capitalist political society 'organised from above downward'. Connolly's trade union based socialism would reduce states, territories, and provinces to 'geographical expressions', having 'no existence as sources of governmental power, though they may be seats of administrative bodies.'

Connolly's ideas met and merged with a vast pre-1914 war wave of strike actions which shook the whole British Establishment. The upturn of the trade cycle was accompanied by sharply rising living costs and a remarkable growth of trade union membership. At the same time, the Labour Party's victorious arrival in Parliament in 1906, had already generated some considerable disillusionment with what some critics were to call the 'decorous and hypothetical socialism of Labour MPs'.

In 1908 there had been a wholesale lockout of woodworkers and a national Cotton strike. Next year and the year after there were major disputes in mining. Also in 1910 the Boilermakers were locked out: so that, in one industry after another it became increasingly clear that the gain of direct Parliamentary representation would be simply ignored if the work of self-defence were not also carried on by an active rank-and-file movement. As this awareness extended itself, so the rolling strike-wave became more and more aggressive, integrated and solid. In 1911 victory after victory was gained, by strikes by seamen, dockers, railwaymen and others. It was no accident that industrial unionists and syndicalists took leading parts in these turbulent events.

While they demanded the democratisation of industry and society, the trade union agitators also tried to rationalise the inherited trade union structure. In 1909, there were 1,168 separate union organisations, and it is not surprising that the call for amalgamation and consolidation aroused very wide echoes.

These were particularly clearly heard on the railways, where the formation of the National Union of Railwaymen, in 1913, embodied for a whole generation of militant workpeople the principles of industrial unionism. Such ideals were summed up in a tract published a little after the birth of the NUR, as 'the permeation of labour with a class spirit' and equipment of the workers 'with an organisation capable of supplanting capitalism'. This was the view of G. D. H. Cole and William Mellor, as expressed in an elegantly printed pamphlet called *The Meaning of Industrial Freedom*, which continued:

'The industrial structure brings into a single union all those who are engaged in a factory, a mine, or a service. It follows the line not of occupation, but of industry: it has regard not to what a man is doing, but to the branch of production in which he is employed. This gives the workers far greater power in fighting the employers, and enables them to negotiate with far greater success . . . but it does far more than that. For the first time, it puts them in a position to end the wage-system.'[6]

It was in pursuit of this goal that the engineers were incited to emulate the railwaymen, amalgamating all their various craft associations into one body, and embracing also the semiskilled and unskilled labourers.

The outbreak of war predictably defused the industry wide strike movement, but it paradoxically heightened the demand for workers' control in the day to day argument on the shop floor, particularly in an engineering industry which was working flat out, to meet an insatiable demand for munitions, under the handicap of great labour shortages. The official union leaderships concluded agreements with the Government to promote 'dilution' (the waiving of traditional training and apprenticeship practices), the outlawing of strikes, direction of labour, and the suspension of many trade union protective practices. This created innumerable grievances, and a veritable upheaval in the working conditions of precisely the most skilled and indispensable part of the work force. There was a remarkable growth in the shop steward movement, which proved under such pressures to be easily open to the doctrines of industrial unionism, syndicalism, and their fashionable variant, guild socialism.

All these currents of thought vied with one another for influence, but they also reinforced each other in criticism and passionate debate. Elsewhere we have documented parts of this argument, which can be very clearly traced in the different appeals made by its partisans within the coal-mining industry, some of whom coupled the call for State ownership with a series of elaborate and detailed proposals for popular self-management, while others counterposed to 'reformist' national-isation proposals the demand for overall revolutionary change. Before the first world war came to an end, the Russian Revolution of 1917 raised yet further hopes, and promoted the idea of Soviets or workers' councils, which bore a remarkable similarity to some of the proposals first advocated in these islands by James Connolly. He himself, however, had meantime been shot, in reprisal for his part in the Easter rising in Dublin in 1916. A remarkable convention, in Leeds, in 1917, brought together all wings of British socialism, and numerous key trade union leaders, to acclaim the first Russian Revolution, and to call for the establishment of workers' and soldiers' councils in this country too. In its earlier years the young Soviet Union appeared to be following a path rather similar to that prescribed by Connolly, and this attracted many industrial unionists, guildsmen and syn-dicalists to the new communist party which grew up in the early 'twenties.[8]

It was in the heat of such passions that the Labour Party ratified its new (1918) constitution, which included a commitment to the 'best obtainable system of popular control' of publicly owned industries.

Revolution was in the air, even though King George V was reassured by Will Thorne, after the Leeds Convention that no ill would come of it. 'This seemed to relieve his mind', wrote the Labour Leader, 'and he spoke to me in a most homely and pleasant way. I was very pleased.' Thorne, however, also told the King that 'there will have to be many political and industrial changes during the next few years'.[9] It was in this context that the Government-appointed Whitley Com-mittee recommended widespread experiments with joint consultation (in 1917) and that (two years later) the Sankey Commission reported in favour of nationalisation of the mines. Instead of reform and industrial peace, though, the trade unions were to suffer prolonged mass unemployment, lockouts, and victimisation. The 1922 Engineering lockout established that the 'prerogative' of management was abso-lute. Shop stewards were sacked in droves. The dole queues provided the overwhelming majority of employers with all the 'consultation' they wanted. And then, in 1926, the defeat of the General Strike registered the beginning of a long moratorium on trade union pressures for greater control over the place of work.

This is not to say that the desire for industrial democracy was extirpated: on the contrary. Throughout the 1930s the issue of workers' control continued to be debated at Labour Party Conferences, and even after the formal victory of the Morrisonian model of national-isation (based upon the experience of Herbert Morrison in the creation of a bureaucratically administered Passenger Transport Board for London, and argued with strenuous appeals to the managerial example of Stalin's Russia,[10] which had long since dispensed with all forms of democracy, including industrial democracy) there remained a continuous and determined opposition which kept alive the ideas of syndicalism, guild socialism, and similar schools of industrial demo-cracy, sometimes in fullblooded forms, and sometimes considerably diluted in a variety of compromise proposals. By the time that a Labour Government could be elected, in 1945, this opposition was in a distinct minority, however.

Nationalisation of Coal, Gas, Electricity, Railways, Road Haulage, Airlines and Steel brought something like a fifth of British industry into public control, under vast centralised corporations. Two concessions were made to the idea of industrial democracy: token trade unionists were usually appointed to the national boards of these industries, and an obligation to establish a framework of joint consultative committees was written into the main nationalisation Acts. The first of these made little difference. In the absence of any direct electoral link with the trade union constituency, or even the most limited forms of account-ability, the union-orientated directors soon came to look exactly like all the others. As George Orwell put it in a different case but a similar situation:

'The animals looked from pig to man, and from man to pig, and from pig to man again; but already it was impossible to say which was which'.

The second expedient was at first more promising: in the earliest days there is some evidence that managers were sensitive to the part which was intended by legislators to be played by joint consultative institutions, and many JCCs began their work with earnest enthusiasm. In at least one case a colliery manager actually handed over powers of decision to such a committee, until a court action (which arose inadvertently) established that his legal responsibility could not be divested, whatever the claims of democracy.

The Limitations of Joint Consultation

In this climate, whatever the hopes in which it began, joint consultation soon came to be seen as at best an inadequate expedient, at worst a positive menace, preventing unions from defending their members as resolutely as they might. Seldom were the committees able to exercise real influence on policy: but they were commonly given responsibility for certain types of personnel questions, such as difficult disciplinary cases, or absenteeism: thus incorporating what might otherwise have been the trade union defence into the management prosecution team.

A very clear example of this was given by Arthur Scargill, in his contribution to a discussion on industrial democracy which was organised by the National Union of Mineworkers:

A number of years ago, the Consultative Committees at colliery level introduced an Absentee Committee to analyse the reasons why men were not attending for work, to interview them and, if necessary, take disciplinary action including dismissal where the Absentee Committee thought it warranted.

I can remember quite well an example of how this worked at a colliery in the Barnsley Area a few years ago.

The members who comprise the Absentee Committee began to look at the statistics and forgot they were representing human beings. They were, in spite of themselves, more concerned with the fact that 20 per cent of the men had been absent over a certain period of time rather than assessing, as Trade Union representatives, why these men had been off work.

When a man advanced an excuse that he had been off work because his wife had been taken ill, or that his children had been taken into hospital, the Committee looked sceptically at the case. They became, in spite of their determination not to, 'management orientated'.

They started to take decisions which were completely out of character with the accepted role of Trade Union representatives. What followed was to show the conflict of interest more clearly than any academic could ever explain.

The man who had been dismissed took his case to the local NUM and asked them to represent him in an attempt to persuade the management to withdraw the notice of dismissal. It should be remembered, of course, that the Union Branch in question had already participated in the decision to dismiss the man concerned and this placed the Miners' Union Branch in an impossible position.

He then took his case to the Branch Meeting and the Branch members overwhelmingly supported his case.

The situation was now bordering on the bizarre, i.e. the representatives of the Union having participated in the decision to dismiss the man had then taken a decision that they could not represent him in negotiations with management because they had been part of the management decision to dismiss.

In effect, the rank and file at the pit were challenging not only the NCB at coal level, but also the NUM at local level. The men at the colliery threatened strike action and the result was that management had a rethink about the case and the man was reinstated and, according to my latest information is still employed at the colliery some 10 years later.'[11]

On the strength of this kind of evidence, Arthur Scargill went on to insist:

'A Union in this situation is completely impotent and can do nothing except watch the rank and file pressurise management and, in effect, the Union to rethink *their* decision.

This has the effect of weakening the Union and discrediting the leadership in the eyes of the miners. It also weakens the Union's ability to negotiate effectively with the management because miners begin to distrust a leadership who are prepared to participate in dismissing a member of the Union when this is clearly a management function and a management decision which can, and should, be challenged by the Union as the representatives of the membership.'

In practice, the institutions of consultation took on somewhat different significance in different areas: where unions were determined to play an adversary role, they could do so: but where they agreed to go along with the pressure to discharge minor policing functions, there were frequently quite similar complaints that the union's identity was being compromised. On the other side of the coin, one beneficial result of the process was that it frequently permitted workpeople to inform (or threaten to inform) higher management of some of the derelictions of middle management so that it could sometimes conduce to a more humane working environment: but this improvement commonly came about as a result of paternalist concern, and could hardly be presented as a form of democratic self-regulation.

Vesting day, (when nationalisation took effect) in the Coal industry, was at the beginning of 1947: by 1948 consultation was already rather obviously less than 'the best obtainable system of popular administration and control', promised in the Labour Party's objects: so that considerable unease was being expressed both in the Labour Party Conference and at the TUC. These protests were muted upon appeal from conference organisers, however, and it was agreed that joint discussions would be initiated between the Party's National Executive Committee and the Congress.

By this time, the international alignments which have dominated the world since 1945 had crystallised: cold war was already raging, and a by-product of it was the circumscription of communist activities in a number of trade unions, some of which determined upon an actual ban on office-holding by communist party members. In 1949, such a proscription was agreed by 426 to 208 votes at the biennial conference of the TGWU. Interestingly, at the same time, by 433 to 170, the conference agreed

> 'that trade union representatives should be placed on the boards and executives . . . with the right of the members to recall such trade union representatives as and when considered necessary.'[12]

These two simultaneous decisions show how far the industrial visions of James Connolly had become separated from the communist doctrine, in the minds of many ordinary union members: they also show how far these workers still desired effective self-government, whatever harm the undemocratic evolution of the USSR might do to the reputation of socialism. Paradoxically, many of those who suffered proscription were themselves ardent supporters of workers' control, who had become communists precisely inasmuch as they believed that Soviet institutions embodied a strong commitment to industrial democracy. An enormous confusion, based upon a vast flow of misinformation, characterised this whole period, and made the whole issue very difficult to discuss.

When, also during 1949, the TUC reported on the questions which it had been set about reform of nationalisation, it confined itself to proposals for improving formal representation by unions on National Boards, and increasing consultation. Two years later, the Labour Government fell, and then, for thirteen years, fundamental democratic restructuring of the nationalised industries was no longer an immediate practical option.

In the meantime, the same cold war which had begun to divide British unions had brought Yugoslavia into conflict with the USSR, and thus created the preconditions for that small country's remarkable experiments in industrial democracy.[13] These were to exert wide influence in later years.

The Content of the Modern Movement

Throughout this time, the movement for industrial democracy in Britain took three connected forms: first, a growth in shop-floor negotiating power and control over specific conditions of employment; second, a lobby for more democratic forms of public ownership; and third, as a result of the intensified difficulties of the British economy, and the consequent demand for Governmental incomes policy, a tendency to create more and more elaborate mechanisms to involve union leaders in some form of overall planning mechanism. Other democratic options, such as the growth of the co-operative idea, were not to mature until a good deal later on.

This modern movement for industrial democracy has had to pilot its way through an extremely complex mish-mash of terminology. 'Workers' control' is an ambivalent term because the word 'control' in the English language is capable of bearing a variety of different meanings. On the one hand, we speak of 'controllers of British industry', meaning the most powerful corporate owners and directors. On the other hand, control can signify a shifting relationship of supervision, surveillance and monitoring. European languages are commonly exempt from this difficulty: control usually means the second type of activities, and a different phrase is used to describe the first. When a Frenchman wishes to speak of the workers taking charge of the running of industry, he calls this process, 'self-management'.[14] Many English trade unionists, however, speak of workers' control when they are seeking to argue for self-management, and this sometimes creates a certain amount of misunderstanding. An increasing consensus limits the use of the words 'workers' control' to cover the extension (encroachment) of direct powers of working people over the immediate environment in which they work. It is in this sense that the growth of shop floor powers is most easily understood. The whole process has been graphically described by Philip Higgs, a convenor in the aircraft industry in Coventry:

'Earnings are one of the principal controls, but by no means the only one. Over the past four or five years, pretty much since I became convenor, a fair part of my time along with other stewards has been spent encouraging and helping workers in a department or section to form a gang. This is a powerful weapon in the struggle for control, because the employer can no longer pick on the individual worker but is forced to negotiate with a collective. Some sections of our plant, such as final assembly of engines, have always worked in gangs because this was the best for the company. So we took the decision that what was best for the company under certain circumstances was good for us all the time. At that time there was real inequality of earnings in some sections and a lack of strength in negotiations with rate-fixers, as well as a failure to be able to control labour-loading. We presented our arguments to the lads: the gang was a collective in which weaker members could be safe-guarded; everyone would get the same wage; there would be more control of conditions; and it could improve earnings when one man—the democratically elected ganger—could be almost full time on rate-fixing problems and the organising of work. Since foremen are usually busy at production meetings, filling in forms or doing progress work, the ganger ends up by having some control over the allocation of work. Of course, this organisation of the work process by the workers themselves in fact helps the company; but when it reaches the stage where the company feels it is losing control over the organisation and earnings of the shop floor, it reacts.

At first, however, the company didn't react, and the gang system started to spread. Usually the most able negotiator would be elected as ganger to negotiate all the prices, and he would get to know the rate-fixer and how he was thinking. Of course, the reverse was also true, but these are facts of life in a factory and we aren't at each other's throats all the time. Yet the ganger knows he has twenty, thirty or forty men behind him; and if he tells a man to put a job on the floor the whole gang will pay that man's wages. I've seen gangs where a man has had a job on the floor for a fortnight. Everyone on the gang is losing only a few pence an hour to pay his wage and eventually the firm has to cave in. The gang is a terrific weapon in the hands of the union . . .

Recently a turning section in my own shop decided they wanted to work the gang system. The company clamped down immediately and refused. Some months before the company had tried to get us to accept a new agreement for gangs which was designed to reassert company control over such things as work allocation, labour-loading and piece-work negotiation. As we were short of work at the time and not in the best position to fight, we left the matter in abeyance until we were in a more favourable position. Now the company announced that no more gangs could be formed until we accepted their terms.

As soon as we knew this, we worked out our best strategy.'[15]

This involved short, considered disputes which were quickly effective at a time when the company was anxious to avoid disruption in other production.

'In a well-organised factory where the strategy is to go for limited advances, long mass strikes shouldn't be necessary. Of course, there are bloody-minded company managements who don't care at all if they are wrong, who prefer a total shutdown to a compromise . . . With each such advance we secure a little more control, a little more of managerial function is taken from management.

For example, the reasons for sacking a worker have been reduced to very bad workmanship or very bad timekeeping, and the incidence of dismissals, which can only be carried out by virtual agreement with the workers as a whole, is a fraction of 1 per cent of the total labour force. Dismissal, in other words, cannot be used for disciplinary reasons. Similarly, with the gang system, management has to get the workers' agreement to engage labour, which gives the gang control over the amount of labour put on to a job and the earning level.

Nothing is won without a fight; and the employers fight back, trying to change the rules of a game which they feel they are losing control of.'[16]

In the same sense, dock workers control hiring and firing in their industry so that no-one may be engaged or turned out without the permission of the dockers' representatives. Yet shop workers quite commonly enjoy no such security. It thus seems reasonable to speak of the dockers exercising greater controls in this domain than the shop workers. Of course, neither dockers nor shop workers have attained anything like self-management.

Encroachment of Powers

Even so, in recent years shop stewards have reached far beyond the point described by Philip Higgs, to wield considerable influence over large areas of decision-making which, comparatively recently, were entirely the property of management. Control of hiring and firing by workpeople became a qualitatively new issue when the prolonged postwar period of full employment began to give place to continued high levels of unemployment. Beginning with an unsuccessful attempt to prevent factory closures and redundancies in the Merseyside plants of GEC, the movement of factory occupations, 'work-ins' and sit-ins became a major phenomenon after the pioneering struggles of the workers at Upper Clyde Shipbuilders, in 1971.[17] Under the slogan of 'the right to work' this exemplary battle soon had imitators all over the country, and within three years more than 200 such initiatives had been recorded. Sometimes these raised the question of co-operative self-management, to which we shall return. More commonly, they were concerned with workers' control in the narrow sense employed in this chapter: they were attempts to limit arbitrary managerial powers by the exercise of joint trade union action.

Naturally, resistance to plant closures or mass redundancies implies a challenge to the decisions which bring these policies into practice: accordingly there have been a whole series of attempts to bargain about such heartland 'management' matters as investment priorities, product-mixes, and alternative corporate planning.[18] The Transport and General Workers' Union began to introduce elements of environmental protection into its claims, during the early 'seventies.[19] Before long, as the demand 'open the books' was taken up both in bargaining around the table, in political action and then in legislative responses, so it became more and more frequent to find investment policies subjected to scrutiny, and sometimes opposition.

This process culminated in two types of action: firstly, the political call for formal planning agreements, intended to be made obligatory in the major multinationals which were dominant in British manufacturing industry, and thus to involve tripartite negotiations between unions, management and Government in determining a range of strategic issues; and secondly, the alternative corporate plan which emerged as a trade union response to the threat of serious contraction in employment at Lucas Aerospace.

Planning Agreements

The first of these approaches was canvassed in the 1973 Programme of the Labour Party:

'The key to our planning effort is the domination of the economy by a few leading firms. For by concentrating our efforts on to these firms—and especially the 100 or so major firms in manufacturing—we can ensure that our planning is kept both manageable and straightforward. We will harness directly the energies of these giants—leaving the numerous smaller firms to our more general planning policies. Two points of principle, however, we must make clear:

First, that in seeking to operate directly upon the activities of these leading firms, we are interested not so much in the day-to-day or month-to-month *tactics* which they will need to employ—how much they should produce, say, of each particular product—but in their medium and longer term *strategies*. That is, we are concerned to influence and shape their strategic programmes on investment, on location, on training, on import substitution and the like.

Second, that we will not attempt to meet precisely a set of over-detailed economic targets or expect to bring about a miraculous spurt in economic growth. Certainly, we do intend to make a major forecasting effort, and to establish—in consultation with both sides of industry—clear and identifiable targets. But our *prime* aim will be to achieve certain very broad objectives in terms of jobs in certain regions, for example, in investment, or in exports. It is the fulfilment of these objectives, indeed, which is critical to our whole economic strategy.'[20]

A far-reaching scheme for monitoring this process was set forth in a seven-point programme.

'To get up-to-date information, on a systematic and continuing basis, from all companies within the system. This information will concern both past performance and *advance* programmes—programmes which can be checked at a later date, against results. And it will cover such areas as investment, prices, product development, marketing, exports and import requirements.

To use this information to help the Labour Government to identify and achieve its planning objectives and to plan for the redistribution of resource which will be needed to meet those objectives.

To get the agreement of the firms within the system—the written Planning Agreement—that they will help the Government to meet certain clearly defined objectives (e.g. a certain number of new jobs in a Development Area)—whilst leaving the *tactics* which will be needed to achieve these objectives to the companies themselves.

To provide for the regular revision of those agreements, in the light of experience and progress.

To provide a basis for channelling selective Government assistance directly to those firms which agree to help us to meet the nation's planning objectives.

To provide a systematic basis for making large companies accountable for their behaviour, and for bringing into line those which refuse to co-operate—using, where necessary, both the extensive powers under our proposed Industry Act, the activities of our new and existing public enterprises, and the powers of public purchasing.

To publish and publicise a detailed annual report to the nation on the record of the companies within the system, and on the progress—or lack of it—towards meeting the nation's economic objectives.'[21]

It was insisted that trade unions 'must have the right to take part' both in drawing up the plans which were to be presented to the Government, and in the consultations about the final agreements.

Later plans were announced to involve the 30 most important companies in such agreements by December 1976, and to comprehend the top 100 by the end of 1978. Twelve items for discussion were listed in the White Paper *The Regeneration of British Industry*:

1. Economic prospects
2. The Company's broad strategy and long term objectives
3. UK sales (sales for each main product line and the Company's market share)
4. Exports
5. Investment
6. Employment and Training
7. Productivity
8. Finance
9. Prices policy
10. Industrial Relations and arrangements for negotiation and consultation
11. Interests of consumers and community
12. Product and process development.[22]

The last five of these items being more complex than the first seven, it was suggested that they might not be tabled for consideration until 1976.

In fact, nothing happened, because the Prime Minister, Mr Wilson, personally intervened to ensure (after his Governmental reshuffle following the 1975 referendum on membership of the European Economic Community) that planning agreements were made 'voluntary' instead of compulsory.[23] Only one such agreement was ever concluded, and this was with Chrysler Motors at the moment between their collapse and subsequent Governmental resuscitation. This agreement was unilaterally abrogated when the company was later taken over by French interests, and no further argument was heard about it.[24] But the idea of such agreements dies hard, and it may well recur if ever a reforming Government comes into office with the will to do anything to widen the scope of economic planning and popular participation.

Alternative Corporate Plans

The Lucas initiative was altogether more elaborate and far-reaching than this fiasco. Shop stewards from the aerospace combine approached Mr Tony Benn while he was Secretary for Industry, with the complaint that contractions in armament budgets would imply serious unemployment unless counter-projects were launched. He invited them to propose alternatives, and after an elaborate programme of discussion and enquiry, the shop stewards' combine committee put forward more than 1,000 pages of reasoned argument about how alternatives might indeed be developed.[25] This involved consultations with 180 leading authorities, universities and institutions outside the firm, and a vast effort inside it. As a result no less than 150 ideas for relevant new or developed products were set forward. These were refined and grouped into six major product ranges, some of which were extensions of existing commitments, (pace-makers and kidney-machines, for instance) while others represented the application of high technology to areas of unmet social need:

> 'Before we even started the corporate plan our members at the Wolverhampton plant visited a centre for children with Spina Bifida and were horrified to see that the only way they could propel themselves about was literally by crawling on the floor. So they designed a vehicle which subsequently became known as Hobcart —it was highly successful and the Spina Bifida Association of Australia wanted to order 2,000 of these. Lucas would not agree to manufacture these because they said it was incompatible with their product range.'[26]

As Mike Cooley, one of the leading stewards involved, reports:

> 'the design and development of this product were significant in another sense: Mike Parry Evans, its designer, said that it was one of the most enriching experiences of his life when he actually took the Hobcart down and saw the pleasure on the child's face—it meant more to him, he said, than all the design activity he had been involved in up to then. For the first time in his career *he actually saw the person who was going to use the product that he had designed.* It was enriching also in another sense because he was intimately in contact with a social human problem. He literally had to make a clay mould of the child's back so that the seat would support it properly. It was also fulfilling in that for the first time he was working in the multi-disciplinary team together with a medical type doctor, a physio-therapist and a health visitor. I mention this because it illustrates very graphically that it is untrue to suggest that aerospace technologists are only interested in complex esoteric technical problems. It can be far more enriching for them if they are allowed to relate their technology to really human and social problems.'[27]

Other prototypes were tested, and some of these aroused worldwide interest. They included a rail-road car which could drive on and off a railway, thus avoiding the need to incur vast expense in laying down railway lines through inclines or tunnels; a hybrid power pack which could both conserve energy and reduce pollution and noise; and a whole area of work on heat pumps.

While the company refused point-blank to negotiate on this alternative corporate plan, although the Government was unwilling to press the company to take up the matter, the argument reached a point at which it became impossible for ministers to ignore the plan, and in 1978 the Labour Party warmly endorsed the whole scheme.

In February 1979 the Lucas shop stewards published a further four hundred-page document: *Turning Industrial Decline into Expansion*.[28] After some considerable initial difficulties with some of the national officials of their various trade unions, the stewards secured the recognition and endorsement of the Confederation of Shipbuilding and Engineering Unions for their Corporate Plan. In the words of Ernie Poland, a TGWU steward:

'It took a lot of persistence, much campaigning and much resolution but eventually, on 25 April 1978, an historic meeting was held in a Brummie pub under the auspices of the Confederation of Shipbuilding and Engineering Unions (CSEU)—we had become legitimate.

This meeting brought the shop stewards' demands right into the orbit of trade unionists most powerful organisation within the engineering industry. Their cause was taken up, endorsed and acted upon.

They won the backing of 2,500,000 workers, whom the CSEU represent, for:—

■ total opposition for any further rundown of Lucas Aerospace within the United Kingdom.

■ full support for no movement of equipment, know-how or transfer of any labour (manual or staff) from any plant under threat and restrictions on all subcontracting.

■ a Parliamentary enquiry into the role of the Department of Industry in its dealings with Lucas and the Company's use of £56 million deferred tax.'[29]

The stewards had discovered that between 1971 and 1977 Lucas had 'made an overall profit of £250 million, paid tax of £10.6 million and yet received grants from the Government of £10.1 million. Since 1973 deferred tax has amounted to £179 milion and in 1978 deferred taxes of about £75 million exceeded the company's profits . . . ' reported the Transport and General Workers' *Record*.

Yet, in the words of *Decline into Expansion*,

'In 1970 Lucas employed 79,431 employees in the United Kingdom, by 1978 this had been reduced to 69,631, a reduction of 12.34 per cent. During the same period the number of employees overseas has grown dramatically. It is difficult to quantify this because the Company reports give only figures for those directly employed by Lucas abroad, whereas the more significant figure would be of those employed in Lucas' associated companies overseas. This method of presenting figures seems to be quite misleading. For example, the Company's 1977 Annual Report gives the number of employees in the EEC countries in total as 4,667 yet, in an advertisement in a French newspaper which appeared in the Lucas House Paper "Lucas Light" of September 1977 the Company states, "There is one British industrial company which guarantees 11,836 jobs in France" . . . (our translation), namely Lucas. Commenting on these developments the Assistant General Secretary of APEX, Mr Ray Edwards, has said "Certainly the relative employment position has deteriorated for the UK based worker. Redundancies have been "the norm" within the United Kingdom for a number of years and factory closures represent a more recent cause for concern. Despite its much publicised Home Investment Plans a considerable amount of money has been raised to finance overseas activities; when this feature is added to the "corporate image" which has been promulgated from the end of 1975, Lucas does not look any different from the other faceless multinationals which proliferate the globe'.[30]

This juxtaposition of trends provides an example in a nutshell of how trade unions recognised the necessity to seek to bargain about investment decisions, at any rate in their relation to manpower commitments. The Lucas campaign has succeeded in preventing the imposition of many redundancies; secured a stay of execution of others; increased the manpower budget at a new plant in Huyton from 500 to 800: and, after stormy and long argument, secured at last some agreement by the company to discuss the stewards' proposals. Meantime, similar projects have been evolved at Vickers, and not unrelated ones at Parsons, the generator manufacturers. At Parsons, constructive and successful negotiations did take place,[31] and the management accepted many of their workers' proposals.

If these were the responses of shop stewards, what was the approach of the central councils of the trade union movement?

Worker Directors and the Bullock Report

From the early 'seventies onwards, the TUC was drawn deeper and deeper into the argument about appointing worker-directors on to company boards, which it had already entered, tentatively, in 1966.

Beginning with reaction to the celebrated Draft Fifth Directive of the European Economic Community, published in 1972, and the EEC's paper on a draft for European Company statutes, the General Council found itself compelled to develop more and more detailed responses on this issue. The EEC proposed to generalise throughout Europe what were essentially variations on current German Company Law, providing for the appointment of works councils representing all employees, whether unionised or not, and for two-tier company boards, separating out 'supervisory' or overall policy functions from 'management' ones. Workers would elect a minority of the directors on the supervisory boards. In reply to Governmental requests for comments on these suggestions, the General Council published a statement on Industrial Democracy in 1974,[32] which argued the case for equality of representation for both workpeople and shareholders upon the supervisory boards of companies employing 2,000 or more workers, provided that worker representatives were elected 'through the trade union machinery'.

Although the Labour Party contested the two 1974 elections on manifestos which included direct commitments to industrial democracy, 'in both the private and public sectors', and specific promises to 'introduce new legislation' no such legislation was ever brought forward. Instead, at the very end of 1975, the Government established the Bullock Committee, comprising a mixture of TUC representatives, industrialists and independents, to look into the effects of proposals to place representative workpeople on boards of directors. This committee reported in 1977,[33] in favour of legislation to require the election of worker-directors on to the single-tier boards of large companies. 'Parity' would require equality of numbers between worker and shareholder representatives, but an intermediary group of directors would be appointed by mutual consent of the two sides, or by an Industrial Democracy Commission in the event of their failure to agree. This was designated the '2x + y' formula, where 'x' was the equal number of directors elected by shareholders and workpeople respectively, and 'y' the smaller quota of independents, who might hold the balance in the event of deadlock between the two 'x' contingents.

Subsequently, although promises of legislation were repeated several times before they were written into the Queen's Speech opening the 1978–79 session of Parliament, no legislation was in fact tabled. But during this prolonged delay, the proposals of Lord Bullock's team were continuously diluted, until from the point of view of the strength of proposed worker representation, they finally reached a specific gravity somewhat lower than that of the original EEC directive, with the publication of a White Paper (Cmnd 7231) in May 1978.

During all this time, the Bullock proposals aroused considerable debate between national union spokesmen. Whilst Jack Jones, general secretary of the TGWU, who had served as a member of the Bullock Committee, called for legislation on its proposals to be tabled the same year, Hugh Scanlon of the AUEW opposed the Report, posing against it a call for

'an extension of collective bargaining, to which we know no limit.'[34]

The lines of argument cut across conventional left-right alignments, uniting both factions of the (normally bitterly divided) AUEW with the (rightwing) EETPU and the (leftwing) Draughtsmen, against any kind of worker representation on the boards of capitalist concerns; and leaving a similarly wide spectrum of forces lined up with the TGWU in favour of implementing the report. The defeat of the Callaghan administration in 1979, however, put an end to this argument for at any rate the time being, since the Conservatives had no interest in enacting any legislation even remotely similar to that proposed either by the TUC, or by the Bullock Committee, or even by the Labour Government's hyper-cautious Cabinet sub-committee on Industrial Democracy.[35]

If the fate of proposals for worker-directors in privately owned industry has not been very encouraging for the advocates of this reform, it does throw light on another issue. Various people have in the past argued that there has been a complete divorce between ownership and control of industry, so that the concept of property has ceased to have any fundamental importance in industrial affairs. Of course, the concentration of economic scale has meant that many small and medium shareholders have been effectively disfranchised in the processes of industrial government: but this process has merely served to augment the real powers exercised by oligarchic minority owner-controllers.[36] How important these powers remain may be diagnosed from the remarkable resistance which was offered to the Bullock proposals, (moderate though they must have seemed to all who thought ownership an irrelevant issue) from the very first moment of their publication.

In the field of the nationalised industries, this problem no longer applies. Since these industries are nominally social property already, many trade unionists would claim that there seems to be no solid reason why they should not be democratically administered, unless it can be proved that democratic forms of administration are inherently incompetent. The same TUC Report in which parity representation was mooted for company boards also addressed the issue of public sector management, and recommended 50 per cent trade union membership of all relevant policy-making boards. The other half of board members 'should be appointed by the Minister, but there is scope for further discussion about the composition of this 50 per cent' the Report went on. Although the October 1974 election manifesto of the Labour Party spoke of 'socialising' the nationalised industries, the terms of reference of the Bullock Committee specifically excluded them. Instead, a separate internal Governmental enquiry was established under the co-ordination of Mr Alan Lord, second secretary at the Treasury. This was a 'private' attempt to monitor the exact position of participatory involvement in different nationalised industries, and it resulted in a memo which tabulated the different stages of participation already reached and offered the opinion that it would be difficult to enforce any single specific policy.[37]

At the level of national trade union initiative, complex discussions took place within the National Union of Mineworkers and between the NUM and the Coal Board;[38] while an experimental scheme involving national union representation in the management of the post office was agreed and began to operate. The real interest in change, however, has made itself more keenly felt lower down. The call for direct forms of self-management has been increasingly frequently heard from workers in the nationalised and about-to-be nationalised industries.

Perhaps the first modern call for a democratic mode of public ownership came from steelworkers, when they were contemplating the renationalisation of their industry during the mid-1960s. After several informal seminars, a programme was drafted,[39] which became the basis in 1967, for a full-fledged programme drafted by the National Craftsmen's Co-ordinating Committee of the Iron and Steel Industry.

'(i)   The corporation should consist of a chairman and twelve full-time members not holding other private directorships.

(ii)   This Public Board should be responsible to Parliament through the Minister.

(iii)   Members to retire in rota, after a maximum term of five years but may be eligible for re-appointment.

(iv)   The Vice-Chairman and four members to be appointed like other members by the Minister, but from a panel of names submitted by agreement among the various trade unions engaged in the industry.

(v)   Fresh panels of names to be submitted at retirements.

(vi)   The Minister to be responsible for issuing general directives from time to time for pricing and investment policies, taking

into account NEDC recommendations and for ratifying the
group structure which the Board recommends.

THE POWERS OF THE CORPORATION

(i)   To mine, import and sell iron ore.
(ii)   To manufacture and sell iron and steel.
(iii)   To fabricate and sell iron and steel products.
(iv)   To manufacture and sell chemicals, gas, electric power, slag,
        and other subsidiary products.
(v)   To operate engineering, processing and other associated
        undertakings.
(vi)   To develop joint operations with state and private companies
        operating overseas.
(vii)   To carry out research and establish training colleges for
        management at all levels.
(viii) To build, own and manage housing, recreational and other
        allied activities either alone or in association with other
        nationalised undertakings.
(ix)   To carry on any other operations necessary to the successful
        work of the Board.

The National board will be responsible for rationalising and
reforming the industry. This process will require the grouping of
companies and, therefore, it is desirable to establish Group or
Combine Boards and provide them with powers appropriate to
them.
In view of the re-organisation which will take place and because of
the past history of the industry, it will be the duty of the National
Board to decide whether to retain both company and brand names.
Moreover, in view of the strong feelings which workers have on this
matter it is desirable that changes be made with the full approval of
the workers.

AT COMBINE OR GROUP LEVEL

(i)   The National Board shall rationalise and reform the national-
        ised sectors by grouping companies and establishing group
        Boards. It is estimated that there will be approximately six
        groups comprising approximately 30 plants in the following
        areas: South Wales, Midlands, North West, Sheffield &
        Scunthorpe, North East and Scotland.
(ii)   The Chairman or managing director of the Operating Board
        should be appointed by the National Board, subject to ratifi-
        cation by a Group Workers Council.

The Group Workers Council will be elected in the following way:

One half of its members would be elected directly by the trade unions in accordance with their strength in the combine or group; the other half indirectly from shop, mill or office committee or from Departmental or Plant Committee depending on the size of the combine.

The Workers Council would have power to receive reports on all policies and to ask for detailed costing of all departments.

(iii) The rest of the Group-board members will be the chairmen of each enterprise.

AT PLANT LEVEL

(i) An enterprise or Plant Board should be established.

(ii) It should comprise the chairman of the enterprise (subject to ratification by the Workers Council); six departmental managers or foremen ratified by departmental committees or shop committees, and six workers elected by the Workers Councils.

AT SHOP, MILL AND OFFICE LEVEL

(i) At the level of all shops, mills and offices, committees should be elected by secret ballot organised by the trade unions. These should cover all white collar as well as manual workers with all members eligible to vote and stand as candidates.

(ii) Appointment of shop managers, etc., deployment of labour, promotion, hiring and dismissing of workers, safety, welfare and disciplinary matters to be subject to ratification by these committees, with appeal to higher committees in the event of disagreement.

(iii) Where appropriate, Department or Plant committees elected from Shop Steward committees, etc., should be provided for with appropriate higher powers to the shop committees, etc., and with special responsibilities also for training and education and other responsibilities delegated from the combine or Group Workers Council.'[40]

The nationalisation measure which was actually brought in was a repeat of those of the late 1940s, except that a token force of 'worker-directors', without specific powers or accountability, was built in at the last moment. These were appointed by management, as one of them subsequently described:

'One morning, our general manager sent for me and said, "Oh, the managing director wants to see you". "What the hell for?", I said, "I haven't done any bloody thing!" '[41]

Twelve such persons, chosen from a list submitted by the TUC without the intervention of any of their workmates, and sworn to preserve the confidentiality of whatever boardroom secrets they might inadvertently uncover, soon came to the opinion 'we're accountable to BSC . . . we're not representatives of the unions at all'.

Setbacks in steel did not prevent others from pressing for greater powers, however. After the work-in at Upper Clyde Shipbuilders, when the demand for nationalisation of the shipbuilding industry was accepted by the Labour Party, a group of workers in the industry at Barrow met with their Member of Parliament, Albert Booth, to discuss plans for a management structure for public ownership. They, too, reached agreement on parity representation on the predominant policy-making board.

But in the aircraft industry, also scheduled for nationalisation by the 1974 Labour administrations, workers raised their sights. Half a year before the return of Mr Wilson to Downing Street, the Bristol workers of the British Aircraft Corporation published a thorough and detailed plan for the administration of their industry by a controlling council of worker representatives, elected by trade unionists, which would hire and fire management. 'We reject worker-directors', they wrote: 'the essence of our system is that management is hired by the workers to run the industry'.[42]

'The TUC's latest proposals, though somewhat unclear, can be seen as a movement towards meeting our objectives although in one basic and fundamental regard they are unacceptable. We discuss this below. Here we reproduce the summary of the proposals for the Public Sector as set out in paragraph 96 of the TUC's latest report:

> "If the proposals put forward above for a form of worker representation on the boards of private industry were adopted, then it would obviously be desirable if similar forms of representation could be established within the nationalised sector. The 1973 Congress affirmed the importance of this principle. However, the present boards of the nationalised industries already include outside appointments representing wider interests, including trade union appointments from outside the industry. In this sense the existing nationalised boards already perform a function not dissimilar to a supervisory board; indeed, in certain nationalised industries there is also an executive or operating board subordinate to the main board. It is proposed that this system—which is in effect a two-tier system—is retained, but that 50 per cent trade union representation should be provided for on the first-tier board (i.e. that concerned with overall policy-

making). This top-tier board would not be the operative body so far as wage negotiations were concerned. The representation should be direct, without involving the Minister, but based on the trade union machinery in the nationalised industry so as to represent the workers employed in the industry. The TUC's role in this would only relate to determining respective unions' interests where necessary. The other 50 per cent of the board should be appointed by the Minister, but there is scope for further discussion about the composition of this 50 per cent. There must therefore be a commitment to a new set of statutes for the nationalised industries."

If this means that the 50 per cent trade union representation shall be directly elected via the trade union machinery in the nationalised industry so as to represent the workers employed in the industry then to that extent it is a movement towards the objectives we have raised earlier. We now come however to our fundamental and basic objection:

What we would ask is the significance of the 50 per cent representation? The question surely is, does this or does it not give control?

If not, it does not matter much whether the representation is 5 per cent, 10 per cent or 50 per cent. On the other hand if it is supposed that the proposed representation could mean the exercise of effective control over decision-making (albeit in certain areas) what are the arguments against a complete break with considerations about what different numerical representations might mean and give overall control to elected worker representatives? The Report would seem to suggest that the trade unionists on a public board can represent workers, help to arrive at decisions and presumably as individuals make an equal contribution as any one of the other 50 per cent nominees, but that they could not be "trusted" to make the "right" decisions on their own. This is a strange reflection when considered in terms of local authorities up and down the country where elected councillors are responsible for the expenditure of considerable public funds and important policy decisions. It might be argued that local authorities have to work within central government's legislative and other constraints but to a lesser or greater extent this is true of the Public Sector in general and would certainly be so as far as a publicly owned aircraft industry was concerned. We cannot therefore understand why both the TUC documents fail even to discuss the proposition that the overall policy-making body of a publicly owned industry could be composed entirely of directly elected trade unionists who work in the industry concerned and that they should be clearly answerable and responsible to those who elected them.'

Similar attitudes were expressed by the dockworkers of Hull and London, when they prepared their plan for the nationalisation of the Ports. With quite unambiguous directness, they spelt out their view of industrial democracy:

'Industrial Democracy does not mean:

- Union leaders (retired or otherwise) sitting on Directors' Boards without any responsibility to the industry's workers.
- that workers' directors are given fat cheques, free meals, and other perks, to hob-nob with the employers, in return for keeping their secrets from the workers.
- that workers' directors or trade unions should meekly agree to "share responsibility" for redundancies, speed-up of work etc.
- that workers and unions should accept "participation" as a "reward" for getting rid of real union control and workers' rules on the job.
- that managers merely "consult" workers after they have made decisions.

Industrial Democracy does mean:

- that Workers' Councils, or Workers' representatives, should be elected by and from workers, to whom they should report back all their proceedings.
- that workers' representatives and Councils should be instantly recallable by those who elected them.
- that all the books, all the commercial secrets, should be open to the inspection of workers' representatives.
- that trade union freedom is preserved and extended, not curbed by restrictive rules against shop stewards, or strike action.'[43]

The New Worker Co-operatives

If the newly nationalised industries came nowhere near to meeting these expectations, they were partially met in the various experiments in co-operation which took place after 1974. Starting in very inauspicious conditions, usually involving bankruptcy, various factory occupations, work-ins or sit-ins, gave place to worker-organised co-operatives. The three largest of these were formed after governmental intervention, at The Scottish Daily News, Kirkby Manufacturing and Engineering, and Triumph Motorcycles at Meriden.[44] By early 1979 the first two had failed from capital starvation, and the third was precariously balanced upon the brink of failure. Yet all three had aroused widespread sympathy, concern and discussion. Smaller co-operatives were considerably more successful, especially in traditional, labour intensive manufactories.[45]

Problems of Technological Innovation

The most recent stimulus to trade union strategic thinking on job control and industrial democracy has come from the introduction of 'new technology' in the shape of the micro-processor. There are two aspects of this development which carry serious implications for trade unionists—the threat of massive job loss, with few prospects of compensating growth in employment in non-automated industries and services, and the threat of more arbitrary managerial control over work.

> 'The new technology offers increased opportunities for management supervision. This is because micro-processors can be programmed to monitor work rates automatically. The exact speed at which people are working can be noted immediately, or stored for later use. This may well make it possible for management to set worker against worker. It certainly means that management will be given the tools to squeeze a greater pace of work from the workers.'[46]

These problems have produced a spate of trade union literature[47] in which the common themes have much to do with the great debates of the 1960s and 1970s on workers' control. The union publications tend to recommend a common strategy, which can be represented by a summary of the TUC's proposals.[48]

The TUC recommends that unions should negotiate New Technology Agreements with companies, and provides a check-list of objectives crucial amongst these are the following:

'a. The first objective should be: "change must be by agreement".'

'b. In companies or industries where collective agreements already contain *status quo* provisions, governing the introduction of new processes or machinery, there may be scope for unions to actively encourage their more vigorous use . . .'

The TUC also insists upon the need for full disclosure of information on management plans for new technology, and for the negotiation of agreed plans for 'maintaining and improving employment'. Not only should there be no redundancies, but 'negotiators should look critically at proposals for using natural wastage to change the size of a workforce . . .' Moreover, 'negotiators can press for exploration by joint management/union teams of new markets for existing products, alternative product ranges, the scope for import substitution . . .' (The influence of the Lucas shop stewards' pioneering initiative is to be noticed here.) The TUC also believes that the health and safety aspects of new technology need careful controls by unions, and that 'no information acquired by computer based systems shall be used for individual or collective work performance measurement.'

Amongst the publications of particular unions, the Model Agreement produced by the Association of Professional, Executive, Clerical and Computer Staffs recommends a clause which reads: 'There shall be no job loss as a result of the introduction of the systems'. A draft Agreement submitted by the TGWU to Reckitt and Colman in Hull during 1979 spells this out even more precisely.

'As new technology is introduced . . . the existing strength of the labour force will be fully maintained by the mutually agreed, phased introduction of the following measures:
(a) redeployment, with full opportunities for retraining and no loss of earnings;
(b) expansion of output and sales of the existing products range;
(c) diversification of the company's operations to manufacture and market new products which are socially useful and commercially viable;
(d) reduction in working time by
  (i)   increased holiday entitlements
  (ii) reduction in working week
  (iii) earlier retirement
  (iv) periods of sabbatical leave
  (v)   reduction of systematic overtime without loss of earnings.'

The same draft spells out the union's demand in the 'control of work' area.

'Union negotiators will be fully involved at the design stage of the introduction of new technology.
Re-programming of micro-processors will not be carried out without mutual agreement.
All storage and use of data relating to personal performance and other details of the work force will be subject to mutual agreement.
No information acquired by computer based systems shall be used for individual or collective work performance measurement.'

It also defines with sharp clarity the general mutuality and *status quo* requirements recommended by the TUC.

'The company and the unions agree that there will be no change by way of the introduction of new technology into the company's operations, except by mutual agreement between the two sides. The company agrees not to introduce new technology until full agreement has been reached on the whole range of negotiating issues raised in Clauses 2 to 8 below of this Agreement.'

Thus, impelled by the practical and pressing problems of protecting their members' jobs and of retaining controls over work, unions are reconverging on the demand for something very similar to planning agreements, and seeking to establish bargaining about their companies' total corporate strategy. In spite of official discouragement, and the inaction of the 1974-9 Labour administration, the idea constantly recurs in the course of practical activities. In demanding the maintenance of existing levels of employment in a company, the unions are in effect drawing attention in a novel way to the social consequences of private company decision-making.

All these initiatives in workers' control or attempts at overall self-management point up complex lessons, and are the subject of a considerable volume of critical study. What is quite clear is that none of them has proved capable of resolving the argument with a simple negative decision: workpeople have proved resilient in their hopes that the next initiative might work. Thus, after the collapse of the newspaper co-op in Glasgow, one of the first acts of journalists locked out by the management of *The Times* was to commission a study of *Co-operative Possibilities for Times Newspapers Limited.*[49]

The fact seems to be that the discussion of industrial democracy is only just beginning, and that it is liable to feed upon its failures, which will provide matter for further analysis and further development of its ideals.

NOTES

1. Sidney and Beatrice Webb: *Industrial Democracy*, WEA edition, London, 1913, pp. 849–50.
2. Allan Flanders: *Trade Unions*, Hutchinson University Library, 1957, p. 118.

3. We have presented a good deal of evidence on this matter in our *Industrial Democracy in Great Britain*, Spokesman, (Three Volumes, Fourth Volume forthcoming). This covers the development of the argument during the twentieth century.

4. Flanders, op. cit, p. 118.

5. Excerpts from this work are reprinted in Volume I of our *Industrial Democracy in Great Britain*, pp. 30–34.

6. Allen and Unwin, n.d., p. 18. This pamphet was printed by the Pelican Press of Francis Meynell, and its typography is a considerable achievement in craftsmanship.

7. *What Happened at Leeds?* in British Labour and the Russian Revolution, (Ed. Ken Coates) Spokesman, 1972.

8. Cf Raymond Postgate's contemporary work: *The Bolshevik Theory* (Grant Richards, 1920) for a good example of this.

9. S. R. Graubard, *British Labour and the Russian Revolution*, OUP, p. 41.

10. Herbert Morrison: *Socialisation and Transport*, Constable, 1933, pp. 208–210.

11. Arthur Scargill: *The Case Against Workers' Control* in *Workers' Control*, Bulletin of the Institute for Workers' Control, No. 37, pp. 13–14.

12. Flanders, op. cit, p. 121–2.

13. The best available account of these is Milojko Drulovic: *Self-Management on Trial*, Spokesman, 1978.

14. We have discussed this terminology in greater detail in *The New Unionism*, Penguin, 1972, Chapter 4.

15. R. Fraser: *Work*, Volume 2, Penguin, 1969, pp. 116–17.

16. Ibid, p. 119.

17. For a brief account, see K. Coates: *Work-ins, Sit-ins and Industrial Democracy*, Spokesman, 1980.

18. For a number of examples, see K. Coates (ed) *The Right to Useful Work*, Spokesman, 1978.
Also:
Vickers' National Combine Committee of Shop Stewards:
Building a Chieftain Tank and the Alternative, Newcastle-upon-Tyne, 1978.
Alternative Employment for Naval Shipbuilding Workers, Barrow, 1978.
Economic Audit on Vickers Scotswood, Newcastle-upon-Tyne, 1979.
C. A. Parsons' Unions Explain: Bulletin of the IWC, No. 36, p. 20.
An Alternative Strategy for Power Engineering: C. A. Parsons' shop stewards. *Workers' Control*, Bulletin of the IWC, New series, No. 1. p. 9.

19. See, for example, the ICI claims of 1971 and 1974. The first was published by the T & GWU under the title *A Positive Employment Programme for ICI*: it proposes joint safety committees with a remit to consider environmental matters.

20. Labour's Programme, 1973.

21. Ibid, p. 18. The promise to publish an annual report was never honoured, because there was never anything to report.

22. HMSO, August 1974.

23. Cf Tom Forester: 'The Neutralisation of the Industrial Strategy' in Coates (Ed) *What Went Wrong?* Spokesman, 1979.

24. Cf Chrysler: The Workers' Answer: *Workers' Control Bulletin*, No. 32, May–June 1976, pp. 12 et seq. There were at least two versions of the Chrysler Agreement, and even the abridged one was marked 'confidential'.

25. Lucas Aerospace Combine Shop Stewards' Committee: *The Lucas Plan*, IWC Pamphlet, No. 55.

26. Mike Cooley: 'Design, Technology and Production for Social Needs' in *The Right to Useful Work*, Spokesman, 1978, p. 201.

27. Ibid, p. 202.

28. Lucas Aerospace Confederation Trade Union Committee, Interim Report, February 1979 (Hayes, Middlesex).

29. Transport and General Workers' Union, *Record*, July 1979.

30. Op. cit. pp. 1.1–1.2.

31. *Workers' Control*, Bulletin of the IWC, New Series, No. 1. pp. 9 et seq.

32. TUC: *Industrial Democracy*, First edition, 1974. Second edition, 1977, Third, revised and expanded edition, 1979.

33. Cmnd. 6706, January 1977. See also K. Coates and T. Topham: *A Shop Stewards' Guide to the Bullock Report*, Spokesman, 1977.

34. *Morning Star*, 27th January 1977.

35. Of which the TUC spoke with less than fierce enthusiasm in the 1979 reprint of *Industrial Democracy*. 'The General Council considered that the Government were proposing a very protracted timetable for the attainment of . . . modest objectives.' (p. 58)

36. This phrase comes from P. Sargant Florence: *The Logic of British and American Industry*, Routledge, 1953 and reprints. See especially Chapter V.

37. John Elliott: *Conflict or Co-opeation*, Kogan Page, 1978, Chapter 17.

38. These talks culminated in a forum at Harrogate in December, 1977, reported in *Workers' Control*, No. 37, pp. 11 et seq.

39. Cf K. Coates and T. Topham, *Workers' Control*, Panther, 1970, p. 385.

40. Coates (Ed) *Can the Workers Run Industry?* Spokesman, 1968, pp. 154–6.

41. P. Brannen, E. Batstone, D. Fatchett and P. White: *The Worker Directors*, Hutchinson, 1976, p. 120.

42. Bristol Aircraft Workers: *A New Approach to Public Ownership* IWC Pamphlet, No. 43, 1974, pp. 10–11.

43. *The Dockers' Next Step*, IWC Pamphlet No. 12, p. 5. Also in Coates and Topham: *Workers' Control*, Panther 1970, p. 428.

44. Cf Coates (Ed) *The New Worker Co-operatives*, Spokesman 1976.

45. As at Grantham, where former Courtaulds' employees established a dressmaking co-operative after the closure of their shirt-factory. See Harold Frayman in *Workers' Control*, New Series, 1978, No. 2, pp. 13 et seq.

46. TGWU, *Micro-Electronics: New Technology, Old Problems, New Opportunities*, 1979.

47. In addition to the TGWU booklet referred to above, see also: APEX, *Office Technology: the Trade Union Response*, 1979; ASTMS, *Discussion*

Document—Technological Change and Collective Bargaining, 1979; NUJ, *Journalists and New Technology*, 1978; POEU, *The Modernisation of Telecommunications*, 1979; AUEW/TASS, *Computer Technology and Employment*, 1978; TUC, *Employment and Technology*, 1979.

See also Clive Jenkins and Barrie Sherman, *The Collapse of Work*, Eyre Methuen 1979; Counter-Information Services, *Report: The New Technology*, (Anti-Report no.23), 1979; and Chris Harman, *Is A Machine After Your Job? New Technology and the Struggle for Socialism*, Socialist Workers' Party, 1979.

For a theoretical discussion see Steve Bodington, *Computers and Socialism*, Spokesman Books, 1973.

48. TUC, op. cit.

49. Job Ownership Limited, *Co-operative Possibilities for Times Newspapers Limited*, February 1979.

Chapter Nine

Trade Unions and the Law

'Law is a technique for the regulation of social powers'.[1] This insight comes (perhaps atypically) from a lawyer, albeit a labour lawyer. Unfortunately for trade unionism, and for the advance of workers' rights, the law as an institution does not acknowledge this rather evident truth. The common law, that is law based on the decisions of judges, is concerned almost exclusively with the rights of individuals, and thus it relates uneasily—indeed commonly in a hostile manner—to the *collective* behaviour of workers in their trade union organisations. A trade union has no place as of right in litigation, although it may represent its members.[2] In cases of unfair dismissal and equal pay, for example, legal proceedings must be brought by individual workers, although in reality it is often collective rights which are in dispute. Yet the law in all these matters has been enacted only during the last decade. At the same time, and indeed for over a hundred years, employers have been allowed to act as a collectivity through the law on limited liability.

Judges and the Law
The social background of the judiciary is one important factor in explaining its historical hostility to labour's interest; but even more significant is the structural place of law in our society, which determines the roles perceived by its practitioners: judges are notoriously 'subject to a compelling professional disposition to conceptualise in terms of individualistic property and contractual rights and . . . are usually impervious to collectivist values'.[3] The statement, by a leading judge of his time, Lord Justice Scrutton, in 1923, has often been quoted but bears repetition for its uncharacteristic honesty concerning this problem.

'The habits . . . the people with whom you mix, lead to your having a certain class of ideas of such a nature that . . . you do not give as sound and accurate judgements as you would wish. This is one of the great difficulties at present with Labour. Labour says "Where are your impartial judges? They all move in the same circle as the employers, and they are all educated and nursed in the same ideas as the employers." How can a labour man or trade unionist get "impartial justice"? It is very difficult sometimes to be sure that you have put yourself into a thoroughly impartial position between two disputants, one of your own class and one not of your class.'[4]

Judges are appointed from amongst the profession of barristers-at-law, who come almost exclusively from the public schools and the ancient universities. Whilst the position is improving, with more sympathetic lawyers emerging both from the traditional and the more modern schools of law, in the past few lawyers cared to specialise in labour law, since there was little money in it compared to other branches. The recent spate of labour legislation does, however, create more demand for lawyers, to whom the employers' side particularly is turning for professional services.

The history of labour law has, for these reasons, revolved around a conflict between the restrictive interpretations of workers' and trade union rights pronounced by judges, and the successive initiatives of the legislature in Parliament designed to meet trade union and reforming pressures for a redress of the balance of forces between capital and labour. Common law has adhered to the myth, the legal fiction, that contracts made between employers and workers are contracts between free and equal parties, whereas in fact the bargaining power of the individual worker seeking employment is commonly very small, while that of his potential employer may be vast. To redress this imbalance, workers must needs act collectively, primarily through trade union organisation. Yet the common law views collective action by workers with deep suspicion, and is always liable to interpret it as 'conspiracy' —a crime and a tort which consequently plays a large role in the history of workers' conflict with the law. This is the foundation of workers' reciprocal suspicion of the law, and the basis of the traditional trade union policy, which has been to keep the law out of trade union affairs as much as possible.

The Outlook of Trade Unionists

This attitude is changing in certain respects, as we shall see. But trade unions still prefer to establish norms and standards in industry through collective bargaining, and in this country agreements made in this way by employers and unions have no legal status; a link with the law is present however, since the terms and conditions established by collective bargaining normally enter into the individual contract of employment. This trade union policy, described as 'a firm belief in collective *laissez-faire*',[5] has meant that there has been no sustained trade union pressure for minimum legal standards in such basic matters as wages and hours of work; parliament has stepped in and established machinery for this purpose, through Wages Council legislation, only in a piece-meal fashion in specific industries, where the normal process of collective bargaining has failed to develop, or when, as in the case of equal pay, a general social pressure—only partially attributable to trade unionism—has made itself felt. It is noteworthy that Rule 2 of the TUC Constitution, adopted in 1922 *did* contain a commitment to seek minimum wage legislation, but this was never the basis of a serious trade union campaign, and was deleted with hardly any debate at the 1978 TUC Congress. Sporadic calls from the TUC in 1946 and 1950, for legislation to enforce a 40-hour week and 2 weeks paid holiday, were never followed through. Thus Britain was, and remains, 'the classical country of collective bargaining,'[6] in contrast to continental countries where, as in France for example, statute law governs hours of work, holidays with pay, and the minimum wage.

In discussing trade union attitudes to 'regulatory law'—which establishes minimum standards, and 'auxiliary law'—which seeks to promote conditions in which collective bargaining can flourish with a minimum of legal intervention, Terry Sullivan has written:

> 'From the trade union side two reasons for their inaction in the area of regulatory law spring to mind. First . . . regulatory law tends to conflict with auxiliary law by producing an alternative to trade unionism. Secondly trade unionists argue that collective bargaining is the way to improve terms and conditions, and anything "won" by negotiation is much more difficult to take away or be altered unilaterally either by the state or the employers.'[7]

This is not to say that trade unions have been wholly neglectful of the potential benefits of regulatory law, but rather that they have been selective in its use, accepting its applicability usually for those workers particularly vulnerable to exploitation, amongst whom trade unionism is weak—traditionally amongst women workers and juveniles, and in selected trades and industries.

In the rest of this chapter, we shall be concerned with the history and current situation concerning both regulatory and auxiliary law, and with the restrictive law emanating from judges, and (less frequently) from parliament. We shall be principally concerned with the law as it affects trade unions, rather than with the whole range of legal rights for individual workers, although we have some things to say about these.

The Development of Labour Law

From as early as 1351, the *Statute of Labourers* had declared combinations of workers to be illegal, and from 1349, the state had empowered local magistrates to fix labourers' wages.[8] By the latter half of the 18th century, the system of statutory regulation of wages was breaking down in favour of 'freedom of contract', and workers' collective efforts to enforce the old laws were increasingly liable to the visitations of the law against combinations, which was made generally prohibitive by the *Combinations Acts* of 1799 and 1800. These laws were the product of the ruling class's dual fear of, and hostility to, collective action by workers both for economic and for political purposes. They were repealed in 1824, but following a wave of strikes, an amending Act was passed in 1825, which gave trade unions only a limited legality, and accompanied this with new crimes in strike situations, such as 'threatening', 'intimidation', and 'molestation'. Criminal prosecutions under this law were frequent in the next decades. Nor were trade unionists free from other hostile laws; the famous Tolpuddle martyrs in 1834 were deported for an offence under the *Unlawful Oaths Act* of 1797. During these years too, workers were constantly harrassed by the various *Master and Servant Acts*, under which a breach of contract of employment by an employee was a criminal offence. Thousands of trade unionists were imprisoned for this crime, under which 10,000 prosecutions a year were brought between 1858 and 1875. (A similar offence of breach of contract by an employer was only subject to the unlikely penalty of damages in a civil court). At the same time, judges deployed a series of common law crimes, such as conspiracy and action 'in restraint of trade' against trade union organisation. The growing organisational competence and confidence of trade unions, particularly amongst skilled workers, and their increasing determination to seek more favourable laws, brought matters to a head in the decade from 1866 to 1875.

In 1867, a judicial decision in the *Hornby v. Close* case found that a trade union, being an organisation 'in restraint of trade', had no legal protection in a case where a trade union official absconded with the union's funds. This undermined the flimsy legal status of trade unions in a fundamental way. In the same year, a Royal Commission on trade unions was set up, instigated by anti-union pressure which built on feeling against the 'Sheffield outrages', a series of violent acts by trade unionists in that town taken against non-unionists. The powerful general secretaries of the leading craft unions mobilised their evidence before this Commission to show that trade unions were peaceful and respectable organisations which sought only for a stable legal base from which to carry out entirely legitimate functions. A re-inforcement for the trade union lobby came with the foundation of the TUC in 1868; moreover the unions' potential for pressurising parliament was increased by the extension of the parliamentary vote to most male urban workers in 1867. The Royal Commission reported in 1869, and it was on the basis of a favourable minority report that Parliament passed, in 1871, the *Trade Union Act*, which effectively nullified the 'restraint of trade' doctrine, thus giving trade unions a more secure legal status, and providing for their voluntary registration with the Registrar of Friendly Societies. Whilst this represented a considerable gain for the unions, this law set a pattern for subsequent legislation in that it provided merely for trade union *immunity* from certain aspects of common law; it did not provide for any general or positive right for workers to organise and to bargain. Moreover in the same year Parliament passed the *Criminal Law Amendment Act* which repealed the 1825 Act, but left in its place provision for the continuing operation of criminal conspiracy charges against strikers. A renewed and effective lobby by the unions against this law resulted in the passing of the *Conspiracy and Protection of Property Act* in 1875, which gave immunity to strikers from the crime of simple conspiracy when they acted in the context of a trade dispute, and which further afforded some legal protection for peaceful picketing. Nevertheless, the Act still contained penalties for specified offences, such as intimidation, persistent following, hiding of tools, watching and besetting; these were always liable to hostile interpretation by the judges. Despite this, it can be said that the *Trade Union Act* of 1871, and the Act of 1875 together mark a significant milestone in the struggle for legal protection for trade unions and for strike action.

But the judges were not finished. Thwarted in their use of *criminal* conspiracy, they turned the weapon of *civil* conspiracy against unions, and in a series of cases aimed against the wave of trade union organisation in the late 1880s and 1890s, found that strike action could be construed as a civil wrong, or tort, for which the injured party, (the employer) could claim damages. The most influential of these cases was that brought by the Taff Vale railway company against the Amalgamated Society of Railway Servants in 1901, in which the union was found liable in tort for damages in a strike action, and had to pay £42,000 in costs and damages. This completely undermined the right to strike; its most immediate consequence was to boost trade union affiliations to the newly formed Labour Representation Committee, which transformed itself in the Labour Party in 1906. In that year, strengthened by the influence of 29 Labour MPs, the unions persuaded the Liberal government to pass the *Trade Disputes Act*, which did for civil law what the 1875 Act had done for criminal law. It prohibited legal action against strikers in tort, and provided a widely-based immunity from judge-made law for trade union action. It set the scene for the growth of collective bargaining free from legal intervention until the 1960s,—although with an aberration between 1927 and 1946, as we shall see. Whilst this provided a more secure base than any previous Act it remained within the category of an 'immunity law'; *individual* strikers were still in principle liable for breach of their employment contracts, although of course this offence had lost its criminal nature in the *Employers & Workmen Act*, 1875.

Within three years of the 1906 Act, the Law Lords found yet another loophole with which to attack trade unions. In the 1909 'Osborne Judgement' they found that it was illegal for trade unions to spend their funds on political purposes, and thus effectively deprived the infant Labour Party of its principal source of income. In 1913, the government redressed this decision in the *Trade Union Act* of that year, which provided that unions may spend money for political purposes, but only out of a special Fund, separate from their general funds. Any individual trade unionist was to be allowed to 'contract out' of paying that part of the union subscription which went into the Political Fund. Moreover a union must hold a ballot of its members to determine whether it shall have political objectives and a political fund. This law obtains to the present day, and is widely regarded as an entirely satisfactory measure. Yet in fact it represents an under-privileged position for the unions, compared with the complete freedom of company directors to contribute to political causes from company funds without consulting shareholders, without operating a separate fund, and with no provision for contracting-out. Trade union rights are in these ways circumscribed; the minority can contract-out of obligations decided on by the majority and the unions may not use their normal decision-making machinery to decide on political involvement. 'The unions operate in a gold-fish bowl, the employers behind a two-way mirror.'[9]

During these decades, the state was taking the first steps to promote industrial conciliation and arbitration, in line with the evolving view of its role as a mediator in the collective bargaining process. In 1891, parliament passed the first of its Fair Wages Resolutions, which stipulated that government contractors should observe the terms and conditions of employment generally operating in their industry. In 1896, the *Conciliation Act* established the practice of the government providing a professional conciliation service in industrial disputes, thus setting a precedent for all subsequent periods, culminating today in one of the key roles of the Advisory, Conciliation and Arbitration Service (ACAS).

A first step of another kind was taken in 1909, with the passing of the Trades Boards Act, which created machinery for the statutory regulation of wages in certain 'sweated' trades,—tailoring, paper-box making, lace and net making, and chain-making. The criterion on which a Board was set up was simply low pay; in 1918 this was broadened to include low levels of trade union organisation, and subsequently enlarged in Wages Council legislation. These measures represent a piece-meal departure from the general principle of state absention in the wages field but they were only applied in industries where collective bargaining had failed to develop to the point at which it could ensure adequate minimum wages.

During the first world war, the *Munitions of War Act* 1915, following mutual agreement between the employers, unions, and government at the Treasury Conference, prohibited strikes and substituted compulsory arbitration as the ultimate stage in industrial disputes. Despite this, industrial unrest reached proportions alarming to the Government, which set up a committee of enquiry under speaker of the House of Commons Whitley, which produced a series of reports in 1917 to form the basis of state policy on industrial relations until the 1960s. Broadly, Whitley recommended the promotion and encouragement of voluntary collective bargaining, with the state's role confined to conciliation, arbitration, and the plugging of loop-holes in the system by means of Trade Boards. One result was the *Industrial Court Act* 1919, which established a permanent arbitration board (not a court, despite its name) to provide a service of purely voluntary arbitration for industry.[10] Both parties to an ordinary trade dispute had to agree to refer a case before the court would hear it, and the award of the court had no legally binding force. Once again this proved to be a precedent followed through in all subsequent amendments of the law, and today these same functions are carried out by the Central Arbitration Committee (CAC). Of course, arbitration awards which result from claims for Fair Wages, Equal Pay, or the 'going rate' (under Schedule 11 of the Employment Protection Act), *are* legally binding on employers. In 1920, the Government, fearing revolutionary outbreaks, or a general strike, passed the *Emergency Powers Act*, which remains today on the Statute Book, and can be called into operation by an Order placed before Parliament. It gives the Government wide powers, including the requisitioning of troops, to secure 'the essentials of life' for 'the community' in cases of serious strikes in industries such as transport and power supply. In itself the Act does not impede the right to strike, but it does give Governments wide scope for strike-breaking activities. In 1927, a Conservative Government, in vindictive response to the general strike of the previous year, enacted the *Trade*

Dispute and Trade Union Act, which outlawed the closed shop in public sector employment, ordained that civil servants must belong to exclusively civil service unions without political affiliations, declared that strikes to 'coerce the government' were illegal, restricted picketing rights, and substituted 'contracting-in' for 'contracting-out' of the political levy. The whole of this law was repealed by the Labour government in 1946. During the second world war, the government once again made strikes illegal through Order 1305, which was not in fact revoked until 1951, when it was replaced with Order 1376, which retained compulsory arbitration for issues where trade unions claimed that an employer was not observing terms and conditions applicable in his industry through collective bargaining. A Tribunal award in these cases became legally binding on the employer. This has proved such a useful weapon in spreading the application of collective agreements that a similar power was retained, and given as an additional duty to the old Industrial Court, by the *Terms and Conditions of Employment Act* 1959, and more recently has been generalised still further in the *Employment Protection Act* 1975. Its effect is to buttress the voluntary collective bargaining system; in effect the state affirms that collectively bargained conditions should prevail, and that where they do not, it will help by enforcing them on recalcitrant employers.

A similar state attitude is displayed in the Fair Wages Resolutions of the House of Commons, the presently applicable one dating from 1946. Along with similar provisions made by local authorities and public corporations, it requires all contractors working for the public sector to observe the collectively bargained rates and conditions prevailing in their industries, and requires that 'the contractor shall recognise the freedom of his workpeople to be members of trade unions'. (Notice that it stops short of requiring him to recognise and bargain with the union.) Otto Kahn-Freund believes that these measures have done more than any other act of state to spread collective bargaining rates throughout industry.[11] Certainly they amount to formidable evidence that the promotion of collective bargaining is a matter of established state policy; the contradiction involved when the state strives to impose incomes policies is patent, and is brought out in our chapter on collective bargaining.

The most recent of the Acts setting up Wages Councils (formerly the Trade Boards of the 1909 Act) was passed in 1959. From its early narrow application to a few trades, the system now covers 4 million workers in over 50 industries, where the state judges that collective bargaining has not developed sufficiently to stand on its own feet and where consequently a Wages Council is given the power to determine statutory minimum wages and conditions. But this method has always been regarded as a substitute for collective bargaining, and the law has always provided for the formal abolition of a Council in any industry where collective bargaining subsequently develops to the point where it can be effectively applied without legal sanction. This object has been further facilitated in the *Employment Protection Act*, which provides for a half-way house in the form of a statutory Joint Industrial Council for industries in transition from Wages Council status.

The 1960s ushered in a whole new phase of legal history. The state became increasingly interventionist, for example to promote labour efficiency and redeployment in such measures as the *Industrial Training Act* 1964, and the *Redundancy Payments Act* 1965. The latter measure, providing workers with a right to financial compensation when dismissed for economic reasons, whilst establishing a new workers' right in this respect, has its ambiguity from a trade union point of view. It was largely motivated by the desire to 'buy out' workers' claims to their jobs, to soften up labour for transfers and for unemployment.[12] Ray Gunter, Minister of Labour at the time, said in the House of Commons when introducing the Bill:

'We see this Bill as an important step in the government's general programme to push forward the modernisation of British industry as fast as possible, and to enlist the co-operation of workers as well as management in this process . . . our object is to encourage mobility of labour by reducing resistance to change.'

But the most startling developments in labour law in the 1960s and 1970s were set in train by the traditional means of an adverse judicial decision in an industrial dispute. In 1964, the judges in the Lords discovered, in the *Rookes v. Barnard* case, an obscure tort of intimidation, and created a new wrong which trade unionists could perpetrate in striking. In the words of the union's counsel, the decision 'drove a coach and four' through the 1906 *Trades Disputes Act*. Although the Labour government in its 1965 *Trades Disputes Act* temporarily restored the 1906 immunities, the stage had been set for a prolonged and intense debate, and a decade of legislation, over the old ground of trade union rights a decade which was introduced with the setting up of a Royal Commission, (the Donovan Commission) on trade unions and employers' associations, in 1965.

From Donovan to Industrial Relations Act

The Commission met in a context of mounting attacks on trade unionism by the media, the employers, and the Conservative Party. There was 'an intense concern, mounting to hysteria'[13] directed against the 'problem' of unofficial strikes; the whole tradition of abstentionism associated with 1875, and 1906, came under challenge. In its evidence to the Royal Commission, the Engineering Employers' Federation called for fines on unconstitutional strikers and for 'other acts of indiscipline', and the CBI called for legally enforceable collective agreements. The Report of the Commission appeared in 1968, and its diagnosis is discussed in chapter 6.

Whilst avoiding commitment to the more extreme programmes for legal controls, the majority of the Commission did propose that the immunity in strikes conferred on all by the 1906 (and 1965) Trade Disputes Acts, should in future be withdrawn from unofficial actions, and that after a period during which collective bargaining procedures should be reformed, legal sanctions would be justified.

'The effect of the reform of collective bargaining will be to greatly reduce the problem of unconstitutional strikes, which may not however disappear. It will then be possible to identify any circumstances in which it would be neither unjust nor futile to apply legal sanctions, because satisfactory disputes procedures are available, and because legal penalties are appropriate where irresponsibility or ill-will is the root cause of their breach.'[14]

Thus Donovan represented the thin edge of the wedge being driven in against the abstentionist tradition. The voice of the unions in all this, represented by the TUC's evidence to Donovan, was confined to a noble and philosophical defence of that tradition.

'The general attitude of abstention on the part of the state arises, be it noted, from the competence of trade unions to safeguard the interests of their members. In other words, it is where this necessary protection is lacking that the state intervenes, because free collective bargaining is absent. Virtually all the traditional activities of the Ministry of Labour in the field of industrial relations can be described as complementary to free collective bargaining.'[15]

The TUC goes on to accept that governments have recently, in measures such as the *Industrial Training Act* and the *Redundancy Payments Act*, intervened more positively in the interests of labour market policy, and believes that these steps are acceptable and beneficial to labour. But

'. . . it should be pointed out that legislation favourable to unions does not logically strengthen the argument for unfavourable legislation as a sort of *quid pro quo*. Improving terms and conditions of employment and enhancing the freedom and dignity of workpeople is essentially a one-way process, just as improving social security arrangements is a continuing process.'[16]

In retrospect, the TUC's tone seems too defensive, too rooted in the *status quo*: there is an absence of any positive demands for a new set of legal rights, a 'workers' charter'. This had to wait until the 1970s and the social contract, after the wave of anti-union enactments which were to come had spent itself and been repealed.

The Labour government initiated the drive for restrictive legislation with the publication of its White Paper *In Place of Strife*, in 1969. This went beyond Donovan's recommendations, to give governments power to order a 28-day conciliation pause in unconstitutional strikes, with fines for defaulters, and compulsory strike ballots. A compulsory recognition procedure was also envisaged. After a serious political conflict between the government and the labour movement, and sustained pressure from the TUC, the government withdrew its proposals winning in return a 'solemn and binding' promise from the TUC to become more actively involved in trying to prevent unconstitutional and unofficial strikes, particularly in cases where inter-union conflict was a factor.

The turn of the High-Tory lawyers had now come; with the election of a Conservative government in 1970 their proposals—first published as a party document in 1968 under the title *Fair Deal at Work*—were carried into law as the *Industrial Relations Act* 1971. This was a comprehensive, restrictive legal code, abolishing overnight the whole foundation of trade union and labour law embodied in the statutes from 1871 to 1906, overtly aimed at curbing trade union action and strikes by means of legal penalties, and at regulating trade union internal affairs by means of a system of state vetting and registering of trade unions and their rule books.

A whole new series of civil wrongs, under the name 'unfair industrial practices' were created under which much official, but particularly unofficial action and action by unregistered unions became liable for damages, and ultimately, through contempt of court proceedings to punishment by imprisonment. The only way a union could avoid liability for the actions of its officers was by disciplining and expelling them; unions were supposed to assume the role of policeman in industry. Collective agreements were made legally enforceable, unless an escape clause was agreed between employer and union. The closed shop was outlawed except in special circumstances, and an elaborate procedure for 'agency shops' was substituted for it. The right to belong, or not to belong, to a union was guaranteed. An unfair dismissal law (the only favourable element in the package) was introduced. The state was empowered to order compulsory strike ballots and a 60-day cooling-off period in the case of serious industrial action. And a new legal authority, the National Industrial Relations Court, was set up to deal with cases under the legislation.

The Act was a complete failure. Far from curbing industrial action it provoked the most serious conflict between government and labour since the general strike. Even more significantly, it was rendered largely inoperative, through both trade union resistance and employers' reluctance to use its provisions. For the Act stopped short of state conscription of industrial relations agencies; it relied for its full effectiveness on action by other parties. In the event, most employers connived at the continuance of past practice. Although no new closed shop agreements could be formalised, most existing ones survived intact. There was near-universal agreement between employers and unions to insert 'TINA LEA' ('This is not a legally enforceable agreement') clauses in their agreements, and rubber stamps were cut for that purpose!

The state itself, after a single salutary experience, declined to use its own emergency powers under the Act. In that one instance, the government ordered a cooling-off period for railway unions which were operating a work-to-rule in pursuit of a wage claim, and then proceeded with a compulsory strike ballot of all railway workers. The result was that 90 per cent of union members, and 66 per cent of non-members, voted in favour of continuing their industrial action. (These emergency procedures were based on the American Taft-Hartley law; the British government could have learned from experience in that country, where cooling-off periods are almost always followed by the stoppage continuing after the ninety days).

But it was the unions' unilateral act of opposition which most effectively nullified the Act. The TUC's policy of instructing its affiliates not to register under the Act was overwhelmingly successful, thus rendering inoperative all those aspects of the Act designed to incorporate unions as state-approved agencies of industrial discipline. The second largest union, the AUEW, steadfastly refused to recognise or appear before the NIRC, even when that court imposed severe fines on it for contempt, and even when union funds were compulsorily sequestered by the court. Ultimately, a national strike of all engineering members against the court's action was only avoided when an anonymous group of business men paid the costs of the union arising from its dispute with the court over an illegal recognition strike.

When, as in the case of the dispute between dockers and container firms, some small and medium sized employers did initiate court action against unofficial shop steward-led industrial action, rank and file defiance of the law powerfully reinforced official union opposition. The TGWU, the dockers' union, was fined £55,000 for its contempt of court in not disciplining its shop stewards, and five of the stewards themselves were sent to gaol for refusing to lift their blacking operation against a container company. This led to the TUC calling for a general strike, which was only called off when the court hastily released the dockers on the flimsiest of legal excuses. By 1973, the Act was almost a dead letter. The whole phase of this historic experience demonstrated the quite extraordinary tenacity and sheer strategic wisdom with which the trade union movement was able to defend its fundamental corporate interests. Moreover, the Act had the result, entirely unlooked-for by its authors, of promoting a new and more positive approach by the unions to the use of the law. For in working out, with the Labour Party, what should replace it, the TUC became committed to a demand for a series of workers' and trade union rights in the 'social contract' legislation which the Labour government enacted between 1974 and 1976.

The 1974 Legislation and After

The first of these laws was the *Trade Union and Labour Relations Act 1974*, (amended in 1976), which repealed the *Industrial Relations Act* (except for the unfair dismissal provisions, which were retained and strengthened) and restored the 1875–1906 position on strike law. The pre-1971 legal immunity was restored to workers and unions taking part in industrial action in the 1974 Act, and was extended in the 1976 Amending Act to cover 'secondary boycotts' such as blacking campaigns and sympathy strikes against suppliers and customers of employers with which workers or unions are in dispute. Action in sympathy with disputes originating overseas was also protected. The legality of closed shop agreements was fully restored only in the 1976 Act, which removed clauses inserted by Tory-Liberal amendments in the 1974 Act which gave legal hoop-holes to non-members and members of minority trade unions. The position now is that where a 'union membership agreement' is in operation, an employer may fairly dismiss a non-unionist, unless the latter can prove a religious objection to membership.

Trade union status at law was restored to that which it had before 1971; the distinction between registered and unregistered unions was abolished, and replaced with the concept of 'independence'. An independent union is one without any dependence upon, or interference from, employers; Certificates of Independence are issued by a Certification Officer. The status thus conferred entitles unions to a number of rights in the *Trade Union and Labour Relations Act*, the *Employment Protection Act* 1975, and the *Health and Safety at Work Act 1974*.

The right to belong to an independent trade union is expressly safeguarded by making dismissal for trade union membership or activity automatically unfair, as is dismissal for refusing to join a non-independent union. Collective agreements are again declared not to be legally enforceable, unless otherwise stated by the two parties in the agreement thus rendering TINA LEA clauses unnecessary. The 1974 Act retained clauses, deriving from the *Industrial Relations Act*, which intervened in trade union internal affairs. Section 5 gave workers the right not to be excluded or expelled from their trade union, branch or section 'by way of arbitrary or unreasonable discrimination.' Section 6 required unions to have rules covering specified subjects. The trade union case against these clauses eventually prevailed, and they were repealed by the 1976 Amending Act. The TUC has set up an independent review body with a lawyer in the chair to hear appeals by workers against exclusion or expulsion.

The *Employment Protection Act* 1975 is designed to encourage and strengthen collective bargaining and to give workers a series of new rights and some greater job security. The former aim is advanced by (1) laying down a procedure for obtaining trade union recognition from an employer; (2) providing for disclosure of information by an employer to a trade union; (3) strengthening and generalising earlier provision whereby unions can claim that the 'going-rate' should be paid to their members in a district or industry; (4) providing that unions have the right to advance warning of, and consultation about, planned redundancies; (5) providing that Wages Councils can be transformed into statutory Joint Industrial Councils; (6) giving statutory rights to trade union representatives to have time-off work with pay for their industrial relations functions and for training; (7) establishing the ACAS as an independent statutory body with functions of mediation, conciliation, and voluntary arbitration.

Individual workers' rights in the Act include (1) the right to a written statement of conditions of employment and periods of notice; (2) the right to trade union membership and activity; (3) the right to time-off work for general trade union duties and for public office such as local councillor; (4) the right to an itemised pay statement; (5) the right to a written statement of reasons for dismissal; (6) the right to pay when suspended on medical grounds; (7) the right to guaranteed pay for short-time working or lay-offs; (8) rights to certain prior payments in the event of the employer's insolvency; (9) the right to maternity leave and pay. The law on unfair dismissal is also augmented in the Act, by providing for re-instatement or re-engagement, protection for trade union membership and activity, and by amending the Redundancy Payments Act to provide for 'unfair selection'.

The Health and Safety at Work Act 1974, although in large part inherited from a Bill prepared by the previous administration, comes properly under the heading of social contract legislation, particularly in respect of its provision for the appointment of trade union safety representatives at all places of work. Their statutory functions, set out in Regulations under the Act, include the carrying out of safety inspections at their work-places, the examination of employers' documentation on safety, and receiving information from the Health and Safety Inspectorate. In its general aspects, the Act is the first comprehensive safety law in our history, covering all workers except those in domestic service. It thus brings under its cover 6 million workers not covered by the earlier piece-meal *Factory Acts, Mines & Quarries Act*, and the *Offices, Shop and Railway Premises Act*. In its provision that safety representatives should only have statutory status if appointed by and from trade unionists, members of recognised independent unions, it consistently reflects the general philosophy of the *Trade Union and Labour Relations Act*, and the *Employment Protection Act*. But it is unique in providing for a trade union agency to supervise the employers' observance of the law, and hence has great potential to raise the level of trade union activity and control at work.

The *Equal Pay Act* 1970 came into full operation only in 1975, and hence constitutes another major piece of legislation needing to be absorbed by trade unionists in this brief reforming period of 1974-6. Covering one-third of the labour force, it represents a dramatic intervention against the principle of collectivist *laissez-faire*; one weighty opinion says that it is potentially 'the most important statute on labour law passed by Parliament since the second world war.'[17] There are still major obstacles to be overcome before its effects are fully operative, notably in applying rigorously equal standards in job evaluation schemes. But it represents, along with the *Sex Discrimination Act* 1975, 'a major attempt to change the mores of a nation.'[18] Both employers and unions are now obliged to end all discriminatory practices based on sex, and the CAC can amend by law any collective agreement which contains any element of discrimination.

The institutions and legal bodies which enforce the new legislation require brief description. Industrial Tribunals are the British equivalent of local labour courts, and consist of a legally qualified chairman, one representative of employers and one trade union nominee. There are some 2,400 lay members of Tribunals, (only 22 per cent of whom are women).[19] In 1976 there were 46,000 applications for Industrial Tribunal hearings, and on any one day about 60 Tribunals will be sitting in the different localities. They deal with claims for redundancy payments, claims under the Sex Discriminaton and Equal

Pay Acts, claims for maternity leave and pay, and claims of unfair dismissal. ACAS was constituted on a statutory basis by the *Employment Protection Act*, and has taken over the conciliation functions formerly undertaken by the Department of Employment. This is an important departure, designed to remove conciliation and arbitration from the suspicion that they were subject to government influence. ACAS is not a government department; it is an independent body corporate, self-governed by a tripartite council of TUC and CBI nominees, together with an academic element, which is not subject to ministerial directions. ACAS handles some 200 conciliation cases a month through its central and regional offices, and achieves settlements in 80 per cent of cases. It provides voluntary arbitration in about 24 cases a month and there is a 100 per cent record of acceptance of its awards. Both in conciliation and arbitration, ACAS activity is at a far higher level than was the work of its predecessors at the Department of Employment.[20] Its other functions include processing and conciliating, reporting and referring to the CAC, in claims for trade union recognition, disclosure of information, and for the 'going-rate'. It is also responsible for preparing Codes of Practice.

The Employment Appeal Tribunal (EAT) is a fully-fledged court which hears appeals from decisions of the Industrial Tribunals. The CAC provides a service of voluntary, agreed arbitration in single disputes (the function which originated in the Industrial Court Act 1919), makes compulsory awards in claims for the going-rate, and compulsory awards of terms and conditions of employment in cases where employers refuse to grant union recognition or to disclose information.

What then, have been the effects of these new laws and institutions? This is a very large question, to which only the most general answers are offered here. We have seen that the *Trade Union and Labour Relations Act* was intended to restore all former legal protection for strikers. We should again note that Britain does not have even now a positive 'right to strike' law, only immunities from legal actions. 'A network of immunities can precariously serve as a substitute for a general principle, but the network is apt to become a labyrinth' and 'the freedom to strike then remains hidden in the interstices of procedural immunities and privileges.'[21] The new strike laws have not in fact remained immune themselves from the traditional judge-made restrictions, and several recent cases since 1976 have given cause for concern at the TUC. In *Gouriet v. the Union of Post Office Workers*, the House of Lords held that the *Post Office Act* 1953, and the *Telegraph Act* 1863, contained provisions which made it a criminal offence for postal workers to wilfully delay or detain a parcel or letter. In the *BBC v Hearn* case, the Appeal Court held that a threat by the Association of Broadcasting Staffs to 'black' coverage of the FA Cup Final because it was to be transmitted to South Africa was not 'action in contemplation or furtherance of a trade dispute'. In *Beaverbrook Newspapers v. Keys*, the Appeal Court held that an instruction by the general secretary of SOGAT to members at the *Daily Express* not to produce extra copies in view of the non-publication of the *Daily Mirror* in London was not action in furtherance of a trade dispute, because SOGAT had no dispute at the *Mirror*. The whole principle of immunity for secondary boycotts and blacking campaigns, supposed to be enacted in the *Trade Union and Labour Relations Act* amendments of 1976, has been put in question by decisions in the case of the National Union of Journalists against the *Daily Express* in 1978. The NUJ had instructed its members on national newspapers not to handle material from the Press Association where a strike had been called in solidarity with its striking members in the provincial press. An injunction granted by a High Court judge was upheld in the Court of Appeal, where Lord Denning said that it was up to the courts to interpret the 1976 Act, and to decide whether a blacking action did in fact 'further' the trade dispute. The president of the NUJ, Denis McShane, said that 'everything Lord Denning said reinforces our conviction that they are trying to destroy the ability of unions to call for sympathetic action'. The House of Lords, in December 1979, upheld an appeal by the union against Lord Denning's judgement, but it is expected that the government will legislate to restore the restriction on sympathetic action implied in the Appeal Court's judgement.

The tendency for the Court of Appeal to limit the scope of the meaning of 'trade dispute' has worried the TUC. Lord Denning has made the general comment, despite the new laws, that trade union immunities might not be appropriate in respect of unofficial and unconstitutional action. The Hon Justice Phillips, retired President of the EAT, has expressed similar views. It is clear that some prominent judges have not accepted the limitation on their powers in the new Acts, and would like to subvert them. The long-term answer to this perennial battle between legislature and judiciary may well have to wait on a radical reform of the legal profession, its sources of recruitment and promotion, and its accountability to sections of the community other than its own narrow elite.

The right to picket—a crucial complement to the right to strike—remains in an extremely insecure state, hedged about with criminal liabilities, police power, and judicial discretion. A reform of the law had been promised in Labour's social contract agreement with the TUC, but in fact the ensuing legislation simply restored the law to the same basis it had in the 1875 and 1906 Acts, wherein there was only a general right peacefully to picket. The police retain huge discretion to determine the number of pickets and to make arrests for a whole range of criminal offences. The experiences of the 1977 pickets at the Grunwick film processing premises in London offer a comprehensive lesson.

'Amongst the many issues highlighted by the Grunwick dispute, one of the most important was the right to picket. The right that exists in law under the *Trade Union and Labour Relations Act* means little in the face of police and judicial hostility. At Grunwick, before the mass picketing, the police varied from day to day their interpretation of the law. On one day they would allow six pickets in front of the gate, on another three and on some days none. Frequently pickets were not allowed to speak to those going in to work. If pickets stood on the footway, they were accused of obstructing it. If they moved into the road, they were accused of obstructing the highway. If they raised their voice, they would be guilty of threatening or insulting behaviour. If they dared ask a policeman the reasons for his interpretation of the law, they would be arrested for obstructing a police officer in the execution of his duty. A Jesus or a Job could not have escaped arrest at Grunwick gate.'[22]

The most serious omission in the law is an absence of any right to stop vehicles entering premises, for the purpose of communicating the pickets' cause to drivers and occupants, a crucial need in an era of motorised transport. Deprived of this right, workers evolved the technique of mass picketing in the 1970s, which was notably successful in the miners' strike of 1972. Yet such techniques are fraught with physical hazard, and a miners' picket was killed by a lorry at a power station in 1972. In the same year, in a sharp and vindictive political reaction to the success of mass and 'flying' pickets, the police and judiciary yet again turned to the conspiracy laws to impose harsh punishment on building worker pickets at Shrewsbury. These pickets were originally charged with the *actual* offence of intimidation under the 1875 Act, but this failed to secure a conviction. Thirteen months after the events, six pickets were then charged with a criminal conspiracy to intimidate, an offence for which the court proceedings are heavily biased in favour of the prosecution (hearsay evidence is allowed), and for which much heavier sentences can be imposed than for an actual offence. On conviction, three pickets were sentenced to 9 months, 2 years, and 3 years imprisonment, a more severe punishment than any in a trade union case since Tolpuddle. The foreman of the jury was moved to cry out 'disgraceful!' and to leave the court, when sentence was pronounced.[23]

The Labour government's *Criminal Law Act* 1977 has now, following the Shrewsbury case, fixed a maximum sentence of three months for conspiracy charges in industrial disputes. Thus, conspiracy has not been altogether removed from industrial law, but it has been made a less attractive option for the prosecution. It remains generally true, as Professor Wedderburn has wryly remarked, that 'the only indisputably lawful pickets are those who attend in small numbers . . . and keep out of everybody's way'.[24] The 1977 Act created a new legal hazard for the modern trade unionist, who in recent years has had recourse to factory occupations in industrial disputes, particularly in defence of the right to work. The Act makes criminal the offence of trespass, which previously was only a civil wrong. Thus the police are brought into situations of factory occupations, and given powers of arrest without warrant, which can lead to convictions carrying gaol sentences.

The new laws, as we have seen, protect the employee's right to join and participate in the activity of an independent trade union. But this law does not apply to *applicants* for jobs, who remain therefore quite without any protection against anti-union employers who make use of the notorious black-lists of trade union activists which are secretly circulated by anti-union organisations such as the Economic League. Since sex and race discrimination have been outlawed in making appointments to jobs, it would seem just to require a similar law on anti-union discrimination of this kind.

How far have the new laws succeeded in advancing collective rights to recognition and collective bargaining? The *Employment Protection Act* laid down the procedure to be followed if a union is denied recognition by an employer. The union appeals to ACAS, which examines the case, makes enquiries, conciliates, and if necessary carries out a ballot or conducts a questionnaire to ascertain the wishes of the employees. Failing a settlement, ACAS must then publish a report, which may include a recommendation in favour of recognition. If the employer still refuses, the only redress is to refer the case to the CAC, which may make a legally binding award, not that the employer should recognise the union, but that he should observe specified terms and conditions of employment. Following the first three years of this law's operation, the unions and the TUC strongly feel the need for its further reform or amendment, since it has proved very unsatisfactory.

Between February 1976 and July 1977, 853 claims for recognition were received by ACAS, of which 248 were settled by conciliation. 216

cases went to the inquiry stage, and 60 reports were issued. Of these, ten recommended that there should be no recognition. Only 27,500 workers achieved recognition through the use of the ACAS procedure; since there are 12,000,000 non-unionists in Britain, the 'impact effect' on the growth of unionism was 0.235 per cent.[25] It is noteworthy that most claims concerned small firms or constituencies; there was an average of only 49 workers per report. The limits of the recognition law were dramatically demonstrated in the Grunwick case.

'Grunwick process films in two North London factories. In 1973 the TGWU failed to get recognition and strikers were sacked. In August 1976 some workers walked out in protest against the sacking of a colleague for refusing compulsory overtime. Pay was very low— 77p an hour—conditions were bad, compulsory overtime of up to 30 hours a week was common, discipline was summary and sackings were frequent. Staff turnover in the mainly Asian female workforce was 100 per cent a year. The workers joined the clerical union APEX, which made the strike official.
The company sacked 137 strikers, APEX asked the Union of Postal Workers and other unions for support, and made a legal claim to . . . ACAS for recognition. Management consistently refused to deal with APEX or ACAS. Supported by the National Association for Freedom and right-wing Tory MPs, Grunwick sought an injunction against the UPW. ACAS conducted a ballot but as the company refused to give the names and addresses of employees, ACAS could only ballot the strikers. It recommended recognition but the company didn't budge. By June 1977 the strikers got support for mass picketing from rank and file trade unionists. Hundreds of pickets were arrested and many convicted. But APEX and the TUC refused to campaign for further mass picketing, the cutting off of essential services or sympathetic action. A court of inquiry recommended reinstatement of the strikers, or compensation, and said recognition of APEX would be "helpful". Grunwick ignored the report and sued ACAS over the way the ballot was conducted. The House of Lords decided that it was lawful to ballot the strikers, but the non-strikers should also have been allowed to vote. So the ballot was invalid and APEX had to start all over again in 1978.'[26]

In this case then, the employer successfully defied ACAS recommendations and also the findings of an official Court of Inquiry (traditionally the 'heavy armour' of governments in seeking a resolution of difficult disputes). Other weaknesses in the law were exposed by the case; it is 'fair' to sack workers for striking, provided they are *all* sacked, and Grunwick therefore complied with the law. The indirect sanction against employers who refuse recognition, (a binding CAC award of terms and conditions) was inapplicable because Grunwick, thanks entirely to the union pressure and publicity, and in order to retain the loyalty of its non-striking workforce, *did* raise its pay to levels comparable with the industry as a whole. Moreover, the House of Lords added insult to injury by castigating ACAS for not doing what the company prevented them from doing—consulting all the workers involved.

This case, and the general experience of the law, suggests that the recognition provisions of the *Employment Protection Act* are almost voluntary for employers. There are other difficulties; the tripartite ACAS Council has failed to agree any general criteria for recognition, and claims can be made which are disruptive of existing collective bargaining arrangements or which conflict with the TUC Bridlington disputes machinery. Delays are built into the system; the average claim takes twelve months to process. Yet the TUC is reluctant to call for greater powers of legal enforceability against unco-operative employers, fearing that this would set a precedent for legal intervention in other forms of trade dispute. And legal enforcement could bring with it additional needs for back-up law to compel an employer to 'bargain in good faith' after the pattern in the USA, with its prospects of endless litigation. One reform in union practice which the TUC is considering would be for unions to by-pass the lengthy ACAS procedure, and proceed straight to compulsory arbitration on a claim for the 'going-rate' under Schedule 11 of the *Employment Protection Act*. The more legalistic solution would be to empower ACAS to have access to all employees, to enter premises, and subsequently to *order* recognition. But this implies an American-type solution, and could still lead to a clash between the law and the Bridlington rules. A way round this may be found by requiring that ACAS takes account of Bridlington decisions. The dilemma involved in moving from voluntaryism to legalism could not be more effectively illustrated, than by the case of recognition law.

The law on disclosure of information was also designed to promote the trade union role in collective bargaining. Independent, recognised unions are given a right to receive information from their employers which is necessary for effective collective bargaining. Failure to comply with a union request for information entitles the union to apply to the CAC, which may ask ACAS to conciliate. Eventually, the CAC may order the employer to produce specified information; if he still refuses, the CAC may award that he must observe specified terms and conditions of employment. Up to April 1978, there had been 28 invocations of this law, 66 per cent from white-collar unions. No CAC decisions had been published. The TUC has found no significance to date in the little use which unions have made of the provision, and notes that the CAC prefers to conciliate rather than make awards.[27]

There are some serious limitations to the law as it stands. An employer has no obligation to reveal any information the uncovering of which would cause 'substantial injury' to his company, nor any information which has been given to him in confidence. He is not obliged to produce original documents, or copies or extracts from them. The unions have no right to inspect accounts or to send in their own auditor to study them. (Shareholders by contrast have the legal right to an independent auditor). Moreover, the employer is not obliged to produce information if this would involve a 'disproportionate amount of time or expense'.

Provision was also made for trade unions to have access to information for purposes connected with the making of planning agreements, in the *Industry Act* 1975, but this aspect of the Act has been a dead letter from the date of its inception. In the *Health and Safety at Work Act* a much stronger obligation is laid on employers to disclose information on health and safety matters to union safety representatives, and Health and Safety inspectors must also pass on information they have obtained on an employer to the safety representatives.

The new provisions allowing trade union representatives to take time-off work with pay for their industrial relations duties and for training, has had a major impact on the number of shop stewards undergoing training in the TUC day-release scheme. The protection of trade unionists from dismissal for their trade union activities includes a provision that Industrial Tribunals can order interim reinstatement or the revival of the employment contract pending a full unfair dismissal hearing. Tribunals have been reluctant to grant these interim orders, preferring to give priority to a speeding-up of the full hearing. A complicated procedure for applying for interim relief, which must be completed in seven days of the dismissal, may be a cause of its infrequent use.

The new obligations on employers to notify the Department of Employment and unions in advance, and to consult with unions, when redundancies are planned, has been found 'generally useful' by the TUC, which also believes that it has had the effect of improving private sector procedures and practices. There have been no prosecutions of employers for failing to notify the Department of Employment of impending redundancies. But the law remains modest; the requirement on employers is limited to *consultation*, and there is no legal obligation on him to bargain and reach agreement with the union if the reduncancies are disputed.

About 60 claims a month are presented by unions to the CAC under Schedule 11 of the *Employment Protection Act*, which allows claims that a particular employer is not paying the 'going-rate' in his industry or district. This is an enlarged version of a law which in one form or other reaches back to war-time compulsory arbitration orders. CAC awards under the new law have been generally favourable to unions, have been immune from the restrictions of government incomes policies, and are enabling unions to tidy up anomalies in the pay field.

Of the remaining provisions for promoting collective bargaining, there has been very little interest by trade unions in the clauses of the *Employment Protection Act* which allow for the conversion of a Wages Council into a statutory Joint Industrial Council. Of the new institutions, ACAS is well regarded by unions in its conciliation role, but is regarded as 'union-biased' by many employers. It has suffered from its involvement in the unsatisfactory recognition procedure. The trade unions expected that the idea of a Certificate of Independence, to be issued by a Certification Officer, who would deny this status to employer-influenced staff associations, would help in eliminating such organisations, particularly in the white-collar field. The practice of the Officer, who has granted certificates to associations regarded as illegitimate by white-collar unions such as the ASTMS, has disappointed the unions. The Industrial Tribunals are criticised by the unions for having developed too legalistic a routine and style, and—self-critically, the TUC is concerned about the quality of the lay members of the Tribunals.

Turning now to the reform of individual employee rights, we can discern a strong tendency for the law to intervene in an increasing number of areas, beginning with the *Contracts of Employment Act* 1963. This laid down rights to minimum periods of notice; since then, rights have been established in relation to redundancy pay, unfair dismissal, equal pay and opportunities, freedom from racial discrimination in employment, rights to maternity pay and leave, to guaranteed pay during lay-offs, and to certain rights in cases of insolvency. Discrimination in employment on racial grounds was first defined and proscribed in the *Race Relations Act* of 1968, yet in 1974 the research organisation PEP estimated that there were 20,000 acts of discrimination a year; hence the need for a stronger Act in 1976.[28] Similarly, the *Sex Discrimination Act* has been found deficient in practice, and extremely hard to enforce. Equal pay has been TUC policy since 1888; the Act of 1970 has not yet by any means removed inequality in pay and conditions for women workers, and

Industrial Tribunals have made unfavourable decisions in equal pay cases, suggesting that women would still do well to rely primarily on trade union organisation and action to achieve equality.

The right to receive a written itemised statement of the make-up of the pay packet is reported to have had a good effect in some backward industries, such as agriculture, where the National Farmers' Union actually opposed this provision before its enactment. The legal minimum standard for the right to guarantee pay during lay-offs and short-time working is a very modest one—a maximum of £6.60 per day for five working days in any quarter (3 months). This is a long way from payment at normal rates, which tends to apply to salaried workers when a company is in economic difficulties, and a long way from the standard achieved in some blue-collar occupations by collective bargaining.

The most significant law on individual rights is that on 'unfair dismissal' which accounts for some 80 per cent of all Industrial Tribunal cases. Traditionally, in British industry, there was no right to any notice of dismissal above one hour, and employers were not obliged to give any reason for dismissal. The power to fire was legally absolute, restrained only by trade unionism and collective action. Inroads in the law began in 1963, with the *Contracts of Employment Act*, which gave workers rights to notice increasing with length of service. These rights have been improved by the *Contracts of Employment Act* 1972 and by the *Employment Protection Act*. At last in 1972 the *Industrial Relations Act* introduced the concept of unfair dismissal, which has been retained and expanded in the *Trade Union and Labour Relations Act* and the *Employment Protection Act*. Industrial Tribunals have the power to order the employer to re-instate or to re-engage, or to pay financial compensation to the unfairly dismissed worker. But an employer who refuses to re-instate or re-engage is not guilty of an offence; he merely risks increasing the compensation charges payable to the sacked worker; in other words the employer retains the ultimate right to discharge. Moreover, those who have been employed for less than 52 weeks (the period when they are often most vulnerable) are not covered by the law, nor are those over 65 years of age, or certain part-time workers. Protection had been afforded in the original Act to those employed for 26 weeks but the period of employment after which protection commences was raised to 52 weeks by the ruling Conservative Government. There seem to be no valid reasons for these exclusions, which are in fact waived in the case of dismissal for trade union membership or activities. Moreover, the financial compensation awarded by Tribunals, which could in law be as high as £11,760 in 1978, was (in 1975) less than £1,000 in 92 per cent of cases, and less than £200 in 49.9 per cent of cases.

Case law established by the EAT has, over the years, made it much harder for workers to win unfair dismissal cases, and in the years from 1975 to 1977, the proportion of cases decided in favour of the employee fell from 40 per cent to 30 per cent.

'Since 1976 . . . the EAT has considerably loosened the constraints upon management . . . recent decisions of the EAT . . . lend no support to the popular notion that managements have been tied hand and foot by the Employment Protection Act and that it is "virtually impossible" for an employer to discharge employees.'[29]

A 1977 study observed that:

'It is still possible for an employee to win an unfair dismissal case, but it is now a lot more difficult than it used to be.'[30]

A 1978 study reported in the Department of Employment *Gazette*,[31] was based on research in firms employing between 50 and 50,000 workers. It found that unfair dismissal had had by far the largest impact on management of any of the new laws, had prompted them to reform and formalise discipline procedures, and had reduced the rate of dismissals, especially where this was very high prior to the introduction of the law. But it found that there was no evidence to support the frequently heard criticism from employers, that it had caused unemployment by making employers reluctant to take on new labour. The author of the survey 'unequivocally rejected' this hypothesis. Nor did it appear that the smallest firms had been most affected by the law, although firms where trade unionism was weak had been. Where there was strong trade unionism, effective procedures for discipline and dismissal had pre-dated the law.

The ACAS Code of Practice on discipline, which is taken into account by Industrial Tribunals in unfair dismissal cases, has been very influential in improving discipline procedures; it is a pity therefore that it does not rule out the barbarous practice of 'instant dismissal', which is still included, for specified 'gross misconduct', in far too many discipline procedures. There is in law no crime—including murder—for which one can be punished without a trial. The same elementary principle should apply to employment and dismissal.

The right to maternity pay (6 weeks, at 9/10ths of normal pay minus social security maternity allowance) and to maternity leave (up to 29 weeks after the birth) is considered by the TUC to be a too modest standard, but it has in fact become the standard one. It is an example of an area of law creating standards which collective bargaining should clearly strive to improve.

It is clear from all this that there has been a substantial wave of new regulatory as well as auxiliary labour law in the past two decades. In this, Britain has acted much later and more minimally than many European countries. (Sweden established the legal right to organise and to bargain as early as 1936). The standards laid down internationally by the EEC and the ILO, are the precedents behind many of the provisions in the *Employment Protection Act*, the *Equal Pay Act*, and the *Sex Discrimination Act*. Laws regulating the employers' power to dismiss preceded that in Britain in France, Belgium, Norway, West Germany, Holland, and Italy. Most European countries provide legal minimum standards on holidays; in Britain such law applies only in Wages Council industries.

'. . . the actual working conditions enjoyed by British workers have fallen behind the standards of other common market countries. Workers in Britain have far less legal protection for public holidays and paid annual leave than in any other common market country, and many of their standards fall well below the minimum standards generally established by law (or by collective bargaining) elsewhere in the common market.'[32]

If continental practice has been a spur to much of the recent labour law, English law remains wedded to the concept of immunities, rather than positive rights, in dealing with strikes. And employees are still compensated largely by pecuniary remedies, rather than by a positive right to work, to information, and to trade union recognition. For all their limitations however, the new laws have undoubtedly spread a stronger confidence and sense of security among workers and trade union representatives, and have at least checked some employer abuses, particularly where trade unionism is weak. The *Health and Safety at Work Act* stands on its own in the advance of workers' rights achieved, because of its vital and unique principle of a trade union-based workers' inspectorate to police the Act. This has opened a whole field of the employment relationship to joint determination, has increased the density of workers' representation on the shop floor, and has led to the foundation of self-help workers' Action Committees and Safety Campaigns in many industrial localities. This is an excellent example of a law stimulating workers' appetites for control. Generally, trade unions show no sign of abandoning their traditional reliance on collective bargaining and trade union solidarity in favour of a dependence on the law. Abstentionism has been re-affirmed in the sphere of strike law, but the restrictive instincts of the judges remain to be dealt with, whilst there is still much room for further reform of individual employment rights. Political circumstances largely determine the direction of labour law, and whilst an incoming conservative administration would be unlikely to repeat all the errors of the *Industrial Relations Act*, it would undoubtedly seek legal change in a number of areas. It would weaken the law on the closed shop, would provide secret ballots, financed by the state, to determine strike decisions, and to elect union officials, and would restrict picketing to the strikers' place of work. Balloting for union office is discussed in the chapter on trade union government. So far as balloting in strikes is concerned, its proponents have undoubtedly forgotten the experience of 1972, and the experience in America. But they clearly expect that it would reduce strike incidence by substituting the influence of the mass media and the private reflections of the hearth and the family, for the collective influence of the work-force on the shop floor. Such a step might therefore itself stimulate the over-due discussion in the labour movement of the need to democratise the mass media. Other legal changes contemplated by conservatives, such as the denial of social security benefit to unofficial strikers' families, and the delaying of tax rebate payment in strikes, are bound to appear provocative to the unions. The situation in labour law remains volatile.

NOTES

1. Otto Kahn-Freund, *Labour and the Law*, Stephens, second edition, 1977. Labour law changes so frequently that its literature soon becomes outdated. At the time of going to press, Professor Kahn-Freund's work is the most authoritative and up-to-date comprehensive account of the current situation. We have drawn heavily upon it in this chapter.
2. Jeremy McMullen, *Rights at Work*, Pluto Press 1978. If Professor Kahn-Freund's book contains the best academic account, Jeremy McMullen's volume is the most complete practical guide to labour law for trade union readers, and we are equally in his debt.
3. Roy Lewis, 'The Historical Development of Labour Law', *British Journal of Industrial Relations*, vol. XIV, no. 1, March 1976.
4. Quoted in several works, including Paul O'Higgins, *Workers' Rights*, Arrow in association with the Society of Industrial Tutors, Trade Union Industrial Studies series, 1976.
5. Roy Lewis, loc. cit.
6. O. Kahn-Freund, op. cit.
7. Terry Sullivan, 'Is there a Cycle in Labour Law?', *The Law Teacher*, April 1977.
8. Roy Lewis, op. cit. is the basis for much of the following paragraphs on legal history.

9. Clive Jenkins and J. E. Mortimer, *The Kind of Laws the Unions ought to Want*, Pergamon, 1968.

10. Formal provision for arbitration had been present since the 1896 Act, and there had been much informal arbitration both before and after that date. The Whitley Committee sought to generalise this experience, and re-printed some existing proposals for an arbitration court, originating in the Labour Department of the Board of Trade.

11. O. Kahn-Freund, op. cit.

12. See R. H. Fryer, *Redundancy, Values and Public Policy*, Discussion Paper no. 8, Industrial Relations Research Unit of the SSRC, Warwick University Nov. 1972.

13. John Westergaard and Henrietta Resler, *Class in a Capitalist Society*, Pelican, 1976.

14. Donovan Royal Commission, *Report*, Cmnd. 3623, 1968, para. 1005.

15. TUC, *Trades Unionism*, published by the TUC, 1968.

16. TUC, op. cit.

17. O. Kahn-Freund, op. cit.

18. O. Kahn-Freund, op. cit.

19. Jeremy McMullen, op. cit.

20. Terry Sullivan, 'Some Comments on Current Labour Law', *Personnel Review*, vol. 7, no. 1, winter 1978.

21. O. Kahn-Freun, op. cit.

22. Tom Durkin, *Grunwick: Bravery and Betrayal*, Brent Trades Council, 1978.

23. C. Ralph, *The Picket and the Law*, Fabian Research Series, no. 331, 1977.

24. K. W. Wedderburn, *The Worker and the Law*, quoted in C. Ralph, op. cit.

25. Terry Sullivan, loc. cit. 1978.

26. Jeremy McMullen, op. cit.

27. See 'Collective Bargaining and Disclosure of Information: A View from Labour Economics,' Terry Sullivan, *Personnel Review*, Vol. 7, no. 3, Summer 1978.

28. Jeremy McMullen, op. cit.

29. Kevin Hawkins, *The Management of Industrial Relations*, Pelican 1978.

30. *Industrial Relations Review and Report*, no. 89, 25th May 1977, quoted in Kevin Hawkins, op. cit.

31. W. W. Daniel, 'The Effects of Employment Protection Laws in Manufacturing Industry,' Department of Employment *Gazette*, June 1978.

32. Paul O'Higgins, op. cit.

APPENDIX TO CHAPTER 9

TUC Response to Governmental Proposals for Law Reform: 1979
This chapter was completed before the installation of the Thatcher administration, and although we were able to update it in minor matters, the central legislative thrust of the new Government really requires separate treatment. It is for this reason that we include, as an appendix, the following carefully-reasoned brief by the TUC which represents its first considered reaction to the Government's draft proposals. Paragraph references in the TUC's text are to the Government's working paper (July 1979) which outline its intentions.

The TUC's Reply to Proposals for new Legislation on Industrial Relations. (November, 1979)

"With regard to the Government's stated *aim* (to enable trade unions to play their indispensable role in furthering the interests of their members responsibility and representatively) the implementation of these proposals would not have this effect but the opposite one. The proposals are irrelevant to the basic issues of improving industrial relations and promoting improvements in productivity, real earnings and job and income security. Worse, they would make it more difficult to achieve progress on these issues because they would introduce highly contentious laws into industrial relations—laws which could be exploited, as with the Industrial Relations Act 1971, by unscrupulous employers and eccentric individuals seeking to disrupt established customary arrangements and to inflame feelings in already difficult disputes.

The Government claim the proposed changes are *'limited'*. They may indeed be limited in relation to the 170-section Industrial Relations Act, but particular proposals have far-reaching implications (see below). Moreover it is important to note that they represent only one part of a wider programme that the Government have in mind with regard to industrial relations legislation. Already, the Government are increasing the qualifying period of unfair dismissal from 26 to 52 weeks and are reducing the period for consultation and notification in advance of redundancy from 60 to 30 days in respect of redundancies of less than 100 employees. Moreover para 12 of the working paper on picketing makes clear that the Government are engaged in a review of the law on trade union 'immunities'. It seems that the

Government may be disclosing its intentions quietly and in stages but the Movement cannot regard the proposed changes as 'limited'. Indeed, the implications for trade unions and industrial relations are immense.

The Government apparently hopes that *voluntary action* to deal with the problems associated with picketing and the closed shop will continue along the lines of the proposed legislative changes. But an increased role for the law would affect the role that trade unions would be prepared to play. In particular, a changed legal framework would make it necessary for the TUC to issue new guidance to affiliated unions, particularly on the conduct of disputes and union organisation.

Picketing

In order to justify their proposals to change the law on picketing, the Government say that there has been a tendency to use picketing to bring pressure to bear on companies not directly involved in the dispute, that picketing has become more effective, and that there are indications of an increasing use of intimidation (paras 3 and 4). The importance of voluntary guidance is stressed (para 5).

The Government propose (para 6–8) to limit the right to picket lawfully to

i. those who are party to the trade dispute which occasions the picketing, and
ii. to the picketing which they carry out at their own place of work.

To picket outside those limits would not be a criminal offence (para 6) but one approach suggested (para 10) is that anyone who picketed outside the limits would not be protected if that picketing induced breaches of contract. It is also suggested that the immunity conferred by section 13 of the Trade Union and Labour Relations Act on all industrial action might be amended so that the immunity the section confers is limited to breaches of contracts of employment (para 11).

The proposed legislation would provide a power for the Employment Secretary to draw up a code covering all aspects of picketing and for this to be submitted to Parliament. He would only make use of this power in the absence of voluntary action which satisfied the Government. It is also suggested that one possibility might be for ACAS to draw up such a Code, subject to Government approval (paras 13–14).

Comments

The General Council have encouraged affiliated unions to give advice to their officials and members about the law and the effective organisation of picketing. The General Council also sought, unsuccessfully to persuade the Labour Government to give trade unionists the legal right to communicate effectively with persons in vehicles. Indeed while the Government complains about picketing having become more effective, there is no doubt that the increased use of motor vehicles has made it less effective in many circumstances.

The Government clearly consider that action by the TUC and unions is not sufficient to control picketing nor do they acknowledge the problems of pickets communicating with persons in vehicles. Moreover, the Government's assertion of an increasing intimidation on picket lines needs to be challenged. The fact is that the vast majority of pickets are conducted wholly peaceably: in the past, just as now, there have only been isolated incidents where violence has occurred and this has never been condoned by unions.

The existing legal constraints on pickets are considerable with the police having powers to deal with pickets because of crimes of obstruction and pickets could be liable at civil law for nuisance—two legal wrong-doings which can cover a wide range of circumstances.

It is not wholly clear whether the two legislative approaches on picketing suggested in paras 10 and 11 are alternative or additional to each other. The opening sentances of para 11 give the impression they are alternatives but para 12 gives the clearer impression that the Government have in mind to introduce both approaches.

In the *first approach*—described in para 10—they are seeking to allow employers to sue pickets, deemed to be acting unlawfully under the proposal, for inducing breaches of contract.

This proposal is intended to prevent a union giving full support to a group of members in dispute. Usually the presence of union members not employed at the workplace where the dispute is taking is designed to show solidarity, give encouragement and boost the morale of the members on strike, and provided such outsiders accept instructions from the person in charge of the picket line, difficulties rarely occur. Now it is proposed that union members showing such solidarity would be acting unlawfully. Besides being objectionable in principle, the proposal raises many practical problems including the following:

i.   the proposals use the term 'picketing' but section 15 of the 1974 Trade Union and Labour Relations Act (which is quoted in para 7 of the working paper) does not mention picketing at all. Picketing is not a legal term. In law there is a right in Section 15 to attend at or near a place for the purpose only of peaceful information or persuasion. It is this right to attend at or near a workplace which the Government is proposing to limit and attendance—the only legal right there is—is not explained. It is not clear, for example, whether a group of workers 500 yards from the factory where the dispute arises would be acting lawfully or not or how near they would need to get before it became unlawful. Presumably the Government have it in mind to leave this to the Courts and, if so, the whole area of picketing will become even more uncertain than it is now;

ii.   The next question is who is 'party' to the dispute. Some disputes have many parties and many places of work. In the Trade Union and Labour Relations Act (Section 29 b.), it is made expressly clear that workers employed by an employer not party to the dispute can be 'parties'. But the working paper implies that in future only workers at one place of work will be regarded as 'parties'. It is also not clear whether a group of workers who have been dismissed and are no longer employees of the employer would be acting lawfully if they picketed;

iii.   what is a 'place of work'? In National Insurance decisions it has been held that a large site owned by one company counts as one place of work. The working paper seems to imply that if one plant on a multi-plant site were to be owned by a different company— even if it was an associated company or subsidiary—then that would be a separate place of work which could not be picketed by workers from the other plants. And it is certainly clear from the working paper that if, for example, workers from Ford Halewood picketed Ford Dagenham it would be unlawful;

iv.   although the working paper states that it would be for the employer concerned to initiate legal action, it appears that it would also be possible for suppliers and customers of the employer in dispute to bring actions against all or any of the pickets for inducing breach of contract and seek injunctions and possibly damages;

v.   full-time officers or any other officers of the union visiting a picket-line would be particularly vulnerable to the imposition of injunctions and being sued for damages because they are likely to be better known. And employers would be encouraged to pick them out, no doubt believing that the union would indemnify officers for payment of costs incurred in any legal action including any damages.

The *second approach*—described in para 11—would involve limiting 'immunity' to inducing breaches of contracts of employment (ie not commercial contracts) not simply in relation to picketing but covering all industrial action. Ostensibly this proposal is directed at other forms of secondary action (eg blacking) as well as picketing and it is said that the effect of this would be to reduce the extent to which S13 of the Trade Union and Labour Relations Act protects interference with commercial contracts.

This is a very dangerous proposal. The effect of the Government legislating on this basis would make unlawful not just secondary action (a term which is in any case very difficult to define), but also primary action where it interferes with a commercial contract (as it is likely to do in most cases). The Trade Union and Labour Relations (Amendment) Act gives trade unionists protection for actions in tort for inducing breach of contract in contemplation or furtherance of a trade dispute. From the Trade Disputes Act 1906 to the 1960s protection in trade disputes against interference with employment contracts seemed to be sufficient to establish trade union rights. But the judges in the 1960s developed a new liability for interference with commercial contracts. It is difficult to conceive of circumstances in which workers would retain the right to strike or take other industrial action against their own employer, or his customer, supplier or other related party without incurring legal liabilty if liability for interference with commercial contracts was resurrected. If the Government makes this change in the law, they will have pre-empted their review of trade disputes 'immunities' because there would be little effective protection left for trade unionists.

The final proposal is for a code of practice on picketing. Unlike guidance provided by the TUC or by an affiliated union which is designed to be applied flexibly with regard to particular circumstances, a code which is to be taken into account by courts would undoubtedly place further restrictions on picketing in addition to the existing extensive range of criminal and civil offences and the proposed new civil offences. For ACAS to be given this task would have implications for the continuation of the TUC's strong commitment to, and support for, the Service.

The Closed Shop

The working paper on the 'closed shop' presents proposals not only on the closed shop but on arbitrary exclusion or expulsion from a trade union. These are separate issues and are summarised and considered separately below.

The Government states that there has been widespead public concern on the 'closed shop' issue and that the UK legislation is to be tested before the European Commission on Human Rights (para 2).

The Government recognise that employers and unions have long had practical reasons for entering into such agreements but aim to ensure that closed shops are only established with the wholehearted support of the workers concerned and that there is a remedy for abuses of individual rights.

At present, the Employment Protection (Consolidation) Act 1978 allows an employer to dismiss fairly an employee who refuses to be or become a member of a trade union under a union membership agreement. There is one exception—where the employee can prove that he or she genuinely objects on the grounds of religious belief to belonging to any trade union whatsoever, in which case the dismissal is automatically unfair.

The Government proposes (para 7) to widen this exception to include:

a.   existing employees at the 'operative date' of the union member-ship agreement who are not members of the union concerned: and

b.   those with a deeply held personal conviction to being a member of any trade union whatsoever; or perhaps to those who object on grounds of deeply held personal conviction to being a member of a particular trade union or those who object on reasonable grounds to being a member of a particular union as in the 1974 Act (this last provision was deleted by the Labour Government in the 1976 Act).

In applications for unfair dismissal in 'closed shop' situations it is suggested that employers (but not applicants) could be able to join unions as co-defendants so that compensaton could be apportioned between the employer and the trade union as the tribunal thought reasonable (para 9). A new 'closed shop' agreement would only provide an employer with a defence against unfair dismissal where it had been introduced following a secret ballot in which an over-whelming majority had voted in favour (para 10). Detailed guidance on the ballots and on the introduction of closed shops would be contained in a Code of Practice which could be drawn up by ACAS or by the Secretary of State (paras 11 and 12). The Code might also contain provisions for reviewing existing agreements (paras 11 and 12).

Comments

The first category of workers who would obtain unfair dismissal compensation if dismissed as a result of a union membership agree-ment would be *existing employees* who did not want to join the union. A large number of union membership agreements (eg Post Office) already exclude some (eg those with long service) or all existing employees. But to turn what is sensible in particular situations into a general legal rule would create the following difficulties:

i. some circumstances would make it virtually impossible for a union to establish an effective union membership agreement, for example, in areas of employment with a low turnover of labour (conversely in areas of employment with high labour turnover, it would be difficult for unions to obtain an 'overwhelming majority' for an agreement in a vote by secret ballot—see below);

ii. the protection for existing employees would cover those who insisted upon belonging to, or maintaining activity on behalf of, a different union from that of those signatory to the union membership agreement. This could be disruptive of collective bargaining arrangements.

The second category of workers who would be able to claim unfair dismissal compensation would be those with a deeply held personal conviction to being a member of any union whatsoever. A number of practical questions arise as follows:

i. would a deeply held personal conviction that the union subscription rates were too high count as an argument for compensation for dismissal?

ii. would a 'political' dislike of unions be sufficient to warrant compensation for dismissal?

If the conviction was to be widened to those who object to being a 'member of a particular union' this would encourage persons to refuse to belong to a signatory union and to join another. The effect, again, would be to disrupt established bargaining arrangements.

A further obstacle to establishing a union membership agreement is proposed. The Government propose that a new agreement must have the support of an overwhelming majority of the workers involved voting for it by *secret ballot*. The details of this proposal would be contained in a code of practice which could also cover the circumstances in which applications could be made to review existing agreements. The following practical questions are:

i. why is an overwhelming, and not a simple, majority of those voting required before an agreement could be concluded?

ii. who would determine the scope of the bargaining unit, who would count the votes and would there be any right for individuals, unions and employers to challenge the conduct of the ballots?

The cumulative effect of all these provisions, if they were widely observed, would be to make it very difficult for unions to establish effective new membership agreements. The need for a ballot and the scale of the exclusions would be such as to make the whole exercise pointless in many circumstances. Areas of employment like retail distribution and textiles where membership agreements are sometimes regarded by employers and unions as the only way to protect bargaining arrangements could be particulary affected if employers were to insist on carrying out the intention of these proposals.

It is suggested that the code could contain a provision allowing for existing agreements to be reviewed. While there is no evidence that significant numbers of workers are dissatisfied with existing compulsory membership arrangements, it can be predicted that this proposal would give opportunities for dissatisfied individuals and groups to disrupt organisational and bargaining arrangements.

On past experience it can also be predicted that these provisions may be widely ignored in industry although there will be occasional and no doubt well-publicised cases where individual non-unionists insist on their legal rights and other workers refuse to work with them. The other areas of possible flash-point is where individuals apply to have an agreement terminated. There is every prospect in these circumstances that this proposed legislation would, like the Industrial Relations Act, make small local issues become large industrial relations problems with serious and far-reaching consequences.

Arbitrary Exclusion or Expulsion

The Government proposes to introduce a right for any person, whether in a closed shop or not and whether in employment or not, not to be arbitrarily or unreasonably excluded or expelled from union membership (para 13). The suggested test would possibly be similar to the 'unreasonableness' test on employers in the unfair dismissal provisions and would not be 'just on the basis of particular union rules'. An alternative might be to lay down detailed criteria. The Government proposes that the aggrieved person should apply to the High Court (para 15).

Comments

The issue was extensively discussed during the drafting of the Trade Union and Labour Relations Act 1974. At that time the General Council firmly opposed the inclusion of these provisions on grounds that most unions had extensive appeals machinery to deal with these matters and the General Council strongly objected to the term 'abitrary' in this context. The TUC had no objection to individuals continuing to have recourse to the ordinary Courts if they were determined to pursue a grievance against a union, but it did not favour a system which would facilitate and encourage disaffected individuals to initiate cases.

At present a member under common law can take a union to Court on the ground that the union's rules have not been adhered to and/or the principles of natural justice have not been observed. However, it is questionable whether there is any existing provision for redress in cases of exclusion (ie refusal of admission) as distinct from expulsion. ('A person who is eligible for membership has no legal or equitable right to be admitted even if membership of an association is essential before he can earn his living in his trade or occupation'—Citrine's *Trade Union Law*; although Lord Denning would say that this proposition is no longer the law.)

There are a number of practical problems with the Government's proposals. For instance, what would be the position of individuals seeking promotion or transfer within a company to a department or section where there is a 'closed shop?' What account would be taken of professional or technical standards? What account would be taken of the suitability of the applicant to work with other union members without causing industrial strife? Would 'oversupply' of labour be a justifiable reason for refusing admission to a union in certain circumstances?

More importantly, however, it would be anomalous that, while an individual worker has no redress against an employer who refuses to engage him because he is a union member or for any other reason, a non-unionist should have the right of action against a union.

There is a reference in para 15 to the 'long standing principle of common law that a man should not be prevented from practising his trade or selling his labour'. It is doubtful if in fact there is any such long standing principle. This particular view had been discredited until revived by Lord Denning in the last two decades. Trade unionists generally hold to a different concept of the right to work namely that of the right of workers to be able to obtain employment on terms agreed with the employer.

In sum, this proposal would give the judges a free hand to decide which union rules were arbitrary or unreasonable and which were not. The TUC could not agree that judges are sufficiently qualified to give reasonable and practical decisions on these matters.

Support from Public Funds for Union Ballots

This working paper proposes legislation to remove major financial constraints on unions holding important ballots. The scheme would initially cover elections to full-time office or union governing bodies, changes to union rules and the calling and ending of strikes (para 4). A trade union could seek reimbursement of at least the cost of using the cheapest postal method and at the discretion of the Certification Officer of the cost of using the first class post (para 5). Views are sought on whether public funds should be available to cover the administrative costs of postal ballots (para 6) or the costs of secret ballots at the workplace (para 7). The Certification Officer would be the public official responsible for administering the scheme.

Comments

Affiliated unions employ a wide range of voting systems in relation to elections, rule changes and the calling and ending of industrial action, including postal ballots and secret ballots at the workplace. Only these last two methods might qualify for State aid.

Unions would have a choice whether to apply for public funds. But if they do so, they must recognise that financial help will not be given from public sources without public accountability. This would have implications for union autonomy if—as appears possible—it led to the Certification Officer developing procedures (which might need to be incorporated in unions' rules) and also supervising aspects of the ballots. Individuals would no doubt have the right to challenge the union and/or the Certification Officer in the courts if they considered that the conduct of the ballot did not comply with the statutory requirements. These issues need to be clarified, and affiliated unions would need to recognise very clearly the implications for their autonomy of accepting money from public sources."

Chapter Ten

Trade Unions and the Labour Party

The Scope of Political Action

The decision which effectively launched the Labour Party was taken at the Trades Union Congress of 1899: 'to ensure that working-class opinion should be represented in the House of Commons by men sympathetic with the aims and demands of the Labour Movement, and whose candidatures are promoted by one or other of the organised movements'.[1] The resultant conference, in 1900, established the Labour Representation Committee, a federation of 41 trade unions and 3 socialist societies, together with 7 constituency associations.[2] One of the socialist societies promptly left for doctrinal reasons, but the number of unions rose to 65, to 127, and then to 165, all within the first four years of the new committee. Affiliated membership passed the million mark in 1907, by which time the 1906 election had seen the spectacular return of 29 Labour members to Parliament.

Rocketing success though this now seems, the unions nonetheless trod very cautiously and defensively into political organisation. The 1902 LRC report states this, rather plainly: 'Menaced on every hand in workshop, court of law, and press, Trade Unionism has no refuge except the ballot box and Labour Representation'.[3] In this tentative way, the unions arrived in the House of Commons as a substantial interest before they announced themselves as a Party, and duly renamed their Representation Committee.

It has often been remarked that the British Labour Party's federal emergence from the unions is quite different from the common continental experience, in which trade unions themselves have often been established from scratch by a pre-existing political party. Socialist parties have been by no means the only innovators in this respect: some of the most successful trade union federations of the post-second world war period were originally established decades earlier by Catholic parties, as a part of the consolidation of their mass-influence. Not infrequently, the doctrine of such unions has been modified, through time, to diverge quite sharply from that of their parent bodies.[4]

The experimental and tentative way in which British unions groped towards a political voice does mean that British Labour politics is perhaps less crystalline, less doctrinaire, and maybe even less 'principled' than some schools of continental socialism. Nonetheless, once political organisation began, argument moved back and forth, and influences were by no means one-directional. More and more trade unions began to reconsider and amend their formal objectives.[5] Before the Labour Party itself was ready to embrace its explicitly socialist constitution of 1918, various major trade union bodies had preceded it. Up to 1918, the Party Constitution stated its sole object as being

'to organise and maintain in Parliament and the country a political Labour Party'.[6]

This was then replaced by a more elaborate set of aims including the famous clause IV:

'to secure for the producers by hand or by brain the full fruits of their industry, and the most equitable distribution thereof that may be possible, upon the basis of the common ownership of the means of production, and the best obtainable system of popular administration and control of each industry or service.'[7]

Much later, when the political leaders of the Labour Party, following electoral defeat in 1959, tried to revise its constitution by deleting that clause, their moves were checked precisely by the resistance of the unions.[8]

The extent of union commitment to socialist objectives does vary through the years, of course: and more significantly, ideas about the main strategic socialist options have changed, and will continue to change, with alterations in the overall political economy which provokes their challenge.

We have discussed these processes in other works,[9] and will excuse ourselves from pursuing them here. But it is necessary to point up one key distinction which helps explain working class responses to the political problems which confront trade unions. This is the distinction, first established in clarity by Antonio Gramsci, and later popularised in England by Perry Anderson,[10] between 'corporate' and 'hegemonic' attitudes and forms of thought. 'Corporate' thinking seeks to defend the perceived interests of working people against 'unfair' actions, or to protect trade unions from employer offensives or judicial interventions, and it leads precisely to the kind of defensive statements made by the LRC during its 1902 Conference, as it prepared to rally support against a variety of hostile 'menaces'. Essentially, such thinking is defensive rather than passive, seeking to prevent adverse changes, and marching behind the banner 'hands off' something or other. It is perfectly possible to be very 'militant' within such a perspective, and often people are.

On the other hand, 'hegemonic' thinking identifies a potential in labour to become the ruling social force, and seeks to challenge all acceptance of subordination whatsoever. In the classic words which Karl Marx used to reproach the unions of his day, it calls upon the unions 'instead of the *conservative* motto: 'a fair day's wages for a fair day's work' . . . to inscribe upon their banners the *revolutionary* watchword 'for the abolition of the wages system!' This appeal takes widely different forms: sometimes, as in the words of the guild-socialists, it is seen as an ethical denunciation of 'the bondage of wagery'. At other moments, it emerges as a call for the establishment of full co-operative self-management, annulling forever the social status of 'employee', and establishing a world in which labour employs capital, rather than the present upside down state in which things lord it over people.

What is plain is that, however staunchly men and women seek to protect their 'corporate' interests, powerful economic forces are constantly undermining all such efforts. Pushed by such a realisation, successive generations of trade unionists seek means of passing beyond the restrictions of defensive politics, into sweeping overall reform of the political-economic structure itself. 'Hegemonic' politics takes different forms, but is to be found in embryo wherever workers' organisations seek to control developments for themselves.

Yet no such imaginative leaps are possible unless labour organisation has developed to the point where ordinary men and women can recognise their own vast collective social power, and this means therefore that unions must become capable of defending their 'corporate' interests before labour movements can develop an awareness of alternative possibilities. How has this process unwound?

Labour Representatives in Parliament

If we take the general elections from 1900 to 1974, we find that the Labour Party has moved from a capacity to field 15 candidates to a regular expectation that it should contest all Parliamentary seats. When we examine the proportion of direct trade union candidates to those from other sources, however, we find that in 1906 35 out of 50 Labour candidates were directly sponsored by their unions, while by 1974 only 141 out of 626 were so sponsored.[11]

In 1910, 95 per cent of all Labour MPs were directly put forward by unions. The proportion has now fallen to 49 per cent, although this itself represents a rise since 1945, when Labour's greatest victory was based upon a considerable influx of new MPs, but when only 30 per

Table X:1
Union sponsored MPs*[11]

Election	Candidates All Labour Party	Candidates All Union Sponsored	Members of Parliament All Labour Party	Members of Parliament All Union Sponsored	Union Sponsored MPs as a % of all Labour Party MPs	Union Sponsored MPs as a % of all Labour Sponsored Candidates
1900	15[b]	?	2[b]	1	50.0	?
1906	50[b]	35[a]	30[b]	21[a]	70.0	60
1910—I	78[b]	?	40[b]	38[a]	95.0	?
1910—II	56[b]	?	42[b]	39[a]	92.8	?
1918	361	163	57	49	85.9	31
1922	414	?	142	86	60.6	?
1923	427	?	191	102	53.4	?
1924	514	?	151	88	58.2	?
1929	569	139	287	115	40.1	83
1931	491	132	46	32	69.5	24
1935	552	128	154	79	51.3	62
1945	603	126	393	121	30.8	96
1950	617	140	315	110	34.9	79
1951	617	137	295	105	35.6	77
1955	620	129	277	96	34.6	75
1959	621	129	258	93	36.0	72
1964	628	138	317	120	37.9	86
1966	622	138	364	132	36.3	95
1970[c]	624	137	287	114	39.7	83
1974—I[c]	627	155	301	127	42.2	82.7
1974—II[c]	626	141	319	129[d]	40.1	91
1979	622	159[e]	268	132	49.5	83

cent of the enlarged total had been put forward by the unions. One figure, however, indicates that unions tend to pick safe-ish seats from which to press their claims: 91 per cent of their nominees got home in the October 1974 election: and as much as 96 per cent of their 1945 team was in fact elected. In 1979, a bad year, 83 per cent were returned and the losses included not only long-established MPs, but also ministers. Not much union money, we may conclude, goes into intentionally contesting marginal seats, and still less into hopeless ones.

Direct trade union sponsorship takes a variety of forms. Its classic shape is to be found in the declining numbers of safe mining seats, in which the NUM (or before that, the MFGB) used to be able to boast that they could weigh the votes necessary to secure their victories. Other occupational concentrations explain how some unions are able to secure representation in particular areas. But more and more union nominees have to win selection as prospective Parliamentary Candidates in open contests with a whole variety of other people, and cannot depend upon a built-in preponderance of their own supporters. The actual membership of the 1974 to 1979 Parliaments included the following union-sponsored detachments.[12]

Table X:2

Individual union sponsorships, October 1974 and 1979

	Total		Elected	
	1974	1979	1974	1979
Transport and General Workers' Union	23	27	22	20
Amalgamated Union of Engineering Workers	23	16	21	15
National Union of Mineworkers	20	17	18	16
General and Municipal Workers' Union	13	14	13	14
Association of Scientific, Technical and Managerial Staffs	13	12	12	8
National Union of Public Employees	7	8	6	7
Association of Professional, Executive, Clerical and Computer Staff	6	6	6	5
National Union of Railwaymen	6	11	6	10
Union of Shop, Distributive and Allied Workers	5	5	5	5
Transport Salaried Staffs Association	4	3	3	3
Union of Post Office Workers	4	4	2	2
Union of Construction, Allied Trades & Technicians	3	4	3	2
Electrical, Electronic & Telecommunications & Plumbing Trades Union	3	4	3	4
Total, including other unions	141	159	129	132
Co-operative Party	24	25	16	16
All sponsored candidates	161	184	142	148

Whilst it is clear that there are mining constituencies, and may once have been 'railway' constituencies, or 'engineering' towns, it is doubtful whether there are ASTMS cities, or NUPE counties. These

Conclusion

Having thus amassed support on the Labour Party's leading committee, carrying an overwhelming preponderance of votes at its Conference, and maintaining a substantial presence in the Parliamentary Labour Party, how effective are British Trade Unions in politics? If one follows reports in the popular press, it seems that the unions rule. But if one examines the actual movement of political events, one may well form a sharply different impression.

First, when Labour is in Government, the pattern of domination follows very precise channels, based upon the pre-eminence of the Prime Minister, who not only appoints all cabinet and Government ministers without needing to consult anyone except the Queen; but who also has sweeping powers of patronage which enable him to create peers, appoint chairmen of nationalised industries, staff a whole variety of ad hoc bodies and quangoes ('quasi-autonomous governmental organisations'), and give (or take away) jobs to (or from) fully one-third of the parliamentary forces on his own side.[27] Second, the parliamentary grouping has developed a species of 'tenure' of its offices which not only insulates it from challenges, but also from new ideas. Thirdly, however precisely unions may develop their industrial policies, they are ill-adapted organs for the refinement of detailed political strategies, with a result that they tend to find themselves reacting to the initiatives of others, rather than assuming any overall innovative role.

Without entering a long discussion of the meaning of day-to-day political issues, which would not be relevant to our present purposes, it seems clear that such major recent events as the formal abandonment of the priority commitment to full employment arose within Government in response to Treasury pressures, and then to direct intervention by the International Monetary Fund, with only the most tardy of responses coming up from the unions.[28] Short of undertaking a detailed analysis of the fate of trade union-supported programmatic commitments, and of trade union legislation (or proposed legislation), we may, however, note that the political development of the unions by no means reflects the uninterrupted growth of support for Labour. In fact, as was seen in table X:6, and is more plainly illustrated in the graph on page 324, the *relative* strength of TUC support for Labour has been declining from a little short of 70 per cent of the total membership in 1957 to just over 50 per cent in 1977.

Of course, during those twenty years trade unionism has grown in membership to its present 12m level: more unions, including white-collar giants such as NALGO and the NUT, have joined forces with the TUC, thus to some degree diluting its erstwhile political linkages,

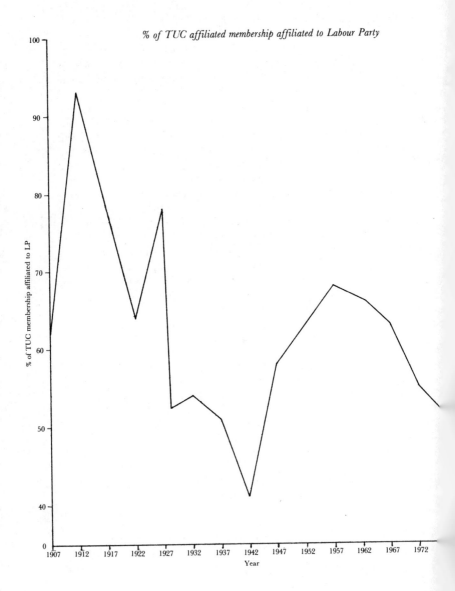

% of TUC affiliated membership affiliated to Labour Party

and, as we have seen, Labour Party member-unions have, themselves, frequently shrunk their proportional rates of affiliation. To this extent, unionateness seems to have suffered a certain type of decline, at the same time that union densities have increased.

It is at this point that the distinction between corporate and hegemonic forms of class consciousness, to which we referred earlier, has considerable relevance, since it can help us to appreciate the meaning of these events. If the Labour Party had proved able to adequately represent the corporate interests of working people, the least result we might have expected would have been a regular increase in percentage rates of membership affiliation, a serious argument among new or recent TUC affiliates raising the question that they might also wish to adhere to the Labour Party; and a certain rise in, or at any rate stability in, the Labour vote. In point of fact, since the Colliery Deputies and the Post Office Engineers decided to join the Party, none of the TUC's more recent major recruitment successes have generated any enthusiasm or even the slightest pressure for additional political affiliations. Such decisions could not be taken without first achieving agreement by a majority in a membership ballot. But decisions to maintain the real level of existing affiliations do not require such a ballot, and can normally be taken by the relevant leading committees. Even so, they have not *been* taken.

As for the popular vote, it has moved adversely:[29]

Table X:9

	Labour Vote (000)	%
1951	13,949	48.8
1955	12,405	46.4
1959	12,216	43.8
1964	12,206	44.1
1966	13,065	47.9
1970	12,178	43.0
1974[a]	11,646	37.1
1974[b]	11,457	39.2
1979	11,510	36.9

It could therefore be argued that the unions are not only not holding their ground politically, but are actually losing out. If the membership felt that their defensive needs were being met, it seems likely that some, if not all these indicators would move differently.

In fact, by the time of the October 1974 election the Labour Party 'seemed to make no advance with trade union members', while, although both parties were more dependent than ever 'on their traditional class vote', nonetheless, because of the growth of minor parties, 'diminishing proportions of the working and middle class are voting for their "natural" party'.[30] 55 per cent of union members voted Labour, the remainder dividing more or less equally between the Conservatives (23 per cent) and the minor parties (22 per cent altogether). Dismal though those figures were from the point of view of the union leaderships, in 1979 they got worse: 51 per cent of trade unionists voted Labour, and 31 per cent Conservative.

It seems likely that the defensive concerns of the unions cannot, in the present framework, be adequately upheld unless their Party moves over to some form of 'hegemonic' politics, involving, as Tony Benn put it at Labour's 1973 Conference, 'a fundamental shift in the balance of wealth and power in the direction of working people and their families'. No such shift took place during the 1974 Labour administration, when not only did officially recognised unemployment pass the 1,400,000 mark, but whole legions of trade unionists subsequently found themselves in heated conflict with a Labour Government about the rudimentary question of wages. Without oversimplifying these crucial and sometimes complex issues, it was clear that as the trade unions readied themselves to enter the decade of the 1980s, they had a lot of political thinking to do.

A number of urgent questions can no longer be postponed, now that a profound and prolonged international crisis undermines and crumbles away the last remnants of the postwar British welfare consensus.

How do the rather chaotic organisations of British labour match and outmanoeuvre the great transnational companies? What kinds of reform do the unions need in their internal structures (combine committees, industrial liaisons) and in their international relations? What joint arrangements can be evolved to control the ill-effects of new technologies and forestall mass unemployment on a continental scale? What detailed programmes of self-defence are involved in meeting the hostile actions of Governments and their judiciaries, and what positive strategies of advance will assure the development of industrial democracy? Above all, what steps are needed to ensure that the British Trade Unions develop a political voice which can address these difficult issues, and the political weight to resolve them?

NOTES

1. Margaret Stewart: *Protest or Power?* Allen and Unwin, 1974, p. 54.
2. Labour Party: *Report of the 45th Annual Conference*, p.35.
3. R. T. McKenzie: *British Political Parties*, Heinemann, 1955, p. 386.
4. Cf Anthony Carew: *Democracy and Government in European Trade Unions.* Allen and Unwin, 1976; Bonety *et al: La CFDT*, Seuil, Paris 1971; K. Coates (ed.) *A Trade Union Strategy in the Common Market*, Spokesman, 1971.
5. Documentation on this process may be found in W. Milne-Bailey: *Trade Union Documents*, G. Bell & Sons, 1929, Part 1, pp. 43-76.
6. R. T. McKenzie, op. cit, p. 479.
7. Labour Party: Constitution and Standing Orders, Clause IV, subsection 4.
8. Cf Mark Jenkins: *Bevanism*, Spokesman, 1979.
9. The New Unionism, Penguin Books, 1974.
10. P. Anderson and R. Blackburn: *Towards Socialism*, Fontana, 1964, pp. 221-290. Also see Anderson's 'The Antinomies of Antonio Gramsci', *New Left Review*, No. 100.
11. W. D. Muller: *The Kept Men*, Harvester, 1977, pp. 29-31. Table X:1, with the exception of 1979 figures, is to be found on page 30. Mr Muller cites the following sources:
    *There is occasional disagreement among various authorities for the actual number of candidates supported by the Labour Party or sponsored by a trade union. This problem is especially acute for the years prior to 1929.
    Sources: Except where otherwise noted, the above table is based on data derived from: F. W. Craig (ed.), *British Parliamentary Election Statistics, 1918-1968* (Glasgow: Political Reference Publications, 1968), p. 54.
    [a]H. A. Clegg, Alan Fox and A. F. Thompson, *A History of British Trade Unions Since 1889*, Vol. 1: *1889-1910* (Oxford: Clarendon Press, 1964), pp. 384, 387, 420-422.
    [b]David Butler and Jennie Freeman (eds.), *British Political Facts, 1900-1967* (Second edition; Macmillan, 1968), pp. 141-144.
    [c]Labour Party, Annual Conference Reports (1970 and 1974).
    [d]Based on correspondence with the Labour Party and detailed analysis of the information given in the Annual Report of the Labour Party for 1974.
    [e]The figure given by the Labour Party's Information Office for 1979 is 149, but this omits 4 NUM sponsorships, 2 AUEW sponsorships, 1 from the GMW, and 1 from the T & GWU, among others.
    For the year 1979 sources are the Labour Party's Press Releases and the Labour Research Department.
12. Butler & Kavanagh provide the 1974 figures in *The British General Election of October 1974*, Macmillan, 1975, p. 217, Table 6. Figures for 1979 from the Labour Research Dept.
13. Repeated efforts have been made to change this situation in the years

since 1974, with limited success. See 1978 *Labour Party Annual Conference Report* for the debate on mandatory reselection.

14.   Their behaviour is best documented in Lewis Minkin: *The Labour Party Conference*, Allen Lane 1978. See also the dated, but useful book by Martin Harrison: *Trade Unions and the Labour Party*, Macmillan, 1960.

15.   *Labour Party Diary*, 1978.

16.   Ibid.

17.   The Labour Party: List of Affiliated Organisations: Brighton 1977, pp. 2-6.

18.   Ibid.

19.   This is discussed in Harrison, op. cit, pp. 62-4. During the late '50s the percentage of levy-paying members affiliated was:

1955	91
1956	91
1957	90
1958	90

Now this percentage has fallen to 80, its lowest since before 1948 (82 per cent). Martin Harrison was right to record, in 1960, that 'the record has improved'. But since then it has sharply deteriorated.

20.   *Annual Report of the Certification Officer*, 1977, p. 23.

21.   *Together We Stand*, June 8th 1979.

22.   *Report of the Registrar of Friendly Societies*, 1974. This report, exceptionally, since it was the final one, covers some matters up to 5th September 1975.

23.   DATA: *Evidence to the Royal Commission on Trade Unions and Employers' Associations*, 1965, pp. 57-8.

24.   This becomes an important issue when union leaders do not evidently respect their own internal decision-making processes in deploying these huge votes. Cf Martin Harrison, op. cit, Lewis Minkin op. cit; Edelstein and Warner, op. cit. Also K. Coates: *The Crisis of British Socialism*, Spokesman, 1971, ch. XII; and Bulletin of the IWC, 1978, December, pp. 2-4.

25.   Martin Harrison, op. cit, shows that 22 unions between them provided all the members of the NEC between 1935 and 1959. 15 of these were represented fairly continuously, the rest extremely infrequently, and briefly at that. (p. 309).

26.   Lewis Minkin, op. cit, pp. 141-2. Cf his Chapter V, on 'Agenda Politics'.

27.   See K. Coates: *Democracy in the Labour Party*, Spokesman, 1977.

28.   The best short account of these developments is Tom Forester: *How Labour's Industrial Policy Got the Chop*, in New Society, volume 45, No. 822. This shows that the TUC 'either because they were intimidated by the crisis atmosphere, felt that somehow it was an internal party or government row, had other priorities, or genuinely regarded the policy as a less immediate . . . matter, . . . didn't make its abandonment a central issue in their negotiations with the government.'

29.   D. Butler and D. Kavanagh, *The British General Election of October 1974*, Macmillan 1975, p. 294.

30.   Ibid, pp. 277-9.

Chapter Eleven

International Affiliations

TUC International Links

British trade unions maintain formal connections with a variety of international organisations, and the TUC as a whole is currently affiliated to three major bodies. These are the International Confederation of Free Trade Unions (ICFTU); the European Trades Union Confederation (ETUC); and the Trade Union Advisory Committee to the OECD. In all, the TUC spent, during 1977, £564,388.97 on these affiliations, and this constitutes no less than 29.4 per cent of its total budget.[1] This is a very large expenditure.

It therefore seems necessary to go a little further into the question of international contacts.

In doing so, we must first of all emphasise that such overseas affiliations are only part of the total TUC investment in foreign relations. In addition, there is a full fledged department at Congress House, which is not separately itemised in the TUC's accounts, but which is totally preoccupied with foreign affairs.[2] Although the costs of its seven specialist teams are not broken down in TUC accounts, nonetheless, reading between the lines, it is possible to assess minimum expenditures. They come out something like this, for the year 1977:

Table XI:1

Estimated TUC international expenditure, 1977

Delegations	£21,358.46
Affiliations:	
ICFTU	£452,878.43
ETUC	£95,036.14
TUAC/OECD	£16,474.40
	£564,388.97
Grants/South African Assistance	£5,947.56
International Department, Salaries	
(say ⅟₇th of total salary bill)	£64,000.00
Post/phone	
(say ⅟₇th of total postage and	
'phone bill)	£4,000.00

The allowance of $\frac{1}{7}$th for the costs of the TUC's own International Department is almost certainly on the mean side, since this department has at least seven direct professional employees at Congress House and an unknown number of clerical and secretarial helpers, and since international work tends to be considerably more expensive than domestic representation. It thus seems likely that, of the £454,000-odd total salary and superannuation bill, and of the overall costs of communications bills, rather more than a one-seventh split goes to the trade union movement's 'foreign office'. Quite apart from any costs incurred in this department, much international work is financed by other departments. For instance, the Economic Department prepares submissions to the International Labour Office, the European Economic Community, and the OECD. Consequently, these costs at least are spread.

Such an allowance would give us a total minimum foreign relations expenditure of around £660,000 for 1977: or something like 34 per cent of the TUC's total expenditure for the year. Obviously, then, the leaders of Britain's unions regard international representation as a matter of great importance. If a third of the TUC's income goes out on such matters, surely it is worthwhile to investigate what union members are getting for their money? It is even more important to look into this question when we realise that what the TUC spends is itself only a part of the total laid out by affiliated organisations on the work of the International Trade Secretariats, the relevant specialised international bodies to which many individual unions find it necessary to belong. In addition, the Government funds the TUC for certain purposes, which have only been separately recorded since 1978.

We have already argued that the rocketing growth of the largest transnational companies makes necessary closer and closer trade union association between workpeople in many different countries. Does this need justify such a rather large investment? It is certainly true that multinational companies are becoming more and more powerful, and exercise a vast influence, not only over the British economy. For all that, it is absolutely clear that very little of the present international work by the unions is effectively directed at controlling and rendering more accountable the colossal concentration of economic power.

Let us take, first of all, the sums laid out by the TUC on international affiliations. They are vast. Since 1961 they have increased by 700 per cent, if one takes simply the cash amounts involved, without allowing for inflation. At no time have they amounted to as little as one fifth of the TUC's total income: commonly they have run at about a quarter of the total, and at times they have absorbed up to 30 per cent of it. (See table XI:2)

Table XI:2
International expenditure as a percentage of total revenue[3]

TUC

	(a) Recorded Total Expenditure	(b) Recorded Affiliations International Expenditure (ICFTU, ISF, ERO, EFTA TU Ctee, TU AC OECD, ETUC) *not* including delegation costs, or costs of TUC International Committee		% (b) of (a)
	£	£	% increase	% of total income
1961	328,278	80,741		24.6
1963	387,584	83,700	+ 3.66	21.6
1965	532,250	164,449	+96.47	30.9
1967	592,507	169,942	+ 3.34	28.7
1969	784,947	195,151	+14.83	24.9
1971	841,875	207,028	+ 6.09	24.6
1973	999,181	214,334	+ 3.53	21.5
1975	1,282,425	334,657	+56.14	26.1
1977	1,917,941	564,389	+68.65	29.4

ICFTU	International Confederation of Free Trade Unions
ISF	International Solidarity Fund (a standing commitment of ICFTU affiliates for part of this period: see Table 4 below)
ERO	European Regional Organisation (taken into ETUC after 1973)
EFTA TU Ctee	The Trade Union Committee of the European Free Trade Association (taken into ETUC after 1973)
ETUC	European Trade Union Confederation: established in 1973, replacing both EEC and EFTA union link-ups, and bringing together, first European ICFTU affiliates; then, the Christian Federations of various countries; the CFDT from France and the CGIL from Italy.
TUAC OECD	An advisory and research body linking unions from member states of the Organisation for Economic Co-operation and Development.

Compared with earlier days, this kind of commitment is truly breathtaking. Back in 1909 there were no comparable trade union international organisations: the total expenditure of the TUC was £7,379 16s. 7d., and, raking through its detailed accounts, we find £323 10s. 7d. allocated to international purposes. This amounts to 4.4 per cent of the total.

By the time that the interwar International Federation of Trade Unions had been reborn, the TUC could spend nearly as much on international work alone as it had received in total income a little more than a decade earlier. This emerges very clearly from a look at the figures during the first half of the 1920s:

Table XI:3

TUC expenditure on international work as % of total, 1923–5

	Total	International	%
1923	£142,792	£6,474	4.5
1924	£107,727	£6,705	6.2
1925	£75,908	£7,353	9.7

These totals vary sharply, but the percentages of expenditure on all foreign relations work remained throughout that period very much lower than they were subsequently to become. During that time a major burden on TUC revenues was the maintenance of the *Daily Herald*, which, of course, provided a constant source of information on foreign affairs for all trade unionists, in addition to its domestic coverage. Perhaps such a commitment to the provision of relevant information to a wide audience is a precondition for any effective democratic trade union 'foreign policy'.

After the second world war, trade union international links became a most complex affair, because of the outbreak of cold war, in which vast efforts were made, first by the Soviet and then by the American Governments, to influence opinion-forming social organisations of all kinds. Much of the influence concerned was undertaken covertly, and a pattern of active intervention in union affairs was established which had very large consequences. It was in this context that trade union expenditures on international affiliations rose to unprecedented levels. Of course, these outgoings reflect a complicated mixture of idealism and genuine solidarity, together with other motives.

Throughout the '60s and '70s, leaving out of account altogether the costs of the International Department itself, a vastly distended budget was laid out in this field. This was at a time when there was no provision of mass-information by the TUC, and the only democratic control over foreign policy consisted of intermittent (and sometimes perfunctory) debates in Congress. The figures are nonetheless very large.

Table XI:4

TUC: some international expenditures, 1961–77

	Dele-gations	% of total	ICFTU	ERO	Int. Soli-darity Fund	EFTA TU Ctee	TU Adv to OECD
1961	3,414	1%	73,161	7,580			
1963	7,380	1.9	74,270	9,430			
1965	6,111	1.2	74,934	9,515	80,000		
1967	8,919	1.5	79,807	10,134	80,000		
1969	8,856	1.1	92,090	9,973	80,000	13,088	
1971	10,059	1.2	148,890	4,768	32,000	18,276	3,093
1973	15,198	1.5	148,796	3,672 ETUC	32,000	21,746	8,119
1975	24,372	1.9	260,157	64,729			9,771
1977	21,358	1.1	452,878	95,036			16,474

The key to the acronyms of the various international bodies is to be found at the foot of table XI:2.

Often international organisation is criticised by the rank and file because it is assumed to involve a high level of junketing. In fact, expenditure on delegations varied between 1.9 per cent and 1.1 per cent of the total TUC annual budget, as compared with the much higher costs of affiliations. Dividing these sums into their component parts, we find that the lion's share of the money always goes to the International Confederation of Free Trade Unions, the Brussels-based organisation which groups 120 trade union centres from 88 different countries, (with a total membership approaching 56 million.) If Britain were affiliated on the TUC's 12 million total membership, then no less than ⅕th of the world-wide membership would be Britons. As things are, the TUC appears to be under-affiliated, since its membership would cost some £600,000 a year if dues were paid in full.

How far do TUC representatives control this large disbursement? It is difficult, from outside, to be sure, but it certainly looks as if the answer is 'not as far as might be expected'. To explore this question we have no alternative but to take a brief look at the chequered story of international trade unionism.

The International Organisations

International organisation of trade unions began as a practical process, for limited purposes. People wanted help for various reasons: to stop strike-breaking by employers who were exporting jobs or importing workpeople, to secure information and support, to move up with or jump in front of adverse technologies. After the initial experiment of the International Working Men's Association, which struggled on for nine years with the active help of Karl Marx, it was not surprising that socialist parties were keen to repeat the same formula: and it is clear that the Second International, the socialist movement which dominated the Labour organisations of the earliest years of the twentieth century, played a major role in encouraging international trade union link-ups.

In 1886 the Scandinavian unions began a federation, to help each other out in strikes. Three years later, the first specialised standing association, or international trade secretariat, of printers, was set up. In 1890 the miners followed on by creating their own international body. Congresses of the Socialist International provided a regular meeting-place at which trade unions could make contact with one another, and in 1903 there was created an international secretariat of trade union national centres. This grew rather quickly, to embrace 14 countries with $2\frac{1}{2}$m members in 1904 and $3\frac{1}{2}$m members in 1906. In 1909 the American Federation of Labour joined in, and the secretariat changed its name, to become the International Federation of Trade Unions. By 1913 this had 16m members in 30 countries.

Meantime, an International Secretariat of Christian Trade Unions had been formed in 1908. Both of these centres appealed for solidarity funds in support of particular actions, but both were pre-eminently concerned with the exchange of information, and the circulation of reports. The political colouration of the IFTU was, at this time, complex. The socialist Germans found themselves joined up alongside French syndicalists and American craft unionists. How these trends of thought would have lived together given time is difficult to predict: but in the event they were wrenched apart by the 1914 war, which wrecked international labour co-operation whilst millions of trade union members put on uniforms and slaughtered one another. In 1917 the Russian Revolution brought the Bolsheviks to power, so that the rebirth of trade union internationalism after the restoration of peace saw the emergence of two federations. The IFTU opened up again, and in 1920 it included 21 centres with 23m members. The Soviets, once they were sufficiently firmly grounded, began a rival Red International of Labour Unions (RILU) in 1921. Although this had a significant propaganda influence, it never gained any really permanent mass basis outside the USSR. However, the existence of two such bodies encouraged others, and the interwar years saw a marked fragmentation of international trade union efforts. Only after Hitler came to power in Germany were minds concentrated in other European countries: and there was, between 1933 and the outbreak of the second world war, a certain convergence of forces. In particular, unsuccessful communist breakaways made their peace with their parent organisations, and in Scotland, France and Canada the IFTU affiliates were restored to sufficient unity to hold unchallenged preponderance over the unions in their countries. Communist influence had been large in Germany and Italy, but all independent unions were crushed by the Nazi and fascist governments. In Britain (apart from Scotland) separate communist unions had been the merest shadow,[4] quickly past, and there was never any very serious opposition to trade union unity.

Partly because the RILU was in these terms largely a failure, and, after the early 'thirties, no big threat to the (mainly) socialist-based trade union centres: and partly because the second world war created a considerable sense of unity among the allies, so that trade union unity became for a time quite thinkable even though there were undoubtedly very great differences of function between the Soviet and West-European labour organisations, there emerged, in 1945, a new body, the World Federation of Trade Unions.

This was established in two international conferences, the first of which (in London) agreed on a drafting committee to prepare a constitution, while the second (in Paris, in October) actually launched the new organisation. Sir Walter Citrine, of the British TUC, played a major role in this work, and became the founding chairman. He has left an interesting description of what happened during the formation of the WFTU in his memoirs.[5] All the major national trade union centres then existing were represented, but there was no participation by workers from the defeated powers, Germany and Japan.

A festival atmosphere was understandable. The war was over, Labour was united, all over Europe socialists and communists were either sharing power in coalition governments, or governing alone, as in England. Trade unions had arrived, it seemed, at the threshold of a new society. But it was not to last. In a very short time the cold war had assumed such intensity that conflict raged in every inclusive international organisation, not excluding the WFTU.

Communist-led federations now represented not only the Soviet and East European organisations, but also those of France and Italy. The argument which broke out during 1947, 8 and 9 was bitter and destructive, because there was no natural mediating influence, and the result was a direct East–West division. This became an irreconcilable split in 1949, and late that year those of the Western unions which were not under communist influence met in London to establish the International Confederation of Free Trade Unions (ICFTU). This set up its headquarters in Brussels.[6]

The formation of a separate international organisation became an occasion for bitter faction fights in some of the national centres. In particular, the French CGT was split, and a breakaway body, Force Ouvriere, (FO) became a founding constituent of the ICFTU. Within the fields of interest of individual trade unions, the International Trade Secretariats, which were continuing in spite of the inheritance of dislocation during the war, to provide functional contacts between unions in particular sectors, had, almost from the beginning, found their relationship with the WFTU imprecise and unsatisfactory. They had no wish to become subordinate desks of WFTU departments, and in addition they began to develop serious political disagreements with the overall international organisation. When they withdrew from the WFTU in 1949, they quickly arrived at an agreement with the founders of the ICFTU, and whilst they remained technically autonomous, they agreed without difficulty to work within broad policy lines determined by the breakaway international. Today there are 16 different International Trade Secretariats: their membership is something over 45 million, and thus is still within reach of being comparable with the claimed membership of the ICFTU itself. At the time of the split in the WFTU, these secretariats had even greater importance, because they represented functional international machinery whilst quarrelling international conferences represented only verbiage, and much of that remained unedifying. Even so, there was an important non-trade union influence at work in the split, and this has dogged the footsteps of trade union internationalism ever since.

During the wartime alliance which had made possible the launching of the WFTU, Stalin had unilaterally dissolved the Communist International, as a concession to the allied governments. Undoubtedly this had impressed many socialists and trade union spokesmen as well. After the war, with the increase of East–West tension, a new communist international body (embracing parties in East Europe as well as the French and Italian organisations) was quickly launched: it became known in the West as the 'Cominform'. All the prewar devices of communist international activity were resumed with greater intensity after the Americans launched the Marshall Plan.

It was in this context that the Americans developed a massive counter-offensive, under the auspices of the CIA (Central Intelligence Agency). In the words of one English critic, this came to carry out 'at a more sophisticated level, exactly the same sort of organised subversion as Stalin's Comintern in its heyday'.[7] Although the whole story is by no means completely clear, it is quite apparent that the CIA played an important role in orchestrating the argument which created the ICFTU. In the words of one ex-employee of the agency who subsequently defected:

> 'Agency labour operations came into being. . . as a reaction against the continuation of pre-World War II CPSU policy and expansion through the international united fronts. In 1945 with the support and participation of the British Trade Unions Congress (TUC), the American Congress of Industrial Organisations (CIO) and the Soviet Trade Unions Council, the World Federation of Trade Unions (WFTU) was formed in Paris. Differences within the WFTU between communist trade-union leaders, who were anxious to use the WFTU for anti-capitalist propaganda, and free-world leaders who insisted on keeping the WFTU focused on economic issues, finally came to a head in 1949 over whether the WFTU should support the Marshall Plan. When the communists, who included French, Italian and Latin American leaders as well as the Soviets refused to allow the WFTU to endorse the Marshall Plan, the TUC and CIO withdrew, and later the same year the International Confederation of Free Trade Unions (ICFTU) was founded as a non-communist alternative to the WFTU, with participation by the TUC, CIO, American Federation of Labor (AFL) and other national centres. Agency operations were responsible in part for the expulsion of the WFTU headquarters from Paris in 1951 when it moved to the Soviet sector of Vienna. Later, in 1956, it was forced to move from Vienna to Prague.
>
> The ICFTU established regional organisations for Europe, the Far East, Africa and the Western Hemisphere, which brought together the non-communist national trade-union centres. Support and guidance by the Agency was, and still is, exercised on the three levels: ICFTU, regional and national centres. At the highest level, Agency labour operations are effected through George Meany, President of the AFL, Jay Lovestone, Foreign Affairs Chief of the AFL and Irving Brown, AFL representative in Europe—all of whom are effective and witting collaborators. Direct Agency control is also exercised on the regional level. Serafino Romualdi, AFL Latin American representative, for example, directs the Inter-American Regional Labor Organisation (ORIT) located in Mexico City. On the national level, particularly in underdeveloped countries, CIA field stations engage in operations to support and guide national labour centres. Its headquarters, support, guidance

and control of all labour operations is centralised in the labour branch of the International Organisations Division.'[8]

Jay Lovestone, who himself played a major role in the history of American communism, (he had been national chairman of the CPUSA in 1929) was intimately familiar with Comintern behaviour and therefore well able to set up a most elaborate countering political organisation. It is not, therefore, surprising that this apparatus bore a marked resemblance to the oppositional machine against which it was ranged. But, whilst in 1949, it is possible that some members of the British Labour Movement might not, had they known of them, have objected very strongly to Mr Lovestone's activities,* it is anything but likely that many people in British unions would have favoured the subsequent continuous manipulation of the ICFTU regional organisations for intelligence purposes and 'counter-insurgency'. It has become clear and undeniable that the CIA has not restricted its use of what it engagingly calls 'dirty tricks' to dictatorships, but has, to the contrary, been particularly active in destabilising democratic regimes in which radical reformers have come to office.[9] The agency's labour desk has not spared the unions their often unwitting involvement in this process. It is claimed, for instance, that

A fourth CIA approach to labour operations is through the International Trade Secretariats (ITS), which represent the interests of workers in a particular industry as opposed to the national centres that unite workers of different industries. Because the ITS system is more specialised, and often more effective, it is at times more appropriate for Agency purposes than the ICFTU with its regional and national structure. Control and guidance is exercised through officers of a particular ITS who are called upon to assist labour operations directed against the workers of a particular industry. Very often the CIA agents in an ITS are the American labour leaders who represent the US affiliate of the ITS, since the ITS would usually receive its principal support from the pertinent US industrial union. Thus the American Federation of State, County and Municipal Employees serves as a channel for CIA operations in the Public Service International, which is the ITS for government employees headquartered in London. And the Retail Clerks International Association, which is the US union of white-collar employees, gives access to the International Federation of Clerical and Technical Employees, which is the white-collar ITS. Similarly, the Communications Workers of America is used to

*Which still continue, of course, since he remains a very active and committed person.

substantial groups of MPs have been adopted in an open process of choice, by constituency organisations which have usually included a wide variety of contending interests. Changes in the Labour Party's federal constitution have reinforced this openness: until the 1960s, local trade unions could send any member who paid to the union's own political fund as a delegate to his or her local party organisation. Now only persons who pay individual party membership contributions as well as corporate affiliation tolls are eligible to serve as delegates to party management committees. This means that the 'selectorate' which chooses Parliamentary candidates is now more restricted. Under the old dispensation, Mr Morgan Phillips, then General Secretary of the Party, sought nomination for the mining area of North-East Derbyshire. NUM delegates came from far and wide to prevent this happening, and instead the local miner's spokesman, Tom Swain, was chosen by a bone-crushing majority. Under the new dispensation, in the area of Ashfield, which is very much a pitman's enclave, an NUM nominee was passed over in 1977 because only a handful of miners were eligible, as individual members of the party, to participate in the selection conference. Subsequently, the non-miner who was chosen was rather spectacularly defeated, and the NUM then regained the nomination, but only after it had undertaken a major drive to recruit, from the mining community, numbers of new individual party members who were willing to participate in the work of the management committee. The Political Committee of the Nottingham Area of the NUM even went so far as to offer to defray the costs of their own members' individual membership subscriptions to the Labour Party, in order to ensure adequate representation on the vital selection conference. This new system of affiliation will certainly change the pattern of trade union representation in Parliament, since it will tend to shrink the power of such traditional lobbies as the miners', while increasing the competition among contending groupings. There is a time-lag in this process, because once adopted, an MP will tend to go on and on until he is either beaten in the polls, or old enough to retire.[13] For this reason, the renewal of trade union representation, just like other representation, is a fairly slow business.

For all the moral weight of their 132 MPs, the unions' political influence is certainly not restricted to their impact on the legislature. Indeed, it is arguable that a more direct and powerful influence is that which is exerted over Labour as a political Party, in determining policy and staffing the national, regional and local machinery of that Party. At national level, unions participate in the Labour Party Conference, at which they cast votes in accordance with their affiliated numbers.[14] At local level, unions may also send delegates to constituency management committees, which arrange the day-to-day local organisation of the Party in addition to controlling the selection of Parliamentary candidates.

Affiliation to the Labour Party

Such local affiliation is based upon the number of trade union Branch members paying political contributions and resident within a particular constituency area. Fees are payable to the constituency organisation at the rate of 3p per member per annum. Since many trade union Branches organise people resident in different areas, it is perfectly possible for one trade union Branch to be represented in several nearby constituency management committees, and this complicates the problem of allocating local resources from the unions' political funds.

At intermediate levels, unions are strongly represented in the Party's regional organisation, and have, within the constitution, some fixed quota of representation in County and other policy-forming bodies. In order to qualify for all these lower levels of participation, a union has to be affiliated nationally.

This turns out to be expensive, the current rate involving a payment to national Labour Party funds of 21p per affiliated member per annum, in addition to local or regional payments and, of course, regardless of special contributions to national election appeals or building funds. 59 unions were so affiliated in 1977,[15] although there are two different estimates of how many members were involved. One Labour Party source gives the total of trade union affiliated members as 5,913,159.[16] Another lists separate figures which add up to 5,802,882.[17]

The full list of unions involved is as follows:

Table X:3
Labour Party: Affiliated Trade Unions, 1977

	a. Members[18] affiliated LP	b. Members affiliated TUC	% a of b
Agricultural and Allied Workers, National Union of	75,000	85,000	88.2
Bakers, Food and Allied Workers' Union	41,713	56,135	74.3
Bakers and Allied Workers, Scottish Union of	5,708	8,693	65.7

Table X:3 (cont.)	a. Members[18] affiliated LP	b. Members affiliated TUC	% a of b
Blastfurnacemen, Ore Miners, Coke Workers and Kindred Trades, National Union of	11,666	16,777	69.5
Blind and Disabled of Great Britain and Ireland, National League of the	859	4,250	20.2
Boilermakers, Shipwrights, Blacksmiths and Structural Workers, Amalgamated Society of	71,000	128,403	55.3
Boot, Shoe and Slipper Operatives, Rossendale Union of	2,857	6,107	46.8
Carpet Workers' Union, Scottish	1,000	n/a	—
Carpet Weavers' and Textile Workers' Association, Power Loom	5,882	6,475	90.8
Ceramic and Allied Trades Union	40,457	46,559	86.9
Cinematograph, Television and Allied Technicians, Association of	1,500	18,682	8.0
Colliery Overmen, Deputies and Shotfirers, National Association of	20,058	20,141	99.6
Construction, Allied Trades and Technicians, Union of	160,000	293,521	54.5
Domestic Appliance and General Metal Workers, National Union of	2,000	5,400	37.0
Dyers, Bleachers and Textile Workers, National Union of	49,000	58,756	83.4
Electrical, Electronic, Telecommunication and Plumbing Union	260,000	420,000	61.9
Engineering Workers, Amalgamated Union of, Constructional Section	13,571	25,000	54.3
Engineering Workers, Amalgamated Union of, Engineering Section	891,879	1,168,990	76.3
Engineering Workers, Amalgamated Union of, Foundry Section	41,440	56,479	73.4
Engineering Workers, Amalgamated Union of, Technical, Administrative and Supervisory Section	70,166	161,607	43.4
Fire Brigades' Union	16,178	30,000	53.9
Footwear, Leather and Allied Trades, National Union of	56,006	66,553	84.2
Funeral Service Operatives, National Union of	200	1,375	14.5
Furniture, Timber and Allied Trades Union	45,000	87,398	51.5

Table X:3 (cont.)

	a. Members[18] affiliated LP	b. Members affiliated TUC	% a of b
General and Municipal Workers' Union	650,000	916,438	70.9
Gold Silver and Allied Trades, National Union of	511	2,447	20.9
Graphical and Allied Trades, Society of	33,742	194,312	17.4
Graphical Association, National	21,157	107,723	19.6
Health Service Employees, Confederation of	50,000	200,455	24.9
Insurance Workers (Prudential Section), National Union of	9,487	25,061*	37.9
Iron and Steel Trades Confederation, The	98,446	104,073	94.6
Lithographic Artists, Designers, Engravers and Process Workers, Society of	7,504	18,239	41.4
Locomotive Engineers and Firemen, Associated Society of	27,768	28,189	98.5
Loom Overlookers, General Union of Associations of	3,053	2,960	103.1
Metal Mechanics, National Society of	16,000	47,882	33.4
Mineworkers, National Union of	248,550	259,966	95.6
Musicians Union	6,000	37,019	16.2
Patternmakers and Allied Craftsmen, Association of	7,000	9,757	71.7
Post Office Engineering Union	76,000	124,535	61.0
Post Office Workers, Union of	176,788	201,099	87.9
Printers, Graphical and Media Personnel, National Society of Operative	15,340	53,396	28.7
Professional, Executive, Clerical and Computer Staff, Association of	100,393	141,766	70.8
Public Employees, National Union of	400,000	650,530	61.5
Railwaymen, National Union of	170,317	180,000	94.6
Scalemakers, National Union of	280	1,842	15.2
Scientific, Technical and Managerial Staffs, Association of	147,000	396,000	37.1
Seamen, National Union of	25,000	41,919	59.6
Sheet Metal Workers, Coppersmiths, Heating and Domestic Engineers, National Union of	30,000	75,049	40.0
Shop Distributive and Allied Workers, Union of	348,633	412,627	84.5
Tailors and Garment Workers, National Union of	66,955	112,783	59.4
Textile Workers and Kindred Trades, Amalgamated Society of	3,200	5,517	58.0

Table X:3 (cont.)

	a. Members[18] affiliated LP	b. Members affiliated TUC	% a of b
Textile Workers' Union, Amalgamated	32,790	44,102	74.4
Theatrical, Television and Kine Employees, National Association of	2,381	16,070	14.8
Tobacco Workers' Union	9,619	21,070	45.7
Transport and General Workers' Union	1,074,000	1,929,834	55.7
Transport Salaried Staffs' Association	59,964	73,842	81.2
Wallcoverings, Decorative and Allied Trades, National Union of	1,764	4,227	41.7
Woolsorters Society, National	100	747	13.4
Total	5,802,882	9,213,727	63.0

*larger total than affiliated sub-section.

As will be seen, this list reveals very great discrepancies in the extent of the commitment of the different unions. Only 8 per cent of the ACTT are affiliated, while 103.1 of the Loom Overlookers were represented during this particular year. Previous years show the Post Office Workers, the Miners, and some other unions to have been affiliated on more than their total TUC strength: there are three explanations for this.[19]

Firstly, there is the problem of 'fiscal drag', in which different accounting years produce a hangover of book representation, after actual membership has declined. Secondly, some unions have special categories of membership, like pensioners, who still pay political contributions after their industrial membership fees have been reduced to half or below. Thirdly, the last explanation is that these figures seem, in some cases, to be quite arbitrary. Taking the unions which nowadays affiliate on more than 100,000 members, we can see this quite plainly in table X:4.

When, year after year, the EETPU is found fielding the same figure of 420,000 to the TUC, it seems clear that this is an administrative approximation. When the same union offers a similarly constant figure of 350,000 to the Labour Party from 1970 through to 1974, even though the TUC figure had originally been 392,000 before steadying off at its present level; and when the revision of Labour Party figures produces a *drop*, in 1976, to 260,000, which also remains constant: then it is clear that we are dealing with arbitrary allocations. A decision has obviously been made to affiliate at a given level, no matter what variations take place in the actual membership.

Table X:4

Labour Party: largest affiliations by TUCs, 1970-77. Figures in 000s

	1970 LP affiliates/affiliates	1970 TUC affiliates	1970 LP % of TUC	1972 LP	1972 TUC	1972 LP % of TUC	1974 LP	1974 TUC	1974 LP % of TUC	1976 LP	1976 TUC	1976 LP % of TUC	1977 LP	1977 TUC	1977 LP % of TUC
APEX	—	—	—	102	118	86.4	100	127	78.7	101	136	74.3	100	142	70.4
ASTMS	65	124	52.4	151	250	60.4	151	310	48.7	151	374	40.4	147	396	37.1
UCATT	—	—	—	183	260	70.4	183	257	71.2	160	275	58.2	160	294	54.4
NUR	175	191	91.6	161	194	83.0	164	174	94.3	161	180	89.4	170	180	94.4
UPOW	183	198	92.4	196	192	102.1	182	194	93.8	181	185	97.8	177	201	88.1
NUM	304	297	102.4	284	276	102.9	263	261	100.8	254	262	96.9	249	260	95.8
EETPU	350	392	89.3	350	420	83.3	350	420	83.3	260	420	61.9	260	420	61.9
USDAW	281	316	88.9	296	319	92.8	293	326	89.9	325	377	86.2	349	413	84.5
NUPE	150	305	49.2	150	397	37.8	150	470	31.9	400	584	68.5	400	651	61.4
GMWU	650	804	80.4	650	842	77.2	650	864	75.2	650	881	73.8	650	916	71.0
AUEW	814	1,131	72.0	853	1,195	71.4	870	1,172	74.2	892	1,205	74.0	892	1,169	76.3
T & GWU	1,000	1,532	65.3	1,000	1,643	60.9	1,000	1,785	56.0	1,000	1,856	53.8	1,074	1,930	55.6
	3,972	5,290	75.1	4,376	6,106	71.7	4,356	6,360	68.5	4,535	6,735	67.3	4,628	6,972	66.4

Sources: The Labour Party, *List of Affiliated Organisations*; TUC *Annual Reports*: each for the years in question.

If we examine the affiliation figures for all the relevant unions (table X:3 again), it becomes possible to construct the following league table:

Table X:5

Labour Party: % of TUC affiliated members affiliated to LP, 1977

Division V (0-20% affiliated)
National League of Blind
ACTT
Funeral Service
NGA
SOGAT
Musicians' Union
Scalemakers
NATTKE
Woolsorters

Division IV (21-40%)
Domestic Appliance & GMW
Gold, Silver and AT
COHSE
Prudential/Insurance Workers
Metal Mechanics
NATSOPA
ASTMS
NU Seamen
Sheetmetalworkers

Division III (41-60%)
Boilermakers
Rossendale Boot, Shoe, Slipper Ops.
UCATT
CEU/AUEW
TASS/AUEW
Firebrigades'
FTAT
SLADE
Tailor & GW
Textile Workers & KT, Ass. of
Tobacco Workers
TGWU
Wallcoverings, etc.

Division II (61-80%)
Bakers
Scottish Bakers
Blastfurnacemen
EETPTU
AUEW (Engineering)
Foundry workers/AUEW
GMWU
Patternmakers
POEU
APEX
NUPE
Amalgamated Textile Workers

Division I (81%+)
NUAAW
Carpet Weavers (90.8%)
Ceramic Workers
NACODS (99.6%)
Dyers & Bleachers
NUFLAT
ISTC (94.6%)
ASLEF (98.4%)
Loom overlookers (103.1%)
NUM (95.6%)
UPW
NUR (94.6%)
USDAW
TSSA

This league table contrasts interestingly with the Annual Report of the Certification Officer for 1977. (The Certification Officer is responsible, not only for maintaining the lists of Trade Unions and Employers' Associations, but also, among other legal duties for 'supervising the statutory requirements' about setting up and operating political funds.)

'Of the 25 major unions with over 100,000 members', he writes, '6 do not maintain political funds. Of those which do, 7 gave the proportion of members contributing to the political fund as more than 90 per cent; these were:

Table X:6
Percentage of contributions to political funds[20]

National Union of Public Employees	99%
National Union of General and Municipal Workers	98%
Transport and General Workers' Union	96%
Union of Post Office Workers	95%
National Union of Railwaymen	95%
Union of Shop Distributive and Allied Workers	93%
Confederation of Health Service Employees	91%

It will be noticed that the affiliation levels of these unions are 61.5 per cent, 70.9 per cent, 55.7 per cent*, 94.6 per cent, 84.5 per cent and 24.9 per cent respectively. Obviously there is no standard policy about levels of representation.

This was most decisively underlined by Martin Linton, in a study published in *Labour Weekly*,[21] which revealed that there was a range of variations between 20 pence and £1.56 per member in the amounts of political levy exacted each year by different unions, and which provided figures for contracting out during the year 1977 which moved from ten per cent in the EETPU to 67 per cent in ASTMS and SLADE. Yet the proportion of levy-payers actually affiliated to the Party fell below half in almost a quarter of the cases studied.

Before the Certification Officer assumed responsibility for the supervision of political funds, this task fell on the Registrar of Friendly Societies. His last Report on the matter, under the old legislation, gave one important additional piece of information which cannot be found in the subsequent Reports of the Certification Officer: the actual numbers of persons paying the political levy. In late 1976, this was

---

*The TGWU subsequently increased its affiliation to 1,250,000. This decision was taken in the year following that on which these figures are based, and took effect in 1979.

7,120,000.[22] At that time the Labour Party had 5,757,000 trade union affiliated members, so that more than 19 per cent of those paying were not represented: a total of 1,363,000 people.

The effect of this under-representation is to shift power from the Labour Party's Executive to the separate executives of the various unions. The monies in political funds will have to be expended on political purposes, but when the Labour Party does not receive them in direct affiliation payments, it has to recurrently negotiate their release as election contributions or other relevant donations, which emphasises its dependence upon those controlling the purse-strings.

One trade union, now affiliated to the TUC, conducts its political affairs differently from the others. All the organisations listed above comply with the Trade Unions Act, 1913, which says that union funds must not be used in pursuit of certain political objectives unless prior approval has been secured in a membership ballot. (If such a ballot reveals a majority in favour, a political fund may be established, but members must be allowed exemption from payment into it if they wish not to contribute. This right, to 'contract out' is a key feature of the Act.) But, as DATA (the Draughtsmen's Union, now called TASS) pointed out in their submission to the Royal Commission on Trade Unions, these requirements:

'are not observed by the National Union of Teachers which also gives support to parliamentary candidates and to Members of Parliament. The NUT has not taken a ballot on the furtherance of political objects, it has not established a separate political fund and it does not provide for 'contracting out'. It is significant that the NUT is one of the very few unions which supports candidates from each of the main political parties. There is, nevertheless, no reason why the Trade Unions Act 1913 should in practice apply only to unions which give exclusive support to Labour candidates or are affiliated to the TUC.

The contention that the NUT is not a trade union and that therefore the Trade Unions Act 1913 does not apply to it is, in the view of DATA, hardly worthy of serious argument. The NUT represents employed persons and furthers their occupational interests by collective bargaining and by other means. There are many other unions, including DATA, which engage in occupational activities other than collective bargaining. DATA, like the NUT, issues statements on professional questions and on general problems affecting the industries in which its members work; it is also a publisher of professional booklets. These activities are fully compatible with trade unionism.'[23]

Trade Union Participation in Labour Party Management

The part played by unions in the actual management of the Labour Party depends first of all on their national participation in its Annual Conference, and secondly on their influence on the election of its National Executive Committee, (NEC). The relationship between union contingents at the Conference and the constituency organisations is made plain in table X:7. With a combined total of 660,000 members affiliated, the constituencies taken together cannot match the votes of either the TGWU, the GMW, or the AUEW, taken singly.[24] If the issues debated at Conference find the unions agreed upon what should be done, then further argument is pointless. Commonly, of course, unions are not agreed, and argument is then unavoidable.

The continuing work of the Labour Party between Conferences is controlled by its NEC. This, although federally structured, gives the major influence to the unions. Directly, they place 12 members on the executive in their own right. One member is appointed by a handful of socialist societies such as the Fabians. Seven are elected by the constituency parties, representing all the individual members of the Party. A further five, the women's section, are chosen in a general ballot in which the unions have the preponderant influence. Finally, the treasurer is similarly chosen. In this way, allowing for the fact that the leader and deputy leader are, up to now, appointees of the Party's Parliamentary caucus, the unions can determine the occupancy of eighteen of the twenty-eight places on the ruling executive.

As far as the direct trade union contingent is concerned, this is generally chosen from a fairly restricted number of organisations. Table X:8 shows how only seventeen unions have provided the necessary dozen victorious candidates during the past decade.[25]

Seventeen organisations is an exaggerated total: the Scottish Motormen joined the TGWU in the middle of this period, so that its candidate then became a TGWU nominee. The AUEW, TASS and the Foundryworkers having conditionally merged, the total is reduced (to the extent that they in fact co-operate) by a further three. This leaves us with a situation in which, during a decade, a cabal of never more than thirteen organisations have been involved in filling twelve places.

Although the five women's nominees are normally put forward by constituencies in fact they each derive consistent support from particular unions, and some of them have very clear associations with those unions. Joan Maynard, MP, for instance, is a former vice-president of the Agricultural Workers' Union, while an unsuccessful runner-up for the women's section, Audrey Wise, is a presidential candidate inside the shopworkers' Union, USDAW.

In recent years, the treasurer, Norman Atkinson, MP, has been an AUEW nominee.

Table X:7
Labour Party and TUC membership 1906–1977

Year	No. TUC		Trade Unions		Individual membership	Socialist & Co-operative membership	Total membership	% of TUC membership affiliated to Labour Party
	Unions	Membership	Affiliated	Membership				
1906	226	1,555,000	176	975,182	—	20,885	998,338	—
1907	236	1,700,000	181	1,049,673	—	22,267	1,072,413	61.7
1912	201	2,001,633	130	1,858,178	—	31,237	1,895,498	92.8
1917	235	3,082,352	123	2,415,383	—	47,140	2,465,131	78.4
1922	206	5,128,648	102	3,279,276	—	31,760	3,311,036	63.9
1927	204	4,163,994	97	3,238,939	—	54,676	3,293,615	77.8
1928	196	3,874,842	91	2,025,139	214,970	52,060	2,292,169	52.3
1932	209	3,613,273	75	1,960,269	371,607	39,911	2,371,787	54.3
1937	214	4,008,647	70	2,037,071	447,150	43,451	2,527,672	50.8
1942	232	5,432,644	69	2,206,209	218,783	28,940	2,453,932	40.6
1947	187	7,540,397	73	4,386,074	609,487	45,738	5,040,299	58.2
1952	183	8,020,079	84	5,071,935	1,014,524	21,200	6,107,659	63.2
1957	185	8,304,709	87	5,644,012	912,987	25,550	6,582,549	68.0
1962	182	8,312,875	86	5,502,773	767,459	25,475	6,295,707	66.2
1967	169	8,787,282	75	5,539,562	733,932	21,120	6,294,614	63.0
1972	132	9,894,881	62	5,425,327	703,030	40,415	6,168,772	54.8
1977	115	11,515,920	59	5,913,159	659,737	43,375	6,616,271	51.3

Dissatisfaction with their Parliamentary leadership has led Labour Party activists to press insistent demands for their Conference to play a greater role in the determination and application of policy, and to invest the Executive with greater authority. In 1979 two constitutional amendments were approved in principle, subjecting Members of Parliament to mandatory reselection by their constituency organisations, and giving the National Executive Committee the main responsibility in the drafting of election manifestos. Both these changes would strengthen the actual powers of the National Executive vis-a-vis the Parliamentary Party while a third proposal, narrowly defeated in 1979, would have provided for the election of the Party leader by an electoral college in which the unions would constitute roughly one third of the selectorate.

But these issues, whilst they are of major political importance, do not by any means exhaust the scope for future argument about the Labour

Table X:8

Trade Union representation on NEC

Union	1969	1970	1971	1972	1973	1974	1975	1976	1977	1978
T & GWU	X	X	X	X	X	X	X*	X	X	X
TSSA	X	X	X	X	X	X	X	X	X	X
Boilermakers	X	X	X	X	X	X	X	X	X	X
EET PTU	X	X	X							
GMWU	X	X	X	X	X	X	X	X	X	X
BISAKTA	X	X	X	X						
NUM	X	X	X	X	X	X	X	X	X	X
Scottish Motormen	X	X	X	X	X	X*				
NUR	X	X	X	X	X	X	X	X	X	X
CAWU/APEX	X	X	X	X	X	X	X	X	X	X
USDAW	X	X	X	X	X	X	X	X	X	X
Foundryworkers	X	X	X	X	X					
TASS				X	X	X	X	X		
POEU					X	X	X	X	X	X
NUS						X	X	X	X	X
AUEW							X	X	X	X
ASTMS										X

*Alex Kitson, formerly representing the Scottish Commercial Motormen, became a TGWU representative after his union amalgamated with the TGWU.

Party Constitution, which will indeed be encouraged by the establishment, again in 1979, of a Commission of Enquiry to report on the Party's organisation and structure.

The Problem of the Block Vote

It is impossible, in this connection, to ignore the difficulties which are developing with the block vote. This system was inherited, for very good reasons, from the nonconformist churches, and it is an ideal method of regulating the affairs of a confederal organisation. Each affiliate of such a federation votes according to its own input of money and members, and this simultaneously guarantees that the Government of the organisation is felt to be representative and fair, and that those whose efforts and contributions are greatest will receive due

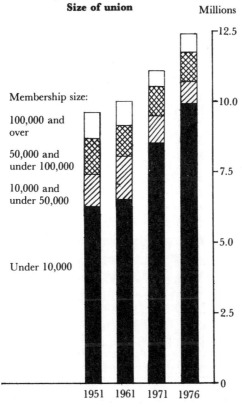

Source: Department of Employment.

recognition of that fact. The federal structure of the Labour Party is a valued resource, since it enables a close, continuing political relationship with the trade unions which is thought to offer a powerful guarantee that the Party must remain close to the people it seeks to organise and represent. But this federal structure obviously needs to be adapted to changing times, if it is to maintain its resilience and relevance.

In the formative years of the Labour Party, the Federation consisted of up to 181 different trade unions, most of them small to medium-sized, so that the million-odd people associated in them were divided into many relatively equal groupings. The growth of trade unionism has been hastened by the concentration of capital, however, which has in turn enforced considerable concentration in the trade union movement itself. At the level of joint negotiations unions need to range over wider fields as companies eat one another up and managements bestride larger and larger collossi. Meantime, the greater complexity of industrial relations legislation, the growth of specialisation in trade union offices, the burgeoning of new services which call for highly trained staff: all these pressures make small unions more and more difficult to maintain, and give the advantage to the vast amalgamations which dominate the modern TUC.

Yet, if growth has been rapid in the past few years, high inflation rates and industrial troubles, taken together, could very well accelerate it still further in the future.

Since 1951, the trend to larger and larger unions has been quite unmistakable. (See the diagram on p. 319).

If this progression merely continues at its present rate, without allowing for sharp speed-up in its tempo, we shall see a qualitative change in the resultant pattern.

From 1968 to 77 the unions in the TUC (in spite of the gain of several important new affiliations) merged themselves down from 160 to 115. This trend extrapolated gives 83 unions in 1986, and maybe 75 in 1990. Of course, there are more reasons to suppose that mergers and takeovers might accelerate than that they will follow the existing trend line.

The largest union, the TGWU, counts well over two million members in 1979. If it grows at the same rate in the next seven years as it has in the past seven, it will number nearly $2\frac{3}{4}$ millions in 1986, and 3 million by the end of the decade. All the other giants will feel the wake of this prodigious movement, and several of them are not merely liable, but likely, to fuse during the same period. Talks have already gone on between the EETPTU and the GMW, the AUEW, and UCATT. Sooner of later one or another initiative will be successful. It would be a brave person who ruled out other marriages among the big league:

NALGO and NUPE, or either of these bodies with others, or a confederation of the major public sector bodies: all seem at least thinkable. But whether these speculations are justifiable or not, union growth and concentration pose a vast problem for the traditional procedures of the Labour Party.

Taking, again, the largest affiliate, since 1978 the TGWU has increased its affiliation, so that it now pays fees on a membership of 1,250,000 to the Labour Party, and votes to that strength. But actual membership now exceeds 2 million, 96 per cent of whom, as we have seen, according to the Certification Officer, pay the political levy. If this last figure has remained reasonably constant, then in 1970 470,000 levy-payers from the TGWU were in fact unrepresented in the Party's Conference votes, and 778,000 in 1978.

Of course, this is not a one-sided question. We have already seen that payments made to the political levy do not all go into affiliations, and the TGWU makes more than usually generous contributions to electoral and other appeals. But it must surely weigh with the leaders of the union that, if they were affiliated to the Labour Party on a figure approaching the 2 million who are by now paying the levy, they would carry, on one card, a third of the combined block vote. And indeed, if the proportion contributing to the levy continues unchanged during a further decade of similar growth, the TGWU could, as we have seen, soon find itself entitled to half that combined total. Surely some of the union's spokesmen must feel that so large a say might be difficult to defend. In the government of a representative and democratic political party there has to be some mechanism to cope with such very large aggregates of power, and the real past forebearance of TGWU leaders is hardly an adequate one. If the TGWU pays up without claiming its due vote, its members may be deprived of their rights whenever the union's proposals are defeated. Yet if it exercises the vote, not merely individual party members, but even many smaller unions, may reasonably feel that the outcome of any argument will be predetermined.

At the same time that the logic of the concentration of the block vote is a cause for concern, so the individual members of the Labour Party, organised in their constituencies, find themselves called upon to assume greater financial and other responsibilities, in spite of their weak voting power. After 1979 individual members will be paying ten times the subscription levied upon affiliated members, and this might well provide a key lever for restructuring the party: since it might seem reasonable to afford such contributors the equivalent, in trade union terms, of a 'financial vote'. An easier and more workable principle, derived from this example, would be to afford the constituency section parity with the trade union section, in the major forums in which policy is deliberated. This proposal was, in fact, canvassed by Jack Jones in the late 'sixties.

Determining Conference Arrangements

Even more spectacular than their heavy presence in the Conference at large and in the NEC has been the consistent union monopoly of the Conference Arrangements Committee. During the whole of the past decade, five unions (AUEW, GMWU, NUM, NUR, TGWU) have consistently occupied all five seats on this key committee, which determines the agenda at the Party's Annual Conference. The capacity to steer the complex compositing of motions, and the order in which they are called, has often influenced the outcome of debates. In particular, during the strong chairmanship of Sir Harry Crane of the GMW, this small committee was widely credited with much responsibility for distorting the shape of debates by artificially encouraging extremely worded motions, to the discredit and possible defeat of milder ones. Conference management may be a fine art as well as a key to democratic development, and sometimes the artistry may have exceeded the democracy by a not inconsiderable factor.

The powers of the Conference Arrangements Committee, (CAC) which is independent of the National Executive, are wide. First, it may exercise the option of applying the 'three-year rule', under which any matters already discussed during the two most recent conferences may be kept off the agenda. Much depends on the stringency of definition, when such a rule is brought into force. Secondly, Labour Conferences normally involve several hundred resolutions, and an equivalent flood of amendments, which have to be composited into a reasonable number of representative motions. A key part of this work is done under the guidance of the CAC. Lewis Minkin cites an example of the pitfalls involved in this process, from the memoirs of Hugh Dalton, who used to dream of

> 'moving a resolution to nationalise the Solar System. This was regarded as a brilliant idea, but towards the close of the debate a Socialist Leaguer got up . . . and moved an amendment to add the words "and the Milky Way".'[26]

A conservative CAC can make lethal use of the demand for social justice in the Milky Way, by encouraging it to be composited into every embarrassing proposal, whether for changes in foreign policy or for reform of the schools. It is therefore noteworthy that constituency representatives do not get chosen for this function which is totally monopolised by delegates from the major unions.

control the Post, Telegraph and Telephone Workers International (PTTI) which is the ITS for communications workers. In the case of the petroleum industry the Agency actually set up the ITS, the International Federation of Petroleum and Chemical Workers (IFPCW) through the US union of petroleum workers, the Oil Workers International Union. Particularly in under-developed countries, station labour operations may be given cover as a local programme of an ITS.'[10]

This matter was raised by Jim Mortimer, then the Draughtsmen's representative, at the TUC in 1967.

'There is, . . . one issue . . . upon which I should like to suggest to Congress and to the General Council it would be most helpful if they could offer us their observations. I refer to the very detailed and specific revelations during the past twelve months of the channelling of millions of pounds from the Central Intelligence Agency of the United States Government under the cover of the international trade union Movement. I am not saying anything about any other trade union.

We ourselves are in this problem. We are affiliated to an ITS against which very detailed charges have been made in United States newspapers. I know there are many other unions here in the same position. There are charges that some of the officials of the ICFTU are CIA agents, I cannot comment on whether those charges are correct or incorrect, but I think it reasonable that the General Council should have a look at the matter and should offer us their observations.

May I just make this point: that the charges have been very detailed indeed and they have come not only from American newspapers, like the *New York Times* and the *Washington Post* but also from a number of American trade unionists themselves. The *Washington Post* said that the total amount of money channelled from CIA into the trade union movement and used for the purposes of the American Government was amounting now to 100 million dollars a year. One of our trade unionists who came to Britain only a few years ago—I remember his fraternal address, but I will not mention his name on this occasion—has, according to reports I have read in the *Washington Post*, confirmed that for six years his union acted as cover for CIA money being poured into an international trade secretariat with headquarters in London.

The UAW—the United Automobile Workers—in February this year withdrew all their officers from the American Federation of

Labour and Congress of Industrial Organisations. They issued a detailed administration letter, a copy of which I have with me at this Congress, and one of the charges made by the UAW is that money has been used through the AFL-CIO for the purpose of the Central Intelligence Agency of the United States Government. Victor Reuther, the international representative of UAW, said that there is a very big story on the financial and policy relationship between the AFL-CIO and the CIA . . .

Very briefly, the way in which this money has been channelled into the trade union Movement, according to the charges made, has been that the CIA has set up a number of dummy charitable foundations—about fifty are named in the *Washington Post*—and then those foundations have passed the money to American trade unions, which have used the money, mainly through the international trade secretariats but partly through the ICFTU, to carry out the policies of the American Government. I hope the General Council will agree that this is a matter that concerns many unions in this Congress and that it is one on which we look to them for their observations.'[11]

There was no debate upon this cogent statement, but George Woodcock, the then General Secretary of the TUC, replied in a brief intervention.

'Mr George Woodcock (*General Secretary*): Let there be no assumption in this Congress that the TUC in any way has had money from any source whatsoever but from the affiliated bodies to Congress. I cannot speak for the trade secretariats; they are not within the control of the General Council of the TUC. We have examined the information from the ICFTU and there is no evidence whatever that any money has been received by the ICFTU from any source other than a trade union source. I do not want it to be thought that the TUC has anything here to hide at all. We have stood firmly, and always will stand firmly, to the view that we are quite capable of doing our own job and paying our own way.'[12]

Whether the General Council really approved this rather laconic reply, or not, it is beyond reasonable doubt that this kind of revelation has been extremely unhelpful to the ICFTU as a whole.

The membership of the Confederation may be measured by three yardsticks. First, how many countries are represented within it? Second, how many national centres are affiliated? This can produce a different answer from the first question, because in some countries there exist more than one national trade union centre. Thirdly, how

Table XI:5
ICFTU membership trends, 1949–75

Year	Number of countries and territories	Number of organisations	Number of individual members represented by affiliates
1949	51	67	48,000,000
1951	59	76	50,500,000
1953	59	97	53,200,000
1955	75	109	54,300,000
1957	88	124	53,800,000
1959	97	137	56,000,000
1962	106	137	56,000,000
1965	96	121	60,300,000
1969	95	123	63,000,000
1972	91	115	48,600,000
1975	88	118	51,800,000
1977	88	120	55,500,000

Source: J. F. Windmuller, op. cit, and TUC Annual Report, 1978.[13]

Table XI:6
ICFTU membership by regions, 1965 and 1975[14]

	1965 Number (000)	%	1975 Number (000)	%
Europe	26,551	44.0	29,973	57.9
Africa	908	1.5	908	1.8
Asia (Far East and South Asia)	5,618	9.3	9,669	18.7
Near East	1,547	2.6	1,434	2.8
Australia and New Zealand	1,050	1.7	1,643	3.2
North America	14,139	23.5	1,516	2.9
Latin America and Caribbean	10,461	17.4	6,605	12.7
Total	60,274	100.0	51,748	100.0

Source: J. F. Windmuller, op. cit.

many individual members are enrolled in the affiliated membership? The answers to these questions are given in table XI:5.

Not all of these unions are strictly comparable, of course. While some are obviously widely representative, others are little more than propaganda desks, sometimes owing very much to the direct support of their governments.

When these figures are broken down for the different regions covered, however, a more precise picture emerges (see table XI:6).

From both these tables, it is clear that ICFTU affiliates as a whole doubled in number between 1949 and 1962, and individual membership rose to a peak in 1969, they have now shrivelled back to a point they had already passed 20 years earlier. During that time, in the advanced European countries, memberships have been growing and this is reflected in the regional figures. But in Africa, nothing has moved. One reason is that various African governments (sometimes for honest and quite understandable reasons, and sometimes solely in order to subordinate the unions to their own wishes) have outlawed both the ICFTU and the WFTU, on the (not altogether unreasonable) grounds that they 'were merely a clever disguise for penetration by one of the major power blocs'. As the Nigerian Government, for instance, reported:

'Both the ICFTU and the AALC supported the United Labour Congress of Nigeria (ULCN) regarded as the main counterbalance to the rival Communist led Nigeria Trade Union Congress (NTUC). From a 1977 report of a government tribunal of inquiry into the activities of the trade unions, the following emerged:

1. So considerable was the ICFTU and US funding to the ULCN that most of the centre's affiliates didn't bother to pay dues to it. Leadership of unions which did pay expected in return financial and other rewards. Money was used to try and bribe union leaders to affiliate their unions with the ULCN.
2. The President of the ULCN had information that the AALC was connected with the CIA. He wrote to two of the AALC staff in Nigeria asking for an explanation. None was forthcoming.
3. In the early 'seventies the ICFTU paid out money for ULCN-run welfare schemes. The inquiry reported: "The projects were established, but with (one) exception they were allowed to fizzle out largely because of lack of supervision of the personnel directly responsible for their operation by the Congress Secretariat. No member of the Congress Secretariat could tell us what had become of the projects—they just did not know. This led us to conclude that they had adopted a carefree attitude to

the projects because the funding went through external sources."

4. In 1973 the ULCN was able to get an additional 10,000 dollars from the ICFTU by pretending it was about to launch an organisational campaign. The inquiry said it "was a specious cover to induce the ICFTU to part with its money."

5. The ICFTU (which prides itself on a non-colonial relationship with affiliated Third World unions) along with the AALC "had a free hand in the running of the affairs of the Congress." Representatives of both took part in policy making meetings.

6. The inquiry found that because of the flow of money and material aid from the ICFTU and the US "there appeared to be a tacit understanding among the officers of Congress of adopting a policy of 'what you have you hold'. The result was that each officer kept to himself/herself what came to him/her be it money, car or scooter and provided he acknowledged receipt of it to the donating organisation, that virtually ended the matter." [15]

And in Latin America, where the CIA depredations have been the most blatant and offensive,[16] membership has dropped right back from ten and a half to six and a half million. It is assumed by informed observers that all these figures are somewhat fictional: but it is certainly no fiction that ORIT, the Confederation's Latin American organisation, to which Philip Agee refers above, has, as he claims, been heavily involved in CIA-funded operations. Of course, ORIT operates on the doorstep of the American unions. The overseas work of the AFL–CIO, whilst it is mainly financed by the United States Government, is also funded by an impressive list of companies:

Table XI:7
Some companies who finance AFL-CIO's overseas work[17]

W.R. Grace & Company	Brazilian Light & Power
Rockefeller Brothers Fund	First National Bank of Boston
International Telephone and Telegraph	United Fruit Company
Pan American World Airways	Anglo-Lautaro Nitrate Corporation
The United Corporation	IBM World Trade Corporation
David Rockefeller	International Basic Economy Corporation
Kennecott Copper Corporation	Sinclair Oil
Standard Oil Co. of New Jersey	Max Ascoli Fund Inc.
Koppers Company	International Mining Corporation
Gillette	Carrier Corporation

Shell Petroleum	Coca-Cola Export Corporation
Crown Zellerbach	Container Corporation of America
The Anaconda Company	Stauffer Chemical Company
ACFE (Venezuela)	American-Standard
King Ranch	International Packers
Sterling Drug. Inc.	Olin
General Foods Corporation	Standard Oil of California
Loeb Rhoades & Company	Warner-Lambard
Owens-Illinois Glass	Corning Glass
Union Carbide Corporation	Eli Lilly & Company
Ebasco Industries	J. Henry Schroeder Banking Corporation
Reader's Digest	United Shoe Machinery
Monsanto	Celanese Corporation
Southern Peru Copper Corporation	Bacardi Corporation
Merck	Schering Foundation
Pfizer International	Bankers Trust Company
Otis Elevator Company	Bristol Myers
Industrias Kaiser Argentina	Chase Manhattan Bank
American Cyanamid	Kimberly-Clark
First National City Bank	Upjohn Company
International Paper Company	Insurance Company of North America
Mobil Oil Company	3M Company
Standard Fruit Company	American International Oil Company
American Telephone & Telegraph	Combustion Engineering
Corn Products	Sheraton Corporation of America
Council for Latin America	Chemetron Corporation
Johnson & Johnson	Motion Picture Association of America
St. Regis Paper Company	Deltec.
American Can Company	

Source: AIFLD, Senate Hearing, 1968, p. 21.
Footnote: In 1977 an AFL-CIO spokesman confirmed that companies still financed part of their overseas programme.

Small wonder that the veteran American Labour leader, George Meany, preaches a form of mirror-image Marxism:

'You can't dictate to a country from any angle at all unless you control the means of production. If you don't control the means of production, you can't dictate. Whether you control them through ideological methods or control them by brute force, you must control them.'[18]

This kind of intervention makes it rather difficult to evaluate the real significance of the different pieces of international machinery. On the one side, virtually none of the rank-and-file affiliated members, either of the ICFTU, or the ITS networks, would endorse the diplomatic objectives of the intelligence operatives, leave alone their 'dirty tricks'. On the other side, the fact that bodies like ORIT have been compromised means that the international body lacks effective organs in a key zone of activity. In political terms the meaning of the ICFTU is complex: in spite of all the abuses of trust, it retains a degree of strong support from key union centres which are nobody's catspaws. So much is this the case that, since the American AFL–CIO walked out, it has even been reproached for being 'soft' on detente.[19] In industrial terms, the political alienation of some of the more dynamic and independent union centres in the third world means a severe restriction of capacity to deal with the practical problems involved in facing up to the multinational companies.

The Growth of Regionalism

All this has pushed the TUC and other European bodies in the direction of greater reliance upon regional organisations.[20] To some extent this development has been a global one, with similar bodies gaining strength in both African and Arab regions.

The European Trade Union Confederation was set up at a founding Congress held at the beginning of 1973 by eighteen of the ICFTU's European affiliates, including all the relevant centres in all the nine EEC countries, except Ireland, together with those of Austria, Finland (2), Iceland, Norway, Sweden (2), Switzerland and Spain. (The additional centre comes from Italy, where, at the time, both the CISL and the UIL were affiliated to the Brussels international office.)

The ETUC knit together previous co-ordinating groups for both the EEC and EFTA: and it specifically set out to mark and pace the growth of transnational companies, at the same time as it sought representation in relevant EEC committees. In May 1974 at an extraordinary Congress in Copenhagen, the Confederation took all the major National Christian Trade Union Centres into membership, and also the radical French centre, the CFDT, together with the Irish Congress of Trade Unions. Within a few weeks the Italian CGIL, (which is a joint communist-socialist federation, formerly affiliated to the WFTU) was also accepted into membership. By 1976, the second (London) ETUC Congress had representation from 30 organisations with 37 million members.

This left outside only the French communist centre, the CGT, which maintained its links with the WFTU, not without certain developing frictions, but which also faced the intransigent hostility of its old breakaway rival, Force Ouvriere. Applications for membership from the CGT were still being rejected up to late 1978.

As of 1974, then, the ETUC comprised the following organisations:

Table XI:8 *Membership of ETUC*[21]

Country		Trade Union Centre	Membership
Austria	*OGB	(Osterreichischer Gewerkschaftsbund)	1,527,000
Belgium	CSC	(Confederation des Syndicats Chretiens)	1,100,000
	*FGTB	(Federation Generale du Travail de Belgique)	950,000
Denmark	*LO	(Landsorganisationen i Danmark)	871,000
	FTF	(Fallesradet for Danske Tjenestemandsoj Funktionarorganisationer)	185,000
Finland	TVK	(Toimihenkilo-ja-Virkamiesjajestojen Keskusliitto)	182,000
	*SAK	(Suomen Ammattiliittojen Keskusjarjesto)	720,000
France	*CGT-FO	(Confederation Generale du Travail-Force Ouvriere)	600,000
	CFDT	(Confederation Francaise Democratique du Travail)	800,000
Germany (Fed. Rep.)	*DGB	(Deutscher Gewerkschaftsbund)	7,200,000
Gt. Britain	*TUC	(Trade Union Congress)	9,900,000
Iceland	*AI	(Althydusamband Islands)	35,000
Ireland	ICTU	(Irish Congress of Trade Unions)	547,000
Italy	*CISL	(Confederazione Italiana Sindacati Lavoratori)	2,000,000
	*UIL	(Unione Italiana del Lavoro)	800,000
	CGIL	(Confederazione Generale Italiana del Lavoro)	2,700,000
Luxembourg	*CGT	(Confederation Generale du Travail)	30,000
	LCGB	(Letzbuerger Christleiche Gewerkschaftsbund)	15,000
Malta	GWU	(General Workers Union)	26,000
Netherlands	*NVV	(Nederlands Verbond van Vakverenigingen)	660,000
	NKV	(Nederlands Katholiek Vakverbond)	340,000
	CNV	(Christelijk National Vakverbond)	240,000
Norway	*LO	(Landsorganisasjonen I Norge)	580,000
Spain	*UGT	(Union General de Trabajadores de Espana)	—
	STB	(Solidarite des Travailleurs Basques)	—
Sweden	*LO	(Landsorganisationen i Sverige)	1,734,000
	*TCO	(Tjanstemannens Centralorganisation)	775,000
Switzerland	*SGB	(Schweizerischer Gewerkschaftsbund)	434,000
	SVEA	(Schweizerischer Verband Evangelischer Arbeitnehmer)	13,000
	CNG	(Christlichnationaler Gewerkschaftsbund der Schweiz)	98,000

Acting in concert, these 30 centres have agreed to create an apparatus of industry committees, six of which were functioning by 1977. These covered metalworkers, farmworkers, postal workers, commercial and clerical workers, miners and entertainment workers. No small amount of friction with the International Trade Secretariats has resulted from the formation of these bodies, and the threat of formation of others.[22] The more that ETUC industry committees secure recognition from EEC agencies, the more conflict there is likely to be with the ITS machinery. The more that campaigns such as that for the 35 hour week, or for five weeks annual holiday, take on grass-roots support, the more real the ETUC as an institution will become, in distinction from both the ICFTU and, maybe, some of the Trade Secretariats.

Once the problem of admitting the last French Centre has been resolved, the ETUC will have become an inclusive organisation, with obvious representative functions, and with active commitments from such diverse bodies as the (part-communist, Italian) CGIL, the (radical former Christian, French) CFDT and the (socialist, Belgian) FGTB.

At first sight, such an alliance is infinitely more useful, and equally less morally suspect, than either of the established overall trade union internationals. But there is a limitation involved in a European regional link-up, which is that, by definition, it is incapable of developing on its own account, direct associations with unions in the third world. If both existing international bodies could be accused of frequently manipulating such unions in the past, and sometimes of very much worse behaviour, this does not lift from our shoulders the burden of need for some sort of open international framework which can knit together the efforts of trade unionists in the over-developed and the under-developed nations, and defend their common interests. The option of regionalisation is perfectly understandable, given the infragrant scent left behind by cold war trade unionism: but regionalism is not enough. Multinationals will continue to shift their operations into ever new territories, and, much as British unions will need closer contact with their European counterparts, they will also need to know who are their natural allies in South Korea, Hong Kong, or the Philippines. To mark, and pace, the modern multinationals, fully international organisation is desirable. Needless to say, it is also desirable that such organisation should serve trade union purposes, and should not be unduly influenced, leave alone bankrolled, by governmental agencies of any power whatsoever.

Some Criteria for International Organisation
Difficult though it may be for the average trade unionist to follow

the story of intrigue and high diplomacy which is knit into trade union internationalism, there remain a series of practical tasks which all trade union members will recognise as requiring a variety of forms of international action.

First, to bargain with a multinational, even on one's home base, one needs adequate information about what one's employer is up to elsewhere. A well-known company in the English Midlands has two foundries, one in Derby, one in Lincoln. For years work was switched back and forth along the railway line which passes both plants, to the frustration of shop stewards, first in one place, then the other. They found this capacity to move work to be a major resource, enabling the employer to offset many perfectly reasonable trade union pressures. Only effective combine organisation could control such movement. How much more true is this of the great transnational companies, which possess footholds (and giant ones, sometimes) in several continents? If the workers at Imperial Typewriters had known what Litton Industries were planning overseas, at the time they were taken over, they could have developed an appropriate political and industrial campaign to defend and expand typewriter production.[23] As things went, Litton consolidated their hold over the English market while they were running down their newly acquired but aged plants in Leicester and Hull, and they shut their production shops at the moment that their distribution plans were advanced enough to allow this. A full flow of information, concerning what was happening at Litton's German plants, for instance, would have been no negligible resource, from the union viewpoint.

Second, beyond information flows, what contacts can be introduced to make bargaining company-wide? At shop-steward level, various rank-and-file initiatives have been taken (by Ford workers, for instance). The most serious and sustained attempt at co-ordination has been that of the Dunlop–Pirelli joint committee, which links British and Italian stewards.[24]

At inter-union level, the TGWU and the AUEW commenced a series of international meetings with the (American) United Auto Workers. Attempts at company level to approach international collective bargaining, even in the broadest terms, have always been repudiated by the big car companies. This is true not only when joint union approaches are made on[25] an ad hoc basis, but also when the International Trade Secretariats are brought into the picture. Some ITSs have set up world company councils for the major transnational companies. In 1972, the Ford World Auto Union Council (convened under the auspices of the International Metalworkers' Federation, an ITS) asked to discuss the company's international investment policy.

The company replied that it preferred to operate its labour relations on a country-by-country basis, 'because labour relations procedures differ'.[26] Slightly more success was obtained by the European Industry Committee for Philips, the Dutch-based Electronic Company. This employs 350,000 people round the world, 285,000 in Europe. 150 European plants exist. For six years the company did talk with the European Committee for the Metal Trades, starting in 1967. They broke relations with the ECMT in 1971, refusing to discuss investment programmes.

This is what the unions are up against. The multinationals reserve the right to operate from a tightly-controlled centre, and to plan all their operations in an integrated way. But they will not discuss those overall plans, at the level at which they have been conceived, with appropriate union representation.

This leads us to a third area of concern: appropriate legislation. If companies will not recognise adequate trade union rights voluntarily, how can they be constrained to do so? Legislation can be a matter for particular national governments, or for pressure upon and through intergovernmental agencies. Reams of paper have been covered in the offensive to enlist aid from these agencies: but whilst national sovereignty retains any validity it is direct pressure on national governments which will remain the principle trade union approach. In Britain, this is reflected in the *Employment Protection Act* of 1975, which charges the Advisory, Conciliation and Arbitration Service (ACAS) with the obligation to prepare and publish codes of industrial relations practice, which will naturally apply to the foreign-based subsidiaries of foreign multinationals in Britain no less than to domestic-based firms. (It will *not*, however, affect British-based overseas subsidiaries in any direct way.) The provisions of the 1975 Act cover not only recognition, but also disclosure questions, but its teeth are not very sharp. International solidarity action by unions receives specific protection under the *Trade Union and Labour Relations Act* of 1976, which repeals the previous restriction, affording protection only to disputes in which it could be shown that those involved had a direct stake in the outcome. The most important legislation in Britain, however, is the *Industry Act* of 1975, which makes it possible for the Government to prohibit foreign takeovers in major industrial concerns, and specifically opens up the issue of investment decisions to tripartite discussion in the framework of planning agreements. Yet, as we saw in chapter 8, planning agreements have been a dead letter, because at the last moment the Prime Minister intervened to fillet the Act of the stipulation that they should be obligatory.

In the context of its actual non-implementation, however, the words of one sympathetic commentator are relevant:

> 'Although the planning agreement concept will bring government and trade unions closer to the activities of foreign-owned and UK-based multinationals it is unlikely that it will give trade unions more information about the basis of transfer pricing and therefore the extent to which multinational companies affect balance of payments performance, decide the level of taxation they might pay, and what is their ability to pay wage increases. By referring only to UK operations of multinationals the planning agreement will not give trade unions much control over decisions by multinationals to invest abroad. At best the arrangements will give trade union representatives the opportunity to ask questions about why investment is being undertaken overseas, and about transfer pricing. The extent to which planning agreements force multinational companies to take full account of national social and economic priorities will remain to be seen.'[27]

By 1979, three years after this evaluation, it has been seen, and it is fair to say that this aspect of the legislation has had no effect at all.

The other major component of the trade union offensive to come within reach of imposing accountability on multinationals was, of course, legislation on industrial democracy, which we have already discussed in chapter 8. By 1979, none of this had been enacted. Undoubtedly, however, the agitation for such legal changes will continue, since the problem of multinational intervention in the British economy, and of British company involvement abroad, poses more acute difficulties for the unions each year.

If national legislation has taken small effect up to now, the resolutions and memoranda of the ICFTU, the ILO, and the OECD have taken less. The OECD Trade Union Advisory Committee has called for a package of internationally co-ordinated simultaneous legislation, which, though it is seen as hyper-moderate by many of the affiliated trade union centres, has not been taken up by the OECD states. Instead, they have drawn up guidelines for yet another code of (voluntary) conduct, and agreed to talk about a set of legal reforms in 1979, if that code fails to take adequate effect. The result of all those conferences, all those declarations, is not, up to date, impressive. As the TUAC explained in November 1978:

> 'The trade unions judge the Guidelines from the point of view of their impact on the real world. Their existence created expectations among the unions who hoped that the climate for their relations

with multinational enterprises would change for the better. Evidence of this, after almost three years of experience, still is not forthcoming. There is little to show that the world of the multinational enterprise has been changed. Furthermore, there is very little evidence that the present voluntary set of Guidelines is being vigorously pursued or that there is effective action to create a framework within which their implementation could be ensured. TUAC underlines that even if its involvement in the follow-up of the Guidelines so far has been active and will continue to be so, it is not primarily for the trade union movement to see to the functioning of the Guidelines. They were agreed upon by Governments, who took upon themselves the responsibility to address them to the multinational enterprises. Consequently, they should also ensure their implementation.

Unless the Guidelines are really implemented, the trade union movement will have to seriously consider their usefulness and also any further support to them. As a compromise, TUAC accepted the Guidelines in 1976 as a first step. At that time, the trade unions clearly envisaged not only their implementation but also further development. If no change to the better has taken place in the real world due to the Guidelines, what was the use of the whole exercise?'[28]

Yet the issue remains urgent. Michael Barratt Brown puts it very clearly:

'Differences in trade union strength reflect national cultural and historical differences between the European countries. But the fact remains that in the countries where capitalism is strong the unions are weak: where capitalism is weak the unions are strong. One is bound to ask which is cause and which is effect. We began by suggesting that there were two new elements in recent capitalist development: the transnational company as the centre of capital accumulation; and the shop stewards committee as the expression of organised labour. In an important sense we are no longer looking only at national centres of capitalism,—British, French, or Italian. These still exist. The City and the CBI are centres of financial and industrial power; the Bourse and the Patronat also. The interlinking of State and private finance is crucial to Italian industry. But, increasingly, national finance—private and state—are the servants of the giant transnational companies. These may have had their origins in Britain or Italy, West Germany or France, in the Netherlands or Belgium and a large number came from the United States; but their attitude to nation states is increasingly opportunistic. National loyalties have been replaced by a hard headed commercial view of the costs and benefits of locating their multifarious activities in this country or that. As in the case of Dunlop and Pirelli, so it is with others. Minerals, oil and other raw materials attract investment to one area; for other areas it will be cheap labour for processing work, a pool of skilled workers for machine making, a docile labour force will all attract investment, while a country with low rates of tax will attract the headquarters and registered offices. Where goods are bulky and transport costs high, production, or at least the final assembly, will be located near the richest and largest markets.'[29]

In chapter one, we called in evidence Karl Marx, who, it may be remembered, spoke, with the voice of a prophet, more than a hundred years ago:

'The battle of competition is fought by cheapening commodities. The cheapness of commodities depends, *ceteris paribus*, on the productivity of labour, and this again on the scale of production. Therefore, the larger capitals beat the smaller . . . '

Now this centralisation has become a vast and universal affair, a continental drift of the major economic forces, squeezing even nation-states until they crack, sometimes in its minor movements. This huge thraldom is answerable to no democratic control, and pursues its own greedy interest across and beneath the frontiers of nations, law and morality, meeting no obstacle which may seriously restrain it in any of the territories over which it holds dominion.

Improbable though it may seem, and fiercely difficult though it will be to accomplish, the only imaginable counter-force upon which to base the future of democracy in the struggle against this unbridled power, is the trade union movement. The last twenty years of the twentieth century will see a major contest in which these elemental economic powers are increasingly opposing and confronting every possibility of humane social development. They may dictate the terms upon which they operate: more and more commonly they buy deeply into newspapers and communications media: where necessary they do not scruple to remove governments. The hopes of far more than this generation may well depend upon the courage, the audacity and the intelligence of the answering response of today's trade unionists. The sooner they merge their resources, the better they will match this task.

NOTES

1. TUC: *Annual Report*, 1977.
2. This has been the object of some controversy, and its head, Mr Hargreaves, has been reproached for maintaining what critics regard as too close a relationship with the Foreign Office. Cf Don Thomson and Rodney Larson: *Where Were You Brother?* War on Want, 1978 for a very interesting documentation on this question. Also Patrick Wintour: 'The TUC's Foreign Policy', *New Statesman*, 2nd March 1979, p. 282-5.
3. Source: TUC: *Annual Reports*.
4. Cf Shirley Lerner: *Breakaway Unions and the Small Trade Union*, Allen and Unwin, 1961, pp. 85 et seq.
5. Lord Citrine: *Two Careers*, Hutchinson, 1967, p. 219 et seq. Soviet delegate Kuznetsov 'seemed to regard the invitation (to Buckingham Palace) with pleasure'.
6. Cf TUC: *Free Trade Unions Leave the WFTU*, 1949. This document states the reasons for the withdrawal of the TUC, the CIO, and the Dutch CFTU from the Executive Bureau of the WFTU in Paris. One sentiment in this report is prophetic: 'Our affiliated unions would not count the cost if real international Trade Unity were developing; but if the General Council have to answer whether the £15,000 now being paid annually by organisations affiliated to the British TUC is being spent profitably . . . the answer is assuredly "no".' Thirty times that sum now goes out annually, but the General Council does not receive many questions.
7. Richard Fletcher: *CIA and the Labour Movement*, Spokesman, 1977, p. 51.
8. Philip Agee: *Inside the Company—CIA Diary*, Penguin Books, 1975, pp. 74-5.
9. Cf *The Pike Report*, Spokesman, 1977. Also Marchietti and Marks: *The CIA and the Cult of Intelligence*, Johnathan Cape, 1974, p. 48 et seq.
10. Agee, op. cit, p. 76.
11. TUC: *Annual Report*, 1967, pp. 487-8.
12. Ibid, p. 488.
13. J. F. Windmuller: 'Realignments in the ICFTU: the Impact of Detente', *BJIR*, XIV, 3, Nov. 1976, p. 249.
14. Ibid.
15. This is the account of the findings of the Nigerian *Report of the Tribunal of Inquiry into the Trade Unions*, (Federal Ministry of Information, Lagos, 1977) given by Thomson and Larson, op. cit, pp. 60-61.
16. Cf Fred Hirsch: *CIA and the Labour Movement*, Spokesman, 1977. Also Cheddi Jagan: *The West on Trial*, Michael Joseph, 1966, pp. 170 et seq. pp. 296 et seq.
17. Cited in Thomson and Larson, op. cit, p. 26.
18. George Meany speaking at the House of Representatives, Committee on Foreign Affairs: 'Winning the Cold War—the US ideological offensive.'

88th Congress, 1st Session, part two, 30th April 1963: cited Thomson and Larson, op. cit.

19.   Cf Windmuller, op. cit, p. 258: 'The current outlook . . . is . . . one of realignment on terms more rather than less favourable to the objectives of the Soviet Union . . .'

20.   B. C. Roberts and Bruno Liebhaberg: 'The European Trade Union Confederation: Influence of Regionalism, Detente and Multinatonals'; BJIR, XIV, 3, November 1976. p. 261 et seq.

21.   Basil Bye and Mel Doyle: *European Trade Union Co-operation*, WEA.

22.   B. C. Roberts and Bruno Liebhaberg, op. cit.

23.   Cf Institute for Workers' Control: *Why Imperial Typewriters Must Not Close*, No. 46.

24.   For a discussion of this and other cases, see Michael Barratt Brown: 'Working Class Internationalism' in K. Coates and F. B. Singleton (Ed) *The Just Society*, Spokesman, 1977, p. 77.

25.   John Gennard: *Multinationals: Industrial Relations and the Trade Union Response*. Occasional Papers in Industrial Relations, Universities of Leeds and Nottingham, 1976, p. 20.

26.   Michael Barratt Brown, op. cit, p. 77.

27.   Gennard, op. cit, pp. 25–6.

28.   ICFTU; Economic and Social Bulletin, XXVII No. 1, Jan.–Mar. 1979, p. 15.

29.   Michael Barratt Brown, op. cit, p. 79.

APPENDIX TO CHAPTER 11

Commonwealth Trade Union Council
A new organisation aimed at strengthening links between trade union centres in the Commonwealth came into being on March 1 1980.

Membership of the Commonwealth Trade Union Council (CTUC) based in London, consists of the 25 million workers who belong to trade unions in over 40 Commonwealth countries. The list of these at the time of the foundation of the CTUC was: Australia, The Bahamas, Bangladesh, Barbados, Botswana, Britain, Canada, Cyprus, Dominica, Fiji, The Gambia, Ghana, Grenada, Guyana, India, Jamaica, Kenya, Kiribati, Lesotho, Malawi, Malaysia, Malta, Mauritius, New Zealand, Nigeria, Papua New Guinea, St Lucia, Seychelles, Sierra Leone, Singapore, Solomon Islands, Sri Lanka, Swaziland, Tanzania, Tonga, Trinidad and Tobago, Tuvalu, Uganda, Western Samoa and Zambia. Announcing the launching of the new body, a press release reported:

'Close ties between Commonwealth trade union organisations have existed for many years and regular meetings have been held during the International Labour Conference each year in Geneva. It was at the 1978 meeting that it was agreed in principle to establish a new Commonwealth trade union body and a special working party was set up to examine the form such a body should take. In 1979 the Commonwealth unions agreed to establish the new Council and at a meeting in Madrid in November Dennis McDermott, President of the Canadian Labour Congress, was elected President, and Carl Wright, formerly Secretary to the Economic and Social Committee of the International Confederation of Free Trade Unions, was appointed the full time Director of the CTUC.

The aims of the CTUC are to promote the interests of workers in the Commonwealth through enhanced cooperation between national trade union centres; to influence Commonwealth institutions and decisions; and to promote acceptance of, and respect for, trade unionism and for the Commonwealth Declaration of Principles of 1971 which sets out the basic relationship between the Commonwealth countries.

The top priority for the new Council is to establish relations with

Commonwealth institutions and governments; (such contacts have been established, from the initiation of the CTUC, between its Director and the Commonwealth Secretary-General, H. E. Shridath S. Ramphal). These contacts are aimed at assessing how the CTUC can best be involved in the follow-up to the Lusaka Heads of Government Meeting and the Valetta Finance Ministers Meeting which took place in 1979, with a view to ensuring that trade union views are taken into account by Commonwealth governments and institutions.

Another priority is an examination of ways in which practical assistance can be given to trade unions in Commonwealth countries. This includes building-up a register of needs of member organisations; approaching relevant aid-giving organisations and initiating specific projects, along with the development of procedures for controlling and reviewing such projects.

As the Commonwealth comprises approximately a third of the independent nations of the world, and contains people of different races, religions and cultures, it is uniquely placed to make a significant contribution towards the development of the 'North-South' dialogue and to promote better understanding between the developed and developing world. This is something which was highlighted in the 1980 report of the 'Brandt Commission'.

Central to its aims is the goal of achieving a fair world social and economic order and highlighting and supporting the role of trade unions in economic and social development.

The executive body of the CTUC is its Steering Sub-Committee, on which sit trade union leaders from the UK and Mediterranean, Canada, Africa, Asia, the Caribbean and Australasia and the Pacific. A general session will be held each year to maintain contacts between member centres and to allow an exchange of views. The first of these was scheduled to be held in Geneva in June 1980 during the International Labour Conference.

Conclusion

We have tried, in this book, to present a picture of the British Trade Union Movement as it actually stands, at the opening of a new decade, the 1980s. We hope it is a fair representation, warts and all, but not more wart than face. A descriptive work, however lovingly composed, is likely to upset various people. Sometimes, the sitter is scandalised. Sir Winston Churchill apparently profoundly resented the most faithful and insightful portrait that was ever painted of him. At other times, the sitters' antagonists are distressed. 'Where is all the villainy, the greed, the smugness, which we associate with this character?', they may ask.

Among twelve million plus people there is a necessary quotient of selfishness, narrowmindedness, and gluttony. A vast newspaper industry ensures that these qualities are adequately advertised. But there is also a rich fund of generous concern, of human warmth, of solidarity; which virtues are not so widely noised about. The British trade union movement is the greatest single community resource of the British people. It stimulates a large and growing voluntary effort, innumerable anonymous acts of self-sacrifice, and a major and vital part of the national commitment to ideals of justice and democracy. Who doubts this must leave reading books, and move among the people who have created the elaborate machinery which is inadequately outlined in these pages.

As we go to press, all this now faces a challenge such as few institutions in history have been able to survive. The economic crisis which generated successive Governmental onslaughts on union rights and liberties, briefly documented above, now in 1980 takes on a convulsive form in which major industries are shivering on the edge of collapse.

During the late 70s a sombre debate began on the question of 'de-industrialisation'. The rickety competitive position of British manufacturing industry had become steadily more disadvantageous, as British entry to the European Economic Community created an acute imbalance in trade in manufactures. Instead of improving investment in this manufacturing industry, the oil boom undermined it: by maintaining a grossly inappropriate rate of exchange, the oil revenues contributed to the throttling of marginal enterprises in one sector after another. By the beginning of the 80s, unemployment was already fixed at around the one and a half million mark. However, all reputable economic forecasters anticipated an early rise to two million or more.

With widespread unemployment, poverty, already endemic, became more and more acute.

In this context, all the principal achievements in the field of welfare provision and humane social organisation, established during the decades following the Second World War, became objects of bitter contention. The postwar decades had previously been marked by a consensus. This broad social agreement assumed continuous improvement in living standards; growing social provision in the fields of education, housing and health; and greater involvement by trade unions in the regulation of an increasingly liberal society. The architects of this consensus would be dismayed by the Britain of 1980. Marked authoritarianism, increasingly obtrusive and arbitrary police powers, surveillance, and frenetic preparations for an impossible war: all marked an end to the postwar settlement, whose dreams had turned into nightmares.

If anyone remains free to write an updated version of this book in 1990, it will very possibly record events which have hitherto been unthinkable. No-one can with certainty predict the outcome of the desperate period into which we are entered: and we do not wish to end this book on a note of vapid optimism. But if the British Trade Unions still need an expositor at the end of the trials which are about to be encountered, then there will remain a real hope that the goals of liberal civilisation, of brotherhood, sisterhood and mutual support, may yet prevail.

If, however, the unions were in fact to be powdered between the pitiless grindstones of official repression and economic ruin, those who dared remember them at all would remember also the democratic promise which they held out, and the large freedoms which were always rooted in their ample support. Books would be burnt, and witches soon after them, on the evil day when the British Trade Unions were compelled to close their offices.

Educated working people may be relied upon to make all these most dire events quite difficult to achieve.

Acknowledgements

We prepared this book to meet the needs of our students, and in the hope that it might be helpful to others who wished to understand the complex structure of the trade union movement. No doubt there remain some errors in our text, and there would have been many more were it not for the generous advice which these students have given us.

We are also extremely grateful to many academic colleagues for their assistance and advice. We must particularly mention Michael Barratt Brown, who has been a constant inspiration; Michael Somerton, who gave us the benefit of a most careful examination of an early draft of the whole work; Graham Winch, Daniel Vulliamy, Professor Norman Lewis and Terry Sullivan, all of whom read parts of the work, and helped us to avoid various mistakes; Don Thomson, whose advice on the chapter on International Trade Unionism was extremely helpful. The scholars whose work we have consulted and reported are listed in a bibliographic index, and our debt to them is quite apparent.

Much of the information recorded in this book is the result of direct enquiries at trade union offices. We wish to thank every research officer who endured our inquisitive questions, and responded to our questionnaires together with all the other numerous officials who have given so much time to answering us. We are most grateful to Tony Benn, Tom Watkinson, Walt Greendale and our colleagues at the Institute for Workers' Control, all of whom provided us with valued advice.

Above all, we wish to thank Ken Fleet, who was an unfailing source of encouragement as well as practical assistance, and Rita Plackett, whose vast patience and unremitting hard work enabled this text to be retyped more times than she or any of us care to remember.

Glossary

AALC	African American Labor Centre Inc.
ACAS	Advisory, Conciliation and Arbitration Service
AFL	American Federation of Labor
BDC	Biennial Delegate Conference (TGWU)
CAC	Central Arbitration Committee
CBI	Confederation of British Industries
CFDT	French, formerly Christian, Trade Union Federation
CGIL	Italian Communist and Socialist Trade Union Federation
CGT	French Communist Trade Union Federation
CIA	Central Intelligence Agency
CIO	American Congress of Industrial Organisation
CPSU	Communist Party of the Soviet Union
CPUSA	Communist Party of the United States
EAT	Employment Appeal Tribunal
ECMT	European Committee for the Metal Trades
EEC	European Economic Community
EEF	Engineering Employers' Federation
EFTA	European Free Trade Association
ETUC	European Trades Union Confederation
FO	French Trade Union Federation
FTGB	Belgian Socialist Trade Union Federation
ICFTU	International Confederation of Free Trade Unions
IFTU	International Federation of Trade Unions
ILO	International Labour Organisation
ITS	International Trade Secretariat
IWC	Institute for Workers' Control
JCC	Joint Consultative Committee
JIC	Joint Industrial Committee
JRC	Joint Representation Committee
LO	Swedish Trade Union Federation
LRC	Labour Representation Committee
MDW	Measured Day Work
MSC	Manpower Services Commission

NEC	National Executive Committee (Labour Party)
NEDC	National Economic Development Council
NIC	National Incomes Commission
NIRC	National Industrial Relations Court
OECD	Organisation for Economic Co-operation and Development
ORIT	American Regional Labour Organisation
PBR	Payment by Results
QUANGO	Quasi-Autonomous National Governmental Organisation
RILU	Red International of Labour Unions
UAW	United Automobile Workers
ULCN	United Labour Congress of Nigeria
UMA	Union Membership Agreement
WEA	Workers' Educational Association
WFTU	World Federation of Trade Unions

Index of Trade Unions

*Alphabetisation follows the practice of the TUC. Initials of
organisations are listed so that readers can decode them.*

A

Actors' Equity Association, 56, 86
Agricultural and Allied Workers, National Union of (NUAAW), 87, 308, 313

ABS	*Broadcasting Staffs, Assoc. of*
ACTT	*Cinematograph, Television & Allied Technicians, Assoc. of*
AEU	*Engineering Union, Amalgamated*
APEX	*Professional, Executive, Clerical & Computer Staff, Assoc. of*
ASBSBSW	*Boilermakers, Shipwrights, Blacksmiths and Structural Workers, Amalgamated Soc. of*
ASE	*Engineers, Amalgamated Society of*
ASLEF	*Locomotive Engineers & Firemen, Assoc. Soc. of*
AScW	*Scientific Workers, Assoc. of*
ASSET	*Supervisory Staffs, Executives & Technicians, Assoc. of*
ASTMS	*Scientific, Technical & Managerial Staffs, Assoc. of*
AUEW	*Engineering Workers, Amalgamated Union of*
AUT	*University Teachers, Assoc. of*

B

Bakers and Allied Workers' Scottish Union, 308, 313
Bakers, Food and Allied Workers' Union, 308, 313
Bank Employees, Nat. Union of, 6, 87, 111
Birmingham and Midland Sheet Metal Workers, 54
Blastfurnacemen, Ore, Miners, Coke Workers and Kindred Trades, Nat. Union of, 309, 313
Blind and Disabled of Great Britain and Ireland, National League of, 309, 313
Boilermakers, Shipwrights, Blacksmiths and Structural Workers, Amalgamated Soc. of (ASBSBSW), 55, 86, 309, 313, 318
Boot and Shoe Operatives, Nat. Union of (NUBSO), 52, 82. See also Nat. Union of Footwear, Leather & Allied Trades (NUFLAT)
British Iron, Steel and Kindred Trades Association (BISAKTA), 73, 318. See also Iron and Steel Trades Federation
British Roll-turners Society, 50
Broadcasting Staffs, Association of (ABS), 51, 54, 280
Building Trade Workers, Amalgamated Union of, 70, 71

BACM	*Colliery Managers, Brit. Assoc. of*
BISAKTA	*British Iron, Steel & Kindred Trades Assoc.*

C

Cardiff, Penarth and Barry Coal Trimers' Association, 46, 59
Carpet Weavers and Textile Workers' Association, Power Loom, 309, 313
Carpet Weavers' Union, Scottish, 309, 313
Chemical Workers' Union, 55, 60
Cinematograph, Television and Allied Technicians, Assoc. of (ACTT), 51, 54, 309, 311, 313
Civil and Public Servants, Society of (SCPS), 51, 87
Civil and Public Services Assoc. (CPSA), 34, 36, 50, 51, 87
Civil Service Clerical Association, 36. See also Civil and Public Services Assoc.
Civil Service Union (CSU), 35, 50, 51
Clerical and Administrative Workers' Union (CAWU), 36. See also Professional, Executive, Clerical and Computer Staff (APEX)
Colliery Managers, British Assoc. of (BACM), 6, 28
Colliery Overmen, Deputies and Shotfirers, 6, 28, 309, 313
Confederation of Shipbuilding and Engineering Unions (CSEU), 45, 55, 162, 163, 191-5
Construction Allied Trades and Technicians, Union of (UCATT), 43, 44, 55, 88, 306, 309, 313, 320
Constructional Engineering Union, 43. See also Engineering Workers' Union, Constructional Section
Coopers' Federation of Great Britain, 55
Coppersmiths, 54
Council of Post Office Unions, 50, 53, 162
Court Officers' Association, 50

CAWU   *Clerical & Administrative Workers' Union*
COHSE   *Health Service Employees, Confederation of*
CSEU   *Confederation of Shipbuilding & Engineering Unions*
CPSA   *Civil & Public Services Assoc.*
CSU   *Civil Service Union*

D

Dock, Wharf, Riverside and General Labourers' Union, 29, 58
Domestic, Appliances and General Metal Workers, Nat. Union of, 309, 313
Draughtsmen's Association, 43, 315, 339. See also Engineers' Union, Technical, etc. section (AUEW/TASS)
Dyers, Bleachers and Textile Workers', Nat. Union of, 52, 74, 227, 209, 313

E

Electrical, Electronic, Telecommunications and Plumbing Union (EETPU), 43, 44, 55, 64, 75, 78, 88, 136, 137, 149, 162, 251, 306, 309, 311, 313, 314, 318, 320. See also Electrical Trades Union
Electrical Trades Union (ETU), 64, 70, 71, 80, 89, 91. See also Electrical, Electronic, Telecommunications and Plumbing Union (EETPU)
Engineering Union, Amalgamated (AEU), 43, 65-6, 70, 71, 85, 113, 189. See also Amalgamated Union of Engineers (AUEW)
Engineers, Amalgamated Society of (ASE), 36, 160. See also Amalgamated Union of Engineers (AUEW)

Engineers and Foundry Workers, Amalgamated (AEF), 55
Engineering Workers, Amalgamated Union of, 21, 34, 35, 36, 42, 43, 50, 54, 62, 74, 75, 76, 77, 80, 85, 86-7, 88, 89, 90, 91, 113, 136, 137, 148, 149, 150, 162, 227, 251, 275, 306, 318, 320, 322, 348
    Engineering Section, 55, 309, 313, 316. See also Amalgamated Engineering Union (AEU) and Amalgamated Society of Engineers (ASE)
    Constructional Section, 43, 55, 309, 313. See also Constructional Engineering Union
    Foundry Section, 21, 43, 55, 309, 313, 318. See also Foundry Workers' Union
    Technical, Administrative, Supervisory Section (TASS), 34, 43, 55, 263, 309, 313, 315, 316, 318. See also Draughtsmen's Union

EETPU   *Electrical, Electronic, Telecommunications & Plumbing Union*
ETU   *Electrical Trades Union*

F

Fire Brigades Union (FBU), 32, 51, 113, 309, 313
Fire Officers, National Association of, 51
Footwear, Leather and Allied Trades, Nat. Union of (NUFLAT), 52, 53, 82, 309, 313
Forfar Factory Workers' Union, 52
Foundry Workers' Union, 43. See also Engineering Workers' Union, Foundry Section
Funeral Service Operatives, Nat. Union of, 78
Furniture, Timber and Allied Trades Union, 309, 313
Furniture Trades Operatives, Nat. Union of, 78

FBU   *Fire Brigades Union*

G

Gasworkers and General Labourers of Great Britain & Ireland, 29
Gas Staffs' Association, 36, 51
General Federation of Trade Unions (GFTU), 94-5
General and Municipal Workers' Union (GMWU), 29, 30-31, 34, 35, 42, 43, 55, 62, 64-5, 70, 71, 74, 83, 86, 88, 89, 136, 141, 149, 161, 162, 205, 227, 306, 310, 313, 314, 316, 318, 320, 322
GLC Staff Association, 51 (GLC = Greater London Council)
Glovers and Leatherworkers, Nat. Union of, 52
Gold, Silver and Allied Trades, Nat. Union of, 310, 313
Government Supervisors and Radio Operators, Association of, 50
Grand National Consolidated Trade Union, 9, 94
Graphical and Allied Trades, Society of (SOGAT), 87, 280, 313
Graphical Association, National (NGA), 310, 313

GFTU   *General Federation of Trade Unions*
GMWU   *General & Municipal Workers' Union*

H

Health Service Employees Confederation of (COHSE), 53, 87, 310, 313, 314
Health Visitors' Association, 49
Heating and Domestic Engineers, 54

Hosiery and Knitwear Workers, Nat. Union of, 52–53
Huddersfield Healders and Twisters Trade and Friendly Society, 46

I

Inland Revenue Staff Federation, 34
Insurance Workers (Prudential Section), Nat. Union of, 310, 313
Irish Transport and General Workers' Union, 223
Iron and Steel Trades Confederation (ISTC), 34, 35, 53, 310, 313. See also British Iron, Steel and Kindred Trades Association (BISAKTA)

ISTC   Iron & Steel Trades Confederation

J

Journalists, Institute of, 53
Journalists, National Union of (NUJ), 53, 86, 87, 263, 280

L

Leather Workers' Society, 52
Leather Workers' Union, 52
Lithographic Artists, Designers, Engravers and Process Workers, Society of (SLADE), 86, 227, 310, 313, 314
Locomotive Engineers and Firemen, Assoc. Society of (ASLEF), 52, 310, 313
London Jewish Bakers, 46
Loom Overlookers, General Union of, 310, 313

M

Manchester and District Caretakers Assoc., 53
Medical Practitioners' Union, 56
Mercantile Marine Services Association, 53
Merchant Navy and Airline Officers' Assoc., 53
Metal Mechanics, Nat. Society of, 55, 310, 313
Miners' Federation of Great Britain (MFGB), 306. See also Nat. Union of Mineworkers
Mineworkers, Nat. Union of (NUM), 28, 37, 43, 44, 73, 74, 76–77, 85, 88, 205, 208, 238–239, 252, 306, 307, 310, 311, 313, 318, 322
Ministry of Labour Staff Assoc., 56
Musicians' Union, 87, 310, 313

MFGB   Miners' Federation of Great Britain

N

National Federation of Building Trades Operatives, 45
National and Local Government Officers' Assoc. (NALGO), 6, 34, 36, 43, 44, 51, 53, 70, 73, 74, 86, 87, 88, 112, 138, 321, 322
Northern Carpet Union, 52

NUAAW   *Agricultural & Allied Workers, Nat. Union of*
NALGO   *National and Local Government Officers' Assoc.*
NATHE   *Teachers in Higher Education, Nat. Assoc. of*
NATKE   *Theatrical, Television & Kine Employees, Nat. Assoc. of*
NATSOPA   *Printers, Graphical & Media Personnel, Nat. Soc. of Operative*
NGA   *Graphical Association, National*
NUBSO   *Boot & Shoe Operatives, Nat. Union of*
NUFLAT   *Footwear Leather & Allied Trades, Nat. Union of*
NUJ   *Journalists, Nat. Union of*
NUM   *Mineworkers, Nat. Union of*
NUPE   *Public Employees, Nat. Union of*
NUR   *Railwaymen, National Union of*
NUT   *Teachers, National Union of*
NUVB   *Vehicle Builders, Nat. Union of*

P

Patternmakers and Allied Craftsmen, Assoc. of, 310, 313
Plumbers' Trade Union, 44. See also Electrical, Electronic, Telecommunications and
    Plumbing Union (EETPU)
Post Office Engineers' Union (POEU), 263, 310, 313, 318, 325
Post Office Executives, Society of (SPOE), 87
Post Office Management Staff Association, 53
Post Office Workers, Nat. Union of (UPW), 40, 53, 208, 227, 228, 283, 306, 310, 311,
    313, 314
Printers, Graphical and Media Personnel, Nat. Society of Operative (NATSOPA), 310,
    313
Printing and Kindred Trades Federation, 46
Professional Civil Servants, Institute of, 6, 112
Professional, Executive, Clerical and Computer Staff, Assoc. of (APEX), 32, 34, 36, 51,
    87, 249, 259, 262, 283, 306, 310, 313, 318. See also Clerical and Administrative
    Workers' Union
Professional Footballers' Association (PFA), 49
Public Employees, Nat. Union of (NUPE), 28, 36, 42, 43, 44, 53, 66-67, 74, 83, 88, 89,
    99-100, 116, 137, 138, 148, 150, 158, 227, 306, 310, 313, 314, 321

PFA   *Professional Footballers' Association*
POEU   *Post Office Engineering Union*

R

Radio Officers' Union, 53
Railwaymen, Nat. Union of (NUR), 21, 28, 29, 34, 35, 43, 44, 52, 70, 74, 85, 235, 306,
    310, 313, 314, 318, 322
Railway Servants, Assoc. Society of, 268
Rossendale Boot, Shoe and Slipper Operatives Union, 52, 54, 309, 313

S

Saddleworth Weavers' Union, 52
Salt and General Workers' Union, 55
Scalemakers, Nat. Union of, 310, 313
Schoolmasters, Nat. Association of, 54
Schoolmasters/Nat. Assoc. of, Women Teachers, Union of, 54, 113
Scientific, Technical and Managerial Staffs, Assoc. of (ASTMS), 33-34, 43, 56-7, 86, 88, 262, 286, 306, 310, 313, 314, 318
Scientific Workers, Assoc. of (AScW), 44, 56. See also Assoc. of Scientific, Technical, and Managerial Staffs (ASTMS)
Scottish Commercial Motormen, 60, 318
Scottish Professional Footballers' Association, 55
Scottish Schoolmasters' Association, 54
Seamen, Nat. Union of (NUS), 51, 80-81, 310, 313, 318
Sheetmetal Workers, Coppersmiths, Heating and Domestic Engineers, Nat. Union of, 54, 55, 310, 313
Sheffield Sawmakers' Protection Society, 46
Sheffield Wool Shear Workers' Trade Union, 46
Shop, Distributive and Allied Workers, Union of (USDAW), 35, 36, 38, 42, 43, 62, 63, 64, 70, 74, 87, 88, 89, 113, 149, 306, 310, 313, 314, 316, 318
Supervisory Staffs, Executives and Technicians, Assoc. of, (ASSET), 44, 56. See also Assoc. of Scientific, Technical, and Managerial Staffs (ASTMS)

SCPS	*Society of Civil & Public Servants*
SLADE	*Lithographic Artists, Designers, Engravers & Process Workers, Society of*
SOGAT	*Graphical & Allied Trades, Soc. of*
SPOE	*Post Office Executives, Soc. of*

T

Tailors and Garment Workers', Nat. Union of, 37, 52, 310, 313
Teachers, National Union of (NUT), 16, 43, 44, 85-86, 88, 112, 315, 322
Teachers in Colleges and Depts. of Education, Association of, 50
Teachers in Further and Higher Education, Nat. Assoc. of (NATHE), 50, 87, 113
Teachers in Technical Institutions, Association of, 50
Textile Workers Union, Amalgamated, 52, 311, 313
Textile Workers and Kindred Trades, Amalgamated Society of, 310, 313
Theatrical, Television and Kine Employees, Nat. Association of (NATTKE), 51, 311, 313
Tobacco Workers' Union, 311, 313
Transport and General Workers' Union (TGWU), 8, 15, 21, 29, 30-31, 34, 35, 36, 42, 43, 48, 51, 58-60, 62, 65, 70, 71, 72, 73, 74, 82, 83, 84, 85, 86, 87, 88, 89, 90, 97, 98, 99, 113, 117, 139, 149, 154, 161, 162, 190, 205, 206, 227, 244, 248, 251, 259, 261, 262, 275, 283, 306, 311, 313, 314, 316, 318, 320, 321, 322, 348
Transport Salaried Staffs Association (TSSA), 34, 52, 74, 306, 311, 313, 318

TGWU	*Transport and General Workers' Union*
TSSA	*Transport Salaried Staffs Association*

U

Ulster Transport Union, 55
United Trades for the Protection of Labour, Association of, 94
University Teachers, Assoc. of (AUT), 6, 112

UCATT	*Construction Allied Trades & Technicians, Union of*
UPW	*Post Office Workers, Union of*
USDAW	*Shop, Distributive & Allied Workers, Union of*

V

Variety Artists Federation, 50
Vehicle Builders, National Union of (NUVB), 55, 60

W

Wallcoverings, Decorative and Allied Trades, Nat. Union of, 311, 313
Waterworks Employees, Union of, 55
Weavers, Amalgamated Assoc. of, 74
Woolsorters Society, National, 311, 313
Women Teachers, Union of, 54
Workers' Union, 135

Bibliographical Index

I *BOOKS AND PAMPHLETS*

Agee, Philip., *Inside the Company–CIA Diary*, Penguin, 1975. p. 353.

Allen, V. L., *Power in Trade Unions*, Longmans, 1954. pp. 79, 90, 91.

Allen, V. L., *Trade Union Militancy*, Merlin Press, 1966. p. 229.

Allen, V. L., *The Sociology of Industrial Relations*, Longmans, 1971. pp. 23, 122.

Anderson, P. and Blackburn, R., *Towards Socialism*, Fontana, 1964. p. 327.

Arnison, J., *The Million Pound Strike*, Lawrence and Wishart, 1970. p. 231.

Barratt Brown, Michael, *From Labourism to Socialism*, Spokesman, 1972. pp. 12, 23.

Barratt Brown, Michael, 'Working Class Internationalism', in Coates, Ken and Single-ton, F. B. (Eds), *The Just Society*, Spokesman, 1977. p. 354

Barratt Brown, Michael, 'The Growth and Distribution of the National Income', in Coates, Ken., (ed.) *What Went Wrong* Spokesman, 1979. p. 190.

Barratt Brown, M., Coates, K., Fleet, K. and Hughes, J., *Full Employment*, Spokesman, 1978. pp. 23, 327.

Batstone, E., Boraston, I. and Frenkel, S., *Shop Stewards in Action*, Blackwell, 1977. pp. 155, 156.

Batstone, E., Boraston, I. and Frenkel, S., *The Social Organisation of Strikes*, Blackwell, 1978 p. 229.

BBC, *Democracy at Work: Trade Union Studies*. p. 90.

Beck, Tony, *The Fine Tubes Strike*, Stage 1, 1974. p. 231.

Beynon, Huw, *Working for Ford*, Penguin, 1973. pp. 156, 189.

Blackburn, R. M., *Union Character and Social Class*, Batsford, 1967. pp. 5–6, 23.

Bodington, Steve., *Computers and Socialism*, Spokesman, 1973. p. 263.

Bonety, R., et. al., *La CFDT*, Seuil, Paris, 1971. p. 327.

Boraston, I., Clegg, H. A. and Rimmer, M., *Workplace and Union*, Heinemann, 1975. p. 156.

Brannen, P., Batstone, E., Fatchett, D., and White, P., *The Worker Directors*, Hutchinson, 1976. p. 262.

Bristol Aircraft Workers, *A New Approach to Public Ownership*, IWC Pamphlet no. 43, 1974. p. 262.

Butler, D. and Kavanagh, D., *The British General Election of October 1974*, Macmillan, 1975. pp. 327, 328.

Bye, Basil and Doyle, Mel., *European Trade Union Co-operation*, WEA, n.d. p. 354.

Carew, Anthony, *Democracy and Government in European Trade Unions*, Allen and Unwin, 1976. p. 327.

Citrine, Lord, *Two Careers*, Hutchinson, 1967. pp. 335, 353.

Citrine, N. A., *Trade Union Law*, Stevens, 1950. p. 23.

Clegg, H. A., *The System of Industrial Relations in Great Britain*, Blackwell, 1970. pp. 37, 38, 39, 48, 122, 154, 230.

Clegg, H. A., *The Changing System of Industrial Relations in Great Britain*, Blackwell, 1979. p. 123.

Clegg, H. A. and Adams, R., *The Employers' Challenge*, Blackwell, 1957. p. 230.

Clegg, H. A., Fox, A. and Thompson, E. F., *A History of British Trade Unions since 1889: Vol. 1, 1889–1910*, Clarendon, 1964. p. 154.

Clegg, H. A., Killick, A. J. and Adams, R., *Trade Union Officers*, Blackwell, 1960. pp. 90, 154.

Clements, Richard, *Glory Without Power*, Barker, 1959. p. 122.

Coates, Ken, *The Crisis of British Socialism*, Spokesman, 1971. p. 328.

Coates, Ken, *Democracy in the Labour Party*, Spokesman, 1977. p. 328.

Coates, Ken, *Work-ins, Sit-ins and Industrial Democracy*, Spokesman, 1980, pp. 23, 261.

Coates, Ken, (ed.) *A Trade Union Strategy in the Common Market*, (Programme of the Belgian FGTB), Spokesman, 1971. pp. 126, 127, 327.

Coates, Ken, (ed.) 'What Happened at Leeds', in *British Labour and the Russian Revolution*, Spokesman, 1972. p. 261.

Coates, Ken, (ed.) *The New Worker Co-operatives*, Spokesman for IWC, 1976. pp. 23, 262.

Coates, Ken, (ed.) *The Right to Useful Work*, Spokesman, 1978. pp. 156, 261.

Coates, Ken and Topham, Tony, *Workers' Control*, Panther, 1970. pp. 21, 24.

Coates, Ken and Topham, Tony, *The New Unionism*, Penguin, 1974. pp. 231, 261, 327.

Coates, Ken and Topham, Tony, *Industrial Democracy in Great Britain*, Vols. 1–4, Spokesman, 1975. pp. 24, 189, 261.

Coates, Ken and Topham, Tony, *A Shop Stewards' Guide to the Bullock Report*, Spokesman, 1977. p. 262.

Cole, G. D. H. and Mellor, W., *The Meaning of Industrial Freedom*, Allen and Unwin, n.d. p. 235.

Cole, G. D. H., *British Trade Unionism: Problems and Policy*, Labour Research Department, 1925. pp. 61–62, 89.

Conboy, Bill, *Pay at Work*, Arrow in association with the Society of Industrial Tutors, 1976. p. 189.

Connolly, James, *Socialism Made Easy*, Irish TGWU various dates, p. 233.

Cooley, Mike, 'Design, Technology and Production for Social Needs' in Coates, Ken (ed.) *The Right to Useful Work*, Spokesman, 1978. p. 262.

The Conservative Party, *The Right to Approach*, October, 1976. pp. 75, 90.

Counter-Information Services, *Report: The New Technology*, Anti-Report no. 23, 1979. p. 263.

Coventry Workshop, *Crisis in Engineering: Machine Tool Workers Fight for Jobs*, IWC, June, 1979. p. 156.

Daniel, W., *Wage Determination in Industry*, PEP, 1976. p. 155.

De Tocqueville, Alexis, *Journeys to England and Ireland* (ed. J. P. Mayer) Faber, 1958. p. 24.

De Tocqueville, Alexis, *Democracy in America (1835)*, OUP, Worlds Classics, 1946 pp. 17, 24.

Docks Workers' Control Group, *The Dockers Next Step*, IWC pamphlet no. 12, 1969. p. 262.

Drulovic, Milojko, *Self-management on Trial*, Spokesman, 1978. pp. 229, 261.

Durkin, Tom, *Grunwick: Bravery and Betrayal*, Brent Trades Council, 1978. pp. 231, 291.

Edelstein, J. D. and Warner, M., *Comparative Union Democracy*, Allen and Unwin, 1975. pp. 79, 90, 91.

Eldridge, J. E. T., *Industrial Disputes*, Routledge and Kegan Paul, 1968. p. 229.

Elliott, John, *Conflict or Co-operation*, Kogan Page, 1978. p. 262.

Evans, E. W. and Creigh, S., *Industrial Conflict in Britain*, Frank Cass, 1977. pp. 201, 229.

Flanders, Allan, *Trade Unions*, Hutchinson, 1957. pp. 260, 261.

Fletcher, Richard, 'Trade Union Democracy—Structural Factors', in *Trade Union Register, 2*, Spokesman, 1970. pp. 81, 91, 92–3.

Fletcher, Richard, 'Trade Union Democracy: The Case of the AUEW Rule Book', in *Trade Union Register 3*, Spokesman, 1973. pp. 78, 90, 91.

Fletcher, Richard, *CIA and the Labour Movement*, Spokesman, 1977. p. 353.

Florence, P. Sargant, *The Logic of British and American Industry*, Routledge, 1953. p. 262.

Forester, Tom, 'The Neutralisation of the Industrial Strategy' in Coates, Ken (ed.) *What Went Wrong* Spokesman, 1979. p. 262.

Fox, Alan, 'The Social Origins of Present Forms and Methods in Britain and Germany', in *Industrial Democracy: International Views*, SSRC, 1978. p. 189.

Fraser, Ronald, *Work vols. 1 and 2*, Penguin Books, 1968, 1969. pp. 24, 261.

Friedman, Henry, *Multi-Plant Working and Trade Union Organisation*, WEA, 1976. p. 156.

Fryer, R. H., *Redundancy, Values and Public Policy*, Warwick University, November, 1972. p. 291.

Fryer, Bob, Fairclough, Andy and Manson, Tom, *Organisation and Change in the National Union of Public Employees*, University of Warwick, 1974. pp. 66-7, 89.

Gardner, Jim, *Key Questions for Trade Unionists*, Lawrence and Wishart, 1960. p. 89.

Gennard, John, *Multi-nationals: Industrial Relations and the Trade Union Response*, Occasional Papers in Industrial Relations, Universities of Leeds and Nottingham, 1976. p. 354.

Gennard, John, *Financing Strikers*, Macmillan, 1977. p. 231.

Gill, C., Morris, R. and Eaton, J., *Industrial Relations in the Chemical Industry*, Saxon House, 1978. p. 190.

Goldstein, J., *The Government of British Trade Unions*, Allen and Unwin, 1952. p. 89.

Goldthorpe, J. H., et. al., *The Affluent Worker*, CUP, 1968-69. p. 89.

Goodman, J. E. B. and Whittingham, T., *Shop Stewards in British Industry*, McGraw-Hill, 1969. p. 155.

Gorz, André, *The Division of Labour*, Harvester Press, 1976. p. 24.

Gowan, Doug., 'The Bargaining System' in *Industrial Studies 2: The Bargaining Context*, ed. E. Coker and G. Stuttard, Arrow in association with the Society of Industrial Tutors, 1976. p. 189.

Graubard, S. R., *British Labour and the Russian Revolution*, OUP, 1956. p. 261.

Harrison, Martin, *Trade Unions and the Labour Party*, Macmillan, 1960. p. 327.

Harman, Chris, *Is a Machine After Your Job? New Technology and the Struggle for Socialism*, Socialist Workers' Party, 1979. p. 263.

Hawkins, Kevin, *The Management of Industrial Relations*, Pelican, 1978. p. 291.

Heath, R. H., 'The National Power Loading Agreement in the Coal Industry and Some Aspects of Workers' Control', in *Trade Union Register, 1969*, Merlin Press, 1969. p. 230.

Hemingway, J., *Conflict and Democracy: Studies in Trade Union Government*, OUP, 1978. pp. 81, 91, 229.

Hirsch, Fred, *CIA and the Labour Movement*, Spokesman, 1977. p. 353.

Holland, Stuart, *Strategy for Socialism*, Spokesman, 1975. p. 11, 23.

Holton, Bob, *British Syndicalism*, Pluto Press, 1977. p. 231.

Hughes, John, *Trade Union Structure and Government, Part 1*, Donovan Commission Research Paper no. 5, HMSO, 1967. pp. 36, 42, 48.

Hughes, John and Moore, Roy, *A Special Case?*, Penguin, 1972. p. 230.

Hunter, R., *The Road to Brighton Pier*, Arthur Barker, 1959. p. 91.

Hyman, Richard, *Marxism and the Sociology of Trade Unionism*, Pluto Press, 1971. p. 90.

Hyman, Richard, *Disputes Procedure in Action*, Heinemann, 1972. p. 190.

Hyman, Richard, *Industrial Relations—A Marxist Introduction*, Macmillan, 1975. pp. 19, 24.

Hyman, Richard, *Strikes*, Fontana, 2nd edition, 1977. p. 229.

Ingham, G. K., *Strikes and Industrial Conflict*, Macmillan, 1974. pp. 229, 230.

IWC Motors Group, *A Workers' Inquiry into the Motor Industry*, CSE, 1978. p. 156.

IWC, *Why Imperial Typewriters Must Not Close*, IWC pamphlet, no. 46, 1975. p. 354.

Jackson, M. P., *Industrial Relations*, Croom Helm, 1977. pp. 228, 231.

Jagan, Cheddi, *The West on Trial*, Michael Joseph, 1966. p. 353.

Jeffreys, J. B., *The Story of the Engineers: 1800–1945*, AEU, 1945. p. 189.

Jenkins, Clive and Mortimer, J. E., *The Kind of Laws the Unions Ought to Want*, Pergamon, 1968. p. 291.

Jenkins, Clive and Sherman, Barrie, *The Collapse of Work*, Eyre Methuen, 1979. p. 263.

Jenkins, Mark, *Bevanism: Labour's High Tide*, Spokesman, 1979. pp. 91, 327.

Job Ownership Ltd., *Co-operative Possibilities for Times Newspapers Ltd.*, February, 1979. p. 263.

Jones, R., Halstead, J. and Barratt Brown, M., (Unpublished) *Report on Sheffield Engineering Shop Stewards 1977*. pp. 154, 155.

Kahn-Freund, Otto, *Labour and the Law*, Stevens, 1972, 2nd edition, 1977. pp. 24, 290, 291.

Kerr, Clark and Siegel, A., 'The Inter Industry Propensity to Strike—an International Comparison', in Kornhauser, A., Dubin, R. and Ross, A., (eds.), *Industrial Conflict*, McGraw-Hill, 1954. p. 230.

Knowles, K. G. J. C., *Strikes: A Study in Industrial Conflict*, Blackwell, 1952. pp. 196, 228, 229.

Knowles, K. G. J. C., 'Strike Proneness and its Determinants' in Galenson, W. and Wiley, S. M., (eds.), *Labour and Trade Unionism*, Wiley, 1960. p. 230.

Labour Party, *Report of 45th Annual Conference* 1946, p. 327.

Lane, T. and Roberts, K., *Strike at Pilkingtons*, Fontana, 1971. p. 230.

Leeson, R. A., (ed.), *Strike: A Live History 1887–1971*, Allen and Unwin, 1973. p. 229.

Lerner, Shirley, *Breakaway Unions and the Small Trade Union*, Allen and Unwin, 1961. p. 353.

Lucas Shop Stewards Committee, *Lucas, an Alternative Plan*, IWC, 1977. pp. 190, 262.

Marchietti, V. and Marks, J. D., *The CIA and the Cult of Intelligence*, Jonathan Cape, 1974. p. 353.

Marglin, Stephen, 'What do Bosses Do?' in Gorz, A: *The Division of Labour*, Harvester, 1976. p. 24.

Marsh, Arthur, *Trade Union Handbook*, Gower Press, 1979. p. 48.

Marsh, A. I., Evans, E. O. and Garcia, P., *Workplace Industrial Relations in Engineering*, Research Paper 4, Engineering Employers' Federation, 1971. p. 229.

Marsh, A. I. and McCarthy, W. E. J., *Disputes Procedures in British Industry*, Research Paper no. 2, Part 2, Donovan Royal Commission, HMSO, 1966. p. 229.

Marx, Karl, *Capital*, pp. 10, 23, 190.

McAuley, Mary, *Labour Disputes in Soviet Russia, 1957–65*, Clarendon, 1969. p. 229.

McCarthy, W. E. J., *The Role of Shop Stewards in British Industrial Relations*, Research Paper no. 1, Donovan Royal Commission, HMSO, 1966. pp. 154, 155.

McCarthy, W. E. J. and Parker, S. R., *Shop Stewards and Workplace Relations*, Research Paper no. 10, Donovan Royal Commission, HMSO, 1968. pp. 154, 156.

McKenzie, R. T., *British Political Parties*, Heinemann, 1955. p. 327.

McMullen, Jeremy, *Rights at Work*, Pluto Press, 1978. p. 290.

Minkin, Lewis, *The Labour Party Conference*, Allen Lane, 1978. p. 327.

Michels, Roberto, *Political Parties*, Constable/Dover, 1950. pp. 69, 90.

Milne-Bailey, W., *Trade Union Documents*, Bell, 1929. pp. 24, 327.

Morrison, Herbert, *Socialisation and Transport*, Constable, 1933. p. 261.

Muller, W. D., *The Kept Man*, Harvester, 1977. p. 327.

O'Higgins, Paul *Workers' Rights*, Arrow in association with the Society of Industrial Tutors, 1976. pp. 290, 291.

Parker, S. R., *Workplace Industrial Relations*, 1972, HMSO, 1974. p. 154.

Parsons, Talcott, 'Communism and the West' in *Social Change* (eds. A. and E. Etzioni) Glencoe, Ill, 1964. pp. 196, 229.

Partridge, B., *Towards an Action Theory of Workplace Industrial Relations*, Aston University Management Centre, Working Paper No. 50, 1976. p. 155.

Passingham, Bernie and Connor, Danny, *Ford Shop Stewards on Industrial Democracy*, IWC pamphlet no. 54, 1977. p. 156.

C. A. Parsons Shop Stewards Committee, 1) 'C. A. Parsons Unions Explain' IWC *Bulletin*, 1977, no. 36, 2) 'An Alternative Strategy for Power Engineering' IWC *Bulletin*, New Series, 1978, no. 1. p. 261.

Pearce, Brian, *Some Rank-and-File Movements*, Labour Review, 1959. p. 90.

PEP, *British Trade Unionism*, 1948. p. 89.

Postgate, Raymond, *The Bolshevik Theory*, Grant Richards, 1920. p. 261.

Ralph, C., *The Picket and the Law*, Fabian Research Series no. 331, 1977. p. 291.

Roberts, B. C., *Trade Union Government and Administration in Great Britain*, Bell, 1956. pp. 89, 90, 91.

Roberts, B. C., *The Trades Union Congress 1868-1921*, Allen and Unwin, 1958, p. 122.

Rolph, C. H., *All Those in Favour—The ETU Trial*, Andre Deutsch, 1962. p. 91.

Ross, A. M. and Hartman, P. T., *Changing Patterns of Industrial Conflict*, Wiley, 1960. p. 230.

Sayles, L. R., *Behaviour of Industrial Workgroups: Prediction and Control*, Chapman and Hall, 1958. p. 155.

Singleton, Norman, *Industrial Relations Procedures*, Department of Employment Manpower Papers no. 14, HMSO, 1975. p. 190.

Smith, Adam, *The Wealth of Nations*, (1776) Everyman Library, pp. 4-5, 17, 23.

Somerton, M. F., 'The Proposals for Changes in the Engineering Procedural Agreement', *Trade Union Register*, 2, Spokesman, 1970. p. 195.

Somerton, M. F., *Trade Unions and Industrial Relations in Local Government*, WEA, 1978, p. 154.

Spokesman, *The Pike Report*, 1977. p. 353.

Stewart, Margaret, *Protest or Power?* Allen and Unwin, 1974. p. 327.

Sweet, T. G. and Jackson, D., *The World Strike Wave 1969-7?* Aston University Management Centre; Working paper series no. 63, 1977. p. 230.

Taylor, Robert, *The Fifth Estate—Britain's Unions in the Seventies*, Routledge and Kegan Paul, 1978. pp. 89, 90, 123, 154.

Turner, H. A., *Trade Union Growth, Structure and Policy*, Allen and Unwin, 1962. pp. 35, 48.

Turner, H. A., *The Trend of Strikes*, Leeds University Press, 1963. pp. 230, 231.

Turner, H. A., *Is Britain Really Strike Prone?* CUP, 1969. p. 229.

Turner, H. A., Clack, G. and Roberts, G., *Labour Relations in the Motor Industry*, Allen and Unwin, 1967. pp. 155, 229.

Turner, H. A., Roberts, G. and Roberts, D., *Management Characteristics and Labour Conflict*, CUP, 1977, p. 231.

Taylor, Mike, 'The Machine-Minder' in Fraser, R., (ed.) *Work 2*, Penguin, 1969. p. 231.

Thomson, Don and Larson, Rodney, *Where Were You Brothers?* War on Want, 1978. p. 353.

Topham, Tony, 'New Types of Bargaining' in *The Incompatibles: Trade Union Militancy and the Consensus*, Penguin, 1967. p. 189.

Topham, Tony, *The Organised Worker*, Arrow in association with the Society of Industrial Tutors, 1975. pp. 189, 190.

Urwin, Harry, *Plant and Productivity Bargaining*, TGWU, 3rd edition, 1972. p. 190.

Vickers National Combine Shop Stewards Committee, 1) *Building the Chieftain Tank and the Alternative*, 1978, 2) *Alternative Employment for Naval Shipbuilding Workers*, 1978, 3) *Economic Audit on Vickers Scotswood*, 1979. p. 261.

Webb, S. and B., *History of Trade Unionism*, London, 1894, WEA edition, 1920. pp. 1, 23, 89.

Webb, S. and B., *Industrial Democracy*, (1897), 1913 edition WEA, 1926 edition, Longman Greeen. pp. 46-47, 48, 157, 189, 190, 260.

Westergaard, John and Resler, Henrietta, *Class in a Capitalist Society*, Pelican, 1976. p. 291.

Wedderburn, K. W., *The Worker and the Law*, Penguin, 1965. p. 291.

Weiner, Norbert, *The Human Use of Human Beings*, Boston, 1950. p. 24.

Wells, H. G., *The Time Machine*, pp. 18, 24.

Wigham, E., *Strikes and the Government 1893-1974*, Macmillan, 1976. p. 230.

II *ARTICLES FROM JOURNALS*

Anderson, P., 'The Antinomies of Antonio Gramsci' *New Left Review*, no. 100. p. 327.

Brown, W., 'A Consideration of Custom and Practice', *British Journal of Industrial Relations*, vol. X, no. 1, March 1972. p. 155.

Brown, W., Ebsworth, R. and Terry, M., 'Factors Shaping Shop Steward Organisation in Britain', *British Journal of Industrial Relations*, vol. XVI, no. 2, July 1978. pp. 154, 155, 156.

Brown, W. and Terry, M., 'The Future of Collective Bargaining', *New Society*, 23rd March, 1978. pp. 155, 156, 189.

Child, J., Loveridge, M. and Warner, M., 'Towards an Organisational Study of Trade Unions', *Sociology*, vol. 7, no. 1. p. 24.

Daniel, W. W., 'The Effects of Employment Protection Law in Manufacturing Industry', *Department of Employment Gazette*, June, 1978. p. 291.

Durcan, J. W. and McCarthy, W. E. J., 'The State Subsidy Theory of Strikes: an Examination of the Statistical Data for the Period 1956-70', *British Journal of Industrial Relations*, vol. XII, no. 1, March, 1974. p. 231.

Elliott, R. and Steele, R., 'The Importance of National Wage Agreements', *British Journal of Industrial Relations*, vol. XIV, no. 1, 1976. p. 189.

Forester, Tom, 'How Labour's Industrial Policy Got the Chop' *New Society*, vol. 45. No. 822. p. 328.

Gennard, J. and Lasko, R. J., 'The Individual and the Strike', *British Journal of Industrial Relations*, vol. XIII, No. 3, November 1975. p. 231.

Goodman, J. F. B., 'Strikes in the UK' in *International Labour Review*, vol. 95, 1967. p. 230.

Hughes, John, 'The Rise of the Militants', in *Trade Union Affairs No. 1*, 1960-61. p. 231.

Hunter, L. C., 'The State Subsidy Theory of Strikes: A Reconsideration' in *British Journal of Industrial Relations*, vol. XII, No. 3, November, 1974. p. 231.

Hyman, Richard, 'The Politics of Workplace Trade Unionism: Recent Tendencies and Some Problems for Theory', in *Capital and Class*, vol. 8, Summer 1979. p. 156.

Incomes Data Services, *Focus*, July, 1976. p. 189.

Incomes Data Service, *International Report, 95*, April, 1979, p. 190.

IWC, 'Chrysler: The Workers Answer', *Workers Control Bulletin*, no. 32, May-June, 1976. p. 262.

IWC, *Workers Control Bulletin*, no. 37, 1977. p. 262.

Institute for Workers Control, *Workers Control Bulletin—new series*, nos. 3 and 4, 1979. p. 90.

Knee, Fred, 'The Revolt of Labour', *Social Democrat, 1910*. p. 157, 189.

Knight, K. G., 'Strikes and Wage Inflation in British Manufacturing Industry 1950-68' in *Bulletin of the Oxford Institute of Economics and Statistics*, vol. 34, 1972. p. 229.

Lewis, Roy, 'The Historical Development of Labour Law', in *British Journal of Industrial Relations*, vol. XIV, no. 1. March 1976. p. 290.

Linton, Martin, 'Together We Stand', *Labour Weekly*, 8th June, 1979. p. 314, 328.

LRD, 'Micro-Electronics: the Trade Union Response', *Labour Research*, June 1979. pp. 178, 190.

McCarthy, W. E. J., 'The Nature of Britain's Strike Problem' in *British Journal of Industrial Relations*, vol. VIII, 1970, p. 229.

Nicholson, N., 'The Role of the Shop Steward: An Empirical Case Study' in *Industrial Relations Journal*, vol. 7, no. 1, 1976. pp. 154, 155.

Nicholson, N. and Ursell, G., 'The NALGO Activists' in *New Society*, 15 December, 1977. p. 154.

Partridge, B., 'The Activities of Shop Stewards' in *Industrial Relations Journal*, vol. 8, no. 4, 1977-8. p. 155.

Rideout, R. W., 'The Content of Trade Union Disciplinary Rules', in *British Journal of Industrial Relations*, vol. 3, 1965. pp. 78, 90.

Roberts, B. C. and Liebhaberg, Bruno, 'The European Trade Union Confederation: Influence of Regionalism, Detente and Multi-nationals', in *British Journal of Industrial Relations*, vol. XIV, no. 3. November, 1976. p. 354.

Sunday Times, 'The Truth About Britain's Strikes', 29 October 1978, and 'The Awful Truth About Strife in our Factories', 12 November, 1978. p. 229.

Silver, M., 'Recent British Strike Trends: A Factual Analysis' in *British Journal of Industrial Relations*, vol. XI, no. 1, 1973. p. 229.

Scargill, Arthur, 'The Case Against Workers' Control', in *Workers Control*, Bulletin of IWC, no. 37. p. 261.

Sullivan, Terry, 'Is There a Cycle in Labour Law?', in *The Law Teacher*, April, 1977. p. 290.

Sullivan, Terry, 'Some Comments on Current Labour Law' in *Personnel Review*, vol. 7, no. 1, 1978. p. 291.

Sullivan, Terry, 'Collective Bargaining and Disclosure of Information: A View from Labour Economics', *Personnel Review*, vol. 7, no. 3, Summer, 1978. p. 291.

Thomson, W. J., Mulvey, C. and Farbman, M., 'Bargaining Structure and Relative Earnings in Great Britain', *British Journal of Industrial Relations*, July, 1977. pp. 189, 190.

Turner, H. A., 'Trade Union Structure: A New Approach' in *British Journal of Industrial Relations*, vol. II, no. 2, July, 1964. p. 48.

Undy, Roger, 'The Devolution of Bargaining Levels and Responsibilities in the TGWU, 1965-75', in *Industrial Relations Journal*, vol. 9, no. 3. pp. 84, 90, 91.

Wilders, M. G. and Parker, S. R., 'Changes in Workplace Industrial Relations 1966-72 in *British Journal of Industrial Relations*, vol. 13, 1975. p. 154.

Winch, Graham, 'Shop Steward Turnover and Workplace Relations', in *Industrial Relations Journal* (forthcoming). p. 155.

Windmiller, J. F., 'Re-alignments in the ICFTU: The Impact of Detente,' in *British Journal of Industrial Relations*, vol. XIV, no. 3, November, 1976. pp. 353, 354.

Wintour, Patrick, 'The TUC's Foreign Policy', in *New Statesman*, 2 March, 1979. p. 353.

III *OFFICIAL REPORTS*

ACAS, *Annual Reports*, 1978 and 1979, HMSO. p. 190.

Bullock, Lord, (Chairman), *Report of the Committee of Inquiry on Industrial Democracy*, HMSO, Cmnd., 6706, January, 1977. pp. 12, 23, 262.

Certification Officer, *Annual Report*, 1977. pp. 314, 328.

Devlin, Lord, (Chairman), *Final Report of the Committee of Inquiry under the Rt. Hon. Lord Devlin into Certain Matters Concerning the Port Transport Industry*, HMSO, Cmnd. 2734, August, 1965. p. 48.

Donovan, Lord, (Chairman) *Report of the Royal Commission on Trade Unions and Employers Association*, HMSO, Cmnd. 3623, 1968. pp. 2, 23, 189, 230, 291.

HMSO, *The Regeneration of British Industry*, (White Paper) HMSO, August, 1974. p. 246.

HMSO White Papers on Incomes Policy, 1) Cmnd. 5125, November 1972; 2) Cmnd. 5205, 5206, January, 1973; 3) Cmnd. 5267, March, 1973; 4) Cmnd. 5444, and 5446, October, 1973; 5) Cmnd. 6151, July, 1975; 6) Cmnd. 6507, July, 1976; 7) Cmnd. 6882, July, 1977; 8) Cmnd. 7293, July, 1978. p. 190.

HMSO, *Industrial Democracy*, Cmnd. 7231, May 1978. pp. 107, 123.

Labour, Ministry of, *Industrial Relations Handbook*, HMSO, 1964. p. 189.

Labour, Ministry of, *Written Evidence* to the Donovan Royal Commission, HMSO, 1965. pp. 189, 190.

Nigerian Ministry of Information, *Report of the Tribunal of Inquiry into the Trade Unions*, 1977. p. 353.

Registrar of Friendly Societies, *Report*, 1974. p. 328.

IV *TRADE UNION PUBLICATIONS*

AEF, *Structure and Functions of the Union*, 1969. p. 90.

AEU, *Trade Unions and the Contemporary Scene*, (evidence to the Royal Commission on Trade Unions and Employers' Associations), 1965. pp. 65–66, 89.

APEX, *Office Technology; the Trade Union Response*, 1979. p. 262.

ASTMS, *Discussion Document: Technological Change and Collective Bargaining*, 1979. p. 262.

AUEW/TASS, *Computer Technology and Employment*, 1978. p. 263.

DATA, *Evidence to the Royal Commission on Trade Unions and Employers Associations*, 1965. p. 328.

ETU, *Submission of Evidence to the Royal Commission on Trade Unions and Employers Associations*, pp. 64, 89.

GMWU, *The General and Municipal Workers' Union—Its History, Structure, Policy, Benefits and Services*, GMWU, 1975. pp. 64–5, 89.

ICFTU, *Economic and Social Bulletin*, vol. XXVII, no. 1, Jan–Mar. 1979. p. 354.

NUJ, *Journalists and New Technology*, 1978. p. 263.

POEU, *The Modernisation of Telecommunications*, 1979. p. 263.

TGWU, *Training Manual*, TGWU, 1960. pp. 65, 89.

TGWU, *Minutes of Evidence to the Donovan Commission*, 1966. pp. 8, 23.

TGWU, *A Positive Employment Programme for ICI*, TGWU, 1971. p. 261.

TGWU, *Report and Balance Sheet*, 1972. p. 48.

TGWU, *The Ford Wage Claim*, TGWU, 1977. p. 190.

TGWU, *Micro-Electronics: New Technology, Old Problems, New Opportunities*, 1979. p. 262.

TGWU, *Record*, July, 1979. p. 262.

TUC, *Free Trade Unions Leave the WFTU*, TUC, 1949. p. 353.

TUC, *Annual Reports*, various years.

TUC, *Trade Unionism*, TUC, 1966. pp. 3–4, 23, 189, 291.

TUC, *Post-Donovan Conferences: Collective Bargaining and Trade Union Development in the Private Sector*, TUC, 1969. p. 190.

TUC, *Good Industrial Relations: A Guide for Negotiators*, TUC, 1971. pp. 154, 190.

TUC, *Industrial Democracy*, TUC, 1974, (2nd edition, 1977, 3rd and revised edition, 1979). pp. 190. 262.

TUC, *Collective Bargaining and the Social Contract*, TUC, June, 1974. p. 190.

TUC, *Economic Review 1979*, TUC, 1979. p. 190.
TUC, *Employment and Technology*, 1979. pp. 190, 263.
USDAW, *Introducing USDAW, The Structure Government and Administration of the Union*, USDAW, 1972. pp. 62-3, 89.

General Index

Advisory, Conciliation and Arbitration Service (ACAS), 105, 109, 125, 126, 177, 178-80, 269, 277, 279, 282, 283, 286, 288, 349
Affiliation fees (Labour Party), 308-16
Affiliation fees (TUC), 122
Agreements, types of, 165
Alienation, 17, 61, 197
Allen, Lord, 115, 126, 127
Allen, V. L., 79, 122, 123
Allowances, 167
Alternative corporate plans, 172, 246-9
Amalgamation, 42, 45, 49, 320
Anderson, Perry, 303
Annual Economic Review (TUC), 100
Arbitration and Conciliation, 177
Arbitrators, single, 179
Arkwright, Richard, 22

Baldwin, Stanley, 180
Baker, F. A., 115, 127
Ballots, 75, 290, 300
Ballot-rigging, 80
Bank employees, 6
Banks, 11
Barratt Brown, Michael, 351
Basnett, David, 115, 127
Batstone, Eric, 143
Beaverbrook Newspapers v Keys, 280
Belgium, 38-hour week, 172
Benn, Tony, 120, 336
Betteshanger Colliery, 204
Bevin, Ernest, 97, 204
Birch, Reg, 115, 127
Block vote, 32, 319-22
Boddy, J. R., 115, 127
Boilermakers, 234
The Boilermaker, 86
Bonuses, shift, 167
Booth, Albert, 255
Boyd, John, 87, 115, 128
Bradley, J. J. W., 67

Bramley, Fred, 122
Branches, 62
Bridlington agreement, 37, 116
British Aircraft Corporation (BAC), 255
British Broadcasting Corporation (BBC) v Hearn, 279-80
British Leyland, 148, 151-2
Broadridge, S. R., 113, 115
Brown, Irving, 337
Brown, J., 115
Buckton, Ray, 115, 128
Buggins Law, 79
Bullock Report, 14-16, 105, 145, 168, 171, 249-57
'Bus strike, London, 97, 206

Carter, D. T., 115
Casey, T. A., 113
Central Arbitration Committee (CAC), 110, 177, 179, 270, 279, 284
Central Intelligence Agency (CIA), 336
Centre for Alternative Industrial and Technological Systems (CAITS), 151
Certification officer, 7, 286, 314
Chalmers, J., 115, 128
Chapple, Frank, 115, 128
Chartism, 9
Chemicals, 33, 175
Christopher, A. M., 115, 128
Chrysler, 152, 171, 228, 246
Citrine, Sir Walter (later Lord), 97, 335
Civil service, 33
Civil Service Department, 124
Clapham, S. F., 115
Clegg, H. A., 37, 122, 126
Clements, Richard, 122
Closed Shop, 296-9
Code of industrial relations practice, 103
Code of practice on discipline (ACAS), 288

Cohen Council, 181
Cole, G. D. H., 61, 95, 235
Collective bargaining, 20, 147, Chapter 6
  development of, 159
  institutions, 163
  issues, 170
  local and national, 166
  procedures, 174, 191
  results, 173
Collective Bargaining Committee (TUC), 100-1
Colliery managers, 6
Colliery officials, 6, 309
Combine committees, 45, 150-3, 168, 246, 253
Commission for Industrial Relations, 102
Commission for Racial Equality, 109, 125
Communications, 10, 85
Communist Party, 82, 205, 214, 240
Competition, 10, 351
Compulsory arbitration, 180
Concentration of capital, 10, 351
Conciliation Act (1896), 177, 269
Conciliation services, 178, 279
Confederation of British Industry (CBI), 107, 216, 273
Confederation General du Travail (CGT) 336
Conference of Public and Professional Service Organisations (COPPSO), 111
Congress House, 121, 329
Connolly, James, 233, 240
Conservative Party, 75
Conspiracy and Protection of Property Act (1875), 268
Construction Industry Manpower Board, 126
Contracts of Employment Act (1959), 286
Contracting out, 315
Cooley, Mike, 247
Cooling-off periods, 102
Co-operatives, 1, 185, 257, 260
'Corporate' interests, 304
Corresponding members, 134
Counter-inflation policies, 182
Coventry Machine-tool Workers' Committee, 152-3

Craft unions, 25, 94
Criminal Law Act (1977), 282
Cripps, Sir Stafford, 181
Crosland, C. A. R., 19
Cousins, Frank, 97, 99, 206, 207

Daily Express, 280
Daily Herald, 87, 119, 332
Daily Mirror, 280
Dalton, Hugh, 322
Daly, Lawrence, 115, 128
Dawn, 88
Deakin, Arthur, 82, 205
Demarcation, 28, 36
Democracy—checklist, 92
Denmark, 12
Denning, Lord, 280
Department of Education (funding TUC), 120
Department of Employment (D of E), 7, 198, 199, 218, 288
Dismissals, 192, 243, 264, 276
Disputes between unions, 36
District committees, 149
Division of Labour, 17, 61
Docks, 36, 257
Domestic procedures, 192
Donovan Commission (Report), 2, 3, 5, 64, 65, 70, 71, 101, 135, 144, 149, 162, 166, 200, 212, 216, 273
Doughty, George, 106, 126
Drain, Geoffrey, 115, 129
Duffy, Terry, 76, 80, 115, 129
Dunlop-Pirelli, 151
Dunlop Speeke, 84
Dyson, F., 115, 129

'Early warning' system, 181
Eastwood, G., 115
Eccles, J. F., 115, 129
Edelstein, J. D., 79
Education Department (TUC), 120
EEC referendum, 246
Elections, trade union, 73
Ellison, Judge, 184, 188
'Employer prerogatives', 174
Employers' Association, 3, 5, 162, 226
Employers and Workmen Act (1875), 269
Employment, 12
Employment Appeal Tribunal, 110, 279

Employment Protection Act (1975), 105, 138, 140, 178, 271, 277, 282, 284, schedule 11: 180, 284, 286
Encroachment, 243
Energy Commission, 109
Engineering, 33
Environmental protection, 244
Equal Pay, 101
Equal Pay Act (1970), 180, 278
Equal Opportunities Commission, 109, 125
Equal Pay and Opportunity Campaign, 90
European TUC, 172, 329, 345
Evans, Mike Parry, 247
Evans, Moss, 83, 115, 129, 149
Expulsion, 299

Fair Deal at Work (1968), 208, 274
Fair Wages Resolutions, 269
Father of the Chapel, 134
Federation General du Travail Belgique (FGTB) (Belgium), 133
Fifth Directive, EEC, 250
Final Appeal Court, AUEW, 85
Finance of strikes, 226
Fiscal drag, 311
Fisher, Alan, 83, 115, 129
Flanders, Allan, 232
Fletcher, Richard, 78, 82
Fords, 151, 152, 209, 348
'Formal' and 'informal' systems of industrial relations, 166
Full-time officials, 70

GEC Merseyside, 243
General Council, election of, 84, 95, 112, 250
General Federation of Trade Unions, 95
General Strike, 97, 161, 203, 233, 237, 276
General unions, 29
    comparison, 31
Gennard, J., 227
Gibson, H. L., 115
Gill, Ken, 114, 130
Gouriet v UPW, 279
Gormley, Joe, 76, 77, 114, 130
Government, local, 33
Gramsci, A., 303

Grand National Consolidated Trade Union, 9, 44
Grantham, R. A., 115
Greendale, Walter, 84, 111, 130
Grieve, C. D., 115, 130
Grunwick, 226, 281, 283
Guide for Negotiators, 170
Gunter, Ray, 272
Guy, L. G., 114, 130

Hare, Sir John, 109
Hartman, P. T., 214-5
Health and Safety at Work Act (1974), 138, 278
Heath, Edward, 187, 209
Hegemony, 304, 326
Hemingway, John, 81
Higgs, Phil, 241
Hobcart, 247
Holland, Stuart, 11, 23, 168
Hornby v Close, 267
Hughes, John, 36, 42
Hyman, Richard, 19, 24, 153

ICI, 170
Incomes Policy, 167, 180-8, 223
Incomes Policy Committee, 100
Income shares, % GNP, 186
Independent Review Committee, 106
Individual Contracts, 3
Industrial Court Act (1919), 178, 270
Industrial Democracy, Chapter 8
Industrial Democracy Commission, 250
Industrial disputes, 96
Industrial Relations Act (1971), 2, 102, 136, 170, 274, 292
Industrial Training Act (1964), 272, 273
Industrial tribunals, 102, 110, 179, 278, 285
Industrial Unions, 27
Industry Act (1975), 171, 285, 349
Industry Committees (TUC), 119
Informal work structures, 146
Information agreements, 170
Ingham, G. K., 215
In Place of Strife, 101, 102, 136, 208, 274
International affiliations, Chapter 11
    bodies involved, 331
    costs, 329-34
International Confederation of Free Trade Unions (ICFTU), 329, 337
    membership, 341

International Labour Office (ILO), 330
International Monetary Fund, 107, 119, 323
International Trade Secretariats, 338-40
Iron Law of Oligarchy, 69
Iron and Steel, 252

Jackson, Tom, 115, 127
Jarvis, F. F., 115, 130
Jenkins, Clive, 114, 130
Jenkins, T., 114
Jersey Mills Strike, 226
Jewish Bakers, London, 46
Joint consultation, 144, 237, 238
Joint Industrial Councils, 160, 277
Joint regulation, 174
Joint Representation Committees, 168
Joint Shop Stewards' Committees, 45
Jones, Bill, 84
Jones, Jack, 70, 84, 120, 149, 183, 209, 251
Journal of the AUEW, 86
Journal of the GMWU, 86

Kahn-Freund, Otto, 271
Kent miners, 204
Kerr, Clark, 214-5
Keys, W. H., 115, 130, 280
King George V, 236
Knee, Fred, 157
Knowles, K. G. J. C., 213

Labour Colleges, 67
Labour Party, 96, 240, 250, 269, 276, Chapter 10
Labour Representation Committee, 95, 268, 303
Labour Weekly, 314
Lawther, Will, 205
Lea, D., 126
Leadership succession, 79
Leeds Convention, 236
Legal enactment, method of, 157
Lenin, V. I., 23
Limited Liability, 9
Linton, Martin, 314
Living standards, 22
Lloyd, G., 114, 131
Locke, John, 47
Lord, Alan, 252
Lovestone, Jay, 337, 338

Lucas Aerospace Joint Shop Stewards' Committee, 151, 172, 246-9, 259
Lyons, J., 114

MacDonald, Ramsay, 97, 122
MacGougan, J., 115, 131
Machine-breaking, 9
Maddocks, A., 115
Maddox, S., 115, 131
Management, 19
Manchester & Salford Trades Council, 94
Manning levels, 172
Manpower Services Commission, 109
Marx, Karl, 10, 184, 304, 352
Master and Servants Acts, 267
McCarthy, Lord, 106, 200
McGahey, Michael, 76
McShane, Dennis, 280
Meany, G., 337, 343
Media—intervention in unions, 76
Mellor, William, 235
Mergers, 41, 49
Metro-Vickers, 204
Michels, Roberto, 69, 153
Microprocessors, 171
Mills, L. A., 115
The Miner, 88
Mineworkers, 28, 208, 209, 238-9, 281, 307
Ministry of Labour (see also Department of Employment), 170, 204
Minkin, Lewis, 322
Montesquieu, 47
Moore, J., 114
Morrison, Herbert, 237
Morris, William, 232
Mortimer, Jim, 339
Morton, J. M., 115, 131
Multinational corporations, 10-16, 168, 185, 348-52
Multiplant firms, 145, 151
Multi-union plants, 145, 162
Mutual Insurance, method of, 157

National agreements, 165, 166
National Board for Prices and Incomes (NBPI), 181
National Coal Board (NCB), 208
National Craftsmen's Co-ordinating Committee, 252

National Economic Development
    Council (NEDC), 98, 107, 108, 126
National Enterprise Board (NEB), 126
National Health Service (NHS), 110
National Incomes Commission (NIC),
    98, 181
National Industrial Relations Court
    (NIRC), 103, 223, 275
National Planning College, 108
Nationalisation, 237, 257
Nevin, E., 114
New Technology Agreements, 172, 258-
    60
Nigeria, 343
Nobel Peace Prize, 151

Objectives, trade union, 21
Officers, full-time, 70
Oligarchy, 69
'Open' and 'closed' structures, 35
Opposition, 80
Order 1305, 205
Organisation for Economic
    Co-operation and Development
    (OECD), 329
Organisational success, 37
ORIT, 337, 343
Orwell, George, 237
Osborne judgement, 269
Overtime, 167
Owen, Robert, 9, 217

Parry, Terry, 113, 115, 131
Participation in union activity, 66
Patronage, 124
Patterson, Marie, 115, 131
Pay Board Third Report, 164
Payment by results (PBR), 167, 169
Pay Pause (1961), 181
Pemberton, Stan, 84, 114, 131
Pensions, 140
Phillips, Hon Justice, 280
Phillips, Morgan, 307
Pickets, 280, 293-6
Planning agreements, 171, 244-6
Plant organisation, 145
Platts Mills, John, 204
Poland, 198, 223
Political strikes, 223
Price Commission, 125
Prices and Incomes Board, 181
Procedural agreements, 174, 191

Productivity bargains, 167, 168, 182
Profits, % share of GNP, 186-8
Public Employees, 88
Public Service, 86, 88

Quangos, 108, 124
    control over, 134
    fees and salaries, 124, 134
    staff costs, 125
    trade union representation on,
        127-33

Railways, 9, 27, 33
Rate-fixing, 207, 242
Reckitt and Colman, 259
Recognition strikes, 226
The Record, 86
Recruitment strategies, 35
Redundancy Payments Act, 272-3
Reform of structure, 39
Regional TUC Councils, 121
Registrar of Friendly Societies, 314
Registration, 103
Research and Development, 11
Road Haulage Wages Act (1938), 180
Road Traffic Act (1960), 180
Roberts, B. C., 122
Roberts, Bryn, 116
Rookes v Barnard, 272
Ross, A. M., 214-15
Rousseau, J. J., 99
Royal Commission on Trade Unions
    and Employers' Associations, 1968
    Report
    see Donovan Report
Rubner, Ben, 115
Rules and rulebooks, 21, 103

Sankey Commission, 236
Sapper, Alan, 115, 132
Scanlon, Hugh, 80, 104, 126, 209,
    251
Scargill, Arthur, 76, 238
Schofield, N., 114
Scottish Development Agency, 125
Scrutton, Lord Justice, 264
Sector Working Parties, 108
Self-management, 198, 241
Separation of Powers, 77
Service Industries, 7
Sheffield outrages, 267

Shop stewards, 45, 71, Chapter 5, 193
  number, 134
  in bargaining, 135, 139
  and union rules, 136
  constituencies, 136
  recognition of, 137
  duties, 139
Shotton Steelworks Committee, 120
Sickness, 201
Siegel, A., 214-5
Silicon-chip technology, 171
Sillitoe, L. R., 115
Simpson, A. E., 114
Sirs, Bill, 114, 132
Sit-ins, 1
Skill changes, 26
Slater, Jim, 81, 114, 132
Smith, Adam, 4, 17
Smith, Sir George, 114, 132
Smith, Hector, 114
'Social contract', 20, 100, 104
Social democracy, 234
Spanswick, Albert, 115, 132
Special Branch, intervention of, 81
Sponsored MPs, 305, 306
Staff representatives, 134
Stalin, J. V., 237, 336
Standing Committees (TUC), 117
'Status quo', 175
Steel, 33, 252-5
Strikes, Chapter 7
  causes, 218
  definition, 196
  measurement of, 198
  economic cost, 200
  numbers of, UK, 202
  international comparisons, 210
Succession, 79
Sullivan, Terry, 266
Supplementary benefit, 227
Sweden, 171, 216
Syndicalism, 95, 217, 233

Taff Vale, 268
Talcott Parsons, 196, 197
Taylor, Robert, 109, 123
The Teacher, 85
Technology agreements, 258
'Technological imperatives', 19
Terminal dates of agreements, 168
Thatcher, M., 187
Thirty-five-hour week, 101, 172

Thomas, K. R., 115, 132
Thorne, Will, 236
Time off for union duties, 138
TINA LEA (this is not a legally
    enforceable agreement), 275
de Tocqueville, Alexis, 17
Tolpuddle, 267
Torode, John, 228
Trade Boards (see also Wages
    Councils), 161
Trade Unions
  branches, basic units, 62
  classification of types, 8, 25
  definition, 1
  democracy in, 46, 61
  full-time officers, 70
  density of organisation, 6, 7, 14, 15
  disputes between, 36
  distribution of members, 38
  legal status, 2
  in larger manufacturing organisations,
    16
  membership, 43
  mergers and amalgamations, 41, 49-
    60
  rules, 21
  research services, 42
  structure, Chapter 2
  subscriptions, 42
  legislation on, Chapter 9
Trade Union Advisory Committee,
    OECD, 329
  guidelines, 350
Trade Union Congress, Chapter 4
  evidence to Donovan Commission, 3,
    5
  formation, 1, 94
  functioning of Congress, 110
  disputes committee, 37
  standing committees, 117
  industry committees, 119
  education, 120
  regional councils, 121
  TUC-Labour Party Liaison
    Committee, 104
Trade Union and Labour Relations
    Act, 1974, 2, 105, 106
Trades Councils, 121
Transfer prices, 12
Transnational companies
  see multinational corporations
Transport Review, 85

Turner, H. A., 198, 208
Two-tier boards, 250
Two x + y, 250

Undy, Roger, 70, 84, 90, 91
Unemployment, 7
Unilateral shop steward controls, 144
Unlawful Oaths Act (1797), 267
Unionateness, 5, 6, 325
Unofficial strikes, 224
Upgrading, 167
Upper Clyde Shipbuilders, 243, 255
USA, 210, 211, 212, 213, 332
USSR, 198, 236, 240, 332
Urwin, Harry, 114, 126, 132

Wage restraint, 84, 98, 181
Wages Councils (see also Trade Boards),
    32, 101, 164, 180, 270, 271, 277, 289
Wages drift, 166
Warner, M., 79
Webb, Sidney and Beatrice, 1, 46, 68, 232
Wedderburn, Lord, 106, 282
Weighall, Sid, 114, 132
Wells, H. G., 18
Welsh Development Agency, 125
White-collar organisation, 25, 150
White Fish Authority, 126
Whitley Committees, 161
Whitley, J. H., 160

Whitley Reports, 160, 270
Williamson, Tom, 205
Wilmott-Breedon, 152
Wilson, Sir Harold, 99, 110, 185, 246, 255
Women in Unions, 73, 115, 316
Wood, J. H., 114
Wood, Les, 132
Woodcock, George, 40, 66, 98, 99, 109,
    340
Work groups, 146
Work-ins, 1, 243
Worker directors, 249-57
Workers' control, 21, 241-57
Workers' co-operatives, 185, 257, 260
Workers' Educational Association
    (WEA), 1, 121
Workplace meetings, 67, 139
World Federation of Trade Unions
    (WFTU), 335-8

Vauxhall, 153
Vertical and Horizontal structures, 32
Vesting day, 239
Victimisation, 148
Vickers, 151
Viewpoint, 88

Yorkshire Miners, 238-9
Yugoslavia, 198, 240